33.72

Nation of Change
The American Democratic System

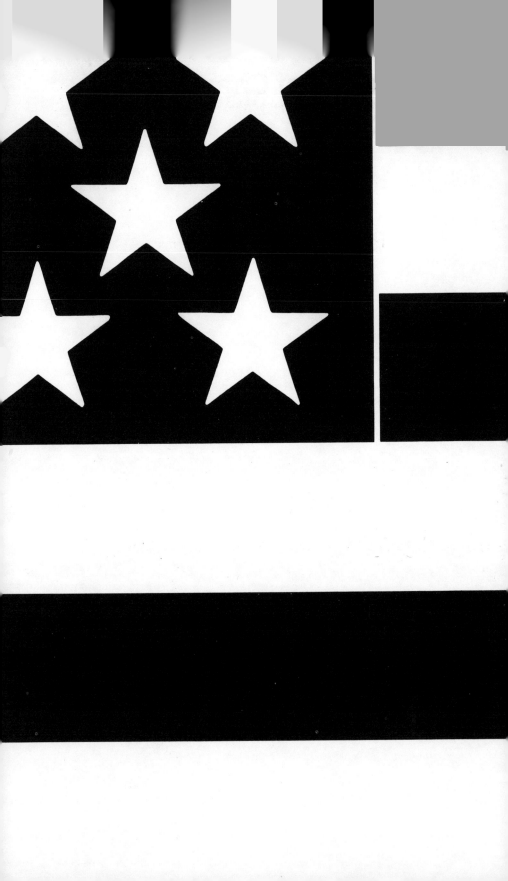

Nation of Change
he American Democratic System

John P. Carney

El Camino College

Canfield Press   San Francisco
A Department of Harper & Row, Publishers, Inc.
New York   Evanston   London

320.473
C289m
1972

Acquisition: *Joseph L. Dana*
Editorial and design supervision: *Brian K. Williams*
Production: *Christine C. Schacker*
Design: *Michael Rogondino*
Graphic illustration: *Ayxa*

To My Wife and Children

Melbaruth

Sean
Angela
Monica

Contents

PART 5   STATE AND LOCAL GOVERNMENT, 417

Preface

Too often a student beginning the study of American government is turned away by a textbook that presents him with what seems to be a bewildering array of unrelated, irrelevant facts. In this book, I have tried to remedy this problem in two ways: first, by giving adequate coverage without going into excessive detail and, second, by showing how the particulars described relate to the overall working of our political system, so that its significance and operations may be better understood. Democracy, for example, is discussed not as an abstract concept but as a part of the American system of power. Political support and alienation are considered not as isolated phenomena but as influences on the political system.

I have tried to make the book extensive enough so it will present the basics an educated person could reasonably be expected to have, yet brief enough so that the instructor may assign paperbacks and other supplementary readings and otherwise spend more time familiarizing students in depth with political issues and behavior. Thus, while the book does not discuss matters of the moment which may soon lose significance, it does describe major problems of current interest. For instance, foreign policy and civil liberties, ignored in so many recently published textbooks, are given two chapters each. At the same time, I have emphasized functional descriptions of government institutions, since, in the United States, the structure of government has a particularly decisive and variable impact on political matters and on how the government operates.

The book is organized as follows: Part 1 discusses the context of American government—theoretical, ideological, constitutional, and federal. Part 2 considers the electoral system, political parties, and political interest groups which make demands on and support the system. Part 3 focuses on the decision-making agencies and activities that constitute the center of the government process. Part 4 considers the rewards and deprivations that result from government decisions. Part 5 describes state and local government, although throughout the book there are comparisons between national and state government and the ways they interrelate and share functions.

I would like to express my gratitude for the criticisms and suggestions of all those who reviewed my manuscript in its entirety: Professors Arthur Aurand, William E. Brigman, Kenneth D. Kennedy, Thomas McEnroe, Gerald Rigby, Charles Sohner, and Fr. John Bradley, O.F.M. In addition, I owe thanks to my colleagues Richard Sherman, Wallace Cohen, Edgar Love, Helmut Bader, Gordon Wilson, William Alexander, and John Cashin for their encouragement and advice, and Helen Puckett and Cheryl Geary for their numerous helpful deeds. Virginia Wagenhals also deserves thanks for her expert deciphering and typing of my manuscript. Finally, a most special thanks to two people at Canfield Press: Brian K. Williams, Managing Editor, who edited the manuscript, and Joseph L. Dana, Social Science Editor, who sponsored it.

I also must acknowledge my debt to all the social scientists from whose research and thinking I have drawn material for the book, although, of course, any errors of fact or judgment are my own responsibility.

J.P.C.

Part 1

The Context of American Government

1 Americans and Their Political System: Support and Alienation

Bonnie Freer, Photo Researchers, Inc.

We the People of the United States, in Order to form a more perfect Union, establish Justice, insure domestic Tranquility, provide for the common defence, promote the general Welfare, and secure the Blessings of Liberty to ourselves and our Posterity...

—Preamble,
The Constitution of the United States

We Americans today are a far different people from what we were in 1789, when our Constitution was written. At that time, there were only about four million of us, and most of us were "WASP"—white, Anglo-Saxon, and Protestant.

WE THE PEOPLE: WHO ARE WE?

Most of us today are still "WASP," although the proportion has declined. Out of a hundred people, eleven of us would be black, more than three Mexican-American, and one another nonwhite (most likely American Indian, Japanese, or Chinese). About thirty would be Roman Catholic and four Jewish. All of us participate to some extent in the total American culture, although the assimilation of some of our subcultures—particularly for those of us who are black, Mexican-American, or Indian—has been a difficult national problem.

Most of us came here from Europe, Africa, or other Western Hemisphere countries or are descended from people who did. Moreover, most came here poor and thus did not transfer all the notions (principally European) of a class system based on inherited wealth. Although we are aware of social and religious differences and tend to measure individual achievement in terms of money, most of us are not notably class conscious: when we think about it at all, about 80 percent of us consider ourselves middle class. Unlike in many other countries, the very poor are a minority—and, understandably, they (and the very rich, also a minority) are most aware of class distinctions. Most of us feel we can "improve our standing." Accordingly, we are not so inclined to work for the advancement of our class or ethnic group—why do so when we have a chance to "strike it rich" on our own?

We are also a geographically mobile people. Most recently, we have moved from East to West, from farm to small town and city, and from central city to suburb. Today, less than six out of a hundred of us live on farms, and the numbers are declining; nine out of ten live in cities or small towns. This geographical mobility is reflected in Figure 1-1, which shows that, in general, the urban states (compare Rhode Island to Alaska here) have populations far out of proportion to their size.

We enjoy probably the highest standard of living in the world. Highly industrialized and technologically advanced, we produce and consume more than any people. In fact, though we are only 6 percent of the world's people, we consume 40 percent of the world's resources. Even with its inequalities, our nation is probably closer than any other to a "worker's paradise." This general prosperity is partly because most of us have received at least a high school education (three-quarters of those of us between twenty-five and twenty-nine finished high school) and partly because most of us who work belong to groups (a fifth of us belong to labor organizations) that protect our occupational interests.

Not all of us share this high standard of living. Many people are not aware of the poor hidden away in slums and other areas of poverty. Public services are also lacking: our government

Figure 1-1. U.S. map is distorted to show state sizes as determined by preliminary 1970 census figures. (Source: *Los Angeles Times*, September 6, 1970. Map by Don Clement.)

spends less proportionately than other countries on schools, hospitals, public transportation, conservation, and pollution control. In health care, for instance, although our governments spend a larger portion of their funds (6.5 percent) than other nations on health services, we rank *eighteenth* in the world in infant mortality—just above Hong Kong. And in 1965 we ranked twenty-second in male life expectancy. Moreover, proportionately, our social security spending is less than half that of the principal European countries—in fact, we rank barely above Portugal.

Our economic system is, of course, predominantly private enterprise. But it is not pure capitalism: government increasingly intervenes in and regulates business and the economy in the public interest. It also itself increasingly engages in economic enterprise, as when it invests millions in the supersonic transport aircraft or when it creates Railpax—a quasi-public corporation—to rescue and run nationwide rail passenger service. Whatever the extent of government involvement, however, our faith in private enterprise is so firmly established that most of us give little thought to changing our economic system radically.

As Americans, we share common attitudes. In general, we identify with the community as a whole, acquiesce in the outcomes of elections, are willing to compromise, are against excessive and arbitrary authority, and are disposed to "fair play"—at least for those who play the game according to customary rules. We take for granted here the presence and preeminence of democracy. Almost unanimously we profess a belief in the abstract ideals of democracy—in majority rule, and in freedom for the minority to criticize—although this unanimity often disappears when it comes to applying democratic precepts to specific instances.

Most of us are proud of things American, often to the point of smugness. We are, in fact, highly ethnocentric; that is, we tend to reject that which is non-American or "un-American." However, personal matters concern us more than political matters—according to one poll, more than one of every four adult Americans never discusses politics.[1]

In attitude we are mostly optimistic, though perhaps not so much today as in earlier times. Yet we do acknowledge that man's nature is imperfect and that we need the inhibiting agency of government and checks on government officials, who might, like ourselves, also surrender to human weakness. We also claim to value competitiveness and individual achievement, even though the competitive ethic conflicts with the religious-moral values we profess ("Nice guys don't win ball games" versus The Golden Rule, for example). Yet, ironically, we also tend to be conformists, to follow the majority will in most matters.

[1] Gabriel A. Almond and Sidney Verba, *The Civic Culture* (Princeton, N.J.: Princeton University Press, 1963), p. 120.

What, then, is the true nature of our society—affluent? materialistic? exploitative? Is it equalitarian? libertarian? individualistic? Should we call it dynamic? violent? racist? The very number and disparity of these terms—not to mention others used to describe us—indicates the awesome difficulty of defining American society.

THE AMERICAN NATION:
BIG, POPULOUS, AND POWERFUL

The United States is among the largest, most populous, and most ethnically and racially mixed (i.e., polyglot) nations. It is also probably the most powerful. How these factors influence our politics is shown below.

A Polyglot People

In the words of John F. Kennedy, the United States is "a nation of immigrants," a mix of races and ethnic groups. But though this country has been a haven for generations of foreign-born, immigration has not always been easy. Some new immigrants have been discriminated against and exploited by earlier arrivals.

The Early Policy of Openness

From colonial times to World War I, American immigration policy was basically one of openness. Great numbers of immigrants were welcomed, since their labor was generally cheap and people were needed to work the land and to increase the nation's population. Most migrated here on their own to seek economic opportunity and individual freedom—the major exception, of course, being the black Africans brought in as slaves.

An important deviation from this open policy began in 1882, when Chinese immigrants were excluded, along with lunatics, idiots, paupers, criminals, immoral persons, and those with contagious diseases.

The Gates Are Narrowed

World War I marked a turning point in immigration policy. Alarmed by predictions that millions of Europeans would pour into this country after the war, Congress tried to reduce immigration by approving a bill, over President Wilson's veto, which excluded immigrants who could not read. President Cleveland had vetoed a similar bill in 1887, arguing, on grounds that still seem appropriate, that ability to read is a test of opportunity, not of intelligence or other qualities making an immigrant valuable to this society.

Not satisfied with the literacy-test legislation, restrictionists enacted a law in 1921 establishing a "quota" or limit for each nationality, and in 1924 they passed a law barring Asians entirely. In 1929, the quota for European immigration was set at about 150,000. This was based on the *national origins plan,* whereby quotas or limits were assigned a nationality according to the total number of persons of that nationality already residing here.

These laws favored immigrants from Northern and Western Europe, where most Americans traced their origins, to the disadvantage of Southern and Eastern Europeans, mostly Catholics and Jews, who comprised most of the immigrants in those early years of this century. Under these laws, immigration decreased so markedly that during the Depression years of 1931 through 1935 more persons emigrated *from* this country than immigrated to it.

The Politics of Immigration Control

As an ideological struggle, immigration control has been a contest between openness and restrictiveness. As a political struggle, it has been between institutions representing a national viewpoint and others representing a local one. Presidents, with their national constituencies and their experiences conducting the nation's foreign affairs, have supported openness. Congress, sensitive to local pressures, has favored restrictiveness. State and local institutions have also supported restriction, but, being limited in their ability to deal with these matters, have directed most of their pressures at Congressmen.

The proponents of openness achieved a minor triumph in 1965, when a bill was passed eliminating the discriminatory country-by-country quotas and increasing the total quota for *all* countries outside the Western Hemisphere to 170,000.[2] Within the quota, preference was given to relatives of persons already in the United States and to individuals whose skills were needed here.[3]

Still a Haven?

On balance, these reforms were somewhat meager. The increased quota of the non–Western Hemisphere nations was actually a percentage decrease, because it failed even to keep pace with the growth of our population. Also, for the first time, a quota (120,000) was placed on immigration from the independent Western Hemisphere countries. Furthermore, reflecting the desires of the powerful Coalition of Patriotic Societies, Congress went against the wishes of the President and gave greater priority to uniting families than to admitting skilled workers and professionals. Still the flow from Northern Europe has been reduced, and there has been a heavy influx from Italy, Greece, Portugal, Taiwan, Hong Kong, and the Philippines. Immigration from Asia and the Middle East has jumped most dramatically, increasing by threefold between 1965 (19,778) and 1967 (57,083). In 1969, total immigration to the United States was over 350,000.

Post–World War II emergency legislation admitting more than 1.5 million political refugees and persons made homeless by war has also been politically motivated. Though the legislation has been partly for humanitarian reasons, there has been a notable tendency to accept refugees from communist regimes more than those fleeing other dictatorships. Recently, most refugees have come from Cuba (about 400,000 since the Castro revolution).

[2] No more than 20,000 may enter in any one year from any single country outside the Western Hemisphere. Under the previous law, Great Britain had the largest quota—65,361—more than 40 percent of the entire quota for non–Western Hemisphere countries.

[3] Every year, many foreign students, businessmen, and government officials are admitted for periods of varying duration without regard to quota restrictions. Several million foreign (mostly Mexican) farm workers have also been admitted since World War II on a temporary basis. Organized labor has generally opposed this immigration, maintaining that these foreign laborers displace American workers.

9

Unlimited numbers of Cubans may enter, but are charged to the Western Hemisphere quota, of which Cubans have used about one-third.

A Bigger and Bigger Population

From 1890 to 1970—as Figure 1-2 shows—the population of the United States has jumped from 60 million to over 204 million. By the year 2000, it may be half again as large, with 300 million—at which time, as Figure 1-3 shows, the earth's population is expected to exceed 7 billion. Many scientists believe that unless some action is taken to correct this population explosion—and soon—this country and the earth will be choked by overpopulation.

Although the federal government has exercised some control over population by regulating immigration, only recently has it tried to discourage childbearing as a way of slowing the increase in numbers of people. One reason it has been slow to act is the opposition from religious groups, particularly the Roman Catholic Church. Another is the general hands-off attitude of the public. As late as 1959, only seven states (all in the South) included family planning as a regular part of their public health services, and President Eisenhower, reflecting the prevailing view in government, could "not imagine a subject more emphatically . . . not a proper . . . governmental activity or responsibility."

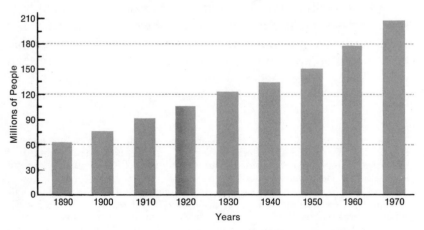

Figure 1-2. An abundance of people. (Source: U.S. Bureau of Census.)

10

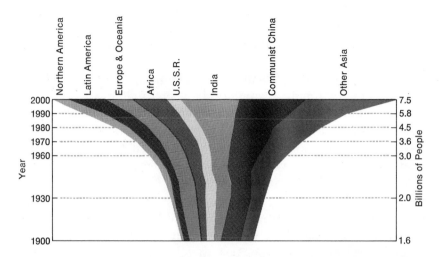

Figure 1-3. The Population Bomb: growth by geographical area (if rate of growth remains the same). Within 70 years world population has more than doubled and is expected to double again by 2000. U.S. population is expected to reach between 280 million and 370 million by then. (Source: Agency for International Development, based on United Nations data; from *Congressional Quarterly Weekly Report,* June 12, 1970.)

By the mid-'60s the mood of the public had changed, and a majority of the states began providing such services. President Johnson specifically advocated federal programs for family planning, and in 1967, Congress began earmarking maternal and child health funds for family planning, requiring that such services be offered to persons receiving benefits under the Aid to Families with Dependent Children program. Not only did family planning become a priority item in the "War on Poverty" in the U.S.; foreign aid funds also began to be used for this purpose in under-developed countries.

The change in public opinion that prompted these developments occurred as a result of the growing awareness of the population explosion and the relationship between overpopulation and poverty in underdeveloped countries, widely publicized by such groups as the Planned Parenthood—World Population organization. Other factors that made political leaders endorse family planning were the development of improved methods of artificial birth control, Pope John's apparent willingness in 1962 to have the Catholic Church reconsider its position on birth con-

11

trol, and a new public awareness of the effect of "overpopulation" on pollution of the environment and depletion of natural resources.

By 1969, more than $100 million was being spent by the federal government for family planning; about $60 million of it was in the U.S., and President Nixon was asking that it be increased to $150 million in five years. In 1970 a Commission on Population Growth and the American Future was created to report in two years on ways to deal with population problems; in the same year, a bill was passed which expanded research in contraceptive development.[4]

Whether the birth control program will be effective remains to be seen. In the papal encyclical of July 29, 1968, the Catholic Church reaffirmed its opposition to all forms of artificial birth control. Some people oppose the program because they believe its real goal is to reduce the high birth rate among nonwhites (about 1.8 times the rate for whites); others feel it discriminates against the poor. Popular attitudes will not change overnight: in the past, people have not paid much attention to the government's telling them the number of children they should have.

Bigness and Sectionalism

Because of its great physical size and varied climate, resources, and topography, the United States is marked off into geographic regions or sections. North, South, East, and West are more than mere geographic expressions (as are also Northeast, Middle Atlantic, etc.). With their different resources and interests, these sections reflect loyalties and political forces that are powerful factors in American politics. *Sectionalism* is probably a state of mind more than anything else. But politicians and voters understand it and behave accordingly. Every analysis of how people vote confirms its significance. One observer has commented on its importance in uniting various classes in our national parties. Sectionalism, he says,

---

[4] However, the law barred use of any funds where abortion is used as a method of birth control.

12

. . . contributes to the multiclass composition of each of the major parties. . . . A politics that arrays the people of one section against those of another pulls into one party men of all social strata. A common interest bound the southern banker, merchant, cotton farmer, and wage earner together.[5]

That feelings about sectionalism are significant is shown by the accusations that President Nixon appealed to Southern regionalism in the 1968 election campaign and during his presidency. Many Southerners continue to fear that their way of life is menaced by other sections of the country.

Still, sectional politics, never a particularly dominant factor in some localities, seems to be losing ground to class and ethnic politics. For instance, the "white backlash"—white hostility to Negro economic and social demands—long associated with the South is now significant in the North as well. This spread shows how population shifts, together with industrialization and urbanization, are lessening sectional differences and producing a national politics. The influence of radio and television may also lessen geographic distinctions and sectional loyalty. Nevertheless, the influence of geography on the political behavior of Americans will endure to some extent.

A World Superpower

Our more than 200 million people live in an area of about 3.6 million square miles, a land blessed with an unmatched (though dwindling) concentration of natural resources and physical advantages. Our Gross National Product, the measure of total production of goods and services at market prices, is more than $1 trillion, well ahead of any other nation's. Only three other countries—the U.S.S.R., Canada, and Brazil—have larger land masses, and only China, India, and Russia have larger populations.

The effects on our politics of our being a superpower are many. Because of our bigness, our great technological resources, and our victory in World War II, we hold a dominant position

[5] V. O. Key, Jr., *Politics, Parties, and Pressure Groups*, 5th ed. (New York: Thomas Y. Crowell, 1964), p. 243.

over about half the globe and are the military and diplomatic mainstay of the Western world. And because we have accepted this role, our government feels it must contend for the loyalty of foreign peoples within its sphere and try to get Americans to support its programs and actions abroad. Its efforts to reduce discrimination in our immigration laws and against racial minorities at home, for instance, are partly because it wants to project a better international image.

Foreign and domestic politics are interrelated. The Indochina war, for instance, has caused many problems at home: inflation, budget deficits, balance-of-payments difficulties, cutbacks in domestic programs, and sharp conflicts in sentiment of the American people. His lack of success in ending the war cost President Johnson a huge drop in popularity and probably a chance for a second term. On the other hand, a successful foreign policy move (or one with foreign policy implications) can help a President's image at home—as did the Apollo 13 moon shot for President Nixon.

But the point is clear: ours is a very powerful country with major interests abroad. How these interests are handled has an important political impact at home. In this sense, American politics do not stop at the shoreline.

HOW WE SUPPORT OUR POLITICAL SYSTEM

That we strongly support our political system is shown by a survey (see Table 1-1) in which people were asked: "Speaking generally, what are the things about this country that you are most proud of?" Eighty-five percent of the Americans immediately mentioned some aspect of the U.S. political system. Similar positive replies by Britons, Germans, Italians, and Mexicans on *their* political systems were nowhere near as high. Germans and Italians expressed the least pride—no doubt because in recent decades (before, during, and after World War II) their countries were so politically unstable.

Also evidence of our support is the lack of major controversy over basic structures and processes. No one expounds, for example, the need for a new Constitution. Almost no one thinks of abolishing the states or the Senate, of popularly electing Supreme

Table 1–1
ASPECTS OF THEIR NATION IN WHICH
RESPONDENTS REPORT PRIDE*

PERCENT WHO SAY THEY ARE PROUD OF	U.S.	U.K.	GERMANY	ITALY	MEXICO
Governmental, political institutions	85%	46%	7%	3%	30%
Social legislation	13	18	6	1	2
Position in international affairs	5	11	5	2	3
Economic system	23	10	33	3	24
Characteristics of people	7	18	36	11	15
Spiritual virtues and religion	3	1	3	6	8
Contributions to the arts	1	6	11	16	9
Contributions to science	3	7	12	3	1
Physical attributes of country	5	10	17	25	22
Nothing or don't know	4	10	15	27	16
Other	9	11	3	21	14

*The number of people in each sample were: U.S., 970; U.K., 963; Germany, 955; Italy, 995; and Mexico, 1007.
Source: Adapted from Gabriel A. Almond and Sidney Verba, *The Civic Culture,* p. 102. Copyright © 1963 by Princeton University Press.

Court Justices, of substituting the parliamentary for the presidential system. People debate whether our convention system for nominating presidential candidates is really workable. But compared to the struggles over the fundamental processes of government that occur in other countries, such controversies are relatively mild.

Such strong support for the political system does not mean, of course, we endorse everything about it. While we may greatly admire high political offices, we also, as Table 1-2 points out, are highly suspicious of political officeholders and of politics in general. Similarly, we are ambiguous in our attitudes about democracy.[6] Though giving it almost unanimous support in the abstract, we are often undemocratic in specific circumstances, as when we persecute Mexican-Americans, blacks, and Indians.

In brief, most of us strongly support our political system for its structure and procedures: majority rule, the Constitution, the

[6] "Democracy" is more clearly defined in Chapter 2.

Table 1-2
POLITICAL INFLUENTIALS VERSUS THE ELECTORATE:
RESPONSES TO ITEMS EXPRESSING CYNICISM TOWARD
GOVERNMENT AND POLITICS* (Some items deleted)

PERCENT WHO SAY THEY AGREE	POLITICAL INFLUENTIALS	GENERAL ELECTORATE
Most politicians are looking out for themselves above all else.	36.3%	54.3%
Both major parties in this country are controlled by the wealthy and are run for their benefit.	7.9	32.1
Many politicians are bought off by some private interest.	43.0	65.3
Most politicians can be trusted to do what they think is best for the country.	77.1	58.9
Most politicians don't seem to me to really mean what they say.	24.7	55.1
Most political parties care only about winning elections and nothing more.	28.3	46.2
All politics is controlled by political bosses.	15.6	45.9

*Number of persons in sample: political influentials, 3020; general electorate, 1484.
Source: Adapted from Herbert McClosky, "Consensus and Ideology in American Politics," *American Political Science Review,* June 1964, p. 391.

presidency, the Congress, the Supreme Court, abstractions like "democracy." However, obviously we do not always support specific officeholders, decisions, or applications of democracy.

ALIENATION FROM THE AMERICAN POLITICAL SYSTEM

Naturally not all Americans support the political system. The black, the young, the Mexican-American, and the white ethnic, to cite the most notable examples, are more estranged and withdrawn—in a word, alienated[7]—than most.

[7] These are not *all* the alienated, of course. Also alienated are Puerto Ricans, American Indians, Asian-Americans, and feminists. Likewise estranged are many so-called "intelligentsia"—persons engaged in interpreting, criticizing, producing, distributing, and inculcating cultural values; such intelligentsia mostly serve art, truth, or pleasure, rather than commercial values. Some also see in poorly educated people's sense of relatively low political efficacy (that is, their feeling that they can or cannot influence government) an indication that they would give the political system less support than the richer and better educated, who think they can influence political decisions.

Alienation Among Blacks

After two centuries of neglect and discrimination, blacks, especially in the last decade,[8] have reacted more and more militantly —with demonstrations, riots, and, finally, calls to revolution. The Kerner Commission—the National Advisory Commission on Civil Disorders, appointed by President Johnson after the 1968 summer riots—grimly concluded that blacks in the urban ghettos held great "alienation and hostility toward the institutions of law and government and the white society which controls them."[9] Tables 1-3 and 1-4 seem to substantiate the fact that blacks believe government is less effective than whites do, and are less satisfied with the work they do.[10]

Yet not all blacks are as alienated as would seem. The Kerner Commission observed that although most blacks sympathized with the rioters, only a few living in riot areas took part in the disruptions. (In Detroit only 11 percent of the blacks in the riot zone participated in the violence, whereas 16 percent actively tried to stop it.) Another survey showed that, in 1968, 70 percent of even the sixteen- to nineteen-year-old males, the most alienated blacks, did not approve of violence to gain Negro rights.

However, a 1970 survey found that 36 percent of the 100,000 black Vietnam veterans agreed that violence is the only way for blacks to obtain their rights.[11] And a 1971 Louis Harris poll found that *51 percent* of all blacks are alienated—a rise of 17 percent since 1966. (The percentage of the total public who felt alienated was 35 percent—up 11 percent from 1966.)

In short, though blacks give considerable support to the American political system, they give less than do whites. Young male blacks and black Vietnam veterans give less than other blacks. And studies show that although active black support for Negro militants may not be widespread, sympathy for them is.

---

[8] Discrimination against blacks is discussed in Chapters 6 and 16.
[9] *Report of the National Advisory Commission on Civil Disorders* (New York: Bantam Books, 1968), p. 205.
[10] See, for instance, William Brink and Louis Harris, *Black and White* (New York: Simon & Schuster, 1966).
[11] James Fendrich and Michael Pearson, "Black Veterans Return," *Trans-action*, March 1970, p. 34.

Table 1–3
EVALUATIONS BY RACE OF HOW THE GOVERNMENT PERFORMS*

ITEM	RACE	EFFECTIVE	INEFFECTIVE
Providing justice for all.	Whites Blacks	79% 60	21% 40
Securing civil rights and liberties.	Whites Blacks	78 55	22 45
Providing a chance to make a good living.	Whites Blacks	85 71	15 29
Make it possible for a person with the means to live where he wishes.	Whites Blacks	75 40	25 60
Seeing to it that everyone who wants a job can have one.	Whites Blacks	63 43	37 57
Insuring equal opportunity to participate in making political decisions.	Whites Blacks	74 68	26 32
Facilitating social mobility.	Whites Blacks	66 36	34 64
Trying to even out differences in wealth and prestige.	Whites Blacks	43 33	57 67

*Sizes of samples vary from 716 to 650 for whites, and 267 to 225 for blacks.
Source: Adapted from Everett F. Cataldo, Richard M. Johnson, and Lyman A. Kellstedt, "Political Attitudes of the Urban Poor: Some Implications for Policy Makers," a paper delivered at the annual meeting of the American Political Science Association, 1968.

Table 1–4
"ON THE WHOLE, WOULD YOU SAY YOU ARE SATISFIED OR DISSATISFIED WITH THE WORK YOU DO?"

WHITES

Year	Satisfied	Dissatisfied	No Opinion
1949	69%	19%	12%
1963	90	7	3
1966	87	8	5
1969	88	6	6

NEGROES

Year	Satisfied	Dissatisfied	No Opinion
1949	55%	33%	12%
1963	54	33	13
1966	69	18	13
1969	76	18	6

Source: *Gallup Index,* May 1969, p. 8.

BLACK POWER

"Black Power recognizes—it must recognize—the ethnic basis of American politics as well as the power-oriented nature of American politics. Black Power therefore calls for black people to consolidate behind their own, so that they can bargain from a position of strength. But while we endorse the procedure of group solidarity and identity for the purpose of attaining certain goals in the body politic, this does not mean that black people should strive for the same kind of rewards (i.e., end results) obtained by the white society. The ultimate values and goals are not domination or exploitation of other groups, but rather an effective share in the total power of the society."

—Stokeley Carmichael and
Charles V. Hamilton*

Though Carmichael's call for Black Power is now over five years old, it lacks an authoritative interpretation. CORE, for instance, emphasizes the idea of a separate black economy based upon traditional forms, while SNCC stresses a politically united black community, and US emphasizes the unity of black culture. The Black Panthers, on the other hand, would impose the philosophies of Marx, Lenin, Stalin, and Mao Tse-tung on black nationalism.

*Stokeley Carmichael and Charles V. Hamilton, *Black Power: The Politics of Liberation in America* (New York: Vintage Books, 1967), p. 47. By permission of Random House, Inc.

Alienation Among Youth

Many young people, particularly left-leaning students, have become disaffected with the American political system. Some have denounced the United States as being imperialist and racist, have refused to obey some of its laws, and have actively protested the Indochina war. The highly publicized "youth revolution"—and the new youth culture involving different kinds of music and art, the use of drugs, different dress, and sexual freedom—has caused a backlash among many adults.

19

But what are these young people's positive goals? Many seek a *democracy of participation,* amenable to evaluation, dissent, and popular crusades. They urge that government satisfy human needs and be closer to the people in the local community—in the neighborhood and the ghetto. They would organize the unrepresented—the black, the poor, and the discontented—and build a new coalition that would overthrow the "establishment" (a synonym for any group of leaders—in government, business, the military, education, finance, the mass media, and other areas) and form a new society devoted to democracy, economic and civil justice, and world peace. Their goals are fundamentally compatible with the traditional concept of democracy. However, they attack traditional democracy largely because they feel it serves the "establishment" rather than the whole people.

But if the more militant students are alienated from the American political system, they probably number less than 10 percent of the 8 million student population. Most college students continue to be wedded to traditional American values. Their chief complaint about their college is that it is too impersonal (see Table 1-5)—the venerable gripe that helped touch off the student protest movement at Berkeley in 1964.

The militants have also alienated the more moderate left students, and as a result, the radical student movement has splintered. As for white radical youths allying themselves with black people, the major signs do not point to such a possibility. Rather, it appears that in the present decade black protest will con-

Table 1–5
STUDENT GRIPES ABOUT THEIR COLLEGE

The Question: What are your chief complaints against the administration and faculty of your college?

No complaints	30.3%
Too impersonal	31.5
Too conservative	12.6
Courses not relevant	8.2
Poor teachers	8.2
All others	32.7

Source: Gallup Poll, *Newsweek,* February 22, 1971, p. 62.

tinue to emphasize black identity, not revolution within a black-white coalition. Still, the militant minority could considerably influence college students, a great many of whom are liberal and independent (see Tables 1-6 and 1-7). This is particularly apt to happen if many students continue to be upset by feelings about war, the draft, black revolt, poverty, and crowding, as well as

Table 1–6
STUDENTS' POLITICAL BELIEFS

The question asked: "How would you describe your political beliefs—as extremely conservative, fairly conservative, middle-of-the-road, fairly liberal, or extremely liberal?"

The following table gives details and shows political beliefs leaning heavily to the left. It also reveals that students who have participated in demonstrations are far more liberal in their political beliefs than nondemonstrators. In fact, one demonstrator in four describes himself as "extremely liberal."

	ALL STUDENTS	DEMON-STRATORS	NONDEMON-STRATORS
Extremely conservative	2%	2%	2%
Fairly conservative	19	10	22
Middle-of-the-road	24	12	29
Fairly liberal	41	48	39
Extremely liberal	12	25	6

Source: *Gallup Survey*, June 1969, p. 37.

Table 1–7
PARTY LABELS LACK APPEAL FOR STUDENTS

Here is the question asked of both college students and the general public: "In politics as of today do you consider yourself a Republican, Democrat, or independent?"

The following table compares the present party affiliation of college students with that of the general public (adults 21 and older):

	STUDENTS	GENERAL PUBLIC
Republicans	23%	29%
Democrats	33	42
Independents	44	29

Students who describe themselves as "Independents" lean decidedly "left" in their political beliefs. Four times as many in this group say they are "fairly liberal" or "extremely liberal" as say they are "fairly conservative" or "extremely conservative."

Source: *Gallup Survey*, June 1969, p. 37.

21

more personal concerns about mass processing, intense work schedules, lack of outlets for their leadership talents, and general sense of powerlessness.

Most Congressmen who voted in 1971 for a constitutional amendment to give eighteen-year-olds the right to vote wished to show that the political system is receptive to legitimate demands.[12] But like most elders who have expressed sympathy for the youth movement, they have been more inclined to seek solutions to the "problem" of communication than to combine with the young to make a social revolution.

Most militants are fully aware that the traditional American way of controlling revolutionary and semi-revolutionary movements is to eliminate or isolate their most militant elements, while putting into effect some of their political, social, and cultural programs. In this way the political system contains revolutionary movements and prevents them from winning over segments of the population not in the movements' original constituencies. This was done to the labor movement and is being done to the black and student movements.

Alienation Among Mexican-Americans

Although our more than 6 million Mexican-Americans[13] are our second largest ethnic minority and antedate the Pilgrims in what is now the United States, perhaps less attention has been paid them than any other disadvantaged minority. This lack of attention has been partly the result of their low level of political participation. In California, for instance, where more than 40 percent of all Mexican-Americans live, fewer than 20 percent of the

[12] The "demands" of the young for the vote may have been exaggerated if the 1970 census surveys of voter participation are indicative. They revealed that in the 1968 presidential election only 33 percent of the eligible eighteen- to twenty-year-olds voted, and that in the 1970 election the figure was just 26 percent.

[13] There is much disagreement concerning the proper term to be used. Generally, the Spanish-surname people of New Mexico prefer to be called "Spanish-Americans," as do many others with Spanish surnames. Others prefer to be called "Americans of Mexican descent," or "people with Spanish surnames," or "Hispanos." Some choose to be known simply as "Americans." Many Mexican-American activists like to be called "Chicanos," which they often describe as Mexican-Americans with a non-Anglo image of themselves.

adult citizens who are Mexican-American were registered voters in 1960, and even fewer yet voted.

Why is it that the Mexican-American, who competes on the lowest rung of the economic ladder with the blacks and poor whites, does not use the franchise to improve his lot? One reason is that before 1950 many Mexicans looked upon voting as an "Anglo" rite, an intangible that was irrelevant to a better life, food, shelter, employment, and education. Another reason is that they have been effectively disfranchised. In Texas, for instance, the required poll tax blocked many who were interested in voting. In California, until it was declared unconstitutional in 1970 by the California Supreme Court, the state required that voters demonstrate an ability to read and write English. Federal law still bars them from citizenship (and thus from voting) if they cannot read, write, speak, or understand English. Most Anglos and blacks do not suffer this disadvantage. Accordingly, it is not surprising that in Los Angeles, which has the country's largest concentration of Spanish-speaking people, there are none on the city council, although there are at least three black councilmen. Nor is it surprising that in Los Angeles county, where Mexican-Americans slightly outnumber blacks, about six times as many blacks are employed by the county.

In New Mexico, where Mexican-Americans have not been required to pay poll taxes or pass language exams, and where there is less prejudice against them, they have been heavily involved in politics and have developed political expertise. As a result, they have long been a major political force there.

Not all of the political weakness of the Mexican-American minority may be attributed to nonvoting. Lack of fluency in English has had a major impact. So also has the discrimination before the law, in employment, education, and housing, which has kept many virtually outside American society.[14] Political weakness has also derived from the Mexican-American's frequently suspicious attitude toward government agencies. He has feared immigration agents who could deport, school authorities who could punish, social workers who could deny him food and clothing, and police

[14] In the 1970 census, Mexican-Americans were for the first time identified as a separate ethnic group.

and other government agencies with even greater authority and sanctions. Justifiable fear of Anglo officialdom has often resulted in uncooperative behavior by Mexican-Americans which, in turn, has tended to reinforce the unfavorable impression many Anglos have of them.

Internal division is yet another problem—for instance, some Mexican-Americans are bilingual; others are literate in Spanish only or English only; and still others are functionally limited in both. Some were born in the United States; some are recent immigrants. Some favor assimilation into American society; others favor retaining Mexican identity and life styles. Some relate to the Spanish heritage, while others maintain close contact with Mexico. Many are cynical or apathetic about politics; others advocate one form or another of political activism. Some are inclined to work with friendly Anglos and blacks; others keep to themselves.

Recently, Mexican-Americans, like blacks, have become increasingly militant. Their leading associations, the Mexican-American Political Association (MAPA), formed in California in 1959, and the Political Association of Spanish-Speaking Organizations (PASSO),[15] organized in Texas in 1960, have engaged actively in politics. Both concentrate on direct political action and have small concern for social assimilation. Essentially they want what blacks want for black people—immediate improvement in their situation.

Alienation Among White Ethnics

A potentially fatal weakness of our racial policy is our neglect of the problems of poor and lower-income white ethnics. On the cutting edge of black gains, and deeply resentful of the Johnson Administration for "giving the Negroes everything," white ethnics have retaliated by voting for George Wallace for President, supporting "law and order" candidates, and forming vigilante groups to defend family, home, and neighborhood. Labeled "white

---

[15] It was thought that this less ethnically partisan name would be more attractive to Puerto Ricans and other Latin Americans who had given significant support to the Viva Kennedy club movement.

racists," "backlashers," "whitelashers," put down and forgotten, they have become increasingly alienated.

Who is the white ethnic? One observer offers this portrait:

> He is the ordinary employee in the factory and in the office. Twenty million strong, he forms the bulk of the nation's working force. He makes five to ten thousand dollars a year, has a wife and two children, owns a house in town—between the ghetto and the suburbs, or perhaps in a low-cost subdivision on the fringe—and owes plenty in installment debts on his car and his appliances. He finds his tax burden heavy, his neighborhood services poor, his national image tarnished, and his political clout diminishing. This too is alienation.[16]

The white ethnic poor are mostly Catholic—and Irish, Polish Italian, Greek, Slovak, Russian, Hungarian, Croatian, or Serb. Although they outnumber black poor, they are not so homogeneous. Furthermore, they are particularly sensitive about being objects of charity. Lacking the political power of blacks, they have benefitted relatively little from anti-poverty programs.

White ethnics are loosely organized in the National Confederation of American Ethnic Groups. Its expressed goal is to show strength so that white ethnics will not continue to "take a back seat" to blacks and other minority pressure groups. It hopes to do this by linking ethnic fraternal societies, the main institutional affiliation for low-income white ethnics. Beneath their anger and fear, white ethnics plead for understanding. Like other minorities, they want representation, and by their own kind.

How dangerous is white ethnic alienation? Robert L. Heilbroner warns that while continued black militancy is needed to secure a further rise in black well-being,

> . . . black militancy, if pushed beyond the never clearly demarcated line of social tolerance, may result in white countermilitancy, with the possibility of an annulment of black gains or even a retrograde movement. If the rise of black power thus opens the way to a long overdue repair of the single greatest

[16] Robert C. Wood, quoted by Monroe W. Karmin, "Polish Hill: The White Ethnic's Complaint," *The Washington Monthly*, August 1969, p. 36.

source of social neglect in America, it also holds the worrisome prospect of a polarization of race relations that could result in major social catastrophe, for whites as well as blacks.[17]

Furthermore, the white ethnics may in desperation turn to right-wing extremists, if a massive effort is not made to understand them and their problems, and if our elites make no effort to help them organize.

Suggested Additional Reading

Anderson, W. (ed.). *Politics and Environment: A Reader in Ecological Crisis.* 1970.

Brink, W., and L. Harris. *Black and White.* 1966.

Dahl, R. A. *Modern Political Analysis.* 1970.

Draper, T. *The Rediscovery of Black Nationalism.* 1970.

Easton, D. *A Framework for Political Analysis.* 1965.

Glick, E. B. *Soldiers, Scholars, and Society.* 1970.

Grodzins, M. *Americans Betrayed: Politics and the Japanese Evacuation.* 1949.

Hacker, A. *The End of the American Era.* 1970.

Langton, K. P. *Political Socialization.* 1969.

Lubell, S. *The Hidden Crisis in American Politics.* 1970.

Nieburg, H. L. *Political Violence: The Behavioral Process.* 1969.

Reich, C. A. *The Greening of America.* 1970.

Roszak, T. *The Making of a Counter Culture: Reflections on the Technocratic Society and Its Youthful Opposition.* 1969.

Samora, J. (ed.). *La Raza: Forgotten Americans.* 1966.

Silverman, S. (ed.). *The Black Revolt and Democratic Politics.* 1970.

Skolnick, J. H. *The Politics of Protest.* 1969.

[17] Robert L. Heilbroner, "Benign Neglect in the United States," *Trans-action*, October 1970, p. 22.

2 Democracy and the Political System

John Kouns, Photofind, S. F.

Thine is not to complete the task, but
neither art thou free to desist from it.
—*The Talmud*

In 1939, Italian political philosopher Gaetano Mosca wrote in
The Ruling Class a theory of a power elite:

> In all societies—from societies that are very meagerly devel-
> oped and have barely attained the dawnings of civilization,
> down to the most advanced and powerful societies—two classes
> of people appear—a class that rules and a class that is ruled.
> The first class, always the less numerous, performs all political
> functions, monopolizes power, and enjoys the advantages that
> power brings, whereas the second, the more numerous class, is
> directed and controlled by the first, in a manner that is now
> more or less legal, now more or less arbitrary and violent.[1]

[1] Gaetano Mosca, *The Ruling Class* (New York: McGraw-Hill, 1939), p. 50.

DEMOCRACY VERSUS POWER

Members of the New Left today also espouse a power-elite theory. They say that, in the United States, those who make the most consequential economic decisions are those who command the mass media, enjoy lofty social position, possess military power, and make the important determinations for our society—behind a façade of government by the people. In this analysis, Congressmen, the President, and other government officials simply rubber-stamp decisions made elsewhere in the power structure.

The idea of a power elite is not palatable to Americans. The theory of democracy familiar to most of us is that power resides in the people, who govern themselves; that the rulers are the ruled; and that government is Lincoln's "of the people, by the people, for the people." But, though we may feel Mosca's system is unknown to us, we still may see the difficulty of translating popular will into policy. Certainly, it is true, in a democracy some people play a more prominent role than others in government decision making. There may be aristocratic, even tyrannical aspects, and at times the system may be powerless to act. Even so, democratic regimes differ from aristocracies or dictatorships. Would it not, then, be more profitable to identify those characteristics than simply to presuppose that Mosca's analysis does not apply at all to democratic political systems?[2]

SIGNIFICANT CHARACTERISTICS OF DEMOCRATIC POWER SYSTEMS

Electoral System of Succession

The method of succession to the principal posts of authority has been a vexing problem in all forms of political systems. In demo-

---

[2] The term *power* does not simply mean orders from above. Actually, the power relationship is reciprocal between the subject and the ruler. As political theorist Harold Lasswell has stated, "power is in interpersonal situation; those who hold power are empowered. They . . . continue only so long as there is a continuing stream of empowering responses." See Lasswell's *Power and Personality* (New York: Norton, 1948), p. 10. The discussion of power in this chapter leans heavily on this book, on V. O. Key, *Politics, Parties, and*

cratic governments, the formula of electoral systems not only happily solves the succession question but also assures that these important power posts will be vacated at frequent intervals without severe convulsions in the commonwealth. Furthermore, as other writers have pointed out,

> . . . an electoral system, designed to turn power over to a particular elite for a limited period of time, can achieve a balance between power and responsiveness: the elites obtain power, yet this power is limited by the periodic elections themselves, by the concern for future elections during the interelection period, and by a variety of other formal and informal checks.[3]

Deference to the Ruled

Another characteristic of democratic power systems, deference to the ruled, depends on there being, first, ways of consulting with the people (or their representatives) and, second, ways of expressing the consent of the ruled. It does not mean the government must defer to the will of *each* person, for this would amount to anarchy. Rather it means the government generally accedes to the will of popular majorities. However, that authority of popular majorities is not unlimited—for instance, it would not be considered legitimate for the majority to do something that divested the minority of such freedoms as the right to express dissent, without fear of reprisals, from governmental actions or the right to associate with others to try to eject the government by voting it out. Even the more extreme expressions of minorities (for instance, one challenging the legitimacy of the government) must be permitted. As U.S. Supreme Court Justice William O. Douglas has observed: "Freedom to differ is not limited to things that do not matter much. That would be a mere shadow of free-

---

Pressure Groups (New York: Thomas Y. Crowell, 1964), and on R. A. Dahl, "The Concept of Power," *Behavioral Science* 2 (1957): 201-15. A recent collection on power and elites is R. Bell, D. V. Edwards, and R. H. Wagner, *Political Power: A Reader in Theory and Research* (New York: Free Press, 1969).
[3] Gabriel A. Almond and Sidney Verba, *The Civic Culture* (Princeton, N.J.: Princeton University Press, 1963), p. 477.

dom. The test of its substance is the right to differ as to things that touch the heart of the existing order."[4]

A Wide Dispersion of Power

A wide dispersion of power is still another characteristic of democratic power systems, particularly the American system. In the United States, authority resides not only in government officials, but also in private groups and individuals. Furthermore, power in America tends to be *situational*—in one situation, the decision of the President may prevail; in another, it may be a compromise negotiated in Congress; in another, the wants of the directors of a few large business corporations, or in still another, agriculture or organized labor. In a study of power in the city of New Haven, Connecticut, political scientist Robert A. Dahl found that influence is exerted by a number of elites, each of which has power over some matters but not others. Dahl reports that:

> the Economic Notables, far from being a ruling group, are simply one of the many groups out of which individuals sporadically emerge to influence the politics and acts of city officials. Almost anything one might say about the influence of the Economic Notables could be said with equal justice about a half dozen other groups in the New Haven community.[5]

Typically associated with the dispersion of power is *competition between power centers*. Although not restricted to democratic political systems, competition arises over many more matters and has different consequences from that in nondemocratic systems. In the American system, the rivalry between dispersed centers of influence and power is so prominent that the very political process itself is one of reconciling these conflicts.

[4] *Beilan v. Board of Eduction*, 1958.
[5] R. A. Dahl, *Who Governs? Democracy and Power in an American City* (New Haven, Conn.: Yale University Press, 1961), p. 72.

PRINCIPAL INSTITUTIONS OF DEMOCRATIC POWER SYSTEMS

Nondemocratic governments, like democratic, have executives, courts, administrative agencies, and even representative organs of a kind. But besides these, democracies have additional institutions which do such things as ease succession to posts of authority, consult with the governed, and accommodate demands of competing power centers. Among these institutions are political parties, electoral systems, representative organs, interest groups, a free press, free educational institutions, although there is other interaction between governors and the governed.

Political Parties

In democracies, political parties are important, first, because they manage the succession of officeholders to power by promoting their candidacy for election, and, second, because they get popular assent to government policy. If they accumulate enough popular support, they can take on governmental authority; if they attract enough discontent, they can oust the government. Either way, parties assist a sizable number of citizens to articulate their wishes and interests.

Electoral Systems

Electoral systems alone do not make power systems democratic; even dictatorships have elections. But elections in dictatorships are only superficial homage to the vigor of the democratic ideology. (In some communist states—for instance, the U.S.S.R.— nearly all citizens vote, but then there is only one party to vote for, the Communist Party.) Democratic elections, on the other hand, are generally carried out as contests between party organizations which offer an alternative to the voters. Although at times the electorate in a democratic system is won over by demagogues, or its elections manipulated by a small group, in the long run, democratic elections produce major deviations in government policy, mark out new courses of public policy, and sanction or repudiate the deeds of an administration.

Representative Organs

Democratic power systems commonly embody some kind of representative organ (or organs)—in the U.S., the Senate and the House of Representatives and lesser bodies—and perhaps other elected officials, such as a President or a governor. These are linked to the voters through elections and the political parties. As the apparatus of representation, they provide the democratic characteristics of consultation with, and consent of, the governed.

Interest Groups

In a democracy, the formal apparatus of government is usually supplemented by nongovernmental organizations—in the United States, *interest* or *pressure groups*. These groups—such as labor unions, business groups, agricultural groups—act as unofficial representative organs for their members by bringing their wishes to the attention of the government or by pressuring the government; sometimes, in fact, the government consults them. Some interest groups ally with a political party (e.g., some labor with Democrats, some business with Republicans); some also try privately to influence voters before elections.[6] At times, the influence of interest groups is so great that they actually determine the government policy—as when the National Rifle Association, some believe, has acted to block legislation to regulate firearms.

A Free Press and Free Educational Institutions

The preservation of a democratic political system depends heavily on a *free press*. "Where the press is free," asserted Thomas Jefferson, "and every man able to read, all is safe."[7] To be most effec-

---

[6] Testimony of California liquor lobbyist Arthur H. Samish before Senator Estes Kefauver's committee in 1951 revealed that he and his clients supported candidates from city councilmen on up.

[7] S. K. Padover, ed., *Thomas Jefferson on Democracy* (New York: Mentor Books, 1946), p. 164.

34

tive, a free press, of course, should not only report information but also reveal conflict in the society. Much has been made of the decline in the number of daily newspapers in the United States (a decrease of 44 percent in the first half of this century in the twenty-five largest cities). However, this has been partly offset by the availability of news from competing media, particularly radio and TV.

There are two other important ingredients of a democratic system. *Free educational institutions* instill the values of freedom of inquiry and self-evaluation. *Academic freedom* allows the free propagation of opposing ideas. Along with a free press, they may expose the evils in society and institutions and encourage reform, thereby keeping the people informed. However, neither is fully effective in any existing democracy.

Other Interaction Between Government and Governed

Still other kinds of interaction between the government and the governed occur when government policymakers are anxious about public opinion. Public officials seldom embark upon important programs without first estimating the popular sentiment and probable response. Their estimates may be based on intuition, on opinion polls, or on mail from constituents. These patterns of interaction are not peculiar to democratic political systems, but in such systems they reach their greatest amplification.

HOW DEMOCRATIC POWER SYSTEMS ENCOURAGE SUPPORT

No political system, whether democratic or not, can exist without support—and the level of support depends in good measure on the system's own actions. The system derives support for itself in two major ways: (1) by satisfying demands and (2) by creating legitimacy for itself.

Satisfying Demands as a Source of Support

The political decisions or policies that a political system makes to gain support for itself may be either negative or positive inducements to members of the system.

Negative inducements threaten members with various penalties or sanctions—for example, detention, a fine, or loss of life. Although coerced support is much greater in despotic than in democratic systems, a certain amount of support in all systems stems from fear of sanctions.

Positive inducements, also used by all political systems, may take the form of, for example, meeting demands of the members. A system need not meet *all* demands made on it, for over the years it stores up reserve support which generates some continuing loyalty to it. Actually, a system need not even satisfy *some* of all the members' demands. However, if it persistently fails to satisfy its members, particularly the most influential members, there may be demands for eliminating the regime or even dissolving the political community. No system, even an autocratic one, can exist solely by coercion.

Legitimacy as a Source of Support

A political system also derives support from the degree of *legitimacy* it enjoys—that is, the members' belief that the system and its institutions are the most appropriate for the society and that its decisions should be complied with.

If a political system is to survive, it must somehow endow its activities with an atmosphere of legitimacy. In part it does this by using *symbols*: the flag, national holidays, folk heroes, political rituals and ceremonies. Symbolic loyalty evokes the support of many members even though they may be dissatisfied.

The system also perpetuates itself through the *political socialization* of its members, so that individuals share the values and practices of the political community, a process of indoctrination that begins in the family and childhood associations and that is reinforced by the schools, the church, the mass media, and other institutions. Although the process of acquiring political attitudes continues in adulthood, apparently most attitudes are absorbed from the family during childhood and adolescent years.

In modern nations the schools are particularly powerful instruments for transmitting values, attitudes, and goals, and typically reflect the outlooks of the society's ascendant members. Schools that deviate and clash with influential groups in the political system experience a compulsion to conform.

DEMOCRATIC IDEALS: LIBERTY, EQUALITY, HUMAN WORTH—AND EMPIRICISM

Liberty and Equality

Individual liberty and *equality* are cardinal catch-words of democratic dogma, but neither is carried to an extreme in American government. Democratic theory affirms human equality—in that each man's life, liberty, and property, and his pursuit of happiness should be respected as much as any other man's. But complete equality is not possible because men are obviously not equal —at least not in ability, virtue, or competency—nor can they be made so.[8] Absolute individual liberty is anarchy, not democracy.

Democratic theory stresses both liberty and equality in this sense, but the emphasis it gives one or the other varies considerably from time to time. This is because the political environment is constantly changing. During the American Revolution, for instance, when people strongly feared arbitrary government, liberty of the individual from government power was emphasized. The rights of the people were principally *restraints on governmental authority.*[9] Although we still believe in freedom from arbitrary government, in recent years we have sought government intervention into economic and social relationships (e.g., fair housing and fair employment practices) in order to maintain the democratic ideals of human dignity and equality.

People argue that imposing equality reduces liberty. No doubt the welfare state, in promoting economic equality, has restricted some traditional liberties of free enterprise; however, we must

[8] Equality has many facets (e.g., human, economic, legal, social, or political). To increase or reduce any of these would increase or reduce equality overall.
[9] The Bill of Rights is an express recital of *limitations on government.* But liberty is also thought of as connoting the individual's faculty to act *positively* toward his chosen goals: that is, not simply to have *freedom from,* but opportunity *to do.*

note two other considerations. First, although the welfare state has circumscribed certain economic liberties, it has increased others—for example, the liberties of labor unions. Second, all legally warranted personal liberties—such as property rights and freedom of speech—restrict the actions of other people (for instance, those who may wish to convert illegally the property of others for their own use or enjoy silence). In brief, the issue is not whether there should be more or less liberty, but more or less of *which* liberties and *whose* liberties.

This is not to say that liberty is not in any way endangered. The increasing powers of government threaten our liberties, just as the unbridled powers of business corporations have. However, these increased government powers are in great part in response to a threat to political and personal liberties from foreign governments (principally Soviet Russia) and to the continuing danger of economic depression.

Human Worth

Behind all the assumptions of democracy is a belief in the supreme worth of the individual. Though nowhere practiced in its consummate sense, this belief includes liberty, equality, and civil rights for all people—good and bad; wise and foolish; rich and poor; white, black, brown, red, or yellow.

The concept of the supreme worth of the individual contrasts sharply with the doctrine of *statism* (as asserted, for instance, in fascist theory), which holds that the state is the measure of all value and that government institutions and policies are good if they further the interests of the state. Democratic theory, on the other hand, asserts that the well-being of the state has no significance except as it promotes the well-being of its individual citizens.

Empiricism

Another great assumption of democracy, *rational empiricism* was first fully explicated by English philosopher John Locke (1632–1704). It holds that all knowledge is derived from experience and that the search for truth is an endless process. To the rational empiricist, today's knowledge or "truth" is much like scientific truth, never immune to questioning—even of fundamentals—and subject to change in the light of new evidence. The empiricist insists on broad and unobstructed expression of the widest range of fact and opinion before an issue is decided. Philosopher Bertrand Russell writes that the rational empiricist says not that "This is true," but "I am inclined to think that under present circumstances this opinion is probably the best." From this point of view we derive the vital democratic liberties of free press, free speech, free association, and free assembly. The chief American exponent of rational empiricism was philosopher John Dewey (1859–1952).

The *political dogmatist* (e.g., Adolph Hitler or Joseph Stalin) is the opposite of the rational empiricist. Thinking he knows the ultimate truth, he rejects the need for further inquiry. He seeks not the truth but the strengthening of his dogma and the suppression of opposing ideas. This tendency (belief) has generally kept Americans cool to the rhetoric of extremists on either left or right, since extreme positions—either communist or fascist—are both characterized by rigid party lines and suppression of free speech, press, and personal liberty.

THE PROBLEM OF DEFINING DEMOCRACY

While we Americans proudly proclaim that the United States is a democracy, usually we have no more than a vague idea what the word means, and even scholars do not use the term uniformly. Though regrettable, this confusion is understandable, for the word *democracy* has been a part of common speech for about twenty-five centuries; and the longer and more widespread its use, the less uniform has been its sense.

Diverse Origins of Democracy

First applied by the ancient Greeks to some of the governments of the Aegean cities, the term "democratic" has been used to describe governments as dissimilar as medieval monasteries and modern Leviathans (like the People's Republic of China). The meaning of democracy is also uncertain, because democracy cannot be attributed to any one philosopher, prophet, society, or document. Nor are there any authoritative books or interpreters whose word is final.

Having no particular philosophical father, no birthplace, and no exact birthdate, democratic theory necessarily reflects a variety of ideas drawn from different philosophies existing in different cultures at different times. The origins of democratic ideas may be seen in the Greek city-states, the medieval Church, the guilds, the dissident religious sects, the New England town meetings, and the self-governing congregations (e.g., Quakers and Congregationalists). Some democratic ideas are found in documents such as *Magna Carta* (1215), a charter dealing mainly with the rights of feudal barons; Pericles' *Funeral Oration* (circa 431 B.C.), a declaration of the ideals of Athenian democracy; the *Agreement of the People*, a classic statement of democratic doctrine and an

> "For really I think that the poorest he that is in England hath a life to live, as the greatest he."
> —Colonel Rainsborough,
>   during the 1647–1648 Army debates
>   over the *Agreement of the People*

appeal for democratic government during England's constitutional crisis of 1647–1648; the *Declaration of Independence* (1776), the American colonists' statement of grievances against the English government, and a democratic political theory; the French *Declaration of the Rights of Man and Citizen* (1789), a hodge-podge of democratic and aristocratic principles; and Lincoln's *Gettysburg Address* (1863), the brief funeral oration which came to be the classic statement of nineteenth-century democracy.

Added to these generally legitimate expressions of bygone times (and adding to the confusion) is the contemporary use of the term *democracy* without warrant either in observation or reason. Today, propagandists for nearly all systems of government, including dictatorships, have made it a standard and repeatedly misused slogan.

Democracy has not always been a positive word. Not until early in the twentieth century, when the United States, England, and France, three of the greatest nations at that time, were calling themselves democracies, did democracy achieve widespread popularity. Even rightists embraced the term. Originally fearful

---

SOME WORDS USED BY THE PREDEMOCRATIC UPPER CLASSES TO DESCRIBE THE COMMON PEOPLE

bog-trotter	hick	potwalloper
chawbacon	looby	rabble
churl	loon	scrub
cinderwench	muckworm	scum
clod	mudlark	vermin
guttersnipe		

—Roget, *Thesaurus of the English Language*

---

of democracy as a threat to property, they came to fear the new bogey of communism much more. Accordingly, they shifted their antagonism against *democracy,* the slogan of the left, to *communism.* Thus, the term democracy came to be almost universally sanctified by democrat leftists and anti-communist rightists alike.

Direct Democracy or Representative Democracy?

Democracy is a form of government in which, as it is said, the people are "sovereign." Taken literally, popular sovereignty would mean a nation of dictators—in the United States more than 200 million of them—and obviously the logistical problems alone of direct popular rule are insurmountable; the problem is one of sheer numbers. Only in the simplest of societies can democracy really be government *by* the people.

Democracy can, however, be representative, that is, government by representatives of the people. In this scheme, the people's representatives serve them through government institutions,

41

representing (in some measure) popular interests. Responsibility is enforced by the people, principally through the ballot.

ROUSSEAU ON REPRESENTATIVE DEMOCRACY

"The people of England regards itself as free, but it is grossly mistaken; it is free only during the election of members to parliament. As soon as they are elected, slavery overtakes it, and it is nothing."
—Jean Jacques Rousseau, *The Social Contract*

Those who share Rousseau's ideas on popular sovereignty today usually accept representative government, but may insist that the people's representatives serve as their *agents,* doing their bidding and reflecting their will rather than serving as *delegates,* or *partisans,* or as combinations of these.

GOVERNMENT BY THE PEOPLE. . . ?

". . . we here highly resolve . . . that government *of* the people, *by* the people, *for* the people, shall not perish from the earth."
—Abraham Lincoln, *Gettysburg Address.* [Italics added.]

. . . OR BY CONSENT OF THE GOVERNED?

We hold these truths to be self-evident, that all men are created equal, that they are endowed by their Creator with certain unalienable rights, that among these are Life, Liberty and the pursuit of Happiness.—That to secure these rights, Governments are instituted among Men, deriving their just powers from the *consent of the governed.* . . .
—*Declaration of Independence.* [Italics added.]

Democracy or Constitutionalism?

Besides being representative, American democracy is also *constitutional.* In a constitutional democracy there are limits on what

TWO IDEOLOGIES THAT RIVAL DEMOCRACY

Fascism

A political system or ideology of the extreme right, it is contemptuous of democratic parliamentarianism and personal liberty. It is anticommunist and seeks to maintain social and economic privilege and destroy personal liberty. It features political dictatorship, a one-party state, and an all-pervasive secret police. Although fascism allows private ownership of land and capital, it regiments all economic and social activity under government control. It depends on national patriotism as its driving force.

Fascism was first fashioned by Benito Mussolini in Italy in 1922 and was emulated by, among others, Adolph Hitler in Germany, Francisco Franco in Spain, and Juan D. Peron in Argentina. Fascist regimes have usually come to power in times of crisis when big land owners or industrialists feared the increasing strength of communism. Despite the defeat of Italian and German fascism in World War II, neofascist military dictatorships have been on the rise in much of the world.

Few Americans espouse fascism, but it appeals to some racists and some strong opponents of socialism, communism, and internationalism.

Communism

Theoretically, communism is an economic, social, and political system in which land and capital are government owned and operated and in which sovereignty resides in the working class or "proletariat." Actual power, however, is with the directors, ruling through a strictly disciplined party.

Communism asserts that class conflict is inevitable and seeks to "liberate" the proletariat from exploitation by capitalists by instituting a socialist system. Where such a system can be achieved by using democratic processes, communism may not advocate force or violence.

Communism claims to extend rather than restrict democracy; under communism the state is supposed to wither away someday and the society is supposed to be classless and democratic. Communism rejects democratic elections in countries such as England and the United

States as being a sham where the political business of the worker is to decide, as Lenin stated, "once every few years which member of the ruling class is to repress and oppress the people."

Established in Russia by the Bolshevik Revolution in 1917, communists prevail in mainland China and most of Eastern Europe and have converted much of the under-developed world. The totalitarian methods of communism are unattractive in the United States and other democra-cies in which the needs of most of the people are fulfilled. Communist party membership in the United States has never exceeded 100,000.

governments may do, even though acting for the majority. Although not everyone agrees on the exact nature and extent of these limits, we agree that there are certain things it may do—only if it uses *proper procedures* and is *fair*. At the very least, government may not deprive a person of life, liberty, or property without due process of law. It should not, however, be thought that because constitutionalism limits majority rule it is antithetical to democracy.

Political, Economic, or Social Democracy?

Definition of democracy, a difficult matter in any event, becomes impossible when the word is used to describe economic and social systems—such as capitalism, socialism, or communism—in addition to political ones.

In this book we have used the word in its political sense, since this is its oldest usage. It emphasizes *processes,* describing how a society is governed, but says nothing about democracy's system of social justice and economic security provided by its laws or about democracy as a way of life—that is, democratic as opposed to authoritarian personalities, families, or educational institutions.

Yet it should not be concluded that political (or parliamentary or liberal) democracy is not concerned with a certain level of economic and social justice and a wide range of civil and political liberties. If the method is to work, it must be. All democracies must make deliberate and successful efforts to provide the material and social basis of an active citizenship.

Democratic socialism, more widespread than political democracy, differs from the latter in that it attempts to combine political *and* economic democracy. *Communism,* on the other hand, emphasizes *economic democracy,* while subordinating political democracy. *Political democracy* reverses the emphasis and stresses *political opportunity and equality. Fascism* rejects democracy outright.

Today, democratic socialism has been partly instituted in much of Africa (e.g., Tanzania), Asia (e.g., India), and Europe (e.g., Italy). In many European countries a social democratic party is the alternative party or leads the opposition. Some regard democratic socialism as the best response to the economic challenge of the communists. Not surprisingly, therefore, communists are hostile to it, fearing that by planning, directing, and regulating the economy and by providing welfare services while retaining some private enterprise in the economy, democratic socialism will correct the weaknesses, "inner contradictions," and evils of capitalism which the communists are counting upon for its collapse. In the United States, conservatives oppose democratic socialism because they believe it would displace the free-market economy and constitute a step toward communism.

AN OPERATIONAL DEFINITION OF DEMOCRACY

Thus far, our discussion has largely been about the origins, characteristics, ideas, and institutions of democracy. But if we are to comprehend democracy fully and put our knowledge to use, we must learn much more than simply the "facts of democracy." We must learn and apply an *operational* definition of democracy— one that describes a functioning democratic system.

One political scientist, E. E. Schattschneider, offers this working definition:

> *Democracy is a competitive political system in which competing leaders and organizations define the alternatives of public*

policy in such a way that the public can participate in the decision-making process.[10]

The chief advantage of this definition over classical definitions is that it describes something that actually happens; it does not make impossible demands on the citizen.

It may seem a contradiction to say that democracy is rule by consent of the governed and also to insist, as Schattschneider does, that leadership is a necessary element of democratic government. Yet we may argue that only when competition exists between political leaders who frame policy alternatives do the people have a choice about policies and candidates. Schattschneider's emphasis on leadership should not be misread—it does not signify that in the American political system an elite despotizes over the rest of the citizens. One reason is that American political leaders are not a socially homogenous group; they emerge from diverse social classes and hold a variety of social interests. Although there are, of course, the Roosevelts, Rockefellers, and Kennedys—all from rich and distinguished families—there are also the Trumans, Johnsons, and Nixons—none of wealthy origins. Another reason is that the division of powers between two levels (national and state) and three branches of government (executive, legislative, judicial) permit many power centers to emerge within the political system. A third reason is that political leaders are only one of many groups in this country that shape public policy. Finally, though neither governors nor governed adhere unreservedly to democratic values, American leaders, having experienced success in democratic politics, seem more inclined to abide by the "rules of the game" and thus support democratic values than do those who have not occupied public office.

In contrast to an operational definition, most Americans are apt to define democracy according to the classical concept of *government by the people.* That is, they define democracy first, instead of first examining existing democracies and *then* arriving at a definition. But this classical definition does not describe

[10] E. E. Schattschneider, *The Semisovereign People* (New York: Holt, Rinehart & Winston, 1960), p. 141.

46

national democracies. It fails to reckon with the great numbers of people involved in modern political units and the resulting impossibility of direct popular government. It also suggests an unreal image of a citizenry that thinks about politics as a Congressman might, daily pressing on government officials their opinions on a multitude of interests. That citizens do not perform this preposterous role has been shown in a study, as depicted in Tables 2-1 and 2-2, of public participation in the United States and four other nations.[11] This study exposes the striking diver-

Table 2–1
PERCENT WHO SAY THE ORDINARY MAN SHOULD BE ACTIVE IN HIS LOCAL COMMUNITY, BY NATION AND EDUCATION

NATION	TOTAL	PRIMARY OR LESS	SOME SECONDARY	SOME UNIVERSITY
United States	51%	35%	56%	66%
Great Britain	39	37	42	42
Germany	22	21	32	38
Italy	10	7	17	22
Mexico	26	24	37	38

Source: Adapted from Gabriel A. Almond and Sidney Verba, *The Civic Culture*, p. 176. Copyright © 1963 by Princeton University Press.

Table 2–2
PERCENT WHO SAY THE ORDINARY MAN SHOULD BE ACTIVE IN HIS LOCAL COMMUNITY, BY NATION AND OCCUPATION OF FAMILY BREADWINNER

NATION	TOTAL	UNSKILLED	SKILLED	WHITE COLLAR	PROFESSIONAL AND MANAGERIAL
United States	51%	34%	52%	59%	73%
Great Britain	39	31	43	50	42
Germany	22	18	20	31	33
Italy	10	8	6	24	14
Mexico	26	26	25	25	42

Source: Adapted from Gabriel A. Almond and Sidney Verba, *The Civic Culture*, p. 176. Copyright © 1963 by Princeton University Press.

[11] Public apathy is given greater treatment in Chapter 6.

gence between the classical ideal of popular rationality and civic participation and the reality of public irrationality, narrowness, and political inertia.

Surely we cannot restore the New England town meeting, though sometimes there seems no other alternative to the complex polity of our mass society and the administrative-bureaucratic state, which are principally responsible for citizen inertia. And representative democracy probably cannot solve all the problems of mass society. But at least it allows the citizen to choose between alternatives created by competing political leaders and organizations, and to determine whether his country's democratic system should be reformed, restructured, or kept as it is (everyone is entitled to his own purgatory). It also allows him to decide if the democratic order is threatened by a domestic power elite (e.g., business, government, military, or liberal establishment), or a mass movement (e.g., Wallacite, radical student, right-wing radical, or black militant), or power elite overreaction to the threat of a mass movement, or by a power elite of another country (e.g., the Soviets of the U.S.S.R.). Here the thoughts of the French observer of America, Alexis de Tocqueville, in his concluding words to *Democracy in America*, seem compelling:

> Let us, then, look forward to the future with that salutory fear which makes men keep watch and ward for freedom, not with that faint and idle terror which depresses and enervates the heart.[12]

A WAY TO STUDY GOVERNMENT: SYSTEMS ANALYSIS

Like the ordinary citizen, or even the professional politician and political scientist, the student beginning his study of government is confronted with a bewildering array of seemingly unrelated facts, events, ideas, and activities. How can one make sense of this jumble?

A first step is to decide how to study politics. An eminent political scientist offers this advice: "The study of politics is con-

[12] Alexis de Tocqueville, *Democracy in America*, vol. II. (New York: Knopf, 1948), p. 330.

cerned with understanding how authoritative decisions are made and executed for a society."[13]

But how might we gain such an understanding? One way is to try to comprehend politics by considering pieces of each of its various aspects. We can scrutinize the operation of such institutions as interest groups, political parties, voting, and government agencies. We can then examine the character and consequences of such political practices as violence, propaganda, and manipulation and the structure within which these practices occur. Then, by combining the results of our studies, we can see approximately what happens in a self-contained political unit.

Yet, by combining our results aren't we implying that we cannot understand one unit unless we understand how the whole works? Why not, then, first seek to understand the system itself?

Our effort to comprehend the American political system might be aided measurably if we had some overall "theory" of politics— a blueprint, as it were, of the political amphitheatre. Political scientists offer such a blueprint in what is called *systems analysis*. Systems analysis is based on three assumptions about politics:

(1) that political life can be separated from other social activities and systems, at least for purposes of analysis;

(2) that politics is a system of related activities which influence how authoritative decisions are made and executed for a society; and

(3) that the system is kept operating by its environment, the culture it influences and which influences it.

Broadly, systems analysis consists of five major elements, as follows (see Figure 2-1):

(1) *The political system itself*—an identifiable whole which can be broken down into interdependent parts called *subsystems* (for example, the congressional, presidential, judicial, and administrative subsystems) and subsystems within subsystems (for example, the Supreme Court within the judicial subsystem).

[13] David Easton, "An Approach to the Analysis of Political Systems," *World Politics*, April 1957, p. 383. Much of the discussion of systems analysis which follows is based upon this article and a later book by Professor Easton, *A Framework for Political Analysis* (Englewood Cliffs, N.J.: Prentice-Hall, 1965).

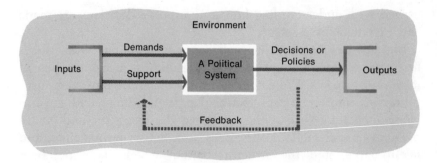

Figure 2-1. The five elements of systems analysis of the political system. (Source: David Easton, "An Approach to the Analysis of Political Systems," *World Politics,* April 1957, p. 384; copyright 1957 by Princeton University Press.

(2) *The environment*—all reality external to the political system.

(3) *Inputs* from the environment—those factors that flow into the political system, affect it, and bring about modifications in it; that is, *demands* upon the system's decision-makers (such as the demands of civil rights demonstrators) and *supports* for the system (such as the support of citizens paying taxes).

(4) *Outputs* into the environment—the system's authoritative decisions which allocate advantages and disadvantages for the entire society (such as civil rights decisions and foreign, military, and economic policies).

(5) *Feedback*—reactions to the system's authoritative decisions; that is, new support given to the system because it satisfied a demand made on it, or a new demand made on it because of some decision (for instance, a demand for government-financed construction of more hospitals as a result of Medicare legislation's providing wider medical care).

HOW SYSTEMS ANALYSIS MIGHT BE USED

How can we use systems analysis to study the American political system? We can start by trying, for purposes of study, to separate the political system from its environment. This is reasonable because the behavior of the political system, like that of the human organism, is determined partly by its own structure and internal needs and partly by the effects on it of the environment. Most of the political system's authoritative decisions reflect these demands and supports, and probably most of the important changes in it reflect environmental changes.

By using systems analysis—that is, by studying the political system itself[14]—the major demands and supports coming into it from the environment,[15] its decision-making activities (interest representation, rule-making, application of rules, and settlement of disputes),[16] and its decisions and actions (outputs)[17]—we may learn how the political system *maintains* itself, and thereby better understand how it works. Although systems analysis cannot be applied to all types of political participation, it is at least an economical way to organize political data so that they can be studied, and it makes the student of government sensitive to a very wide range of political relationships.

Suggested Additional Reading

Adorno, T. W., *et al. The Authoritarian Personality.* 1950.

Aron, T. *Democracy and Totalitarianism.* 1969.

Bell, T., E. V. Edwards, and R. H. Wagner. *Political Power: A Reader in Theory and Research.* 1969.

Clark, J. M. *Alternative to Serfdom.* 1948.

Dahl, R. A. *A Preface to Democratic Theory.* 1956.

———. *Who Governs? Democracy and Power in an American City.* 1961.

Ebenstein, W. *Today's Isms: Communism, Fascism, Capitalism, Socialism.* 1970.

Eisenberg, D. *The Re-emergence of Fascism.* 1968.

Encyclopedia of the Social Sciences. 1930. (See also *International Encyclopedia of the Social Sciences,* 1968, which complements and updates this encyclopedia.)

Freedman, L. *Issues of the Seventies.* 1970.

Hartz, L. *The Liberal Tradition in America.* 1955.

---

[14] Covered principally in Chapters 1 through 5.
[15] Covered principally in Chapters 6 through 9.
[16] Covered principally in Chapters 10 through 14.
[17] Covered principally in Chapters 15 through 19.

Hayek, F. A. *The Road to Serfdom.* 1955.

Heilbroner, R. L. *The Future as History.* 1959.

Hoffer, E. *The True Believer.* 1951.

Jacobs, D. N. *The New Communisms.* 1969.

Kennedy, R. F. *To Seek a Newer World.* 1968.

Kirk, R. *The Conservative Mind.* 1960.

Lasswell, H. *Power and Personality.* 1948.

McCarthy, E. *First Things First: New Priorities for America.* 1968.

Mosca, G. *The Ruling Class.* 1939.

Ortega y Gasset, J. *The Revolt of the Masses.* 1932.

Padover, S. (ed.). *Thomas Jefferson on Democracy.* 1946.

Redford, E. *Democracy in the Administrative State.* 1969.

Riker, W. H. *Democracy in the United States.* 1965.

Rose, A. *The Power Structure.* 1967.

Rubinstein, A. Z., and G. W. Thumm. *Ideas and Issues.* 1970.

Schattschneider, E. E. *The Semisovereign People.* 1960.

Tocqueville, A. *Democracy in America.* 1948.

3 The Philadelphia Story: A New Scheme of Government

He that goeth about to persuade a multitude that they are not so well governed as they might be shall never want attentive and favorable hearers.

—*Thomas Hooker*

On a very hot day in the summer of 1787, in the imposing red-brick State House in Philadelphia, fifty-five delegates gathered from twelve American states.[1] Because of their upper-class social graces and the smallness of their number, they found intimate and agreeable acquaintance not difficult. Several were men of age and maturity, but the comparatively young men—those in their forties—were the more active and influential.[2]

THE DELEGATES AND THEIR "MANDATES"

Although an able group, these gentlemen were not particularly representative of the American people, whose constitution they

---

[1] Altogether, seventy-four delegates were selected in the twelve states, but only fifty-five of them participated. Rhode Island, dominated by those who favored inflation and were suspicious of the undertaking, was never represented.

[2] The average age of the delegates was forty-three.

were preparing to draft. None had been elected directly by the people, and none were spokesmen for the poor and debtors. The delegates had been selected by state legislatures whose members in turn had been chosen by a property-holding electorate, since in those times only owners of property—about 80 to 95 percent of the adult, white males—had the right to vote. Furthermore, the instructions given them by the Congress of the Articles of Confederation in calling the convention clearly restricted them to meet "for the sole and express purpose" of revising the Articles, the then-existing Constitution. None had been given specific authority by his state to draft a new constitution.

The "Great Agreement"

The delegates realized that major disagreements would arise once discussions began. Therefore, they held their sessions entirely in secrecy, with guards posted at the doors, and wisely chose not to advertise their dissensions. Also, they did not wish to be put in a position of having to answer politically for their voting record at the convention.[3] Voting was not by individuals but by states, with each state having one vote.

Deliberations had barely begun when the wisdom of maintaining secrecy became apparent. On May 30, Edmund Randolph of Virginia, then only thirty-four, proposed "that a *national* Government ought to be established consisting of a *supreme* Legislature, Executive, and Judiciary." His suggestion meant that the delegates would have to cast aside the Articles and fashion a wholly new governmental system in which both the national and state governments would draw their authority directly from the people and in which the laws of the national government would be supreme. Approval of this proposal would also mean the triumph of the nationalists over those who were more sensitive about the "rights" of the states and who had fought most strongly against the imperial centralization of the British Empire.

[3] The official records of the proceedings at the convention were very sketchy and were not released by General Washington to the State Department until 1796. They were not printed and released until 1819. James Madison's notes, our best source of information on the convention proceedings, were not published until 1840, three years after his death.

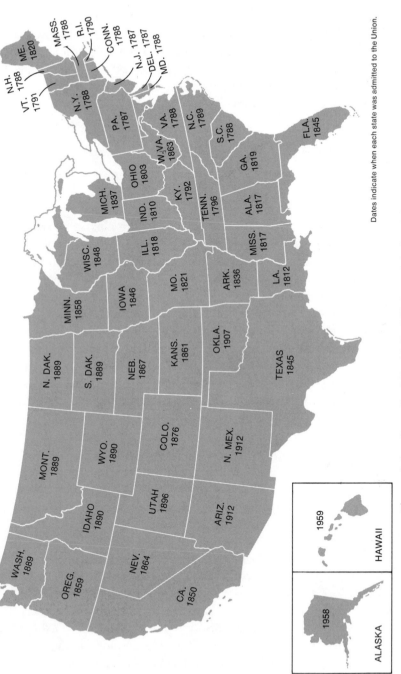

Figure 3-1. Growth of the United States, state by state.

Dates indicate when each state was admitted to the Union.

With each state delegation casting one vote, Randolph's resolution, which became known as the Great Agreement, was passed with only three dissenting votes. Would the original proposal for a convention have prevailed had the Congress and the people anticipated, as George Washington expressed it, this "radical cure of the Articles"? No one can say.

The Great Men of Philadelphia

It is fortunate that these were undeniably great men at the Philadelphia gathering—"demigods," Thomas Jefferson called them. Most were gentlemen of learning and ideas as well as men of affairs. Many had a scholarly knowledge of the classic works on Greek and Roman government and the writings of great political philosophers such as Aristotle, Cicero, Harrington, Locke, Montesquieu, and Rousseau, and they drew heavily on this knowledge during the convention.

The great majority had served as governors, members of Congress, state legislators, and judges, and more than half were lawyers. They were familiar with their own state governments as well as European political systems, and had a detailed knowledge of the Articles and its several weaknesses. Fortunately, many were also old hands at constitution making in their respective states. Obviously, they were rich in experience from which to draw ideas for a new governmental system.

No one delegate dominated the proceedings. George Washington, only fifty-five at the time, although aloof and reluctant to attend the convention, was nevertheless selected presiding officer. Though he was not active in formal discussions, his enormous prestige helped to quiet tempers inflamed by the tension of the debates and the oppressive summer heat. Furthermore, the delegates knew, the expectation that he would be elected the first President of the United States would help make the convention acceptable to the public and would increase the likelihood that the states would ratify the new constitution. Benjamin Franklin, then eighty-one, was second in prestige only to General Washington. Although he was indiscreetly talkative in his old age, the wisdom and humor of this elder statesman saved the day more than once; for instance, on June 30, he advised the delegates by saying that when the "planks" do not fit, a little should be shaved from each to create a "good joint." James Madison of Virginia, who was later to become a leading figure in Congress, Secretary of State, and President of the United States, also made notable contributions to the Constitution. His knowledge of the federations and confederations known to history was immense, and his detailed notes on the proceedings are our best source on the Convention. Finally, there was the brilliant conservative Alexander Hamilton, a New York lawyer and comrade-in-arms with General Washington. Then only thirty, Hamilton was actually not very influential at the Convention, largely because of his rather extreme views on many matters and his irregular attendance. His five-hour speech on behalf of his plan for a superpowerful central government, for instance, gathered only one "yes" vote—his. Hamilton's major contribution came later, in the struggle over ratification.

Many of the great leaders of the American Revolution were absent. The fiery Patrick Henry, ardent champion of states' rights, "smelt a rat" and refused to attend. Thomas Jefferson, the author of the Declaration of Independence, who would doubtless have been a great asset to the Convention and a strong liberal voice, was in Europe as minister to France. The pamphleteer of the Revolution, Thomas Paine, was also in Europe. Sam Adams was not there, nor was Richard Henry Lee, who introduced the Declaration of Independence. John Hancock was not elected because of his strong anti-federalist leanings.

Those who occupied the stage at Philadelphia were not the stormy architects of revolution. They were conservative men, skilled in the difficult art of fashioning stable political systems.

The Delegates as Nationalists

To many public figures of the day, and especially the nationalists, the government created by our first national constitution, the Articles of Confederation (1781–1789), cut a sorry figure indeed. Internationally, its feebleness invited abuse and disrespect. Domestically, it was too impotent to deal with the quarreling states or to withstand agrarian-debtor revolts such as Shays' Rebellion in Massachusetts. It lacked both a separate executive and a system of

59

courts and power to compel obedience to its mandates. While its one-house Congress, the single constitutional organ of its central government, was given power to conduct foreign relations, determine war or peace, regulate the coinage system, borrow money, regulate Indian affairs, establish post offices, maintain an army and navy, and make requisitions on the states for money and men, it depended completely on the states for income as well as execution of its laws. Furthermore, it was *denied* power to tax and to regulate commerce, deficiencies which proved to be its undoing. Having announced their sovereignty in the Declaration of Independence (1776), and having exercised it in the Second Continental Congress (1775–1781), the states were unwilling in 1781 to grant full sovereign powers to a central government, be it at London, Philadelphia, or anywhere. This stance of the states reflected current popular opinion that only through strong *local* governments, not through a strong and potentially dangerous *central* government, would the goals of the American Revolution be realized.

Washington, Madison, and Hamilton were nationalists. They had little confidence in the state legislatures and they feared what they considered these states' democratic excesses. Noting with apprehension the public's continual questioning of the established economic and social order, the nationalists realized they could expect no help from the legislatures. Only a strong central authority, they concluded, could deal effectively with foreign nations, establish the public credit, restrain state barriers to trade, and stimulate national loyalty. They therefore decided on a peaceful overthrow of the government of the Articles, the then-existing government of the United States.

Areas of Agreement Among the Delegates

Not all of the delegates wanted a strong national government based on a union of the entire American populace, that is, a popularly elected government. Some, called *federationists,* and led by William Patterson of New Jersey, wanted a union of states. The state, they held, should be the important unit of government, close to the people and exercising the most power. Fortunately, most of the delegates were not dogmatic theorists and, because of their business dealings and their participation in government, were accustomed to practicing the art of compromise. Furthermore, they were aware of the consequences if they failed.

History has perhaps overemphasized the heated clashes of the delegates. Yet they agreed that their government was not functioning effectively, that immediate remedies were needed, and obviously there was general agreement on other matters, otherwise the gathering would have broken up. What were some of these areas of agreement?

As friends of property and business, the framers were generally in accord on economic matters: they insisted on sound money (i.e., currency that could be redeemed for gold) and on the protection of private property. They were also in substantial agreement on political matters: they wanted a stronger central government, strong enough to cope with the problems that had frustrated the Congress created by the Articles of Confederation, but with the central government's powers divided among three branches—executive, legislative, and judicial—so that each could check the other. The majority of the delegates further agreed that Congress should have the power to levy and collect taxes and to regulate commerce between the states and with foreign nations.

The framers also believed the government should not be controlled by a minority ruling as it wished, yet at the same time they were nearly unanimous in rejecting majoritarian democracy based upon complete manhood suffrage (e.g., the issuance by some states of legal tender paper money for paying debts and the extending of the time within which debtors had to pay off mortgages), for they attributed much of the recent public misfortunes to the headway democracy had been making among the new state governments. They preferred a republican form of government in which different economic and social groups would be represented in a balanced way.

POLITICS AND THE DELEGATES' BUNDLE OF COMPROMISES

Most of the important provisions of the Constitution issued from compromise rather than from principles and theories of sound government; they were the by-products of political adjustment or exigency. Still, this does not mean that principle was unimportant in the drafting of the Constitution or that expediency was the framers' sole guide. Individual delegates strove for or against certain provisions because of principle; and it is unlikely that the framers would have entered into proffered compromises had they thought them unreasonable or assuredly hurtful. The most significant of these—the Great Compromise, the "Three-Fifths" Compromise, the commerce and slave-trade compromises, and the major compromises concerning the presidency—are discussed below.

The Great Compromise: Nationalists Versus Federationists

Probably the most critical compromise issued from the confrontation of the nationalists, representing the large states, and the federationists, representing the small states. The large states supported a scheme, authored principally by James Madison and promoted by delegates from populous Virginia (population 747,610), known as the *Large-State Plan*. This proposal called for a strong national government of three branches, executive, legislature, and judiciary. Its two-house national legislature would have had formidable powers, and representation in it would have been apportioned among the states according to population or wealth. The small states, fearing domination by the more populous and powerful states, backed a plan presented by tiny New Jersey (population 184,139), known as the *Small-State Plan*. This proposal would have protected the equality of states by providing for their equal representation in a single-house Congress, as under the Articles of Confederation. Big-state opponents of the New Jersey proposal argued, and correctly, that it would merely revise the Articles, while small-state opponents of the Virginia proposal balked at the prospect of a radical shift of power to the larger states and the central government.

It appeared that the Convention might becomes hopelessly deadlocked; however, after prolonged and bitter debate the delegates arrived at the so-called *Great Compromise*. Fashioned by the Connecticut delegates (though probably authored by Benjamin Franklin), it granted the smaller states equal representation in the Senate; at the same time it appeased the big states by basing representation in the House on population. In the exchange the larger states yielded more. They were, however, in part compensated by the provisions that all bills for raising revenue must originate in the House—where population determined voting strength—and that federal judges be chosen by the President with Senate confirmation, rather than by the Senate alone. Having earlier got their way in the Great Agreement, on a three-branch national government, large states now were ready to make concessions. The successful conclusion of the Convention seemed within reach.

The Three-Fifths Compromise

The decision of the Great (or Connecticut) Compromise to base representation in the House on population created a major dispute over the counting of slaves for this purpose. Should the voteless black slave of the South be counted a person? Southern states, wanting to maximize their representation in the House, said yes; middle and Northern states, having few slaves, said no. As a compromise between total inclusion or total exclusion it was decided that—incredible as it may seem to us now—a slave should be counted as three-fifths of a person.[4] Further, to placate the Southern states, which thought they had received less than their due in the "Three-Fifths Compromise," the Convention agreed that direct taxes levied by Congress be apportioned among the states on the same basis as representation.[5]

Commerce and Slave-Trade Compromises

Sectional differences also flared over two other significant issues: the power Congress would exercise over commerce, and the question of the slave trade. Industrial states north of the Potomac, acutely interested in trade, wanted Congress to have full power to regulate commerce and navigation. Southern agricultural states,

[4] Article I, Section 2, para. 3. In 1868, following the Civil War, this clause was superseded by Amendment XIV, Section 2, which counted "the whole number of persons in each State, excluding Indians not taxed."
[5] The federal income taxes were excluded from this limitation by the Sixteenth Amendment (1913).

on the other hand, feared that Congress would tax the export of their products and in other ways discriminate against them.

The states were similarly divided on the slave-trade issue. Most states favored immediately shutting off the importation of slaves from abroad, and even the Southern states were not united on the issue. Maryland and Virginia, for instance, being already well supplied with slaves, did not take a strong stand. Only Georgia and South Carolina, wanting slave labor to work their rice paddies and clear their swamps, protested mightily. A compromise finally pacified all elements: Congress was assigned broad powers to regulate both navigation and foreign commerce, but could not tax exports nor interfere until 1808 with the importation of slaves.[6]

Compromise Concerning the Presidency

The Convention decided that there should be a single chief executive, a President, rather than the plural executive composed of two or three men of equal power some delegates preferred, and that his term should be four years instead of six, seven, or even longer, as some wished.[7] Another compromise was arranged in choosing the manner of his selection. There was little sentiment for direct popular election; some delegates had favored selection by Congress, others by the legislatures of the states, and still others by a separately established electoral body. The delegates finally agreed upon indirect election through the Electoral College arrangement. Under this method, each state was to select, in a manner its legislature indicated, a number of electors equal to the total number of Senators and Representatives to which it was entitled. Interestingly, several delegates from large states supported the compromise because they anticipated that the electors would seldom agree on a President and that the House

[6] Article I, Section 9, para. 1. As soon as the clause lapsed, Congress halted the trade.

[7] The Convention turned down, by only a 6–4 vote, a proposal that he serve "during good behavior," meaning life tenure. At one time or another, the Convention approved a six- and seven-year term. Delegate Rufus King of Massachusetts had proposed a term of twenty years; Elbridge Gerry of Massachusetts suggested fifteen; Luther Martin of Maryland, eleven.

of Representatives, given the authority in that event, would usually make the choice.

Franklin's Plea for Unity

In a closing plea for the delegates' support of the draft Constitution, the venerable Benjamin Franklin defended it thus:

> I agree to this Constitution with all its faults, if there are such; because I think the general government necessary for us. . . . I doubt whether any other Convention we can obtain may be able to make a better Constitution. For when you assemble a number of men to have the advantage of their joint wisdom, you inevitably assemble with those men all their prejudices, their passions, their errors of opinion, their local interests, and their selfish views. . . . Thus, I consent . . . because I expect no better and because I am not sure that it is not the best.

Despite Franklin's rational, eloquent plea, the Constitution did not win unanimous support. Of the forty-two delegates present during the signing of the document, three (Elbridge Gerry of Massachusetts and Edmund Randolph and George Mason of Virginia) declined to subscribe their names, and some of the thirteen delegates absent at the time were critical. Actually, few if any of the delegates were completely satisfied, yet on September 17, 1787, General Washington and thirty-eight other delegates completed the final acts and under Article VII released the result of their deliberations for the ratifications of the states.

RATIFICATION OF THE "SHOCKING DOCUMENT"

The people were shocked by the proposed new Constitution. So effectively had secrecy been maintained throughout the Convention that they had no prior hint of its contents. They had expected that the old Articles of Confederation, after needed surgery, would be presented to the states for approval in a constitutional manner. Instead, they were handed a radically differ-

ARTICLE VII

The Ratification of the Conventions of nine States, shall be sufficient for the Establishment of this Constitution between the States so ratifying the Same.

Done in Convention by the Unanimous Consent of the States present the Seventeenth Day of September in the Year of our Lord one thousand seven hundred and Eighty seven and of the Independence of the United States of America the Twelfth. *In Witness* whereof We have hereunto subscribed our Names,

G:° WASHINGTON—
*Presidt, and Deputy
from Virginia*

New Hampshire	{ John Langdon Nicholas Gilman
Massachusetts	{ Nathaniel Gorham Rufus King
Connecticut	{ Wm Saml Johnson Roger Sherman
New York	Alexander Hamilton
New Jersey	{ Wil: Livingston David Brearley Wm Paterson Jona: Dayton

---

ent plan, one in which precious state sovereignty would be relinquished.

Having exceeded their authority by setting aside the Articles, the Convention delegates had not hesitated to ignore its Article XIII, which had prohibited any amendment unless approved by the old Congress created by the Articles and *all of the state legislatures.* Calculating that there was little chance of securing approval from the legislatures, the delegates had moved audaciously and declared a revolutionary method of ratification. The Constitution, they stated, would become effective between the states

Pennsylvania	B Franklin Thomas Mifflin Robt Morris Geo. Clymer Thos. FitzSimons Jared Ingersoll James Wilson Gouv Morris
Delaware	Geo Read Gunning Bedfor jun John Dickinson Richard Bassett Jaco: Broom
Maryland	James McHenry Dan of St Thos. Jenifer Danl Carroll
Virginia	John Blair — James Madison Jr.
North Carolina	Wm Blount Richd Dobbs Spaight Hu Williamson
South Carolina	J. Rutledge Charles Cotesworth Pinckney Charles Pinckney Pierce Butler
Georgia	William Few Abr Baldwin

that approved it as soon as it was ratified by specifically elected conventions in *nine,* rather than thirteen (or twelve), states.

An Appeal to the People

What the framers were attempting was an appeal to the people—that is, to those who could vote—over the heads of both the Congress that had called the Convention and the twelve state legislatures that had chosen delegates. Seeing little alternative, the Congress of the Articles reluctantly voted to submit the document to the states on this basis, without indicating approval or disapproval. And as the document became known to the people there immediately ensued one of the great debates of American history.

Supporters of the new government shrewdly appropriated the name *federalists* in an effort to quiet fears that they were bent upon devouring the states and erecting an all-powerful national government. To call themselves *nationalists* (which they actually were) would, of course, have been suicidal for their cause. They cleverly called those who opposed them and the stronger central government *anti-federalists*, making them appear negative and obstructionist.

The Battles Over Ratification

Candidates were popularly elected to state ratifying conventions on the basis of their pledges either in favor or against the new Constitution. Most elections were hotly contested, with people in the tidewater South and on the eastern seaboard favoring the Constitution more than did those in the upcountry areas. Townspeople also favored it more than did country folk. Economic lines were evident but not sharp. Hard-money creditors, slaveholders, merchants, bankers, and large land owners were more inclined toward ratification than were debtors who had secured favorable state legislation, small farmers, shopkeepers, and artisans. Persons whose fortunes were closely connected with commerce, whether rich or poor, tended to favor the Constitution.

Proponents and opponents of the Constitution did not divide strictly along class lines, since there were wealthy persons on both sides of the debate. "The only generalization that can stand the test of facts," concludes historian Samuel Eliot Morison, "is that the cleavage was one of age against youth. . . . The warmest advocates were eager young men.[8]

Although in three states—Delaware, Georgia, and New Jersey—the vote in favor was unanimous, in many the battle over ratification was close and bitter. Anti-federalists, who supported con-

[8] Samuel Eliot Morison, *The Oxford History of the American People* (New York: Oxford University Press, 1965), p. 313.

federation, opposed granting more power to a central government, which they considered far removed from the people and insensitive to their needs. They feared that, after throwing off the yoke of the British monarchy, they were now being asked to accept another kind of despotism.

The first state to ratify was Delaware, the smallest of the thirteen. In general, the smaller states ratified first, for they had fared much better than might have been expected.

The contest in Massachusetts was an acid test. Its ratifying convention, at first predominately anti-federalist, was particularly dismayed by the absence of a bill of rights. Only after securing a promise from the federalists that the first Congress would propose a bill of rights to the states as amendments to the Constitution, did the Massachusetts Convention ratify, and then only by 187 to 168.

The efforts of James Madison, Edmund Randolph, John Marshall, and the impelling influence of General Washington won approval in the Virginia convention by an 89 to 79 vote. The favorable vote in New York was even closer: 30 to 27. Greatly aiding the federalist cause in that state was the publication in newspapers of eighty-five essays by Hamilton, Madison, and Jay explaining the meaning of the Constitution and attempting to allay fears about it. These essays were published as a book in 1788, under the title *The Federalist*. Although clearly campaign documents and representing only one side, they are among the most masterly works of their type ever produced.

By July 26, 1788, only two states remained out—North Carolina and Rhode Island. Both later entered, but not until the new government had been in operation for several months. Rhode Island held out longest—until May 29, 1790, more than one year after Washington was inaugurated as President—and then ratified by a vote of only 34 to 32.

A NEW SCHEME OF GOVERNMENT

The Constitution framed at Philadelphia was much more than a "bundle of compromises," for it inaugurated an entirely new scheme of government. No single feature of the new Constitution was strikingly innovative—precedent could be found for each in an American colonial charter, in a state constitution, in the Articles of Confederation, or in American or British custom. But in combination its features were unexampled anywhere.

The seven most important basic features of this new system of 1787 (see box) are discussed below. Together they comprise a governmental system that is uniquely American.[9]

SEVEN BASIC FEATURES
OF THE AMERICAN CONSTITUTION OF 1787

1. Representative democracy
2. The federal principle
3. Separation of powers, and checks and balances
4. Limited government
5. Supremacy of national law
6. Judicial review
7. Civilian supremacy

Representative Democracy

The delegates who had met in Philadelphia to frame the American Constitution had been alarmed by what democratic majorities had done in the states. In general, they agreed, most men tended to be foolish—Shays' Rebellion, they felt, was but a portent of what infuriated masses might do in the future.[10] In their analysis of democratic excesses, turbulence, and follies they differed not at all from political theorists and statesmen up to that time, most of whom rejected democracy out of hand. What distinguished the Convention delegates was that although they agreed that democracy had certain inherent weaknesses and dangerous tendencies, they did not reject it completely. Indeed, the American people would not have permitted them to do so.

---

[9] Except with respect to federalism as a descriptive concept in state-local relations, all of these "basic features" of the federal government are operative at the state level.

[10] Shays' Rebellion (Massachusetts, 1786–1787) was led by Shays and sought relief for the debtor class.

Perhaps the delegates were not really democrats by choice. The evidence indicates that they sought to make government sufficiently popular that it would not excite popular opposition. Yet whatever their motives, of greater importance is that, although they erected numerous safeguards against what Madison termed "the inconvenience of democracy," they did it in a way consistent with the democratic form of government. The presidency, the Senate, and the federal judiciary, for example, were put at least one step beyond immediate popular control; however, they did empower the people to choose the members of the House of Representatives from their states and guaranteed that their state governments would remain "republican" in form.[11] Furthermore, they made the original undemocratic features of the Constitution flexible and alterable. As a result, the election of the President became more democratic without any change in the written words of the Constitution. Also, by the formal amendment procedures written into the Constitution, Negroes and women have been enfranchised, poll taxes in federal elections have been abolished, and United States Senators have been made directly elective. Finally, with the power to decide who may vote left to them by the Convention delegates, the states have broadened the franchise.

The Federal Principle

Necessity compelled the delegates to fashion their greatest achievement—the "federal principle," or "federalism." Why the federal form? Why not the unitary or confederation forms? Apparently there was some sentiment at Philadelphia for the creation of a unitary system. Alexander Hamilton, for one, favored this. However, he, as well as the other delegates, knew it was a hopeless cause, that the people would not tolerate the subordination of their states to a central government. The vast size of

[11] The term "republican" means having the characteristics of a republic— that is, a government in which sovereignty resides in the voters, who exercise their authority through representatives who are elected by and are responsible to them. Monarchies are not republics, though, even if they have representative institutions, because sovereignty theoretically resides with the monarch, not with the people.

**COMPARISON OF THE FEDERAL AND
ALTERNATIVE SYSTEMS**

Federal System

Governmental powers are divided on a territorial basis between a central or national government and constituent governments. Neither level acting alone can alter the division. Among present-day federalisms are the governments of the United States, the U.S.S.R., India, Mexico, Canada, and Australia.

Unitary System

All power to govern rests with one central government. Acting alone, it may alter at will the powers of the constituent governments, which derive all their authority from it. Examples of unitary systems are Great Britain and Israel. The system is not unknown to Americans, for the relations between our states and their counties, cities, and other subdivisions is of this order.

Confederate System

This loose league or association of sovereign states usually has a central government which may act on matters of common concern. However, the operations and even the very existence of the central government is at the sufferance of the member states. Employed by the United States in 1781–1789, this form is not widely used today.

the country, the regional and political differences, and the slowness of communication and transportation also worked against unitary government. Not surprisingly, it was never proposed at the Convention. Nor did the delegates wish to continue with a confederate form after their unhappy experience under the Articles of Confederation. They had seen quite enough of this system.

Thus, the delegates, having really no other choice, settled upon a federal system. Under it, the states maintained their constitutional, geographic, and political integrity, but surrendered enough authority to establish a national government with substantial powers. Both governments performed separate functions while sharing others; Americans held citizenship in both.

A chief characteristic of our federal system is that power is diffused—most local issues are decided locally and national issues such as the conduct of foreign relations and the maintenance of a sound economy are handled nationally. Thus, divisive local issues generally are not thrust upon national political leaders and parties for solution. However, some people believe this diffusion of power is a disadvantage, holding that it is difficult for a national majority to implement national programs effectively unless it controls not only the three branches of the national government, but the state governments as well. This American innovation will be discussed in Chapter 5.

Separation of Powers and a System of Checks and Balances

Just as the Founding Fathers knew that the proposed Constitution would be disapproved if they rejected democracy or abolished state governments, so they perceived that the people would probably spurn any government that did not erect barriers against tyranny. Besides, the delegates themselves believed that amassing all powers of government—executive, legislative, and judicial—in the hands of one person or group would surely result in despotism. They followed also in this regard the dictum of the philosophers John Locke and particularly Baron Montesquieu favoring the separation of powers.[12]

The delegates, though intending that Congress be the dominant organ, distributed constitutional authority among the three branches of the national government instead of concentrating authority in the legislature (as in the present British system). However, believing that even this division of power would not prevent the three branches cooperating to exercise tyranny, they made each branch responsible to a different political constituency. The President was to be chosen by a group of electors, Senators by state legislators, congressional Representatives by the people in local districts, and the judges by the President with the approval of the Senate. Election periods of national officials were

---

[12] See *The Federalist* No. 47 (Madison).

also staggered and terms of office set at varying durations. The President would have a four-year term, Representatives two years, Senators six, and judges life terms. Thus, a popular majority or faction could win control over only part of the government at a time.

Each of the three branches was empowered to perform some functions in conjunction with the others and to control some operations of the others. In this the delegates agreed with Madison's observation:

> . . . The great security against a gradual concentration of the several powers in the same department, consists in giving to those who administer each department the necessary constitutional means and personal motives to resist encroachments of the others. . . . Ambition must be made to counteract ambition.[13]

Today, although Congress passes laws, the President can veto them, and Congress can by two-thirds vote pass them over his veto. The President sees that the laws are executed, but Congress may refuse him the funds he requests for his administration. The Senate and House may reject bills or proposals for constitutional amendments passed in the other. The Supreme Court can rule laws and executive actions unconstitutional, but the President appoints the judges, and the Senate concurs. A multitude of other examples could be given. Obviously, our national government is not one in which powers are strictly separated, but one in which three separated branches share powers.

Critics see the separation of powers and system of checks and balances as a needlessly complicated and unwieldly method of governing. It invites, they say, needless delay and deadlock, encourages logrolling by private factions at the expense of the general welfare, and does not, as its proponents claim, promote deliberation. They further hold that it makes responsible government virtually impossible, particularly when rival parties control different branches of the government. Even when one party con-

---

[13] *The Federalist* No. 51.

trols both the presidency and Congress, the policies they agree upon may not pass muster when challenged in a Supreme Court case. Furthermore, the traditional rivalry between the branches causes uncertainty in the formulation of both domestic and foreign policy. Finally, it is held that the system provides the forces of reaction a vehicle for hindering social change.

Defenders point out that under the present system the United States has become the most powerful democratic republic in the world; that while social changes may have been slowed by the separation of powers and system of checks and balances, it has not prevented them; and that invariably the three branches act in concert in time of national emergency. Besides, they say, the separation of powers and system of checks and balances, by helping insure that change will be orderly and measured, helps guarantee that social change will indeed come and that social gains once made will not be easily lost.

Limited Government

The Constitution did not specifically provide for limited government; yet it undeniably instituted it. Even the manner in which the document was ratified, that is, *by consent of the governed,* bears this out, as does the Constitution's firm base on *rule of law* instead of arbitrary political power. The separation of the powers of government, the arrangements of checks and balances, the popular elections of members of the House, and guarantees of popular rights included in the body of the Constitution and in the Bill of Rights—all safeguard the rights of the people.

The delegation of certain powers to the national government and the reservation of others to the states also provide a two-way limitation on government. The delegation limits the national government to its *enumerated powers* (plus those which could reasonably be implied from them), and limits the states to the extent that powers have been delegated to the national government. Finally, numerous specific limitations are placed on the national government by Section 9 of Article I, and on the states by Section 10.

Supremacy of National Law

Anticipating frequent conflicts between national and state laws, and realizing the advisability of avoiding them as much as practical, the Convention delegates stated, in Article VI, the supremacy of national law in clear and precise terms:

> This Constitution, and the Laws of the United States which shall be made in Pursuance thereof; and all Treaties made, or which shall be made, under the Authority of the United States, shall be the supreme Law of the Land; and the Judges in every State be bound thereby, any Thing in the Constitution or Laws of any State to the Contrary notwithstanding.

This left no doubt of the supremacy of the national government *when operating within its delegated powers.*

Judicial Review

If it was clear that federal law was superior to state law, what about the differences in interpretation of the Constitution which would inevitably arise? Who was to be the final arbiter? The Constitution does not provide a satisfactory guide; it does not, as some might think, specifically give the courts this function.

There is evidence that the delegates at Philadelphia thought the courts should be empowered to rule *state* legislation unconstitutional; however, it is not clear whether they intended that the courts have the same review power over national laws. Alexander Hamilton believed that they should have this power, and Chief Justice Marshall stated in the celebrated case of *Marbury* v. *Madison* (1803) that he could see the basis for it in the supremacy clause (Article VI) of the Constitution. At any rate, today it is an established principle that the courts have the power to void all legislative and executive acts that they find conflict with the Constitution, and that the U.S. Supreme Court serves as the ultimate regulator of federalism, a most important role. As Justice Holmes stated more than five decades ago, "the United States would [not] come to an end if we lost our power to declare an act of Congress void. I do think the Union would be imperiled if we could not make that declaration as to the laws of the several states."[14]

Civilian Supremacy

Like the leading political theorists of their day, the founders of the American republic believed that military domination and free government were incompatible. For that reason they wrote a number of precautionary provisions into the Constitution. For instance, the President, an elected official, was made commander in chief of the armed forces; army appropriations were limited to a two-year period; the states retained authority to train militias and select their officers; Congress and not the President was authorized to declare war; and limitations were placed upon the suspension of the writ of habeas corpus. Furthermore, during the debates over ratification, proponents of the Constitution agreed to amendments which limited the government's authority to quarter troops in a house without the owner's consent (Third Amendment). Additional precautions, such as the requirement that the Secretary of Defense and the heads of the military departments be civilians, were added by Congress.

In modern times it has become increasingly difficult to maintain civilian supremacy over the military. This is due largely to our drastically increased foreign involvement and commitments; the enormous growth of our defense establishment; the increasingly powerful lobby of the military bureaucracy supported by veterans organizations, "patriotic societies," and interests benefiting from armaments production (one in ten people depend directly or indirectly on the military for their jobs); and increased domination of the state militias (National Guard) by federal authority.

Many have warned of the dangers of militarization to individual freedom. Probably the best known admonition was that of President Eisenhower to the American people:

[14] Oliver Wendell Holmes, "Law and the Court," in *Collected Legal Papers* (New York: Peter Smith, 1920), pp. 295–96. This American innovation (federalism and the presidential form are the other two) is discussed in Chapter 14.

In the councils of government, we must guard against the acquisition of unwarranted influence, whether sought or unsought, by the military-industrial complex. The potential for the disastrous rise of misplaced power exists and will persist.

Some cited the dangers inherent in the development of a military caste in the United States as a compelling argument against President Nixon's proposal for an all-volunteer professional military to replace the military draft.

WHY HAS THE CONSTITUTION ENDURED?

What accounts for the great endurance of the United States Constitution—the oldest written constitution of any nation? It was described in 1878 by the British statesman William E. Gladstone as "the most wonderful work ever struck off at a given time by the brain and purpose of man." Elegantly written,[15] it reflects centuries of experience, extending back to Magna Carta and beyond, plus a masterful adaptation of old forms and practices to the American environment. Furthermore, much about it has been proven by experience to be wise in the writing of a fundamental charter. It is flexible, based on compromise, and has very high overall technical quality.

The Constitution is also short, much shorter than most state constitutions: even with all of its amendments, it totals little more than seven thousand words. Limited to essential principles and provisions, it is not cluttered with unnecessary details, though it is generally precise enough where it needs to be. The Philadelphia delegates fully realized the pitfalls of attempting to provide for every exigency. This task they wisely left for future generations. As they perhaps anticipated, the brevity of the Constitution and its silence or lack of specificity on many matters have permitted it to grow as needed. Probably these characteristics, plus the relative stability of American society, have been most responsible for its endurance.

[15] The Constitution's lucid and polished style may be credited largely to Pennsylvania delegate Gouveneur Morris, who wrote out the completed document in his own hand.

Suggested Additional Reading

Beard, C. A. *An Economic Interpretation of the Constitution.* 1913.

Brown, R. E. *Charles Beard and the Constitution.* 1956.

Corwin, E. S., and J. W. Peltason. *Understanding the Constitution.* 1970.

Farrand, M. *The Records of the Federal Convention of 1787.* 4 vols. 1937.

Garrity, J. A. *Quarrels That Have Shaped the Constitution.* 1964.

Hamilton, A., J. Madison, and J. Jay. *The Federalist Papers.* 1787.

McDonald, F. *We the People: The Economic Origins of the Constitution.* 1958.

Nevins, A. *The States During and After the Revolution.* 1924.

4 Patterns of Constitutional Development

Legislators and would-be founders of any constitution . . . will find that the work of construction is not their only or principal business. The maintenance of the constitution is the thing which really matters.

—*Aristotle*

We Americans hold our Constitution in honor and esteem. Though we may disagree about how it should be interpreted or about which programs should be developed under it, we agree that it is a charter which should be scrupulously observed. If we sometimes challenge Supreme Court interpretations of it, we do not attack the Constitution itself.

POLITICS AND THE CONSTITUTION

What is the political meaning of the great respect we pay our Constitution? Primarily it means that the Constitution and its traditional uses are important in creating legitimacy and support for the political system—much as the monarchy does in Britain. Significantly, some of this respect also carries over to the institutions and procedures the Constitution created. Thus, a particular decision that is warranted by proponents as being prescribed or licensed by it tends to be conceded a certain legitimacy and hence is given more support than it might get otherwise.

Another fact about the Constitution that is politically significant is that, in founding the principal institutions of government and bestowing and withholding powers, it apportioned advantages and disadvantages to the several interests. For instance, the Philadelphia delegates awarded advantages to the landed and commercial interests of the time by forbidding taxes on exports and by prohibiting the states from issuing paper money or from passing laws impairing the obligation of contracts. We must not, however, exaggerate the importance of this apportioning of advantages to the rich. Although the framers initiated general rules which did this, they left considerable leeway for their interpretation and application.

The fact of the Constitution's flexibility also has political significance. Much of this results from its ambiguities, from the difficulty of pinning down precise meanings. For example, the Fifth and Fourteenth Amendments guarantee that no persons be deprived "of life, liberty, or property, without due process of law." Exactly what does "due process of law" mean? The Fourth Amendment provides that "The right of the people to be secure . . . against unreasonable searches and seizures shall not be violated." But what is an "unreasonable" search or seizure? The Sixth Amendment guarantees a defendant in a criminal proceeding a "speedy" trial. But what does "speedy" mean? The Fifth Amendment guarantees that property shall not "be taken for public use, without just compensation." But what constitutes "taking," "public use," and "just compensation"? Similarly, what is meant specifically by the Eighth Amendment provisos that (the emphasis is added) "*Excessive bail* shall not be required, nor *excessive fines* imposed, nor *cruel and unusual punishments* inflicted"?

Even certain clauses of the Constitution which appear quite clear are open to interpretation. The Fourteenth Amendment, for instance, forbids a state to deny anyone within its jurisdiction the "equal protection of the laws." But what would constitute denial of equal protection? Another example is the commerce clause of

Article I, which states that Congress shall have power to "regulate Commerce . . . among the several States," but does not define "commerce."

The point is this: the Constitution is such that several interpretations may be made of important provisions. As a result, advantages and disadvantages are in great measure apportioned not by the Constitution but by decisions made within the political system.

ALTERING THE LETTER OF THE CONSTITUTION

The delegates to the Philadelphia Convention preferred that it not be too easy to modify their handiwork. They hoped that the adoption of the Constitution would begin an indefinite period of stability, and that the principles of government they instituted would be impervious to temporary waves of popular feeling. At the same time, they knew that no constitution could be so perfect or farsighted that amendments would not be needed from time to time. They themselves had experienced troubles because procedures for amending the Articles and various state constitutions were inadequate.

So it was that the framers approached the task of fashioning an amendment clause. They provided that formal amendments could be made, but only by unusually large majorities. So troublesome did the delegates make the formal process that only twenty-six amendments have been secured since 1789. The difficulty may be seen in the four methods of formal amendment now provided in the Constitution, shown graphically in Figure 4-1, which are:

(1) proposal by two-thirds vote in both houses of Congress and ratification by legislatures in three-fourths of the states;

(2) proposal by two-thirds vote in both houses of Congress, and ratification by specially called ratifying conventions in three-fourths of the states;

(3) proposal by a national convention called by Congress on the request of legislatures in two-thirds of the states, and ratification by legislatures in three-fourths of the states;

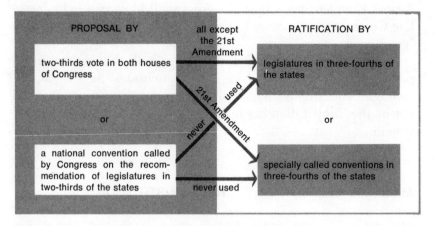

PROPOSAL BY

two-thirds vote in both houses of Congress

or

a national convention called by Congress on the recommendation of legislatures in two-thirds of the states

all except the 21st Amendment

21st Amendment used

never

RATIFICATION BY

legislatures in three-fourths of the states

or

specially called conventions in three-fourths of the states

never used

Figure 4-1. Four methods of formally amending the national Constitution.

(4) proposal by a national convention called by Congress on the request of legislatures in two-thirds of the states, and ratification by special ratifying conventions in three-fourths of the states.[1]

Congress determines which method of ratification will be used. The President has no part in the process of formal constitutional amendment.

The first method described above was used for all amendments except the Twenty-first (repealing national liquor prohibition), which was adopted through the second method because Congress feared that state legislatures dominated by the "drys" would vote against repeal. The third and fourth have never been used, for Congress has never called a constitutional convention.[2] In any event, Congress prefers to respond to demands for change by legislating or by proposing amendments itself, being aware that a convention could presumably propose as many amendments as it might choose, and might even propose an entirely new Consti-

[1] A state that has rejected an amendment may later ratify it. However, a state having ratified cannot reverse its ratification.

[2] Thomas Jefferson and other early leaders thought that each new generation should call a national constitutional convention to engage in a general constitutional revision. This has not been necessary, largely because of the flexibility of the Constitution.

tution. Perhaps its recollection of the fate that befell the Congress of the Articles in 1787 influences Congress's calculations.

THE TWENTY-SIX FORMAL AMENDMENTS

The number of amendments to the United States Constitution is strikingly small. The first ten amendments (The Bill of Rights),[3] adopted in 1791 and dealing with individual freedom, changed no provisions in the original document and were so closely tied to its adoption that they are virtually a part of it. The Eighteenth ("Prohibition") and the Twenty-first ("Repeal") Amendments counter-balance each other, leaving only fourteen as actual alterations.

Eleventh Amendment (1798)

The Eleventh Amendment was added after anti-federalists and states' rights advocates had been angered by the Supreme Court's 1793 decision in *Chisholm* v. *Georgia* that Article III of the Constitution permitted a citizen of one state to sue another state in federal courts. It ensured that thereafter no state would thus be summoned before the federal judiciary.

Twelfth Amendment (1804)

The Twelfth Amendment provided for separate election of President and Vice-President instead of on the same ballot as required in the original Constitution.[4] The need for this change became apparent during the election of 1800, when each Republican member of the Electoral College cast his ballot for Thomas Jefferson and Aaron Burr (each elector was to vote for two persons with his ballot), thus causing a tie. Everyone knew that the Republican electors meant Jefferson to be President and Burr

---

[3] Discussed in Chapters 16 and 17.

[4] Under the original Constitution, the candidate who received a majority of the electoral votes would have been President. The candidate who received the second highest number would have been Vice-President.

Vice-President, but the Constitution specifically stated that in the event of a tie vote, the House would decide. It took thirty-six ballots before the House, dominated by "lame duck" Federalists, finally agreed to give the presidency to Jefferson. To avoid a repetition of this incident, the Twelfth Amendment was adopted.

Thirteenth Amendment (1865)

The first of three so-called "Civil War" Amendments (the Fourteenth and Fifteenth are the others), this amendment ended the "peculiar institution" of slavery. It also prohibited "peonage," a form of involuntary service, usually to work off a debt.

Fourteenth Amendment (1868)

This amendment reversed an 1857 Supreme Court ruling, *Dred Scott* v. *Sanford,* that Negroes were not American citizens. It also defined citizenship, asserted the supremacy of national over state citizenship, and guaranteed individuals protection against certain state action: depriving any person of life, liberty, or property without due process of law; abridging the privileges or immunities of United States citizens; or denying to any person within its jurisdiction the equal protection of the laws.[5]

Fifteenth (1870), Nineteenth (1920), Twenty-third (1961), Twenty-fourth (1964), and Twenty-sixth (1971) Amendments

All of these amendments furthered the suffrage. The Fifteenth gave Negroes voting rights; it prohibited preventing a citizen from voting because of his "race, color, or previous condition of servitude." The Nineteenth gave women the right to vote. The Twenty-third allowed citizens of the District of Columbia to vote in presidential elections. The Twenty-fourth abolished the use of the poll tax in federal elections in five Southern states. The newest amendment, the Twenty-sixth, extended voting rights, both in federal and state elections, to eighteen-year-olds.

[5] The amendment is discussed extensively in Chapters 16 and 17.

Sixteenth Amendment (1913)

The Sixteenth or "Income-Tax Amendment" makes constitutional a federal income tax.[6] Under this authorization Congress has levied direct and progressive taxes on incomes, with great effect on the American economy and society. Their major impact has been twofold. First, by being *progressive* taxes—that is, the higher one's taxable income, the higher the *percentage* of taxes he must pay—the burden of financing the federal government has shifted more from the poor to those more able to pay.[7] Second, as tremendous revenue raisers, income taxes have permitted a vast expansion of public services, from which poorer Americans generally derive most benefit. Opposition to Sixteenth Amendment has come from those who fear that it is the basis for instituting socialism in the United States.

Seventeenth Amendment (1913)

Although Representatives had always been popularly elected, and the election of the President had been brought under control of the voters by the development of popular political parties, United States Senators were not made popularly elective until 1913. Before that they had been chosen by state legislatures. This frequently meant that special interests or state party machines actually decreed who would be sent to the Senate from the state. The Seventeenth Amendment finally extended popular control to all parts of the political branches of the federal government.

Twentieth Amendment (1933)

The passage of the Twentieth or "Lame-Duck" Amendment was precipitated by the long delay between Franklin D. Roosevelt's election to the presidency and his inauguration. It moved forward the beginning dates of the terms of President, Vice-President,

---

[6] In *Pollock* v. *Farmers' Loan and Trust Co.* (1895), the Supreme Court had ruled that income taxes would be invalid unless apportioned among the states.

[7] Most state and local taxes remain regressive, bearing more heavily on the poor than on the rich.

Senators, and Representatives. Before that, Congressmen defeated in the November elections had continued in office during the following December session, while newly elected Congressmen did not take office until thirteen months after being elected, unless the President called Congress into special session. Furthermore, the President and Vice-President did not take office until March following the November election. The Twentieth Amendment moved the date forward to January and also provided for filling the office of President if the President-elect died or failed to qualify, or if a President was not chosen before inauguration day. This latter provision was designed to avoid situations such as the disputed Tildon-Hayes election of 1876, when a President-elect was not chosen until a few hours before inauguration.

Twenty-second Amendment (1951)

This amendment overruled the decision of the Constitution's architects that the President be permitted to run for the office as many times as he chose. It made the two-term "tradition" a constitutional mandate by providing that:

> No person shall be elected to the office of the President more than twice, and no person who has held the office of President, or acted as President, for more than two years of a term to which some other person was elected President shall be elected to the office of the President more than once.

Proposed in Congress in 1947, the Twenty-second Amendment was a reaction by those who were outraged by President Roosevelt's election to four terms. It is too soon to judge the effects of this amendment, but it may lessen rather than increase popular control, by limiting the voters' option to keep a President they believe is effective. This limitation might be particularly troublesome in time of sustained major crisis.

Twenty-fifth Amendment (1967)

The Twenty-fifth Amendment improved arrangements to deal with presidential succession and disability, matters on which the

Constitution was not a sufficient guide. Its provisions are discussed in Chapter 12.

KEEPING THE CONSTITUTION CURRENT

That we have the oldest written constitution of any nation should not be misread, for it is not the simple document of 1787, but rather one of the most elaborate known to history. This is largely because it has been changed over the years, not only by the formal process of amendment, but also by custom, by judicial, executive, and legislative interpretation, and by state action. This living Constitution and its fundamental provisions—provisions that must be interpreted and applied—are the legal basis of American politics. An understanding of how it has changed is essential if one is to comprehend our political system.

Change Through Custom

"Time and habit," observed George Washington, "are at least as necessary to fix the true character of governments as they are to the evolution of other institutions." The accuracy of this remark about the force of custom has been demonstrated over and over again in American political experience. Custom now determines much of our Constitution.

One of the important customs related to the Constitution is the political party system. Long indispensable to American democracy, parties are not even mentioned in the written Constitution, nor does the document make any reference to pressure groups. The President's Cabinet also developed through custom, as did presidential nominating conventions and the committee and caucus systems in Congress. Custom has decreed that members of the Electoral College, instead of having a free hand in electing a President, are practically fifth wheels. Custom determines that the Senate does not confirm appointments to federal offices within a state against the wishes of the Senators from that state. Finally, the "requirement" that members of the House be residents of the districts they represent is customary only: the practice developed

89

probably because people did not elect them if they were not residents.

Change Through Court Interpretation

Decisions of the United States Supreme Court may have the same immediate effects as formal constitutional amendments. In fact, it is primarily from such decisions that the Constitution is best understood, since practically every clause has been before the Court at one time or another. The Court has changed the working constitution so much that lawyers of an earlier day would find it quite unfamiliar. For instance, now Congress may regulate manufacturing and agricultural production; public schools may not segregate on the basis of race nor require Bible reading or prayers; and the democratic ideal of "one man, one vote" is a constitutional command (the United States Senate and the Electoral College excepted). Does this mean that the Constitution is what a majority of the Court says it is? In practical terms, yes. Until the Court has decided an issue, Americans generally assume that the Constitution has not yet been interpreted, at least not officially. When it does decide, almost invariably Congress and the President, as well as lesser officials and bodies, yield to its judgment. This interpretive power is what is meant by the Court's being the final arbiter.[8]

Change Through Executive Interpretation

While it is true that the Constitution is often what a majority of the Supreme Court Justices say it is, it is also sometimes what the political branches say it is, for they also interpret it. For example, largely because various Presidents have exercised the type of leadership the American people have wanted, the President is now the "chief legislator" as well as chief executive, and the presidency has displaced Congress as the central institution in the national government. Furthermore, it is also because of presidential actions that conflicts on foreign soil are waged without declaration of war, executive agreements with other countries are used increas-

[8] Judicial review is discussed in Chapter 14.

ingly instead of formal treaties, and the office of Vice-President is growing in prominence.[9]

Change Through Legislative Interpretation

Congress also interprets the Constitution, and many of its fundamental acts are considered part of our "living Constitution." It is by act of Congress, for instance, that the number of members of the House of Representatives is determined. Furthermore, it is also by law that the number of Supreme Court Justices is set, federal courts of appeals and district courts established and their jurisdictions assigned. The Constitution merely provides that there be one Supreme Court and "such inferior courts as the Congress may from time to time ordain and establish." Similarly, Congress legislated into existence the eleven great executive departments. Although their creation was anticipated in the Constitution, only three very incidental references were made to them in the entire document.

Congress has also provided for succession to the presidency in the event of the death, inability, resignation, or removal of *both* the President and Vice-President, the Constitution being silent on this question. Furthermore, by broadly interpreting its powers, Congress has created myriad administrative boards and commissions, provided for a multitude of different services (e.g., Social Security) and taken measures to regulate the complex social and economic life of the country—all in ways far beyond the powers mentioned in the Constitution of 1787.[10]

Change Through State Action

The national Constitution has also been amplified informally through state action. Among the most significant examples have been the broadening of suffrage by the states, the method of selecting presidential electors, the division of their electoral votes,

[9] Executive interpretation is also discussed in Chapter 12.
[10] Its very extensive amplification of the meanings of the commerce and tax powers are discussed in Chapter 5.

the evolution of the process of selecting candidates for federal office, and the national party conventions.[11]

Suggested Additional Reading

Corwin, E. S., and J. W. Peltason. *Understanding the Constitution.* 1970.

Holcombe, A. N. *Securing the Blessings of Liberty: The Constitutional Systems.* 1964.

Kelly, A. H., and W. A. Harbison. *The American Constitution: Its Origin and Development.* 3rd ed. 1963.

Leedham, C. *Our Changing Constitution.* 1965.

McBain, H. L. *The Living Constitution.* 1927.

Orfield, L. B. *Amending the Federal Constitution.* 1942.

Pritchett, C. H. *The American Constitution.* 1968.

Swisher, C. B. *American Constitutional Development.* 1954.

[11] Many of these are examined in Chapter 8.

5 Evolving Federalism

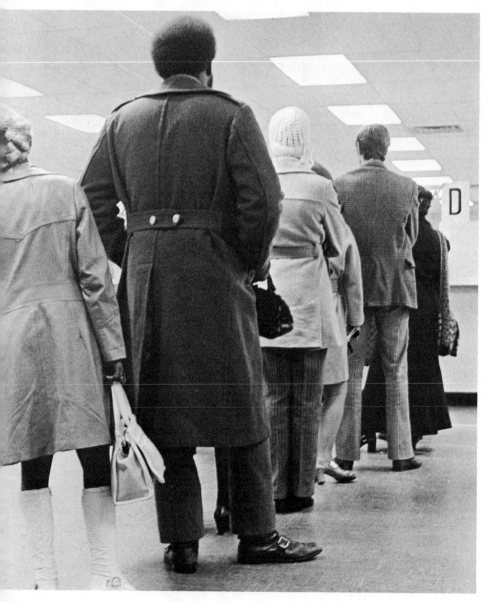

This government is acknowledged by all to be one of enumerated powers. The principle that it can exercise only the powers granted to it . . . is now universally admitted. *But the question respecting the extent of the powers actually granted is perpetually arising, and will probably continue to arise, as long as our system shall exist.*

—Chief Justice John Marshall
[Emphasis added]

Whatever the party in power in Washington—Federalist, Jeffersonian Republican, Whig, Democrat, or Republican—the national government's activity has continuously increased. Although some people lament this increase, very likely the government will continue to expand.

GROWING PERVASIVENESS OF THE FEDERAL GOVERNMENT

The federal government has grown large not primarily because the Constitution has been formally amended but because there have been changing interpretations and applications of it, for the division of powers between the national and state governments is not unchangeable. The Constitution sets the rules, but the political system interprets and applies these rules and thus determines their precise sense. In practice, then, the powers of the national and state governments are not as explicitly defined as the traditional theory of federalism indicates.

The role of the national government has expanded not because of plotting and power grabbing by certain men in Washington, nor because of any preconceived plan. Instead, it has expanded because of the need to deal with extensive economic and social changes. These changes have occurred as scientific and technological developments have transformed this country from a small, primarily agrarian society to a large industrial nation, and as the slow, skeletal communication and transportation systems have become massive and rapid. Problems that did not exist before or were local in character are now national concerns.

Obviously, states, counties, or cities cannot effectively regulate television, radio, telephone, telegraph, railroads, and air travel. Nor can they effectively deal with the increasingly centralized American economy, with giant corporations, labor unions, and "agribusinesses." Their capabilities are overtaxed by the problems of expanding interstate commerce, urbanization, racial conflict, economic recessions, and automation. The preeminence of international affairs and their domestic impact are also considerations which the states alone are largely helpless to deal with.

HOW THE FEDERAL ROLE HAS EXPANDED

The built-in flexibility of our Constitution is partly responsible for the extensive federal expansion. It has allowed the Supreme Court, Congress, the President, and also the people to utilize and adapt federal powers as needed. Among them, the commerce, war, and taxing and spending powers have been most important.

Expansion Through the Commerce Clause

Few economic transactions are excluded from Congress's power to regulate interstate commerce, as given in Article 1, Section 8; nor is this an entirely recent development. Almost from the beginning of the republic, "commerce" was interpreted by Congress and the Supreme Court to mean not only the transporting of goods, but the movement of services and people as well.[1] As various new methods of transportation and communication developed, they too were included in the definition, along with production, buying, and selling.

Not until 1936–37, however, did the present vast scope of national authority over our economy become established. During that period, the Court ruled that manufacturing, or any other form of productive undertaking, was interstate commerce if constituted on a national basis and conducted in two or more states.[2] This interpretation opened the door for a vast amount of federal legislation regulating commerce, particularly in the areas of agricultural production, minimum wages–maximum hours, employer-employee relations, civil rights, and child labor. As more and more commercial activities have since become regional, national, and international, they have come under the authority of the national government, and the scope of state action has diminished. Even *noncommercial* activity is now also regulated by Congress. For example, federal laws prohibit the use of interstate commerce to rob banks, or to steal automobiles; they also make it a crime for hotelkeepers to refuse service to interstate travelers on the basis of race, color, national origin, or religion. Also prohibited are interstate travel to incite or take part in a riot[3] and the interstate transportation of explosives or firearms with the knowledge that they are to be used in a civil disorder that would obstruct commerce.

[1] See especially *Gibbons* v. *Ogden* (1824). In this case, involving New York's effort to establish a monopoly on steamboat transportation on its waters, the Supreme Court ruled that states must yield their power to regulate commerce when Congress has "preempted" the field by adopting regulations of its own.
[2] *National Labor Relations Board* v. *Jones and Laughlin Steel Corporation* (1937). Jones and Laughlin had fired several employees for union activities in production units at one of its plants and had subsequently asserted that the federal government lacked jurisdiction to interfere in the firings because the men were engaged in manufacturing, which was not interstate commerce.
[3] The 1968 Safe Streets Act was specifically aimed at revolutionary leaders who threatened protest at the 1968 Democratic Convention in Chicago. The resulting indictment of "the Chicago Eight" for conspiracy to incite riot was the first action taken under this law.

Expansion Through the War Power

Federal powers have also expanded because of the total nature of modern warfare—its complex organization, technology, and propensity for destructiveness—and the ever-present danger of war occurring. Not only does the federal government organize and direct national efforts during all wars, but afterward it reconverts manpower, machines, and goods for peacetime purposes. Furthermore, it controls the nation's resources so as to keep up its war-making ability by such measures as conserving and allocating natural resources, encouraging scientific study, maintaining a strong economy, and drafting manpower. In past all-out wars, the government has also rationed goods (in World War II, such items as gasoline, rubber, and sugar) and controlled prices, wages, and rents. In short, in this age of continual danger of unlimited thermonuclear conflict in which an entire country—not just its armies—must be engaged in struggling to protect itself, the federal government may exercise almost unlimited power to promote national defense in time of war or prepare for war during peacetime. Obviously, therefore, the activities of state and local governments in this area are necessarily subsumed under the federal effort.

Expansion Through Federal Financial Powers

Federal authority has also been extended through the financial powers of Congress. Education, agriculture, and state highway construction, for instance, have been subjected to some federal regulation because Congress appropriates money for their support and attaches conditions as to how the money is used. Under the 1964 Civil Rights Act, federal authorities may refuse federal funds to school districts, colleges, and hospitals that deny admission to or segregate persons because of race. Another example is the program of unemployment compensation now in all states, established after Congress in 1935 levied a payroll tax on employers but permitted them to deduct this federal tax from the taxes they paid to their states for compensation of employees who were out of work—if such a system existed in their states. Naturally, after this legislation passed, *all* states proceeded to adopt unemployment compensation programs. The tax power has also been used to control such activities as the sale of narcotics and professional gambling.[4]

Expansion Through Civil Rights System

When the Fourteenth Amendment was adopted in 1868, the protection of civil rights, once mainly the responsibility of the states, come under federal jurisdiction. The amendment provided that no state could "deprive any person of life, liberty, or property, without due process of law; nor deny to any person within its jurisdiction the equal protection of the laws." Under this new amendment, state practices which had supposedly deprived persons of their civil rights were subjected to the review of federal courts.

For many years this provision was narrowly construed and added little to federal power. In 1925 (*Gitlow* v. *New York*), however, the Supreme Court began to apply the Fourteenth Amendment to what states were doing in limiting free speech and press, then by 1947 extended it to take in the other First Amendment freedoms of assembly, petition, and religion, and finally expanded it to cover nearly the entire Bill of Rights.[5] Later, commencing in the 1930s and accelerating after 1964, the Court extended its coverage to discrimination in public facilities, schools, housing, criminal justice,[6] and to unequal apportionments of legislative seats. This broader interpretation, plus national legislative and administrative actions in these areas, has thrust

[4] However, in 1968, in *Marchetti* v. *United States*, the Supreme Court ruled that the registration provisions of the federal wagering tax statutes violated the Fifth Amendment privilege against self-incrimination in criminal prosecutions.

[5] For the exceptions—jury trial of civil cases and grand jury indictment for serious crimes—see the discussion of the Fourteenth Amendment "due process" clause in Chapter 15.

[6] The second section of the Thirteenth Amendment (1865) also gave Congress some power in the area of civil rights. It was with this authority that Congress passed an 1866 statute barring racial discrimination in the sale or rental of all property. However, in the decade after the Reconstruction period the Supreme Court, in a series of cases, spelled out its basic assumption that none of the Civil War amendments had been intended to give Congress any new power to enforce civil rights. Their only function was to forbid certain state actions and enforce them against the states, not against individuals.

the federal government into fields once almost solely the jurisdiction of state and local governments. Not surprisingly, federal entry has been strongly criticized and resisted.

Expansion Through Abdication by the States

Some argue that the federal government has grown because the states have abdicated their responsibilities. It is true that some state governments are inefficient, graft ridden, and without necessary resources, tax bases, and borrowing power to provide for even the most minimal public needs, and that in general the states have proved largely inadequate in crises such as the Great Depression of the 1930s. Nevertheless it appears that even if all states performed ideally, the federal government would still expand to satisfy national needs. Outstanding performances by some states in providing for the public needs of their citizens (e.g., California's relatively high compensation for disabled workers) have actually resulted in increased federal activity to satisfy demands in the other states that services be brought up to the higher standard.

Expansion Through Admission of New States

The gradual admission of thirty-seven states since 1789 obviously extended the geographic dimensions of the national domain; it has also extended federal authority. Unlike the original thirteen states, which might claim some rights because the national government was created by their consent, the later states owe their statehood to acts of Congress.[7] Not only could Congress have granted or denied entry but it could also have placed conditions on admission—and in some cases did. (Utah was admitted in 1896 on condition its constitution outlaw polygamy; Alaska, admitted in 1959, was forbidden ever to claim lands legally held by an Eskimo, Indian, or Aleutian.) Congress is limited only in that

---

[7] Thirty were administered as territories by the national government prior to admission. Five more—Kentucky, Maine, Tennessee, Vermont, and West Virginia—were admitted after separating from other states. The independent Republic of Texas was admitted directly to statehood, as was California, ceded by Mexico in 1848.

(1) it may not create a new state by taking territory from one or more existing states unless it secures the consent of the state legislature or legislatures involved, and (2) the conditions it imposes for admission may be enforced only when they do not compromise the independence of a state to manage its internal affairs.

Expansion Through the Doctrine of Implied Powers

When the architects of the Constitution divided powers between the national and the state governments, they realized that federal-state jurisdictional conflict was inevitable. Anticipating this, they inserted into the Constitution the supremacy clause of Article VI, which made federal law—"the supreme Law of the Land"—superior to state law and also limited state jurisdiction to fields not preempted by the federal government.

However, not all questions were thereby solved, for the extent of federal powers remained undefined. Furthermore, with the President, Congress, and the states all interpreting constitutional prescriptions, differences were bound to arise. To resolve them, the framers provided a Supreme Court to umpire the federal system.

Before the republic was a year old, sharp controversy arose over the precise limits of national power when Alexander Hamilton proposed the creation of a national Bank of the United States to establish a uniform currency, to care for the property of the United States, and to help establish a national economy. Secretary of State Thomas Jefferson and other states' righters saw in the national bank a threat to state powers over local economic affairs. They argued vigorously against the idea, pointing out that there was no specific authorization for it in the Constitution, that all powers not categorically granted to the central government were reserved to the states, and that therefore only the states had the power to charter banks.

Hamilton retorted that the creation of a national bank to carry out the expressly delegated powers of the national government to tax and to regulate trade was not only "proper" but "necessary." Although he agreed that the Constitution did not authorize the bank in so many words, nevertheless he believed that by in-

101

ference—that is, by virtue of *implied powers*—Congress could do so. Implied powers are those which may be reasonably inferred from the express powers granted. These implied powers are based on the so-called *elastic* or *necessary and proper clause* of Article I, Section 8, which provides that Congress shall have power "to make all Laws which shall be necessary and proper for carrying into Execution the foregoing Powers, and all other Powers vested by this Constitution in the Government of the United States, or in any Department or Officer thereof." Federal authority is not, however, without limits; regardless of the elastic clause, the government's activities must be based upon specifically delegated powers, since otherwise the activity may be challenged as unconstitutional. In essence Hamilton argued for a "loose" or "broad" interpretation of the Constitution—and his views prevailed. His eloquent arguments were accepted by President Washington, and the first Bank of the United States was chartered by Congress in 1791.

The Supreme Court supported Hamilton's contention in its famous 1819 decision in *McCulloch* v. *Maryland*. This case was the result of an attempt by the Maryland legislature (in 1818) to destroy a branch of the Bank of the United States by imposing a heavy tax on the bank's notes. The cashier of the Baltimore branch of the bank refused to pay the tax and was convicted of violating the law by the Maryland courts. Maryland, basing its argument on the states' rights interpretation of federalism, insisted that the bank was unconstitutional. However, the Supreme Court declared that the Bank *was* constitutional and denied Maryland the right to tax it. In a classic exposition of the *doctrine of implied powers*, Chief Justice John Marshall, writing the Court's opinion, ringingly asserted:

> The powers of government are limited, and its powers are not to be transcended. But we think the sound construction of the Constitution must allow to the national legislature that discretion with respect to the means by which the powers it confers are to be carried into execution, which will enable that body to perform the high duties assigned to it in a manner most beneficial to the people. Let the end be legitimate, let it be within the scope of the Constitution, and all means which are appro-

THE CONSTITUTIONAL DIVISION OF POWERS

The national government has only those powers delegated to it by the Constitution, but its constitutional acts are supreme. The states possess *all* powers not granted to the national government *except* those denied them by the Constitution. Some powers are denied to both the state and federal governments; others are denied either one or the other; others are shared.

The National Government: Delegated, Implied, and Inherent Powers

The national government is one of *delegated powers.* Many are expressed in eighteen paragraphs of Article I, Section 8 of the Constitution; others are expressed elsewhere in the document.

The national government also has *inherent powers*, principally in the area of foreign affairs, simply because it *is* the government of the United States. Since these powers were exercised by the United States before the Constitution was drafted, it may be inferred that the framers assumed they would be exercised also by the new national government. In any event, their use is not limited by any theory of delegated powers. Even so-called "inherent powers" may be classified as implied powers. For example, the power to recognize foreign governments may be implied from the treaty power, and the power to regulate immigration from the power to regulate foreign commerce.

The State Governments: Reserved Powers

The states have governments of *reserved powers*; they possess all powers not delegated to the national government nor prohibited to them. The Tenth Amendment (1791) made the division specific: "The powers not delegated to the United States by the Constitution, nor prohibited by it to the States, are reserved to the States respectively, or to the people." Because state powers are reserved, or *residual*, they are nowhere enumerated.

Shared Powers

Some powers are *shared* by the national and state governments. For instance, while the federal government may tax and borrow, define and punish crimes, enact bankruptcy

103

> laws, condemn private property for public use, or set
> standards or weights and measures, so also may the states.
> Even the power to control interstate commerce is shared,
> for although federal authority and responsibility are para-
> mount, state regulation of certain phases of commerce
> would be valid if not in conflict with federal regulations.
>
> ### Forbidden Powers
>
> Some powers are *forbidden*. For instance, as a protection
> to the states, the national government is forbidden to favor
> the ports of one state over those of another. Many other
> powers are denied the states in favor of the national gov-
> ernment. Fourteen are listed in Article I, Section 10 alone.
> Numerous other limitations are placed on the states or the
> national government, or both, to protect civil rights and
> liberties.

priate, which are plainly adapted to that end, which are not prohibited but consist with the letter and spirit of the Constitution, are constitutional.

Marshall further stated that:

> ... if the right of the states to tax the means employed by the general government be conceded, the declaration that the Constitution, and the laws made in pursuance thereof, shall be the supreme law of the land, is empty and unmeaning declamation.

The principles thus enunciated became part of our constitutional law. Even the Jeffersonians, after gaining control of the government in 1801, invoked them. And Congress has time and again based important legislation on the most meager evidence of constitutional authorization, usually with the Supreme Court's subsequent support.

Still, the precise boundary between federal and state power has never been settled, and the debate goes on. States' rights versus federal authority was, for example, a primary cause of the Civil War, and today Southern states' righters vigorously oppose federal civil rights programs as unconstitutional invasions of areas reserved for the states. It is unlikely that the debate of states' rights versus federal powers will end as long as our federal system remains, for the essence of this system is the relationship between governments. Inherent in this relationship is change, and thus dispute over the specific relationship at any one time.

COOPERATIVE FEDERALISM AND FEDERAL GRANTS-IN-AID

To understand American federalism we must consider not only the constitutional framework, but also how the system works within that framework. How does federalism operate?

Much government activity is *cooperative;* that is, it is shared by all levels of government—federal, state, and local.[9] Most federal activities are administered locally, with about 90 percent of federal civilian employees working outside Washington, D.C. Federalism does not, therefore, operate as a hierarchy with a remote federal government at the top, state governments in the middle, and local governments at the base. In this sense, American federalism is not and never has been a system of separated powers, responsibilities, and functions.

Federal Grants to State and Local Governments

Most responsible for reshaping federalism in the twentieth century have been federal grants-in-aid. By making federalism a cooperative activity between national and state governments, these grants have immensely strengthened the federal system and have brought better public services to the people.

These grants are not new: in the eighteenth century, federal land and money were given to the states for education, agriculture, roads, and canals; but it is only in the last few decades that they have been widely used. Currently these grants-in-aid amount to more than $25 billion annually (see Figure 5-1) and are earmarked for such diverse uses as Social Security, public health,

[9] Among the areas where greatest sharing occurs are law enforcement, civil defense, selective service, conservation of natural resources, public health, disaster relief, urban renewal, housing, civil aviation, agriculture, education, welfare, employment security, and vocational rehabilitation.

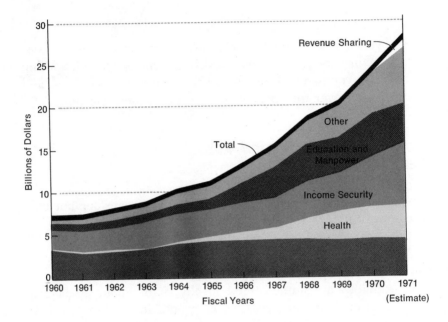

Figure 5-1. Federal aid to state and local governments, 1960–1971 (estimated). (Source: *Congressional Quarterly Weekly Report,* February 6, 1970, p. 378.)

pollution control, crime fighting, civil defense, forestry, highway and airport construction, urban mass transportation, general education, vocational education and rehabilitation, and school lunch programs. In 1971, there were over 1400 grant-in-aid programs.

Most federal grants-in-aid are *conditional;* that is, they are given only if the states comply with detailed standards. Usually, this means a state must spend the money only for the purpose and in the manner indicated by the federal government, and must match the federal funds with at least an equal amount. The state must also have a suitable administrative body to deal with the federal government about the project, must hire, retain, and promote employees on the basis of fitness instead of party or personal loyalty, and must accept federal regulations, policies, plans, minimum standards, and inspection.[10]

---

[10] Some federal grants require that states agree to only minimal conditions, and some require states to contribute less than the federal government. A few require no state contribution at all.

Advantages and Disadvantages of Grants-in-Aid

Many people feel there are at least two advantages to having grants-in-aid. First, they enable the national government to re-distribute funds collected from personal and corporate income taxes in the affluent areas to the poorer states, thus raising the standard of public services. This investment by the national government is sound, its advocates believe, because persons with inadequate education or poor health may be actually national as well as local liabilities. Second, such grants enhance the role of the states and avoid complete centralization in the federal government by stimulating modernization of state administration, increasing state activity, and raising the level of competence of state employees.

However, opponents of grants-in-aid believe there are at least three drawbacks to the system. First, to secure sufficient funds for the grants, the national government has had to broaden the federal tax base, making it more difficult for states to raise their own revenue and in turn stimulating pressure for more and more grants. At present, the states depend upon federal grants-in-aid for about one-fifth of all their income. Second, states are tempted to put up matching funds to secure federal grants for prescribed purposes, even when their limited funds might be better spent for other projects. Third, because the basic administrative provisions are established by the federal government and are uniform, state initiative in creating administrative machinery and state independence are seriously undermined.

Unconditional Grants—An Alternative

How could the above drawbacks be overcome? Some people have proposed that the government should make federal subsidies without attaching detailed conditions. The grants could be marked for general areas, such as education, highways, and public health. States would thus have greater independence and initiative to work out programs most suitable to their needs. Discussion and debate of the general grants idea was greatly stimulated by President Nixon's 1971 proposal for a $16 billion program of general-purpose grants to states and cities. According to the

President, this so-called *revenue-sharing plan* would give Americans a new chance to participate in government and would provide states and localities with more money and less interference.

Those who oppose such *unconditional* (or *general*) *grants* do so largely because they feel the states would substitute these unmatched funds for their own appropriations and would look more and more to Washington for tax money. Furthermore, these critics hold that many desirable influences of the conditional grants-in-aid would probably be eliminated or reduced: For instance, perhaps the greatest advantage of the present grants pattern—the accomplishing of near-uniformity of program without centralization of administration—would be lost.

Federal Grants to Cities

Not until the 1937 Housing Act did the federal government begin giving aid to local government agencies. Today, federal grants to cities are vastly expanded. Urban areas receive federal funds for housing, airports, street construction, mass transportation, civil defense, slum clearance, urban renewal, poverty programs, and many other activities. This increased federal initiative has largely come about because the problems of the modern city have multiplied and the city constituencies have generally had greater influence with the national government—particularly with the executive branch—than with traditionally rural-minded state legislatures. Also, of course, neither the states nor the cities have the tax resources to deal effectively with these problems anyway.

The scope of this federal-urban cooperation will probably increase, as indicated by the creation in 1965 of the Department of Housing and Urban Development (HUD) to administer the principal federal assistance programs for housing and city development.

The Future of Federal Grants-in-Aid

The federal grant system is unlikely to be soon overturned or fundamentally altered. Its constitutionality has been strongly affirmed (in 1923 in *Massachusetts* v. *Mellon,* which sustained a federal program of grants for maternity care) and, rhetoric to the contrary, there is little pressure against it out of concern for the states. Rather, pressures are directed against expanding grants for specific purposes, such as highway construction, education, and public health.

The grant system has not solved all problems, nor is it free from abuse. Yet by building on existing institutions, keeping program administrators subject to local control, and providing improved public services, it seems better than a system of direct national administration or no system at all. Commenting on the program, a presidential commission concluded that, where federal aid is necessary, federal grants "represent a basically sound technique."[11]

"HORIZONTAL" COOPERATIVE FEDERALISM

Just as cooperative federalism and the local administration of federal programs have helped deter the development of immensely centralized government, also there have been cooperative efforts among the states themselves to develop relatively uniform government services and programs. Among the devices of this "horizontal" cooperative federalism (as opposed to the "vertical" cooperation between states and federal governments) are interstate compacts, uniform state laws, and consultation.

Interstate Compacts

Interstate compacts are agreements, between two or more states, that deal with common problems. Since 1920 well over one hundred such agreements have been concluded. They cover such diverse matters as boundary disputes, construction of airports, diversion of water, oil conservation, construction of bridges over and tunnels under rivers serving as boundaries, conservation of

[11] The Commission on Intergovernmental Relations, *A Report to the President for Transmittal to Congress.* (Washington, D.C.: Government Printing Office, 1964), p. 81. The permanent Advisory Commission on Intergovernmental Relations has concurred in this opinion; see its *The Role of Equalization in Federal Grants* (Washington, D.C.: Government Printing Office, 1964), p. 81.

natural resources, harbor development, and sewage pollution. Congressional approval is not needed—except, the Supreme Court has ruled (in *Virginia* v. *Tennessee*, 1893), for those agreements "tending to increase the political power of the states."

An outstanding example of a successful compact is the Port of New York Authority, established in 1921 by agreement between New York and New Jersey. The Authority deals with common transportation problems between New York City and neighboring communities in New Jersey and is directed by twelve commissioners, six from each state. Among its most important projects are the Holland and Lincoln tunnels, the George Washington Bridge, and three giant airports—Kennedy, La Guardia, and Newark.

In the 1920s it was hoped the states would use the compact extensively to deal with regional matters, as an alternative to greater centralization in the federal government. However, although a number of compacts have been successful, the device has not been widely used. Yet it is a significant way in which states cooperate on common problems. A recent example is the Tahoe Regional Planning Compact between California and Nevada. Finally approved in 1968, it permitted the formation of an agency to regulate air pollution, waste disposal, outdoor advertising, and to provide watershed protection in the Lake Tahoe basin astride the California-Nevada border.

Uniform State Laws

Another way states may cooperate is to enact uniform state laws to make it easier to do business across state boundaries. The leading organization promoting this cooperation is the National Conference of Commissioners on Uniform State Laws, founded in 1892, which has representatives appointed by the governors of the fifty states. The conference has drafted and ratified more than one hundred uniform laws, a number of which, particularly in the field of commercial law, have been widely adopted by the states. However, these laws have been adopted at least as much to simplify and to have better law as to have uniformity. Furthermore, these laws are still interpreted differently in states adopting them. An outstanding example of a uniform law is the Uniform Narcotic Drug Act.

Interstate Consultation

There are a number of organizations set up for interstate consultation, the two most important being the Council of State Governments and the Conference of State Governors.

The *Council of State Governments,* organized in 1935 and having all states as members, promotes interstate cooperation by research and publishing (including the biennial *Book of the States,* the major source on state developments, and the monthly periodical *State Government*), and by serving as a secretariat for such organs as the American Legislators' Association, the National Association of State Attorneys General, and the Conference of Chief Justices. Through its state commissions and national and regional conferences on such matters as crime, water pollution, fisheries, and conservation of natural resources it promotes uniform state legislation, and encourages improved state administrative organization. The Council also lobbies in Washington for the states' rights point of view. In 1962 it launched a campaign to get the state legislatures to call a constitutional convention to adopt three states' rights amendments which, if adopted, would have made the United States more a confederation than a federal union. Although thirty-three of the required thirty-eight legislatures approved the package, the amendments got so little public attention that they have been called the "silent amendments."

The *Conference of State Governors,* established in 1908, meets annually to consider cooperative action. However, these gatherings of state chief executives have had mostly the flavor of social affairs and have not lived up to earlier expectations. Regional conferences of state governors have actually been much more productive.

STATE-LOCAL GOVERNMENT RELATIONS

While national-state relations are *federal,* state-local relationships are largely *unitary.* This means that whereas the states are guaranteed their own powers as well as territorial and political integrity in the federal Constitution, local governments are generally creatures of the state legislatures and have no power in their own right. This is not, however, to say that all local governments are powerless and at the mercy of the state governments. In many states the legislature no longer regulates specific local governments with special laws nor determines their structure or processes—these are done instead by constitutional provisions. Furthermore, in some states, certain local governments enjoy "home rule"—that is, they may manage their own affairs with little interference from state officials. The "federal principle" is thus unofficially operating here.

Like the federal government, states have enormously expanded their activities, largely because of new social and economic matters which local governments cannot adequately manage, and because problems once thought to be local are now seen to be state problems. Sometimes these formerly local matters are to some extent taken over by the state; sometimes they are handled by the state's making grants to local governments (usually with strings attached). In any event, more and more, state officials supervise local officials, particularly in the fields of health, law enforcement, highways, and social security.

FEDERAL OBLIGATIONS IMPOSED BY THE CONSTITUTION

Article IV of the Constitution imposed three obligations upon the national government in its relations with the states. "The United States" it said, must (1) guarantee each state "a Republican Form of Government," (2) "protect each of them against invasion," and (3) protect each "against domestic violence."

States Guaranteed a Republican Form of Government

While the Constitution guaranteed every state a *republican form,* it left key questions unanswered: what, for instance, is meant specifically by "Republican Form" and who is to enforce the guarantee? On the first question, the framers indirectly provided a guideline. They generally used the term "Republican Form" to distinguish it from monarchy, oligarchy, or direct democracy. Still unspecified, however, was the branch of the government of the United States responsible for enforcement.

While refusing to enforce the guarantee or even to interpret it, the Supreme Court has indicated that the guarantee is not a *legal* but a *political* matter and is therefore the responsibility of the executive and legislative, that is, the political, branches. Both branches may act on the matter—Congress, for instance, could exclude Senators and Representatives from states not having a republican form; the President could use the armed forces to preserve a state's republican form. The President could also decide between contending factions claiming legal authority within a state. In fact, when President John Tyler did this in 1842, during the Dorr Rebellion against the government of Rhode Island, which was functioning under the original constitution of the state, the Supreme Court supported him (*Luther v. Borden,* 1849),[12] holding itself bound by his decision, and refusing to decide any questions concerning the legitimacy of either rival faction in Rhode Island. Dorr's supporters had drawn up a new constitution and elected him governor.

States Protected Against Invasion

Article IV of the Constitution also obliged the national government to protect each of the states against invasion—a matter that does not require comment, since obviously an invasion of any state would be an invasion of the United States. It is a logical companion to the primacy of the federal war powers and the prohibition of state armies and navies.

States Protected Against Domestic Violence

Article IV further required the national government to protect the states "on Application of the Legislature, or of the Executive (when the Legislature cannot be convened) against domestic violence." Involved here are complex political and constitutional issues, for all branches and levels of government are frequently involved in these tense undertakings.

[12] Luther was a follower of Thomas Dorr. Borden, an official of the charter government, entered Luther's home to arrest him. Luther sued Borden, charging him with trespass and bringing into question which was the legal government of the state.

Although Congress was authorized by Article I, Section 8 "To provide for calling forth the Militia to execute the Laws of the Union, suppress Insurrections and repel Invasions," primary federal responsibility lies with the President. He may act either on the request of the state legislature or executive or entirely on his own authority. For instance, in 1894, President Grover Cleveland sent federal troops into Illinois—despite the protest of the governor of the state—to intervene in a strike against the Pullman Company in order to keep open the flow of interstate commerce and to ensure mail delivery. Similarly, in 1957, President Eisenhower sent troops to Little Rock, Arkansas, over the opposition of Governor Orville Faubus, to prevent interference with federal court orders requiring the admission of nine Negro students to Central High School,[13] and again, in 1962, President Kennedy ordered federal marshals and troops to the University of Mississippi to ensure compliance with federal court orders on the enrollment of black student James Meredith. In 1970 President Nixon sent federal troops to New York to move the mail during a postal workers' strike.

STATE OBLIGATIONS IMPOSED BY THE CONSTITUTION

Article IV also imposes three obligations upon each state in its relations with sister states. Each must (1) give "Full Faith and Credit" to one another's "public Acts, Records, and judicial Proceedings"; (2) return fugitives "to the State having Jurisdiction of the Crime"; and (3) extend to any other's citizens "all Privileges and Immunities" it accords its own.

Give Full Faith and Credit to Other States

The "Full Faith and Credit" clause requires each state to enforce the civil (but not criminal) judgments of the other states and to recognize their statutes and administrative actions. The most

[13] The President is specifically authorized, by legislation passed in 1792 and 1795, to take action "whenever the laws of the United States shall be opposed, or the execution thereof obstructed, in any state, by combinations too powerful to be suppressed by the ordinary course of judicial proceedings."

common application of this clause is in connection with judicial proceedings. For instance, if Smith sues another person in the Texas courts and obtains a judgment for $5000, but the second person immediately moves himself and his property to New York and refuses to pay, New York would not *automatically* enforce the judgment awarded by the Texas courts. However, if Smith brings an action in the New York courts to enforce the Texas judgment, he would not have to satisfy a New York jury or judge that he is entitled to payment. Once the New York courts found the Texas judgment properly authenticated and without fraud, they would give full faith and credit to the Texas judgment and issue an enforcement order of their own, without examining the merits of the case.

But what about the quick and easy divorces that some states grant? Must the other states give full faith and credit to *these* judicial proceedings? Apparently not always. In *Williams* v. *North Carolina* (1942) the Supreme Court upheld North Carolina's refusal to recognize the validity of a Nevada divorce granted to two North Carolinians on the ground that Nevada did not have jurisdiction because the parties were not *bona fide* residents of that state. The case involved a Mr. Williams and a Mrs. Hendrix, who were married, but not to each other. Both were residents of North Carolina, a state with stricter divorce laws, who had gone to Nevada, where they stayed for six weeks in order to fulfill Nevada's residency requirement necessary to obtain a divorce, then divorced their respective spouses, married each other, and returned to North Carolina. They were arrested and charged with bigamy, North Carolina contending that a six-week stay in Nevada for the sole purpose of obtaining a divorce did not constitute legal residence nor give Nevada courts jurisdiction over a North Carolina resident. It is important to note here, however, that although a state need not accept the "quickie" divorce granted by another state, states seldom arrest for bigamy recipients who later remarry.

Render Fugitives

As noted above, the full-faith-and-credit clause does not require a state to enforce the *criminal* laws of its sister states; its only obligation here is to "render" or return fugitives. According to the Constitution:

> A Person charged in any State with Treason, Felony, or other Crime, who shall flee from Justice, and be found in another State, shall on Demand of the executive Authority of the State from which he fled, be delivered up, to be removed to the State having Jurisdiction of the Crime.

Furthermore, Congress has supplemented this clause by passing legislation which makes the state governor responsible for demanding the return of fugitives. However, it has not provided for enforcement of the laws, and the federal courts will not require a governor to return fugitives.[14] Thus, governors can, and sometimes do, refuse to honor a request for rendition. Frequently their refusals are for humanitarian reasons or because they believe that other circumstances warrant a refusal. Even though federal authorities may make arrests in such cases (because it is a federal offense to cross a state boundary to avoid prosecution or imprisonment), they often prefer to avoid involvement. Occasionally a governor's refusal to render a fugitive gets wide publicity, but by and large the obligation is quietly observed.

Extend Privileges and Immunities to Citizens of Other States

The Constitution forbids a state to deny to citizens of other states the privileges and immunities it extends to its own citizens. Among these are full protection by the state and local governments, and the rights to acquire and dispose of property, travel freely through or reside in the state, engage in a lawful occupation, have access to the courts, and be exempt from higher taxes than are paid by citizens of the state. This protection does not, however, extend to political rights such as voting, holding public office, or serving on juries. A state may require a minimum period

---

[14] See *Kentucky* v. *Dennison* (1861). In this case, the Supreme Court refused to compel William Dennison, the governor of Ohio, to turn over to Kentucky authorities a free Negro who, while in Kentucky, had violated Kentucky law by helping a slave escape to Ohio. Chief Justice Taney, commenting on the case, stated that the governor was morally obliged to render fugitives, but could not be legally compelled to do so.

of residence in counties and polling districts as a prerequisite to the exercise of political rights. Nor does this protection apply to those engaged in professions or trades requiring special skills. For instance, medical doctors, lawyers, barbers, teachers, realtors, engineers, and others licensed in another state may be required to take state examinations to test their competence to engage in their occupations in the states to which they may move. Furthermore, a state may restrict hunting, fishing, or attendance at a state educational institution to its own citizens, or it may charge nonresidents higher fees for these privileges.

FUTURE OF THE STATES AND LOCALITIES

The opinion is often voiced that the national government has grown so large that the states are threatened with obsolescence. The weakness of this gloomy analysis, however, is easily demonstrated. The states and their local governments have also become more pervasive within their territorial limits. Thus, their role in the federal system is increasing, not decreasing. Today they perform more public services, spend more money, and employ more personnel than ever before. In fact, in recent years they have expanded more rapidly than the federal government has.

In the past twenty years the number of state and local government employees has nearly tripled, while federal civilian employment has not increased appreciably. By 1967 there were 7.6 million full-time state employees, and only 2.9 million full-time federal employees. Furthermore, in that year, state employment increased by 416,000, while federal employment rose by only 32,000. Data on their respective expenditures reveal the same pattern: during the 1950s the rate of growth of state expenditures was more than six times that of the federal government's nondefense spending.[15] In addition, by 1970 the states were receiving about $25 billion annually in federal grants-in-aid, nearly three times more than they were in 1960.

Furthermore, states and localities remain the power bases for

[15] On the other hand, in 1968, defense-generated employment was 2,932,700 —an increase of nearly 900,000 over the 1965 level.

our great national parties. They have equal representation in the Senate, and state and local constituents decide on who sits in Congress. Also, states serve as laboratories where party tactics, new types of legislation, and new administrative techniques may be tried and evaluated. In state government, future statesmen and federal judges gain experience and are tested. Finally, states continue to assume the major responsibility for such important functions as education, law enforcement, and highway construction and maintenance.

THE NEW FEDERAL DISTRICTS: TOWARD A DECENTRALIZED BUREAUCRACY?

In the past two decades, hundreds of new programs have been fashioned to clear slums, feed hungry people, retrain unskilled workers, reduce pollution, upgrade schools, improve police departments, better our highways, and to do other worthy things. By 1970, the annual federal outlay to the states for these activities amounted to more than $27 billion. Yet we all know that the slums have not been cleared, that there are still those of us who are hungry and lacking in marketable skills, that the air we breathe and the water we drink is still fouled, that the crime rate continues to go up, and that the schools are not doing the job of educating we expect of them.

But if money alone is not the answer, what is? Both the Nixon and Johnson Administrations (and also the New Left) have concluded that greater progress in solving these problems may be made by moving a major share of decision-making away from Washington and into local communities. In 1969, President Nixon, building on a reorganization study made in the Johnson Administration, ventured a first step in this direction by announcing the institution of ten federal regions, as shown in the map in Figure 5-2. The new regional system applies to three federal departments—Health, Education, and Welfare (HEW), Housing and Urban Development (HUD), and Labor. Its machinery includes a regional council in each of the ten regional headquarters. Comprised of ranking field officers from the three executive departments, the council chooses its chairman and meets as fre-

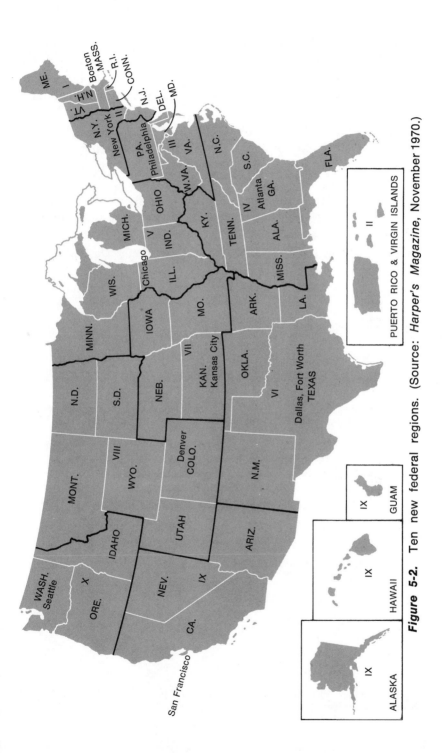

Figure 5-2. Ten new federal regions. (Source: *Harper's Magazine*, November 1970.)

quently as necessary to handle problems. In addition, the Bureau of Budget and Management has a "desk man" for each region. On his frequent visits he mediates controversies between bureaucracies, and reports to Washington on the performance of each agency.

The most impressive result of this decentralization is quicker processing of local applications for federal funding of intergovernmental projects. Overall, the time has been reduced by about half. Some of the speed-ups have been most spectacular. For instance, HUD, which previously had spent an average of ninety-six days to make up its collective mind, now decides for or against a mayor's petition for a rehabilitation loan in an average of five days.[16] Red tape has also been slashed. While these gains are not yet earth-shaking, they are significant steps toward making government more responsive and human.

Suggested Additional Reading

Anderson, W. *The Nation and the States: Rivals or Partners?* 1955.

Carney, J. P., and W. A. Alexander. *California and United States Governments.* 1967.

Elazar, D. J. (ed.). *American Federalism: A View From the States.* 1966.

Goldwin, R. A. (ed.). *A Nation of States: Essays on the American Federal System.* 1963.

Graves, W. B. *American Intergovernmental Relations: Their Origins, Historical Development, and Current Status.* 1964.

Martin, R. C. *The Cities and the Federal System.* 1965.

Riker, W. H. *Federalism: Origin, Operation, Significance.* 1964.

Wheare, K. C. *Federal Government.* 1964.

Wildavsky, A. (ed.). *American Federalism in Perspective.* 1967.

[16] John Fischer, "Can the Nixon Administration Be Doing Something Right?" *Harper's Magazine*, November 1970, p. 36.

Part 2

**The People and Channels
of Popular Influence**

6 Voters, Voter Behavior, and Problems of the Franchise

Carl Iwasaki, *Life* Magazine, ©Time Inc.

Having solemnly resolved that all men are created equal, we shut our eyes and waited for the formula to work.

—Jacob Riis

When we think at all about the typical American, most of us probably prefer to think of him rather as follows: He is honest and hard working, not distinguished by a great deal of formal learning or sophistication, but nevertheless reasonably well informed. He is a man of sound common sense, has an abiding interest in his country, and is very concerned about its well-being. When he votes, he ponders carefully and casts his ballot for candidates whom he thinks are best qualified.

THE AMERICAN VOTER

Unfortunately, recent research does not support such a happy view. Apparently, the typical American gives political matters a rather low priority. If he bothers to vote at all, he chooses on the basis of self-interest, emotion, or ill-defined inclinations, not on the basis of a political ideology or philosophy.[1] It is not surprising, then, to find that his opinions are based on little correct information. How much can be expected of a person who has such a limited interest in, and concern for, political affairs? And how much political information can we expect a person to retain when he does not fit specific political issues into an overall ideology or philosophy?

If we Americans can be characterized thus, on what basis do we vote for candidates? Most of us have an association with one of the major parties, and we generally vote on the basis of that affiliation. This is not to say that there are not major defections in some elections. As Table 6-1 shows, in the 1964 presidential

Table 6–1
PERCENTAGE OF VOTE FOR DEMOCRATIC PRESIDENTIAL
CANDIDATES, 1952–1968

ELECTION YEAR	DEMOCRATS* STRONG	DEMOCRATS* WEAK	INDE-PENDENTS	REPUBLICANS* WEAK	REPUBLICANS* STRONG
1952	84%	62%	33%	6%	1%
1956	85	63	27	7	1
1960	91	72	46	13	2
1964	95	82	66	43	10
1968	85	57	26	10	3

* Strength of party identification was determined by asking respondents whether they were "strong" or "not so strong" Democrats or Republicans.
Source: Benjamin I. Page and Raymond E. Wolfinger, "Party Identification," in Raymond E. Wolfinger (ed.), *Readings in American Political Behavior*, 2nd ed. (Englewood Cliffs, N.J.: Prentice-Hall, 1970), p. 291.

election, for instance, many Republicans crossed party lines to vote for Lyndon Johnson. And in 1968, many Democrats voted for Richard Nixon. Still, the American voter typically tends to take the easy route and vote for the nominees of the party with which he affiliates.

[1] A. Campbell, P. E. Converse, W. E. Miller, and D. E. Stokes, *The American Voter* (New York: Wiley, 1960), pp. 89, 249.

124

HOW VOTING AND PUBLIC OPINION INFLUENCE
GOVERNMENT DECISION-MAKERS

How can a public that is uninterested in politics, is relatively uninformed, lacks an overall integrating ideology or philosophy, and votes simply on the basis of party association effectively influence government decision-makers? And how can people influence their Congressman when they do not know how he votes and may not even know his name? It would appear they cannot, yet government decision-makers act as if public opinion and elections *do* affect their decisions. They are aware that even an inert public will notice conditions that cause hurt to a major part of the population—and will act accordingly. Riots, an unpopular war, inflation, or depression will arouse public notice, and will often result in unfavorable attitudes toward the party or administration in power. In the 1968 election, for instance, the Democrats—and the Johnson Administration in particular—were held to account by the voters for four years of the frustrating, seemingly endless war in Vietnam, for race riots, and for increasing student unrest. The result was President Johnson's decision not to seek reelection, Republican gains, and the election of Republican candidate Richard Nixon.

In short, although public consciousness is usually quite limited, major troubles increase public consciousness and influence voters negatively toward government leaders. This reaction occurs regardless of whether the troubles resulted from the ineptness of the leaders or occurred because of events beyond their control. Comprehending this usual pattern of voter behavior, officeholders make every effort to head off such troubles.

Public opinion also influences government officials by setting certain limits upon their behavior. If a Congressman is caught taking a bribe or misappropriating public funds, supports the abolition of Medicare, advocates unilateral disarmament, joins the Communist Party, attacks labor unions while representing a district with many union members, or supports the Arab position in the Middle East while representing a district with a large Jewish population, he will find that the public in his constituency, though usually unaware of his name or the policies he supports, will very quickly become aware of him. Accordingly, he can anticipate severe defections by the voters from him the next time he stands for election. He will pay a price for going outside the boundaries set by public opinion.

Two other considerations tend to make public opinion and elections a significant influence over the behavior of government leaders. One is that these leaders tend to overestimate the knowledge the public has of their actions and they therefore behave accordingly. Uncertain about the exact extent of their visibility, they usually decide that it is in their best interest to overestimate rather than to underestimate public awareness of their actions.

Finally, even though the public is uninterested and unaware, and usually votes largely on the basis of party affiliation, *opinion leaders* among the public do pay attention to political matters and have an integrating philosophy. More importantly, they try to influence others to embrace their opinions. An opinion leader may hold no official position; he may be a party or interest-group official, a newspaper editor or columnist, or a TV or radio commentator. In any event, he watches governmental decision-makers and passes his knowledge, in generalized form, on to the public. Thus, by a circuitous and two-step process, acts of government officials make impressions on public opinion that are reflected in election results.

BASES OF PARTY PREFERENCE

The party preferences of Americans are uncertain—first, because Americans do not fit into tidy political categories and, second, because their preferences result not from one but from a variety of often indistinct factors. Still, we may make some observations about party preference. Studies reveal, for instance, that the young tend to associate with the party of their parents. This is possibly the most common basis of party membership.[2] Yet, taken alone it tells us little. Left unexplained is whether filial devotion or shared circumstances is the true determinant. Most children

---

[2] Herbert McClosky and Harold E. Dahlgren, "Primary Group Influence on Party Loyalty," *The American Political Science Review,* September 1959, p. 775.

share common racial, religious, sectional, class, and other characteristics with their parents.

Much the same is true of other apparent bases of party membership. The Michigan Survey Research Center (see Table 6-2) has demonstrated, for instance, that voters in large cities generally favor Democrats, whereas suburban voters tend to favor Republicans. Yet the reason is not geographic or environmental. Blacks,

Table 6–2
VOTING PATTERN OF MAJOR SOCIAL GROUPS
IN THE UNITED STATES

GROUP CHARACTERISTIC	VOTE REPUBLICAN	VOTE DEMOCRATIC	OTHER	NOT VOTING
Education				
1948				
Grade school	16%	35%	4%	45%
High school	29	34	4	33
College	54	17	8	21
1956				
Grade school	35	24	1	40
High school	41	34	1	26
College	62	28	–	10
1960				
Grade school	29	37	1	33
High school	38	42	1	19
College	57	32	1	10
Occupation of Head of Family				
1948				
Professional and managerial	58	14	3	25
Other white collar	38	38	5	19
Skilled and semiskilled	15	52	4	29
Unskilled	12	33	5	50
Farm operators	13	25	4	58
1956				
Professional and managerial	57	27	1	15
Other white collar	48	30	1	21
Skilled and semiskilled	39	32	1	28
Unskilled	24	29	–	47
Farm operators	40	34	–	26
1960				
Professional and managerial	46	39	3	12
Other white collar	46	37	1	16
Skilled and semiskilled	31	44	3	22
Unskilled	27	41	–	32
Farm operators	50	25	2	23

127

Table 6–2 Cont.

GROUP CHARACTERISTIC	VOTE REPUBLICAN	VOTE DEMOCRATIC	OTHER	NOT VOTING
Trade Union Affiliation of Head of Family				
1948				
Member	13	55	5	27
Nonmember	32	26	4	38
1956				
Member	36	39	2	23
Nonmember	46	25	1	28
1960				
Member	27	48	2	23
Nonmember	44	35	1	20
Type of Community				
1948				
Metropolitan areas	32	46	5	17
Towns and cities	30	28	5	37
Rural areas	12	25	4	59
1956				
Metropolitan areas	43	35	1	21
Towns and cities	46	25	1	28
Rural areas	38	29	1	32
1960				
Metropolitan areas	34	46	2	18
Towns and cities	41	36	1	22
Rural areas	40	35	2	23
Religion				
1948				
Protestant	28	25	5	42
Catholic	25	49	5	21
1956				
Protestant	44	25	1	30
Catholic	43	36	1	20
1960				
Protestant	47	28	1	24
Catholic	16	68	1	15
Race				
1948				
White	29	33	4	34
Negro	10	18	8	64
1956				
White	46	29	1	24
Negro	12	23	1	64
1960				
White	42	38	1	19
Negro	15	36	3	46

Source: University of Michigan Survey Research Center, as cited in Fred I. Greenstein, *The American Party System and the American People* (Englewood Cliffs, N.J.: Prentice-Hall, 1963) pp. 24–25.

Jews, Catholics, and blue-collar workers—all traditionally Democratic voters—concentrate in the cities, whereas managerial, professional, and other higher-income groups, traditionally Republican, concentrate in the suburbs.

Sectionalism has also been an important basis of party membership. For instance, the South has been traditionally solid for the Democrats, while New England has been a Republican stronghold. But this has been only partly a matter of sectional and cultural dissimilarities. Economic differences have also been important. Furthermore, since 1932, the influence of section on party affiliation has declined. For instance, in four recent presidential elections—1952, 1956, 1964, and 1968—the Republicans carried a number of Southern states. In 1968, the Democrats carried only one Southern state—Texas. In New England, on the other hand, even Maine and Vermont, usually overwhelmingly Republican, voted Democratic in 1964.

Some political scientists believe the old sectional politics are breaking down and a new class politics is taking its place; however, this does not seem total or imminent. Thus far, voters have not divided sharply on class lines. Most consider themselves "middle class"; this feeling is obviously a deterrent to class politics.

For many voters—perhaps a majority—party preference is rather casual. If economic and social conditions change, they are likely to shift political preferences. About one-fourth do not affiliate at all, and these independents tend to cast their ballots for candidates, not for parties.

THE "PROBLEM" OF NONVOTING

Usually, only slightly more than 60 percent of the potential American electorate take the trouble to vote in presidential elections. The showing in primaries is even worse—about 35 percent. By contrast, a turnout of 85 to 90 percent is common in democratic elections in Europe and elsewhere. Is our relatively poor showing a bad or good sign? Why is it and what does it signify? What, if anything, might be done to increase voter participation?

None of these questions is easily answered; however, we may

make some observations about low voter turnout. For one thing, many potential voters are disfranchised through no fault of their own. Some were away from their home districts at election time. Others changed residence too recently to qualify to vote under state residence requirements. Others did not go to the polls because of physical disability. Nevertheless, millions of Americans who are qualified to vote do not bother to do so, and their main reason is not technical or legal or lack of education, but simple lack of interest. Studies reveal that nearly one-third of adult Americans are apathetic about politics and uninformed about candidates and issues.[3] Despite the exposure of most to a great deal more formal education than their forebears, and the increased relevance of political decisions, their voting record is far poorer than their grandfathers'.

As Table 6-3 shows, women, blacks, young people, workers, persons with low income and low education, and rural dwellers constitute a disproportionately high percentage of nonvoters. Many of these see little connection between political decision making and their conditions of life, and some are doubtless alienated from the political system and cynical about politics and elections.

When, as in 1968, about 40 million potential voters fail to participate, many observers fear for the good health of our democracy. Politicians and civic leaders often react by attempting to increase popular participation. Some seek reform of the election process; they advocate, among other things, improving registration systems and absentee ballot provisions, removing still-existing discrimination bars, decreasing the number of elections and elective offices, and shortening the sometimes excessively long ballot. Some seek to simply "get out the vote"; this is attempted through political education and by drives led by civic, labor, civil-rights, and party organizations.

The first approach may be worthwhile, even if only partly successful. However, the second may not be in the public interest. Although a big vote turnout could help keep small, unrepresentative minorities from controlling elections, and might

[3] See Charles E. Lindblom, *The Policy-Making Process* (Englewood Cliffs, N.J.: Prentice-Hall, 1968), p. 44.

Table 6–3
SOCIAL CHARACTERISTICS CORRELATED WITH VOTER TURNOUT
IN THE UNITED STATES AND WESTERN EUROPE

HIGHER TURNOUT	LOWER TURNOUT
High income	Low income
High education	Low education
Occupational groups:	Occupational groups:
Businessmen	Unskilled workers
Government employees	Service workers
Commercial-crop farmers	Subsistence farmers, peasants
Miners	
Whites	Negroes
Men	Women
Middle-aged people (35–55)	Young people (under 35)
Older people (over 55)	
Old residents in community	Newcomers in community
Workers in Western Europe	Workers in United States
Crisis situations	Normal situations
Married people	Single
Members of organizations	Isolated individuals

Source: Seymour M. Lipset, *Political Man: The Social Bases of Politics,* p. 184.
Copyright © 1960 by Seymour Martin Lipset. Reprinted by permission of Doubleday & Company, Inc.

look good for the political system, or help a party or group, it might not actually be beneficial. Induced participation seems to add little except numbers. Some studies have revealed that of those who were uninterested in presidential election campaigns or results, more than one half voted anyway, but only because they felt it was their duty or simply felt it was the usual thing to do.[4] Perhaps, therefore, the interests of effective democratic government are best served when the uninformed and unmotivated do *not* vote.

Another way to look at nonvoters is that, as some observers suggest, perhaps their failure to vote results much less from alienation and apathy than from complacency, and that many Americans do not vote because the government is already operating to their general satisfaction. In any event, the real reasons

[4] Campbell *et al., The American Voter,* pp. 31–32.

why Americans do not vote (not simply the reasons they give) are indeed elusive, and whether they should be encouraged to is a difficult question.

THE BALLOT BOX

Perhaps the strongest point commonly made for the American political system (and against communist states) is that our elections are essentially free. It matters not, we contend, that high voter turnouts are recorded in communist countries, or that they may have social and economic democracy—still no real choice is offered the voters.

But if our elections are to be meaningful, should there be any indefensible limitations on who has the right to vote? Shouldn't government guarantee that voters not be defrauded in some manner—as for example, by having their voting district lines drawn to benefit one party or faction over others (gerrymandering")? Regretfully, during most of our history our system has been far from perfect. However, before going further, let us identify the constitutional basis for the suffrage, and briefly review the more important defensible qualifications for voting.

WHO MAY VOTE?

The Constitution does not define who the electorate should be. However, it does stipulate that persons who vote for members "of the most numerous Branch of the State Legislature"—that is, the house of representatives or lower house in their state—may vote for United States Senators and Representatives, and that presidential electors should be appointed by the states in a manner to be decided by each state legislature. The Constitution also restricts the authority of the states to define the electorate in four important respects: The Fifteenth Amendment provides that: "The right of citizens of the United States to vote shall not be denied or abridged on account of race, color, or previous condition of servitude."[5] The Nineteenth prohibits abridgement on the basis of sex,[6] and the Twenty-fourth forbids the use of poll taxes as qualifications for voting in federal elections. The Twenty-sixth prohibits denial on the basis of age, if a citizen is eighteen or older.

DEFENSIBLE SUFFRAGE QUALIFICATIONS

United States citizenship, a minimum period of residence, and a *minimum age* are universal qualifications for voting in the United States. Most states require one year of residence in that state, but a few states in the South require two. Some states of the North and East require only six months. There are also requirements for shorter periods of residence in the county and district within the state. The primary reasons for limiting the vote to actual residents are, first, to prevent repeat voting and, second, to ensure that the voter has a primary interest in the community in which he votes. These laws do not take into consideration that voters in a given location often feel little commonality with their neighbors except proximity, that they may feel closer to people with common economic or social interests or occupations. Another important drawback is that residence requirements temporarily disfranchise some voters because they change their residences too close to election time to qualify at their new addresses[7]—a fact that particularly disadvantages poor migrant workers. This general situation was improved somewhat in 1970 by a provision of the federal Voting Rights Act which established a uniform thirty-day residency requirement for voting in presidential elections.

[5] The Fourteenth Amendment empowers Congress to reduce the congressional representation of any state which disfranchised a part of its adult male citizens except for participation in rebellion or other crime. This penalty has never been enforced.

[6] At the time the amendment was adopted, fourteen states permitted women to vote in presidential elections.

[7] Residence is achieved by maintaining a legal home, one which a person leaves from for a trip and returns to after a trip.

All states (except Texas) also require some form of *voter registration* to reduce election fraud by providing time enough before an election so that interested persons may inspect the list of qualified voters. Most states have adopted the permanent registration system, by which a voter remains on the rolls unless he moves, dies, or fails to vote during a stated time period. A few states retain the *periodic registration system,* compiling new voting lists at regular intervals.

All states *disqualify* certain persons from voting—generally inmates of prisons or insane asylums, vagrants, and violators of election laws. Usually, those who have been dishonorably discharged from the armed forces are also disfranchised. Some states bar persons convicted of serious crimes, even after their release from prison.

THE EIGHTEEN-YEAR-OLD VOTE

The minimum age for voting was twenty-one in all states until 1944, when Georgia gave the ballot to eighteen-year-olds. Kentucky did likewise in 1955. In 1959, Hawaii set the minimum age at twenty—see one result of this in Figure 6-1—and Alaska set it at nineteen.

Proponents of reducing the voting age have pointed out that the practice of franchising citizens at age twenty-one comes not from American experience, but from medieval England.[8] Often they argue that young men may be drafted at age eighteen, and that a man old enough to fight is old enough to vote. They also point out that young people have longer to live, and assert that eighteen- to twenty-one-year-olds are more alert and better educated than their grandparents and better equipped to deal with the vast and rapid changes of our age. Governor Ellis Arnall, in successfully promoting the idea in Georgia, observed that the "fresh viewpoint of youth is needed in politics and that young people would benefit from political participation." Of course, some have opposed lowering the voting age, holding that the

[8] In 1970, the British lowered the voting age to eighteen.

Figure 6-1. A fascinating feature of Hawaii's 1970 campaign for the U.S. Senate was the candidacy of Neil Abercrombie, a thirty-two-year-old graduate assistant at the University of Hawaii. His advertising, as in the poster of the Captain America–type hero above, illustrates, as he put it, his "stunts and statements" campaign. (Source: *San Francisco Sunday Examiner & Chronicle.*)

younger people are too immature and too indifferent to political matters to be entrusted with the ballot.

As early as 1942, Senator Arthur Vandenberg proposed that the federal Constitution be amended to enfranchise eighteen-year-olds. President Eisenhower asked for similar action in 1954, in his State of the Union address. Then, in 1968, President Johnson proposed a constitutional amendment to Congress to lower the voting age to eighteen. A month after his inauguration in 1969, President Nixon added his voice to those who supported a constitutional amendment. However, he opposed federal legislation that would do this, saying that any method of extending the vote to eighteen-year-olds, other than by constitutional amendment, would be "an unconstitutional assertion by congressional authority in an area specifically reserved to the states." Nevertheless, in 1970, Congress extended the vote to eighteen-year-olds in a rider attached to the Voting Rights Act, and President Nixon ("reluctantly," he stated) signed the measure. The law took effect on January 1, 1971, enfranchising 11 million persons.

The law was to cover all elections; however, in 1971, the Supreme Court ruled that the law was valid only in federal elections. Congress reacted by proposing a constitutional amendment which read in part:

> The right of citizens of the United States, who are eighteen years of age or older, to vote shall not be denied or abridged by the United States or any state on account of age.

This became the heart of the Twenty-sixth Amendment when the thirty-eighth state legislature (Ohio's) approved it on June 30, 1971. Ratification by the states was completed in only three months—five months faster than had been done with any other amendment.

ENFRANCHISING THE SOUTHERN BLACK

Southern opposition to granting the franchise to blacks has deep historical roots in the post–Civil War reconstruction period, when the Southern black—illiterate, uneducated, and politically naïve —was enfranchised at a stroke. At the same time, his political

136

domination was assured through the disfranchisement of whites who were active on behalf of the Confederacy. Allied with and advising the blacks were whites from the North and certain Southern whites. This alliance was aided and protected by the Union army and the radical Republicans of the North. When military government ended, Southern whites lashed out at those who had controlled the South. White allies of the blacks fled. Only the mass of blacks remained exposed to the wrath of Southern whites.

To maintain white supremacy, several barriers to black voting were erected. Most important among these were *long residence requirements, poll taxes, white primaries,* and *literacy tests.* Mississippi led the way when in 1890 it amended its constitution to require that voters reside two years in the state and one year in their election district, pay a poll tax of $2, and be literate. This so-called "Mississippi Plan" was copied by other Southern states. As a result, many migratory blacks who followed the crops were disfranchised by the long residence requirements, and the uneducated blacks were disqualified by the literacy tests.

Considerable and widespread agitation against poll taxes arose largely because they disfranchised blacks in the South. The tax was ultimately eliminated in all but five states. In 1964, it was outlawed in national elections by the Twenty-fourth Amendment. After that only Alabama, Mississippi, Texas, and Virginia still retained the poll tax for state and local elections. In 1966, the Supreme Court (*Harper* v. *Virginia*) declared the tax unconstitutional in any election.

After 1921, another barrier to black voting was erected, the *white primary.* First Texas and then other Southern states passed legislation excluding blacks from the Democratic Party primary. In these one-party states an electoral victory in a Democratic primary was tantamount to election, so exclusion of the blacks was effective disfranchisement. However, in 1944, the Supreme Court (*Smith* v. *Allwright*) ruled the white primary in its various forms unconstitutional.

To guard against disfranchisement of blacks through literacy tests, the *Civil Rights Act of 1964* established certain regulations to ensure fair administration of the tests provided that evidence of successful completion of the sixth grade of school constituted literacy. Later, President Johnson asked Congress to outlaw the tests entirely in certain states, and Congress essentially did so in the *1965 Civil Rights Act,* the so-called "Magna Carta of black voting rights." It suspended the literacy test in any state or county where fewer than 50 percent of the voting-age population were registered on November 1, 1964, or voted in the 1964 presidential election. In addition, the law stated that successful completion of the sixth grade in an American territory school was sufficient proof of literacy, even if classes were conducted in a language other than English. The primary purpose of this provision was to enfranchise New York's Spanish-speaking Puerto Ricans who could not pass the state's English literacy test. A 1970 amendment to the law eliminated literacy tests entirely.

The 1965 Civil Rights Act also banned tests of moral character, of understanding, and of educational achievement, and requirements that a person be certified by other registered voters. It also provided penalties for attempts to prevent qualified individuals from voting, and established federal voting registrars. These registrars could be sent by the Attorney General to any county where he believed that there was a pattern of discrimination. They could enroll voters and appoint poll watchers. The results of the 1965 bill may be seen in the fact that, between 1965 and 1967, on the average, the percentage of nonwhites who were registered more than *doubled* (from 25.7 to 54.7 percent) in the six Southern states of Alabama, Georgia, Louisiana, Mississippi, South Carolina, and Virginia. In fact, in Mississippi such registration jumped nearly ninefold, from 6.7 to 58.8 percent.

GERRYMANDERED VOTERS AND "ONE MAN, ONE VOTE"

The gerrymandering of electoral districts so that some voters are cheated of full voting power has been a major scandal of American elections. This practice has occurred at all levels of government and is as old as the republic itself. Actually, it took its name in 1812 from Elbridge Gerry, who was held responsible for rigging electoral districts in Massachusetts (see Figure 6-2). City and suburban voters, union members, Negro, Mexican and other minorities, and members of minority factions and minority political parties have been its usual victims.

Shocking examples of *malapportionment* abound. Perhaps the

138

Figure 6-2. The original "gerrymander" as drawn by Elkanah Tisdale in 1812, who in this cartoon represented Elbridge Gerry's districting of Massachusetts as a salamander.

worst was in the California State Senate elections where, as late as 1965, it took the votes of approximately 428 residents of Los Angeles to equal one voter in a rural district in the state. The basis of this disparity was that this most populous urban district was far larger in population than the smaller rural district, but still was represented by the same number of state senators—one. This inequity resulted from the California constitution's provision that no county could have more than one state senator.[9]

Other inequities have resulted from state legislatures' having yielded to the temptation to malapportion. That is, they have drawn both the state legislative districts and congressional districts within the state in such a way as to give the majority party or faction which controls the legislature an advantage which many believe to be unfair. This has been done by arranging dis-

---

[9] The California Senate was reapportioned on a fairer basis by the state legislature in 1965—by order of a federal court.

tricts so that the opposition was uniformly strong in all districts, but still unable to elect any representatives. Or, the districts were laid out so that the opposition carried a few districts by strong majorities, but left the others safely in the hands of the party or faction which was doing the districting.

The legislatures have also gerrymandered legislative and congressional districts by establishing districts of unequal population. In Michigan, for instance, the 1960 census showed that the largest district in the state was nearly five times the size of the smallest.

The "silent gerrymander" has also been common. It resulted when the dominant party or faction failed to redistrict after significant shifts in population. The gerrymander in its various forms has given the rural interests, in particular, much greater representation than they deserve.

Quite suddenly, and very rapidly, this traditional pattern of malapportionment is changing. In 1960 (in Gomillion v. Lightfoot), the Supreme Court for the first time ruled a gerrymander unconstitutional. Involved was a gerrymander by the Alabama legislature of the city of Tuskegee, which removed from the city all but four or five of the 400 black voters. The Court ruled this action a denial of voting rights to Negroes in violation of the Fifteenth Amendment. Prior to this decision, the Court had consistently refused to grant injunctive relief from inequality of representation, holding that this was not a legal but a political issue.

In 1962, the Court ruled (Baker v. Carr) that federal courts have jurisdiction to hear cases where city voters have been arbitrarily denied fair representation in their state legislature. This decision, a landmark step toward reform of the system of representation, was cited as a precedent when, in 1964, the Supreme Court in the sweeping decision of Reynolds v. Sims held that both houses of the state legislatures must be based on districts of substantially equal population, and that this must be the dominant standard for determining legislative representation. It also asserted that the democratic ideal of "one man, one vote" is a constitutional command, the United States Senate and the Electoral College being the only specific exceptions.

These decisions, based primarily on the equal-protection clause of the Fourteenth Amendment, have some truly revolutionary implications. Since 1962, virtually every state legislature has undergone some reapportionment. Also, most states have redrawn their congressional districts to confer more equality of representation.[10] The voices of black voters, and those of city and particularly suburban voters have accordingly been increased.

In one important respect the gerrymander remains quite intact: nothing has been done to prevent legislatures from arranging districts in distorted shapes to favor a faction or party (that is, some voters), even though observing the one man–one vote principle.

POLITICS AND SUFFRAGE: "NATIONAL" VIEWPOINT VERSUS "STATES' RIGHTS" VIEWPOINT

The political struggle over Negro suffrage and the gerrymander has been a battle between equality and special privilege. But it has also been a contest between institutions reflecting a national viewpoint—the Supreme Court, the presidency, and to a much lesser extent Congress—and those representing primarily state and local interests.

The Supreme Court, practically immune from state and local pressures, has led the way. It carried virtually the entire battle against the gerrymander, supported mostly by city and suburban groups. The Court did not, of course, escape attack. State groups which faced loss of power fought doggedly. Fighting with them were numerous allies in Congress, including Senate Minority Leader Everett Dirksen. In the end, however, their attempts to overrule the Court's edicts, principally by seeking constitutional amendments, proved unsuccessful.

The Supreme Court has also led the way in the contest over equal voting rights for Negroes, striking down numerous unconstitutional inequities devised by certain states, mostly Southern. But the Court did not do the entire job alone. The executive branch entered the fray vigorously in 1948, when President Harry

---

[10] Actually, any variance from the mathematical average must be justified by the state (*Wells* v. *Rockefeller*, 1969).

Truman urged Congress to enact a comprehensive civil rights package that contained provisions protecting the right to vote. However, none of the measures passed. Southern white supremacists used their power in Congress to block this and subsequent voting rights proposals. Throughout the 1940s and 1950s, they could depend upon their control of key committee posts, or their venerable coalition with conservative Republicans, or if these failed, their ultimate weapon—the filibuster—to block strong voting rights legislation. Southern governors supported their efforts.

Lacking legislation, federal action on behalf of equal voting rights could come only through institutions other than Congress. But it was plain to the growing and increasingly impatient coalition of black and white civil rights advocates that executive and judicial action alone, however spirited, was inadequate. A strong statutory basis was needed. Accordingly, national efforts to achieve this end were sharply intensified. Two weak laws were passed, one in 1957, and another in 1960. However, not until the passage of the Civil Rights Act of 1964 was the power of Southern states' rights forces to block strong civil rights legislation finally broken. This marked the end of an era, and a triumph for the national equal-voting-rights viewpoint.

Suggested Additional Reading

Berelson, B., P. Lazarsfield, and W. McPhee. *Voting.* 1954.

Campbell, A., P. E. Converse, W. E. Miller, and D. E. Stokes. *The American Voter.* 1960.

Council of State Governments. *Book of the States.* (Biennial publication which contains articles and tables on matters such as voter qualification and election laws.)

Easton, D., and J. Dennis. *Children in the Political System: Origins of Political Legitimacy.* 1969.

Free, L. A., and H. Cantril (ed.). *The Political Beliefs of Americans.* 1968.

Lang, K., and G. E. Lang. *Voting and Nonvoting: Implications of Broadcasting Returns Before Polls Are Closed.* 1968.

Lippman, W. *Public Opinion.* 1922.

Porter, K. H. *A History of Suffrage in the United States.* 1918.

Rosenbloom, D. L. *Electing Congress: The Financial Dilemma.* 1970.

Sanders, M. K. *The Lady and the Vote*. 1956.

White, T. *The Making of the President 1968*. 1969.

Williamson, C. *American Suffrage: From Property to Democracy, 1760–1860*. 1960.

7 Political Parties

Jeffrey Blankfort, BBM

No America without democracy, no democracy without politics, no politics without parties, no parties without compromise and moderation.

—*Clinton Rossiter*

American political parties perform at least five functions that make them indispensable to the survival of our democracy.

First, they nominate and publicize candidates, and thereby give our society an orderly way in which contending groups may assemble voter support in pursuit of public office.

Second, they provide two important components of a political system: (a) officeholders, aspirants to office, and full-time professional party workers, and (b) the "party in the electorate"—the part-time party workers and the traditional party voters.

Third, in our pluralistic system, the parties are nationwide coalitions; they conciliate different attitudes by invoking values and articulating interests (reflected in the candidates they present) that are widely supported by the society.

Fourth, when a party is in power it helps to increase cooperation and coordination between public officials, and to surmount the obstacles imposed by the system's separation of powers and checks and balances so that decision making is easier. When a party is out of power it is important as a critic of the party in power.

Finally, political parties provide the voter with alternative solutions, for of all groups only the parties submit themselves to the acid test of democracy—free elections.

THE EVOLUTION OF AMERICAN PARTIES

The history of our national party system is nearly as long as that of the nation itself. In becoming what it is today—each of the two parties a coalition of multifarious interests that unite quadrennially to capture the presidency—the system passed through four stages: the gestatory period (1789–1793), the first party system (1793–1824), the second party system (1828–1860), and the third party system (1860–present).

The Gestatory Period: 1789–1793

Personality has been a mighty force in the development of American parties. For instance, during Washington's first term, urbane Alexander Hamilton of New York City stated his plans for a commercial and industrial America and for a government with centralized power and strong executive leadership. As a result, the Virginia planters, who were suspicious of the plutocracy of New York and Boston, rallied around Thomas Jefferson, himself a Virginia plantation owner. An egalitarian, legendary man, Jefferson favored decentralized and limited government, a strong legislature, and policies that would benefit farmers, planters, workers, and small shopkeepers. President Washington, although he preferred to be nonpartisan, came to accept the policies of Hamilton, the first Secretary of the Treasury, over those of Jefferson, the first Secretary of State. Early in Washington's second term, Jefferson left the cabinet to organize and head his own opposition party. First called the Anti-Federalist Party, by 1796 it became known as the Jeffersonian-Republican Party, and finally in 1828 as the Democratic Party.

The First Party System: 1793–1824

The most remarkable thing about the birth of the Jeffersonian-Republican Party was its anticipation of today's Democratic Party —assembling men of diverse interests who submerged their differences to gain victory over an opponent they disliked even more than each other. The joining together of Jefferson, leader of the rural, agricultural South, and Aaron Burr, leader of the urban, laboring North, was enormously important for the future of American politics; the uneasy alliance they formed has characterized the Democratic Party to this day. The victory in 1800 of the party of Jefferson over the incumbent Federalists was also truly momentous in that it confirmed the legitimacy of peaceful party opposition. The Jeffersonian-Republicans went on to yet more spectacular wins in 1804 and 1808—so spectacular, in fact, that after the election of 1816 the celebrated Federalists were sent into oblivion. Thus ended the first party system, which was followed by eight years of benevolent one-party rule—the so-called "Era of Good Feeling"—in which partisanship declined and personality rose as a force in national politics.

The Second Party System: 1828–1860

The second party system differed markedly from the first: the suffrage was vastly expanded by the extension of the vote to all adult white males by most states and by provision of direct popular election of presidential electors. The political leaders were mostly popular folk heroes, like Jackson and Harrison, or men with organizational abilities. Also, unlike the first parties, which were shaped by small elites and which reflected sharply disparate policies, the parties of the second system consisted of broad, pragmatic coalitions of interests and began at the grass roots. The Democratic Party of this period was formed in 1828 by the opponents of President John Quincy Adams who coalesced around Andrew Jackson, the first "man of the people" to become President. The other major party, the Whig, began in 1834 with the uniting of anti-Jackson factions (mostly conservatives, including Southern planters who supported Calhoun's claim that a state could nullify federal laws, National Republicans who had backed

Adams and Clay in the 1824 election, anti-Masons, and other dissident groups). Comprised of fragile coalitions, this second party system was wrecked by the divisive issue of slavery: in 1860 the Democratic Party split into Northern and Southern wings, each nominating its own presidential candidates. The Republican Party, formed in 1854 by Whigs, dissident Democrats, and third-party members, elected Abraham Lincoln as their first President.

The Third Party System: 1860–Present

The third party system consists of the Republican and Democratic parties. During its early years, from 1860 to 1876, the Republican Party was dominant. A product of a spontaneous eruption of political sentiment, it was probably the most powerful authentic "grass-roots" movement in American history. It was essentially progressive during these years and based upon ideals such as anti-slavery, the preservation of the Union, and free land, as much as interests; it gathered leaders and voters from every party and group in America. The Democrats, weakened by the Civil War and left essentially with the conservatives of the North and the former slaveowners of the South, at first remained a splintered and ineffectual opposition. From 1876 to 1896, however, the two parties competed on a comparatively equal basis.

During this third era two significant realignments tooks place, one in 1896 and the other in 1932. In the election of 1896, the once progressive Republican Party became conservative and business oriented by gaining new voters from Eastern corporate interests, urban workers favoring sound money, and Western grain producers. As a result, the party was able to dominate both houses of Congress and the presidency most of the time between 1896 and 1932.

The second realignment of party voters began in 1928 when the Democrats, under presidential candidate Al Smith, gained the support of a considerable number of the urban voters, industrial workers, Catholics, and the foreign born. However, it was not until 1932 that, with the help of the Great Depression, the Democrats formed the successful and lasting coalition of the solid South, ethnic minorities, intellectuals, many industrial workers, small farmers, and some small businessmen. Since then, the Republicans have won the Presidency only three times: Eisenhower in 1952 and 1956, Nixon in 1968. And they have had a majority in one or both houses of Congress only twice: 1947–1949 and 1953–1955.

Today a realignment may be occurring in the social and regional groups that make up the two parties. Since 1952, for instance, Republican presidential candidates have made gains among the white voters of Southern states. As Figure 7-1 shows, whereas in the 1948 presidential election, the Republican candidate (.Dewey) carried only one Southern state, in 1968 Nixon won eight Southern states while Humphrey won only three (as compared to Truman's eleven in 1948).

DISTINCTIVE FEATURES OF THE AMERICAN PARTY SYSTEM

If we consider the American political party system, we will find these major tendencies: (1) the persistence of a two-party arrangement, (2) a relatively low level of ideological orientation, and (3) a decentralized party organization.

A Two-Party System

Clearly, an important characteristic of American politics is that we have a two-party system. In no other large democracy do third parties generally have so little influence. The vote for George Wallace as the American Independent Party's candidate for President in 1968 was an exception. Reflecting a mass movement of lower-income whites reacting to black demands, it was a true threat to the two-party system. Why is it that most Americans vote for the candidates of the two major parties? Though we have no scientific answers, there are various conjectures. Some people say two parties are natural because some people are temperamentally liberal and others conservative, and therefore each group will fall into a party reflecting this attitude. However, this opinion fails to consider that a person is often conservative only on *some* matters and liberal on others. Furthermore, neither of the two major parties is really liberal or conservative, though both have *wings* that are liberal or conservative.

149

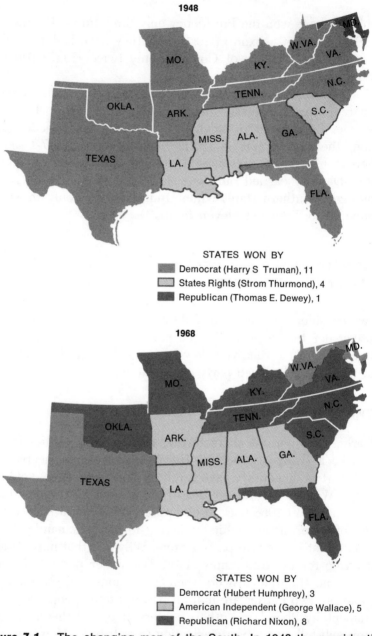

1948

STATES WON BY

▨ Democrat (Harry S Truman), 11
☐ States Rights (Strom Thurmond), 4
■ Republican (Thomas E. Dewey), 1

1968

STATES WON BY

▨ Democrat (Hubert Humphrey), 3
☐ American Independent (George Wallace), 5
■ Republican (Richard Nixon), 8

Figure 7-1. The changing map of the South. In 1948 the presidential winners, their parties, and the total number of Southern states were: Harry S Truman, Democrat, 11; Strom Thurmond, States Rights, 4; Thomas E. Dewey, Republican, 1. Twenty years later the winners were: Richard Nixon, Republican, 8; George Wallace, American Independent, 5; Hubert Humphrey, Democrat, 3.

150

Another belief is that the two-party system is based on a persistent division of opinion over states' rights versus centralized government. However, this overlooks the fact that the party in power nationally—whether Democrat, Republican, or Whig—has generally been nationalist.

There are, though, some more likely explanations for our two-party pattern. To begin with, we *inherited* a two-party tradition from Britain, and in time it has become psychologically entrenched in America. Moreover, our elections help perpetuate it, for elected public officials are usually chosen by plurality vote (not always a majority) in single-member districts. Consequently, our elections are win-or-lose propositions: one of the two major parties invariably wins and the minor parties, unable to gain a plurality—that is, the greater share—almost always lose. Probably only if districts were multi-membered, and elective posts were divided among parties in proportion to their popular vote, would candidates of many parties be elected and a multiple-party system develop.

The method of electing the President is also "winner take all," for *all* of a state's electoral votes go to the presidential candidate receiving the *greatest number* of popular votes. This encourages various interests to form coalitions to seek electoral victory with their combined strength. Inevitably, the major parties, with their broader appeal, win nearly all the electoral votes.

Minor parties have been only modestly successful in the United States. Seldom do they elect members to public office, although there have been recent exceptions in New York with the 1969 election of New York City Mayor John Lindsay on the Liberal Party ticket and the 1970 election of U.S. Senator James Buckley on the Conservative Party ticket. In general, however, third parties lack jobs (patronage) or favors to dispense, and face constitutional and legal disadvantages (e.g., a single-member district system, or a requirement that a party have an indicated number of supporters to qualify for a position on the ballot), and are therefore generally unable to attract strong candidates. Few prominent persons are interested in challenging Democratic or Republican candidates and bucking the traditional preference of voters for the major parties.

This is not to say that minor parties have been completely impotent, for they have at times affected the outcome of presi-

TWO-PARTY AND MULTI-PARTY SYSTEMS

Two-Party

The two-party pattern is not common: it exists only in the United States, Great Britain, and a few other democracies. In it, two major parties compete for victory, and alternate as the government party and the opposition party. Minor parties generally have little chance to achieve power or even to affect the struggle between the major parties. Two consequences of the system are: (1) it gives one party a popular mandate, plus a strong enough legislative majority to implement its program (though in the U. S., with its separated powers, the executive and legislative branches may deadlock), and (2) since each party must attract enough support to gain power, major parties tend toward compromise and consensus, which tends to moderate group conflicts and unite the citizenry.

Multi-Party

Proponents of this system, which occurs in most of Western Europe, believe it provides more faithful representation for various political viewpoints, whereas two-party systems do not give the voters' choice much meaning because both parties have similar programs. Critics say that although many countries have reasonably effective multiparty systems, partisan support and organization is dispersed and may have detrimental results—e.g., because governments are comprised of coalitions of parties, government and opposition are not clearly distinguishable, and no single party may be held responsible by the voters. Such coalitions are also always threatened by the withdrawal of some members, and no alternative party exists if voters become dissatisfied with the coalition. Another drawback is that if the ruling coalition is replaced by another, the new one may still contain some parties from the old, and the party the voter supports may not even be in it. Even the leader of the new ruling coalition is uncertain, since the legislature determines this by compromise after the election.

ONE-PARTY AND "NO-PARTY" SYSTEMS

One-Party

This system exists not only in fascist or communist totalitarian states; they represent only one of four forms.

A second form, common in developing countries, is that more than one party may exist, but one is dominant, governing alone, without a coalition. (An example is India's Congress party, dominant largely for four reasons: because it was the party that won independence, because of the strong leadership of Gandhi, Nehru, and Shastri, because other parties have not united, and because India's electoral system favors it.)

A third form is to have one dominant revolutionary party. (An example is the Mexican *Partido Revolucionario Institucional*, which originated in the 1910 revolution and is a revolutionary party, not an independence movement. It has won the presidency and congressional majorities since 1924. Other parties exist and are permitted freedom of speech, press, association, and assembly, but since the PRI is almost synonymous with the government and its major social and economic reforms, only it wins elections. The focal point of national loyalties and an alternative to Mexico's tradition of nearly constant civil war, the PRI increasingly unites the people behind it by compromise and persuasion.)

In the fourth form, one party dominates and others are severely restricted or banned. (Examples are the systems of the African countries of Chad, Dahomy, Ivory Coast, Liberia, and Niger.)

No-Party

Some nations have no parties at all. (Examples are Ethiopia and Saudi Arabia, ruled by royal autocrats who have outlawed parties.) Other nations have had parties in the past but are now ruled by dictators (Haiti) or by military governments (Egypt and Thailand). While parties continue to exist in some of these countries, they are only shadows of the real form.

dential elections, as when the Progressives of 1912 propelled Woodrow Wilson into the presidency, and one of them—the Republican Party—became a major party. Furthermore, they have often influenced the public on economic and social matters, and have sometimes revealed the drift of public opinion.

Being more radical than the major parties and freer of the need to win elections, they can also develop issues much for their own sake. In the past, the Populists exposed the wrongdoing of state legislatures, railroads, and banks, the Socialists the injustices and weaknesses of capitalism, and the Prohibitionists the evils of demon rum. Issues that have demonstrated substantial vote-getting potential for minor parties have frequently been taken up by the major parties—for example, the income tax; regulation of railroads, banks, and various utilities; aid to farmers; and women suffrage.

Major Parties Are Ideologically Similar

Compared to parties in other countries, the major American parties are mainly without ideology, without doctrine. This does not mean they advocate no ideology at all, yet nevertheless it is hard to differentiate between them. Both parties, for instance, say they are committed to the Constitution, to democracy, to private enterprise, to free public education, and to religious freedom—and the reason for this ideological similarity is that most Americans do not sharply divide on ideological perspectives.

Most differences between the two parties are not in ideology but in emphasis. In a very general sense, Democrats have (at least in their rhetoric) taken a more positive attitude than Republicans have toward government involvement in people's lives. The Democrats have been more innovative than Republicans in supporting government programs to ameliorate the conditions of the unfortunate and the poor, to regulate the economy in the interest of the worker, and to promote public power projects. They have also generally favored lower tariffs on imported goods and broader international commitments. In addition, the Democrats have tended to emphasize the equality of individuals, whereas the Republicans have tended to emphasize the liberty of individuals (especially in the economic realm).

Republicans, on the other hand, have been more inclined, at least in recent years, to speak out against the dangers of "big government," to oppose large federal involvement in citizens' affairs, and to emphasize free enterprise and private initiative instead of government social welfare programs and economic security. In international relations, they have usually espoused more vigorous military measures to counter the actions of communist countries.

But, for all these differences, both parties shift their positions and subordinate their ideology to the practical purpose of winning elections. Moreover, both have much good to say for the average American, the taxpayer, the middle class, moderation, the American Way, and so on—none really issues. Even so, we cannot dismiss them as being mere carbon copies of each other or as being devoid of ideology or principles.

Major Parties Are Decentralized

Unlike the centralized national party systems of other democracies such as Britain, our system is decentralized and diffused. The different American pattern largely results, first, from the sheer force of federalism and, second, from the system of separation of powers. Because our parties are organized around *units* of government, they are accordingly decentralized into national, state, and local units, and diffused into legislative and executive branches. Thus, we have national, state, and local parties, presidential Republicans and congressional Republicans, presidential Democrats and congressional Democrats, as well as party groups organized around other elected officials on the national, state, and local levels.

American parties are essentially state organizations, not national, and as such they enjoy enormous strategic advantages. For instance, in most states they control the innumerable nominations for state and local offices, and enact and enforce most legislation governing party organization, party finance, and nominations and elections. Furthermore, they do not have to depend on federal patronage and can survive electoral defeat of the national party ticket. On the other hand, even the President and Vice-President, with their nationwide constituencies, must win states to get elected.

Because this decentralized pattern has become thoroughly institutionalized, and state and local party leaders have become accustomed to it, little centralization is likely to occur in the future. From their strongholds, these local leaders can successfully resist any attempt to centralize party control, and national leaders, not wishing to incur their collective wrath and suffer certain disaster, are apt not to challenge the system.

Decentralization means that state and local party organizations are not disciplined by national party leaders. The President has only moderate control over the votes of his party colleagues in Congress, and his control over state and local leaders is negligible. Even when the national party convention meets to nominate candidates for President and Vice-President and to write the national party platform, control is not centralized but is diffused among a number of powerful politicians. Furthermore, most candidates for offices other than President and Vice-President are not selected by party officialdom, but by the voters.

Party discipline in Congress is also weak, far weaker than party discipline in European parliamentary democracies. European parties require their members in public office to follow the policies of the national organization, and undisciplined members may be deprived of campaign funds, removed from party or government positions, or expelled from the party. A member of Congress, on the other hand, may run for office on the party label without having to accept the platform of the national convention and be largely exempt from discipline by the national party.[1] The reason is that most of his campaign funds, workers, and supporters come from his own constituency, and thus his chief loyalty is to the voters of his district, not to the national party or voters in other districts.

THE STRUCTURE OF AMERICAN PARTIES: A FEDERAL PATTERN

Each of the two major parties is federal; that is, each is decentralized around national, state, and local units of government and has a pyramidal structure. At the top is the national organization—the national convention and national committee. Beneath that are the fifty state organizations, and within each state are the county committees, followed by the municipal and township committees. At the base of the pyramid are the ward and precinct organizations.

[1] President Nixon's purge of New York Senator Charles E. Goodell in the 1970 election was an exception. Goodell, a Republican, had opposed a number of the President's policies.

Although it may seem that the real power is at the apex, actually the opposite is true: the parties are weak—almost shadowy —at the top; the state and local organizations at the bottom are far better organized and financed. Moreover, the relationship between the levels is not authoritarian but cooperative; the essence of the relationship is loyalty that runs in both directions.

The National Party Organization

The two major national parties in this country are really alliances of local parties; their chief national goal is to win the presidency and the patronage and other advantages which accompany the office. Not surprisingly, they are most active in presidential election years.

The National Convention.   The supreme authority of a party is its national convention, which meets for only a few days every four years. The delegates to the convention are responsible for the critical task of selecting the party's candidates for President and Vice-President and for writing the party's national platform. Most of the time, however, the direction of the party is given over to party executives and its two arms, the national committee and its chairman.

The National Committee.   The national committee is composed of one man and one woman from each state (and also territories and possessions, such as Guam and the Virgin Islands).[2] They are selected most commonly by state delegations to the national convention, state party conventions, or party primaries. Despite being the highest tier of the party hierarchy, the committee is not very powerful. Its chief function is to assist the presidential campaign and to make arrangements for the national convention.

Chairman of the National Committee.   Since the national committee seldom meets, the party organization is run by the chairman of the committee and the permanent staff of the party.

[2] In addition, the GOP includes the Republican chairman of each state that casts its electoral votes for the Republican candidate for the President at the preceding election, or has a Republican governor, or a Republican majority in its congressional delegation.

Chosen by the party's presidential candidate after the national convention (the national committee rubber-stamps his choice), the chairman's main task is to manage the presidential campaign. Backed by the presidential candidate, he provides some direction and unity for the party. If his candidate wins, he becomes the chief dispenser of the President's patronage and is the person through whom the President runs the party nationally. However, if his candidate loses, he has no jobs to offer and thus little real power; control of the party may then shift to congressional leaders.

Congressional Campaign Committees. Each major party has a congressional campaign committee and a senatorial campaign committee. Composed of members of the House and Senate respectively, these committees send money and speakers into states and congressional districts to help party candidates facing serious election opposition. Although overshadowed by the national committee in presidential election years, they assist the national campaign in off-year elections.

State Party Organization and the State Chairman

In the past, the supreme party authority in a state was the state convention. Today, however, it is the state central committee and its chairman. In many respects, they resemble their national counterparts.

Like the national chairman, the state chairman is generally the central figure; working with the state central committee, he directs the state-wide election campaigns. Since he is also influential in distributing state and national patronage if his party wins, his position is much sought after.

Although sometimes the chairman is the state party's boss, more often he is dominated by the governor, by one of the state's U.S. Senators, by a powerful party leader, or even by a coalition of local leaders.

District and County Committees

Below each of the fifty state organizations are myriad congressional and state legislative district committees. Usually made up of representatives of county committees in the districts, they support candidates for these offices. Frequently not well organized, they do not generally function very effectively.

County committees occupy the next lower level. They raise money, sometimes select candidates for local offices, and direct local election campaigns. Composed of township and municipal representatives, they are usually most active in small towns and rural areas.

Grass-Roots Organization

The basic grass-roots party units are the *precinct* organizations. In the cities they cover part of a ward and include a neighborhood of several blocks,[3] usually having a voting population of several hundred. They are also present in rural neighborhoods.

Precincts, when they are politically organized at all, are headed by precinct captains or *committeemen,* who perform favors and services for their constituents (e.g., fixing traffic tickets or giving advice on welfare benefits). They are particularly active in areas where political interest is great and the party well organized (true in Chicago, but not so in Los Angeles). Effective performance at the precinct or ward level is, in some localities, a means of political advancement, since membership in higher party levels is drawn from below.

Of the local organizations, *city committees* of large cities are generally most powerful. They exert immense influence over the choices of national and state candidates, party policy, and in the allocation of patronage. They also have the most complete party organizations. A classic example is Mayor Richard Daley's extremely traditional machine in Chicago.

AMERICAN PARTIES AS UNIFIERS AND COORDINATORS

As noted, our two major national parties, unlike European parties, are not centralized, disciplined, or ideological. Nevertheless, they

---

[3] Precincts and wards are governmental units as well as territorial subdivisions for the convenience of administering certain public services (e.g., police administration).

do perform an organizing and unifying role in the American political system. They are conspicuous in organizing Congress, since they are the basis for selecting congressional leaders and assigning committee chairmanships. They also are prominent in the legislative process in Congress by ensuring the direction, continuity, and coordination of the formal congressional leadership. Furthermore, to get support for his program, the President may appeal to the loyalty of his fellow party members in Congress or capitalize on their concern for the party's fate at the next election. In addition, as party chief, he has sanctions he may use to gain their backing—for instance, threatening to withhold his cooperation in their future election campaigns. Party is also conspicuous when the President appoints judges and bureaucrats.

Party is not the only, or even most effective, organizing force in the political system—the President is a stronger one, and his fellow partisans in the upper bureaucracy help coordinate his administration. Still, because the American political system is, as has been observed, one of "separated institutions sharing powers," party helps bind these institutions together.

Suggested Additional Reading

Chambers, W. N., and W. Burnham (eds.). *The American Party Systems: Stages of Political Development.* 1968.

Eldersveld, S. J. *Political Parties: A Behavioral Analysis.* 1964.

Fenton, J. *Midwest Politics.* 1966.

Goldman, R. M. *The Democratic Party in American Politics.* 1966.

Greenstein, F. *The American Party System and the American People.* 1970.

Jones, C. O. *The Republican Party in American Politics.* 1965.

Key, V. O. *Politics, Parties, and Pressure Groups.* 1964.

———. *Southern Politics in State and Nation.* 1949.

Lasswell, H. D. *Politics: Who Gets What, When, How.* 1946.

Lawson, K. *Political Parties and Democracy in the United States.* 1968.

Monsma, S. V. *American Politics.* 1969.

Rossiter, C. *Parties and Politics in America.* 1964.

Schattschneider, E. E. *The Semisovereign People.* 1960.

Sorauf, F. J. *Politics in America.* 1968.

8 The Parties in Action: Nominations and Elections

Larry Tiscornia, San Francisco *Chronicle*

The people can never err more than in supposing that by multiplying their representatives beyond a certain limit, they strengthen the barrier against the government of a few.

—*Alexander Hamilton*

The two basic methods of nominating candidates for public office in the United States are *primaries* and *nominating conventions*. Most successful candidates for public office are nominated by the voters in *direct primaries*. These are very important in all states, but particularly in those having one dominant party in which a candidate's nomination is tantamount to his election. Mostly these states are in the South, where the Republican Party is weak and the Democratic Party strong.[1]

THE PRIMARIES AND CONVENTIONS: PRELIMINARY ELECTIONS

First used in Wisconsin in 1904, primaries are intended to democratize the nominating process by permitting voters to select

---

[1] In these states, a second or *runoff primary* may be held to select the party nominee from the two higher candidates.

candidates who will run in the general election, rather than to let them be selected by party delegates in a nominating convention. They are also intended to reduce the power of party bosses and political machines. At present, each of the fifty states employs at least one of the two major types of primaries—the closed and the open. Of the two, the *closed primary* is the most widely used. It is closed to all voters but party members, so that some measure of party regularity may be maintained. The *open primary,* now used in only seven states, permits a voter to participate in the primary of any party he chooses without facing any test of party affiliation. However, except in the state of Washington, where he may vote for the candidate he prefers, regardless of party,[2] he may participate in only *one* party's primary.

The open primary system is deplored by party officials because it allows voters to enter the primary of a rival party and vote into nomination weak candidates whom they expect can be more easily defeated in the general election. It also allows nonpartisans to influence what party officials consider an internal party matter. Thus, the open primary is preferred by independents, by those not wishing to reveal their party affiliation, and by those who want a free choice of the party contests in which they may vote.

The *nonpartisan primary* is also used to nominate candidates for certain state offices and a great many local offices in which no party designation of candidates is permitted. If no candidate for a given office wins a majority, the two top vote getters usually engage in a runoff at the following general election—again without party designation.

The *convention system* is used nationally to select candidates for President and Vice-President of the United States and in some states to choose delegates to the national conventions and candidates for a few offices. Conventions are composed of party leaders and other party activists who convene to nominate candidates for office. Since the party's goal, naturally, is to win, whether nomination is by primary or by convention, party leaders, who are very influential in the nominating process, feel pressure to promote the candidacies of those who represent the chief interests of

---

[2] This can be done because the state of Washington uses a "blanket" ballot, that is, one which contains the names of all candidates of all parties.

the voters (as well as are popular, of course). Thus, indirectly at least, popular interests get representation in the nominating process.

BALLOTING

The *Australian ballot* (so called because first used in Australia) was adopted first in Kentucky and Massachusetts (1888), and is now used throughout the United States. Its chief attractions are these characteristics, which guard the secrecy of the vote: (1) The ballots are printed at public expense and are uniform throughout a given voting region. (2) They are available only at the polling place on election day and may be marked only there. (3) They have no distinguishing characteristics that would identify the voter. Finally (4), they are marked in secrecy by the voter. Spurred on by the agitation of labor and reform groups who were convinced that bribery and intimidation of voters was hurting their cause, a majority of the states adopted this method of secret voting by 1900.

These ballots are of two general types, the party column and the office group. The *party column* (or "Indiana") *ballot* has the names of candidates listed in vertical columns under the name and symbol of their party (e.g., the Democratic Donkey and the Republican Elephant). Typically, a circle or square is at the top of each column, making it easy to vote a "straight ticket" by making one cross or pulling one master lever on the voting machine. The *office group* (or "Massachusetts") *ballot*, on the other hand, has candidates listed or grouped under the offices they seek. This form discourages straight-ticket voting, and is less favored by most politicians.

Voting machines used now retain the advantages of honesty and secrecy, but add speed and greater accuracy to voting and the vote count. However, these machines are expensive (costing about $2000 apiece) and often subject to breakdown. A new device, which is relatively inexpensive and promises to be very effective, is the IBM Votomatic. It features a ballot printed on a punch card. The voter punches out his choice with a needle, and the punched holes on the cards are then counted by computers.

The Votomatic provides a permanent record which may be checked to discover fraud and analyze voter behavior.

NOMINATING A CANDIDATE FOR PRESIDENT

To become President, one must win first his party's nomination by getting a majority of the votes of the delegates to the party's national convention—not an easy task—and, second, the presidential election by getting a majority of the nation's electoral votes.

Usually, a presidential aspirant starts his campaign for the nomination a year or two before the party's national convention. John F. Kennedy, following an activist strategy, campaigned even longer—more than three years—before the 1960 Democratic Convention, and Richard Nixon followed a similar strategy in capturing the 1968 Republican nomination. Both vigorously sought the votes of convention delegates by entering state primaries and by contacting delegates chosen in state party conventions or committees. Both also impressed state party politicians by making strong showings in public opinion polls and in state primaries. Kennedy was particularly impressive in his primary victories, whereas Nixon drew strong support from party organization people, a result of his years of hard work for the party and its candidates. No doubt these strategies—which won both candidates first-ballot nominations—will be emulated by future presidential hopefuls.

There are other routes to the nomination. An incumbent President may arrange his own renomination (as did Harry S Truman in 1948) by, if nothing else, simply trading on party allegiance. Or a candidate may remain silent about his plans and quietly line up delegates by making various arrangements (e.g., promising the vice-presidency to the chairman of a large state delegation), perhaps even staying out of the primaries. This was Hubert Humphrey's 1968 pre-convention strategy, although his campaign was not typical because it was complicated by two unforeseen events—the late decision of President Johnson not to seek reelection and the assassination of Senator Robert Kennedy, a leading rival for the nomination.

THE NATIONAL CONVENTION

The time and place of the national convention are set by the party's national committee. In 1968, the Republicans chose to hold theirs in early August, the Democrats in late August. The choice of the site is determined by, among other things, the city's hotel, communication, and other convention facilities available, and the monetary inducements made by the city's business interests. In recent convention years, cities have paid as much as $1 million into a party's coffers for the convention.[3] In return, of course, a city hosting a convention reaps not only millions of dollars worth of free publicity but also the dollars of visitors using its hotel, restaurant, and recreational facilities. Chicago has been the most popular city; it has hosted conventions twenty-four times, the first being the 1860 Republican Convention which nominated Abraham Lincoln.

Makeup of the Conventions and Selection of Delegates

In 1968, the number of delegate votes in the Democratic Convention was 2,622, and the number in the Republican Convention was 1,333. Within these figures, each party gave representation to states in proportion to their populations. At the same time they awarded bonuses, in the form of allowing extra delegates, to states that supported the party in the previous presidential election. The exact formula is devised by the party's national convention (see box).

In recent years, Republican and Democratic formulas have differed mainly in that the Republicans have rewarded voting for President, Congressmen, and governors, whereas the Democrats have rewarded voting for President only. The effect of the Democratic formula is to reduce the delegate strength of Southern states, which typically vote heavily Democratic for governor or Congressman, but much lighter for President. This penalty is not, of course, just a coincidence; the goal is to limit the influence of the South in the selection of a Democratic candidate for President.

[3] In 1968, Chicago offered the Democrats $750,000 in cash and $300,000 in services. Miami Beach offered the Republicans $800,000 in cash and services.

DELEGATE FORMULAS FOR 1968 CONVENTIONS

Republicans

• four delegates-at-large for each state.

• two delegates-at-large for each Representative-at-large.

• six additional delegates-at-large for each state that voted Republican for President in 1964 or elected a Republican U. S. Senator or governor in 1964 or later.

• one district delegate for each congressional district which cast 2000 votes or more for the presidential nominee in 1964 or the Republican U. S. House candidate in 1966.

• one additional district delegate for each congressional district which cast 10,000 votes or more for the Republican presidential nominee in 1964 or for a Republican U. S. House candidate in 1966.

• nine delegates for the District of Columbia, five for Puerto Rico, and three for the Virgin Islands.

Democrats

• three delegate votes for each of the electors from that state in the Electoral College.

• bonus of one convention vote for each 100,000 popular votes (or major fraction thereof) which were cast in the state in 1964 for presidential electors pledged to the national Democratic nominees.

• victory bonus of ten votes for each state which cast its electoral votes for the 1964 Democratic nominees.

• one vote each for the Democratic National Committeeman and Committeewoman from that state.

• eight convention votes for Puerto Rico, and five each for the Canal Zone, Guam, and the Virgin Islands.

• twenty-three delegate votes for the District of Columbia.

The method of delegate selection is established by state law. In about one-half of the states, including most of the more populous states, delegates are chosen by the people voting in presidential primaries. In most of the others they are selected by conventions or party committees. A combination of these two methods is used in three states. The convention and party committee methods allow less popular control because they generally give control over delegate selection to a party "establishment." Since the 1968 national conventions the trend has been strongly toward adopting the presidential primary system.

State Presidential Primaries

The two most widely used forms of state presidential primaries are: (1) election of delegates, who may be pledged to vote for a particular presidential candidate at the convention or who may be unpledged, and (2) popular expression of preference among presidential candidates. A few states provide for both.

Usually the presidential primary is not a decisive factor. One reason is that many delegates chosen in primaries are pledged to their state's "favorite son," who is generally the party's leading officerholder in that state, such as Senator or governor (Governor Ronald Reagan, for instance, was California's "favorite son" at the 1968 GOP Convention). This is usually a convenient subterfuge to permit the state delegation to bargain with serious candidates. Furthermore, only five or six states have genuine primary contests involving leading candidates. Candidates may even stay out of the primaries entirely (as did Hubert Humphrey in 1968), or make poor showings (as did Herbert Hoover in 1928), and still be nominated. Success in the primaries may, however, contribute decisively (as noted, they helped John Kennedy in 1960) or at least significantly (Barry Goldwater in 1964, Richard Nixon in 1968). On the other hand, primary victories may be disregarded by party leaders: in 1952, Tennessee Senator Estes Kefauver demonstrated strong popularity with Democratic primary voters, but party king-makers passed him over for Illinois Governor Adlai Stevenson, who had not entered any primaries.

Primaries are certainly not entirely without value. As mentioned, they do provide aspirants a means of capturing the nomination and often give some idea of the strength or weakness of candidates. Also, primaries are popular with the voters, stimulate interest in nominating presidential candidates, and permit more voter participation.

Opening Ceremonies

The organization and procedures of both parties' national conventions are similar. Both run about four or five days. On the first day, the chairman of the national committee calls the meeting to order and presides until temporary officers, including a temporary chairman, are selected. These in turn officiate until permanent officers are elected by the convention. Early in the convention sessions, either the temporary chairman or some prominent party member with oratorical ability delivers the "keynote" address. He will invariably extol the virtues and record of the party and its great leaders both past and present, and highlight the weaknesses, poor record, and miserable potentiality of the opposition party. His address is designed to get the convention off to a good start.

Action of Convention Committees

The next order of business usually takes place on the second day and consists of the reports of the four principal committees selected by the convention.[4]

The *credentials committee* decides which are the official delegates. Its decision may vitally affect the outcome of the balloting for a candidate. In the 1964 Democratic Convention, for instance, the committee established a bar to racial discrimination in the selection of delegations to future conventions.

The *committee on permanent organization* submits, for the delegates' approval, a slate of officers to direct the convention during its remaining sessions and the *committee on rules and order of business* submits rules governing the convention proceedings.

The *committee on the platform and resolutions,* also relatively important, draws up the party platform and recommends its adoption by the convention. The platform covers major subjects of national policy, reflecting the forces that are ascendant or the

[4] The platform and resolutions committee is composed of one man and one woman from each state. All other committees are composed of one delegate from each delegation. Committee members are named before the convention by each state delegation from among its membership. The convention confirms their choices.

skill of party leaders in contriving language that adjusts differences. But the platform is one of the less important indicators of what the party and its elected candidates will do. It is much less significant, for instance, than the expressed views of the presidential candidate. On the other hand, platform fights may badly weaken the party, as they did the Republican Party in 1964 and the Democratic Party in 1968.

Nomination of Candidates

Often it is the third day before the convention begins its main work—nominating a candidate for President of the United States. First, the roll of states is called. In the past, it has been called in alphabetical order beginning with Alabama, and each state could, if it wished, nominate its "favorite son" or another person (or yield to another state or pass). In 1971, however, the Democrats changed the rules to shake up the traditional alphabetical roll call and make the nomination of favorite-son candidates all but impossible. Beginning at the 1972 Democratic Convention, the roll call of state delegations is decided by lot beforehand. Delegates are still free to vote for favorite sons, if they wish, but their names cannot be placed in nomination unless they can secure the written backing of delegates with at least fifty votes, with no more than twenty from any one delegation. (Hitherto, favorite sons have usually drawn all their support from one state.)

The real test of a nominee is his *availability*—that is, whether he would be a strong vote-getter, has not alienated a large racial, economic, ethnic or religious group, is not bound to a narrow faction, or is not unrepresentative of major popular interests, and appears to have presidential stature. He must, of course, also satisfy the Constitution's not-too-difficult requirements: that is, be at least thirty-five, an American-born citizen, and a resident within the United States for fourteen years.

Nominating and seconding speeches have traditionally been occasions for vigorous oratory describing each nominee in turn as possessing all virtues and talents, including, of course, that he is capable of being elected President. As each candidate's name is put in nomination, it is followed by noisy "spontaneous" floor demonstrations (actually planned weeks in advance) and usually several long seconding speeches. Here too, however, the Democrats have changed the rules for the 1972 convention, banning demonstrations altogether and limiting nominating and seconding speeches for any one candidate to 15 minutes, with no more than three speakers. After the seconding speeches the balloting on candidates begins.

Balloting on Presidential Candidates

In both parties' conventions, a simple majority of votes cast is sufficient to nominate a presidential candidate. Voting is by states, again in alphabetical order, with the chairman of each state delegation announcing its vote. The vote may be all for one candidate or divided among two or more. Before 1936, the Democratic Party required a two-thirds vote to select the party's candidate. The rule was supported by the Southern Democrats to avoid being outvoted by the larger Northern wing of the party. Its use led to many deadlocks, the worst occurring in 1924, when 103 ballots and nine days were needed to nominate John W. Davis. Another disadvantage of the two-thirds rule was that it sometimes resulted in the nomination of a weaker compromise candidate. James K. Polk and Franklin Pierce were such compromise (or "dark horse") Democratic candidates.

When a candidate gains a majority of the delegate votes, near pandemonium breaks out. Almost simultaneously a delegate who has voted for another candidate moves that the nomination be unanimous. This being accomplished, there is a second burst of approbation. In a moment of great general excitement and anticipation, the victorious candidate is usually transported from a nearby hotel suite, from which he has been guiding his cohorts at the convention, to the convention hall. Flanked by his smiling (or tearful) wife, and perhaps other family members, he thanks the convention delegates for their confidence in his leadership and promises a winning campaign.

Selecting the Vice-Presidential Candidate

The selection of a vice-presidential candidate is almost an anticlimax. It is now the fourth or perhaps even the fifth day, and the delegates are by now tired and anxious to go home. And besides, the actual choice is usually made by the party's presidential candidate anyway. Not since 1956, when presidential candidate Adlai Stevenson "threw open" the Democratic Convention, have the delegates actually made the selection of vice-presidential candidate. Nevertheless, the convention goes through the same formal procedures of nominating and seconding speeches and balloting.

A number of considerations may influence the decision of a running mate. The choice might be made to placate an important group in the party which lost the battle over the presidential nomination or the platform and thus widen the interests represented on the ticket, or it may be made as a reward to a favorite son who threw his support to the successful presidential candidate, or to improve the party's chance of winning a large doubtful state. Attention will also be given to balancing the ticket by selecting a person who contrasts with the presidential nominee. It is not likely, for instance, that both will be Catholics, Easterners, or liberals, or represent identical policies and approaches. Unfortunately, often precious little consideration is given the vice-presidential nominee's qualifications to succeed to the presidency.

Closing Acts

In keeping with a precedent set by Franklin D. Roosevelt in 1932, the presidential candidate mounts the rostrum on the final day of the convention and delivers his acceptance speech. The drama of the occasion is felt by all. Party enthusiasm peaks, and members leave girded for battle. The convention then closes after formally electing members of the new national committee.

WEAKNESS OF THE CONVENTION SYSTEM: WHY NOT A NATIONAL PRIMARY?

The strongest defense of the convention system is that it works reasonably well. Not only have a number of great men been selected in this manner, but its nominees usually represent party consensus rather than a wing or faction of the party. Furthermore, in recent years the conventions have almost always selected candidates who were favored in public opinion polls. Thus, to some extent, and at least indirectly, the interests of the voters are represented.

Still, the national convention is much criticized, especially the manner of selecting delegates. Opponents say the delegate-selection processes are too complicated and too much manipulated by state party bosses. Furthermore, they assert that the presidential candidate is actually picked by party bosses away from the convention floor, making deals in "smoke-filled rooms," and that mostly they select mediocre party men to head the ticket.

Certainly the convention system is not perfect—even its supporters agree on that. But if not the convention system of nominating, what else?

Senate Majority Leader Mike Mansfield, in the wake of the widespread criticism of the general turmoil in the city of Chicago and on the floor at the 1968 Democratic Convention, proposed that conventions be abolished entirely and be replaced by a direct national primary. Mansfield's proposal has been seconded by many others engaged in politics or its study, and opinion polls show that the public also favors it. The idea, however, is not at all new. As early as 1913, Woodrow Wilson, in a message to Congress, proposed a national primary, and ever since it has been quietly debated by politicians and political scientists.

There is, of course, a surface attraction to a proposal that rank-and-file Democratic and Republican voters be allowed to choose their own presidential candidates by direct vote. Obviously, the plan would eliminate state as well as national conventions, including those dominated by party professionals. It would have the added advantage of making the primary system uniform. Yet the idea raises a host of questions. How would we decide which aspirants are eligible to run in the national primary? And how many would there be? An open primary might be more democratic, but it would doubtless produce a crowded field. Furthermore, divisive, expensive, and time-consuming runoff elections would probably be needed. We would then end up with several national elections before getting a President. And who would pay for the expensive national primary and runoff campaigns— the government? The parties could not be expected to, and many attractive candidates would not have the money.

Then what about the independents? Would they be allowed to vote in the national party primaries? At least in theory, na-

174

tional nominating conventions, anxious to select a winning ticket, take the reported desires of independents into consideration. But if party members alone make the choices, might they not often select candidates who are unappealing to the broad mass of the voters? It is quite possible that, under this plan, candidates representing extreme wings of the party would run first and second in a large field. In this event, moderate candidates would be eliminated.

Another question is whether the primary should be open or closed. If it were open, with no test of party affiliation, unfriendly elements could raid one party's primary to nominate the weaker candidate. On the other hand, a closed primary would protect the integrity of the parties but exclude millions of independents from a vital stage of the election process. Furthermore, provision would have to be made for selecting a vice-presidential candidate and for writing the party platform. However, this problem is not insurmountable. It could be done by national party conventions called after the national party primaries.

With all of these unanswered questions and drawbacks, perhaps it would be wiser to reform the existing convention system. Doubtless there will be those who wield disproportionate power in any scheme; yet the methods of selecting convention delegates could be improved, and the entire system simplified and made clearer to the voter. Perhaps it would also help if the parties held annual or biennial sessions or conventions where issues could be considered and platforms framed. In this way, complete attention could be given to nominating candidates and adopting platforms at separate conventions, without either function needlessly impinging on the other. In any event, it should be kept in mind that it is more important that the major interests of the people get representation than that machinery we can tag "democratic" be adopted.

ELECTING A PRESIDENT

The modern presidential campaign is vast, grueling, tense, and costly. It usually begins in September, not many days after the national conventions, and lasts until the eve of election on Tuesday after the first Monday in November.

The Grand Campaign

Although the type of campaign depends largely on the personality and talents of the candidate, one characteristic is certain: the incumbent, or the nominee of the party controlling the White House, will defend the administration's record, while the opposing candidate will criticize the administration and promise improved policies. The candidates are also likely to emphasize certain general themes (e.g., "law and order" or "It's time for a change") they feel will be effective, making variations and adjustments as the campaign proceeds. Generally, the presidential candidate carries the brunt of his party's campaign, making personal appearances in all sections of the country and tailoring his topics and remarks to his audiences. Usually, he gives his greatest attention to doubtful states with large populations and therefore large electoral votes.

A campaign manager, selected by the candidate to run the campaign, directs such diverse activities as establishing headquarters, raising funds, coordinating publicity, arranging speaker activities, distributing biographies of all party candidates, supplying information to state and local party workers, providing brochures and other literature, and preparing mailings. He also coordinates the national campaign with local, state, and congressional campaigns.

The use of airplanes and television has supplanted campaigning by train; however, much of the warmth of the whistle-stop campaign is now captured by use of motorcades that make frequent stops at suburban shopping centers and the like where the candidate delivers a short speech. Being aware that the voters wish to see him face to face, the candidate always tries to project a pleasing image and to come across as friendly, understanding, and interested in their welfare. The emphasis on personality assumes that many voters choose more on this basis than on issues. In fact, many candidates feel that evasion of issues is an effective tactic. However, this need not be so. Harry Truman and John Kennedy, for example, won after taking fairly definite stands on issues. In 1948, President Truman explicitly championed the chief components of the New Deal under the label of the Fair Deal, and also espoused civil rights legislation. In 1960, Kennedy met squarely the issue of his Catholicism.

In recent years, radio and particularly television have loomed large in campaigns, and in the future the ability of the candidate to perform well on "the tube" will no doubt weigh heavily in his favor. Many observers believe that John Kennedy made an impressive showing in his four televised debates with Richard Nixon in 1960 and that this contributed to Kennedy's victory. Hubert Humphrey, after losing the 1968 presidential election—an election in which Nixon had depended heavily on television during his campaign—said that his failure to learn how to use television effectively was perhaps the biggest mistake of his political career. As Figure 8-1 shows, ads on radio and television have also assumed greater importance in recent years.

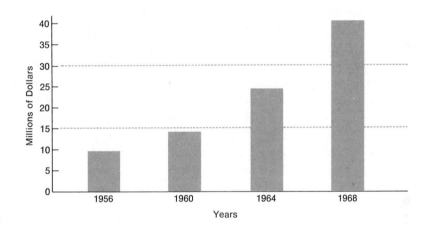

Figure 8-1. Rising political investment in TV and radio—general election expenditures, 1956–1968. (Source: Federal Communications Commission.)

A significant result of candidates' increasingly using the mass media is that they increasingly depend on public relations men for advice in organizing campaigns. These professional persuaders, who have long experience using the media to reach and move vast audiences, today are solicited by aspirants for even the humblest offices. Although some observers decry this—Adlai

177

Stevenson stated that "the idea that you can merchandise candidates for high office like breakfast cereal is the ultimate indignity to the democratic process"—nevertheless, since 1956 both major parties have worked closely with public relations firms.

Campaign Strategies

Although few election campaigns are purely of one specific kind, it is nevertheless helpful to identify them by type. The candidate running a *party-oriented* campaign stresses his party affiliation and tries to ride into office on the crest of his party's popularity. He has only to make clear his party identification and activate those who support his party. Naturally, a candidate will not use this strategy unless his is the majority party in his constituency. Thus, it is not often used in presidential campaigns, since nationally the parties are too equal in strength.

A *candidate-oriented* campaign emphasizes the candidate and his personal qualifications. His past accomplishments and his desirable personal qualities are played up, and his positions on issues and his partisan connections are played down. This strategy is often used by the "outs"—the minority party, or the party that has an exceptionally attractive (i.e., popular) candidate like an Eisenhower, a Kennedy, or a Lindsay.

The *issue-oriented* campaign stresses issues, but in a general or emotional way rather than in a specific or detailed way. This strategy was employed by Humphrey in his 1968 campaign. Because of the difficulty of catching and holding the public's attention, such campaigns are likely to be expressed in slogans such as "We must have law and order" or "We must bring an end to the senseless war in Vietnam," rather than in careful and dispassionate discussions of complex matters. Still, interests do get some representation in this type of campaign.

Frequently, a campaign will combine an issue-oriented with a candidate-oriented strategy, as Nixon did in his 1968 campaign.

THE POPULAR VOTE AND THE ELECTORAL COLLEGE VOTE

The real test of the campaign strategy—its moment of truth—is the election. In a presidential election year it is a particularly spectacular event. The excitement and suspense of anticipating the outcome is nearly overwhelming. The real show comes on the evening of election day when, with much of the nation glued to radios and TV sets, news commentators, with all the excitement with which they would announce a great heavyweight championship fight, give a blow-by-blow account of early national and regional "rundowns." Anticipation mounts as early trends are identified. Finally, the event reaches a climax as the computers predict the election results, sometimes before the polls close.[5]

But the President and Vice-President are not really elected directly by the American people. Rather they are elected in meetings of the Electoral College. Composed of electors designated by the states, each state having the same number of electors as in its congressional delegation (U.S. Representatives and Senators), it currently has 538 members.[6]

Originally, the electors were commonly selected by the state legislatures, but with the spread of democratic sentiment and the rise of political parties, they have become popularly elected, and now merely register the voters' decision. Today, when a person votes for President he really is registering his choice between rival slates of electors drawn up by the state convention or other state party organizations. Usually, the entire slate is pledged to a particular candidate. The candidate receiving the greatest number of popular votes in the state captures the state's entire electoral vote. This winner-take-all or "unit-rule" arrangement is not mandated by the Constitution, but is followed because it maximizes the state's influence over the nomination and election of the President. If a state split its electoral vote, it would correspondingly reduce its potency.

Because of the unit rule, a President may be elected who actually received fewer votes nationwide than one of his opponents. This happened in 1876, when Rutherford B. Hayes was elected over Samuel Tilden, although he received about 250,000 fewer votes, and in 1888 when Benjamin Harrison won over Grover Cleveland with about 100,000 fewer votes.

[5] In the 1964 presidential election, explicit predictions of a Johnson victory over Barry Goldwater by the three major networks came at 3:48 P.M., at 4:43 P.M., and at 4:50 P.M. Pacific Time, long before the polls closed in California and a number of neighboring states.
[6] The District of Columbia also has electors, the same number as Alaska, Delaware, Nevada, North Dakota, Vermont, and Wyoming—three.

Not until early December, after the general election, are the President and Vice-President *really* elected. At this time (first Monday after the second Wednesday) the electors meet in their respective state capitols to cast ballots. Although they are expected to vote for the candidate to whom they pledged, there are no federal regulations binding them to do so, and only fifteen states require this.

Elector Fidelity and Unpledged Electors

Elector fidelity has not been a real problem. In the entire history of the United States, only five electors ever ignored their party and election mandate and voted for another party's candidates. More critical, however, is the problem of electors who refuse to be pledged,[7] or who run with the intention of making their votes negotiable. This strategy was used by the Dixiecrat (States' Rights) electors pledged to Strom Thurmond in 1948. They were prepared to switch their votes as part of a Southern "deal" with one of the major parties for a Southern veto of national policies, particularly on the race question. In 1968, electors pledged to George Wallace could have followed a similar strategy, if neither Nixon nor Humphrey had won an absolute majority in the Electoral College (see Figure 8-2).

Counting the Electoral Votes

Electoral College votes are counted in a joint session of the two houses of Congress on January 6, the President of the Senate presiding. If any candidate for President receives an absolute majority, he becomes President-elect, and the same applies to any candidate for Vice-President. Both take office on January 20.

How Disputes Are Handled

What if conflicting totals of electoral votes are sent in from a state? This happened in 1876, in the Tilden-Hayes election, when

[7] In 1960, Mississippi voters elected eight unpledged electors, who then voted for Harry F. Byrd for President. (There were also six Alabama electors pledged to Byrd.)

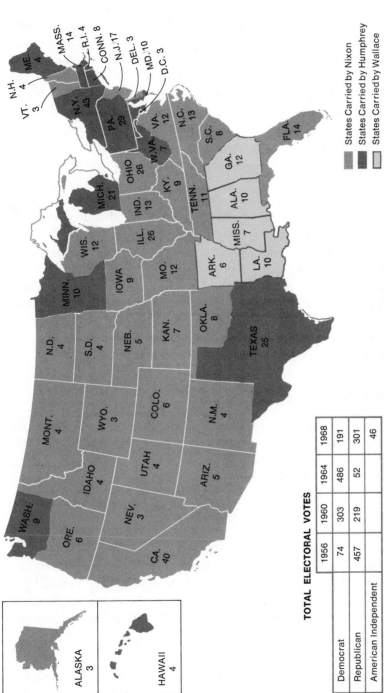

Figure 8-2. 1968 electoral votes by states. (Source: *Congressional Quarterly Guide to Current American Government*, Spring 1969, p. 13.)

States Carried by Nixon
States Carried by Humphrey
States Carried by Wallace

TOTAL ELECTORAL VOTES

	1956	1960	1964	1968
Democrat	74	303	486	191
Republican	457	219	52	301
American Independent				46

MASS. 14
R.I. 4
CONN. 8
N.J. 17
DEL. 3
MD. 10
D.C. 3
ME. 4
N.H. 4
VT. 3
N.Y. 43
PA. 29
VA. 12
N.C. 13
S.C. 8
FLA. 14
W.VA. 7
OHIO 26
KY. 9
GA. 12
TENN. 11
ALA. 10
MICH. 21
IND. 13
ILL. 26
MISS. 7
WIS. 12
MO. 12
ARK. 6
LA. 10
IOWA 9
MINN. 10
N.D. 4
S.D. 4
NEB. 5
KAN. 7
OKLA. 8
TEXAS 25
COLO. 6
N.M. 4
MONT. 4
WYO. 3
UTAH 4
ARIZ. 5
IDAHO 4
NEV. 3
WASH. 9
ORE. 6
CA. 40

ALASKA 3
HAWAII 4

Congress received two conflicting sets each from Florida, Louisiana, and South Carolina. One electoral vote from Oregon was also in dispute. In all, twenty-one electoral votes were contested. Tilden, the Democratic candidate, won a popular majority and 184 electoral votes, just one short of the number needed to be elected; Hayes, the Republican, received 165 electoral votes, and needed all twenty-one disputed votes to be elected. After much bickering, Congress created a fifteen-man electoral commission (five Senators, five Representatives, and five Supreme Court Justices) and agreed to abide by its decision. The commission decided strictly along party lines, with the eight Republicans outvoting the seven Democrats to award all disputed votes to Hayes. To avoid a recurrence, Congress passed a law in 1877— a law still in force today—placing responsibility for settling electoral vote disputes with the state itself, but providing that if conflicting returns make their way to Washington, and the houses of Congress cannot agree on which returns are valid, those certified by the governor would be honored. Fortunately, with but rare exceptions, the counting of these votes, and their certification by state canvassing boards, has been merely a formality.

Possible Election by Congress

If no candidate receives a majority of the electoral votes, the House of Representatives names the President from among the three top contenders, and the Senate the Vice-President from among the two top contenders. In the House, each state delegation has one vote, but in the Senate, each Senator votes as an individual, and to be elected, a candidate must have a majority vote.

The House has elected the President twice.[8] In 1801 it elected Thomas Jefferson over Aaron Burr, after each candidate had received the same number of electoral votes because all the Republican electors cast two ballots, one for each of them for President. This happened because the Constitution at that time

[8] In 1827, the Senate chose the Vice-President when Richard M. Johnson, Martin Van Buren's vice-presidential running mate, won one less than an absolute majority. It elected Johnson, the front runner, over the runner-up in the electoral vote, Francis Granger.

allowed each elector to cast two votes for President, with the candidate receiving the greatest number becoming President and the one receiving second greatest number becoming Vice-President. To avoid a similar deadlock in the future, the Constitution was amended in 1804 to provide for separate election of President and Vice-President. In 1825, when none of the four candidates got a majority of the electoral vote, the House elected John Quincy Adams President over Andrew Jackson, William H. Crawford, and Henry Clay, even though Jackson had won more electoral votes than Adams.

WEAKNESSES OF THE ELECTORAL COLLEGE SYSTEM: WHY NOT DIRECT POPULAR ELECTION?

Though the Electoral College system has worked reasonably well, it has some weaknesses. In the first place, as mentioned, individual electors *may* legally cast ballots for whomever they like, regardless of what the outcome of the popular election was in their state. This is dangerous: a small number of maverick electors *could* frustrate popular preferences for President. This possibility could be eliminated by simply abolishing the Electoral College. Or we could eliminate the present winner-take-all, unit-vote system, which poses the ever-present possibility that the winner of a majority of the country's electoral vote will have received fewer of the country's popular votes than an opponent. This has happened only twice since the Civil War,[9] but it could have happened in many other elections, had a relatively few popular votes gone the other way in certain key states.

A second weakness, which loomed large in the 1968 election, is that no candidate might win an absolute majority of electoral votes, with the election then being thrown into the Congress. This danger is particularly acute when third parties capture electoral

[9] Besides the "minority Presidents" Hayes and Harrison, there were twelve other instances when Presidents were elected in spite of their party's having received only a plurality of the popular vote. These are Polk (1844), Taylor (1848), Buchanan (1856), Lincoln (1860), Garfield (1880), Cleveland (1884 and 1892), Wilson (1912 and 1916), Truman (1948), Kennedy (1960), and Nixon (1968).

183

votes. Election of the President by the House has many disadvantages, the most important perhaps being that the President might be encumbered with heavy political debts, the outside chance that a minority party could control most of the state delegations (which each have only one vote), or that no candidate could gain a majority of the state delegations.

In 1969, President Nixon proposed eliminating individual electors and distributing the electoral vote in each state so as to more closely approximate the popular vote. This would probably strengthen the political position of rural, small-town conservatives. He also favored making 40 percent of the electoral vote enough to elect a President and holding a popular runoff election if no candidate received over 40 percent, the winner being the candidate receiving the largest popular runoff vote.

Some conservative Republicans and Southern Democrats favor having a system whereby an elector is chosen from each congressional district instead of by the present unit-vote procedure; this would lessen the influence of groups in the North and West (such as Catholics, labor, and ethnic groups) which tend to hold the balance of power in presidential elections.

For several years, many people have urged abandoning the Electoral College system in favor of direct popular election of the President. In 1970, in fact, Congress even considered proposing a constitutional amendment that would do this. But there have been several arguments against the proposal: (1) that the plan to hold a runoff election if no one received 40 percent of the popular vote would be time-consuming, costly, and an invitation to political bargaining; (2) that it would encourage vote fraud in close elections; (3) that it would deprive minority groups of political leverage in some states; (4) that it would erode the federal system by making state boundaries unimportant; (5) that it would take away the political power of small states; and (6) that it would weaken the two-party system. Even if Congress should propose such an amendment, getting the necessary constitutional approval of thirty-eight states would be difficult. If only thirteen states refused to approve it—and in fact thirty or more states stand to lose some political influence under direct elections —the reform proposal would be dead.

Whatever its faults, therefore, the reasonably effective performance of the present Electoral College system, combined with the confusion over what the consequences might be of changing it, appear to make major reform or abolition doubtful.

THREE TYPES OF ELECTIONS

A "normal" vote, some say, is one in which each voter casts his ballot in keeping with how he perceives his party affiliation. But, of course, no election has been a normal vote in this consummate sense. Nevertheless, from our viewpoint, there are advantages in thinking what a "normal" vote is, and noting the shift from one party to another. Using a model of a normal-vote election, we may divide presidential elections into three categories.[10]

The Maintaining Election. Here there is not enough deviation from the normal voting pattern for the principal minority party (currently, in our history, the Republican Party) to be elected. The elections of Truman in 1948, of Kennedy in 1960, and of Johnson in 1964 were maintaining elections.

The Deviating Election. Here the minority party is able to win by getting enough votes of those who normally affiliate with the majority party. Still, the pattern of party affiliation of the majority remains intact. The elections of Eisenhower in 1952 and 1956 and of Nixon in 1968 were of this variety.

The Realigning Election. Perhaps this might better be called realigning elections, for the realignment process may take place over a number of elections. The elections of Roosevelt in 1932 and 1936 are examples.

The importance of the foregoing description is that while Americans generally vote according to their perception of their party affiliation, they will sometimes alter their voting pattern or their affiliation. When they do, they may exert an immense influence.

[10] For a more thorough discussion of the three types of elections mentioned here, see Angus Campbell, Gerald Gurin, and Warren E. Miller, *The Voter Decides* (New York: Harper & Row, 1954), pp. 531–38.

MONEY AND ELECTIONS

Whether for the presidency or for a state legislative seat, a political campaign is a costly enterprise. In the 1968 election it cost $96,000 for half an hour of network television time during the evening hours when the largest audience could be reached. A candidate for a local office had to pay $1250 for a half hour of "prime" time on a first-class metropolitan station. Currently, more than $250 *million* is spent in presidential election years for all national, state, and local contests. Most of the financing—e.g., contributions of $500 or more (see Figure 8-3)—is by a small,

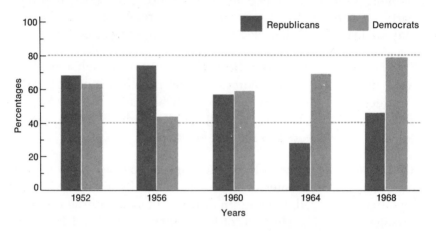

Figure 8-3. Contributions of $500 or more as percent of all contributions by individuals to national-level committees, Democratic and Republican parties, 1952–1968. (Source: *Voters' Time.* Twentieth Century Fund Commission on Campaign Costs in the Electronic Era, The Twentieth Century Fund, New York, 1969.)

well-heeled minority with some special interest. Suspicions that he who "pays the piper calls the tune" have inspired state and federal laws regulating campaign finances. Most are directed not at the objects of spending but at the amounts spent and at the sources of the money.

State Laws on Corrupt Practices

Party finance in this country has always had its nether side. For instance, fund raisers, hard pressed to get contributions, have resorted to virtual extortion, forcing persons vulnerable to prosecution for some wrongdoing (e.g., saloonkeepers who are threatened with revocation of their liquor licenses because they have violated the law) to give, and exacting contributions from contractors who supply services and goods to government agencies,[11] and from officeholders who fear for their jobs or of being passed over for promotion. On the other hand, more reputable party finance committees have had to fend off some people who are only too eager to deposit some greenbacks into party coffers. A contribution from a person notoriously involved in shady economic activities or who is bordering on trouble with the district attorney might seriously embarrass the party.

Today, nearly all states have laws against unfair campaign financing. Typically, they require political candidates to make public disclosure of campaign contributions and expenditures, limit expenditures on behalf of candidates, prohibit civil servants from actively participating in campaigns, and outlaw forced contributions from officeholders. Unfortunately, these laws have reflected more a legislative deference to the popular desire that the power of money in elections be limited than a belief that rigid limitations can be enforced. In any event, they have not been very effective.

Federal Laws on Corrupt Practices

Congress has enacted similar laws, though mostly they also have proved ineffectual. The Hatch Acts of 1939 and 1940, for instance, limit the size of individual contributions to the campaign of any candidate for federal office to $5000 in a calendar year. However, a donor may avoid this "limitation" by arranging for other members of his family to contribute a like amount. He may also, of course, contribute to as many other campaigns as he chooses. The Hatch Acts also limit national political committee receipts and expenditures to $3 million in a calendar year. But this limitation has simply resulted in a proliferation of clubs and committees

---

[11] In major statewide primaries in Georgia, for instance, at least 50 percent of the money managed by state party headquarters has come from liquor dealers and highway contractors. See J. L. Bernd, "The Role of Campaign Funds in Georgia Primary Elections: 1936–1958," *Georgia Journal,* October 1958, p. 3.

which receive and spend money, thus largely negating the restriction. Furthermore, state and local committees are not limited at all by the law.

There are also ceilings on Senate and House campaigns. Federal statutes limit the amounts spent to from $10,000 to $25,000 by a candidate for the Senate, and $2500 to $5000 by a candidate for the House. The major weaknesses are that the limitation does not apply to primaries at all, covers only certain types of expenditures, and applies only to those expenditures made by the candidate or with his knowledge. Candidates for the Senate or House, and national "political committees," must also report their campaign receipts and expenditures. However, the requirement does not extend to primary elections, nor to money spent without the knowledge and consent of the candidate. Furthermore, it exempts "educational committees" and political committees operating in only one state.

Corporations and labor unions are barred from contributing to political campaigns. However, the restrictions do not extend to organizations *associated* with unions, or to contributions by *officers* of corporations, or to lobbying expenditures. Thus, both corporations and labor unions circumvent the law with little inconvenience.

Probably the greatest disadvantage of the present system of financing campaigns is that it makes candidates dependent upon a relatively small number of groups and individuals. Many solutions have been suggested to avoid this, among them stricter requirements on public disclosure of political contributions and expenditures and encouraging middle- and lower-income donors to contribute by permitting them some form of tax deduction.

Suggested Additional Reading

Alexander, H. E. *Financing the 1964 Election*. 1966.

Downs, A. *An Economic Theory of Democracy*. 1957.

Felknor, B. L. *Dirty Politics*. 1966.

Goldman, E. F. *The Tragedy of Lyndon Johnson: A Historian's Personal Interpretation*. 1968.

Kelly, S., Jr. *Professional Public Relations and Political Power*. 1956.

Lang, K., and G. E. Lang. *Voting and Nonvoting: Implications of Broadcasting Returns Before Polls Are Closed.* 1968.

Levin, M. B. *The Alienated Voter.* 1960.

McGuiness, J. *The Selling of the President, 1968.* 1969.

Nordlinger, E. A. *Politics and Society: Studies in Comparative Political Sociology.* 1969.

Polsby, N. W., and A. B. Wildavsky. *Presidential Elections.* 1968.

Pomper, G. M. *Elections in America: Control and Influence in Democratic Politics.* 1968.

Scammon, R. M. *America Votes: A Handbook of American Elections* (biennial since 1956).

White, T. *The Making of the President 1960.* 1961.

_____. *The Making of the President 1964.* 1965.

_____. *The Making of the President 1968.* 1969.

Wilmerding, L., Jr. *The Electoral College.* 1958.

9 Pressure and Protest

Candy Freeland, BBM

Woodpecker and sparrow
With froggy and gnat,
Attacking *en masse*, laid
The elephant flat.

—*The Panchatantra*

A *political interest group* (or pressure group) is any private organization that seeks to influence public policy on any level of government in any way. Interest groups have participated actively in American politics since the time of our first governments and are intrinsic to our political system. In fact, their power and diversity have been one of the system's outstanding characteristics. This is partly because our political parties are geographically decentralized, poorly organized, and lacking in discipline and cohesion, and thus have been unable to devise well-defined national policies. The resulting power vacuum, therefore, has in large part been filled by pressure groups.

Interest groups have also become prominent because of a certain weakness in our system of representation—namely, that elections for Congress and the state legislatures are on a geographical basis. Interest groups, on the other hand, more directly represent

---

HOW INTEREST GROUPS AND PARTIES DIFFER

1. Interest groups try to influence government decisions without being responsible for operating the government machinery. They run no candidates for public office, nor do their members take public office as their spokesmen.

2. Although interest groups seek to influence government policy, they represent minority viewpoints and thus cannot seriously compete for power in the American constitutional system with the two major political parties.

3. Interest group members share an occupation, principles, goals, special experiences (such as prior military service), or personal attributes (such as race or nationality).

4. Interest groups usually have stronger internal discipline than do parties, thus giving them greater cohesion in pursuing group objectives.

5. Interest groups often require members to seek admission and pay dues.

6. Interest group members may also belong to other interest groups with conflicting objectives. Parties do not have this particular problem of internal cohesion.

---

people's economic or social interests. And since some voters feel more common ties with those having similar socio-economic goals than with those having a common geographical residence, they see themselves better represented by an interest group than by their Congressman or legislator. A medical doctor, for instance, may feel more in common with fellow physicians in other districts than with residents of his state or congressional or legislative district, and thus believe his interests are better served by his medical association than by his elected representatives. The same may be true of a union member, a farmer, a black, a Mexican-American, or a businessman.

Thus, interest groups perform a vital task that is not adequately performed by our political parties and elections—namely, they give their members *functional* representation. As mentioned, our political parties are not issue oriented; their primary purpose is to make nominations and staff the government with people who can win more votes than their opponents. Necessarily, they represent a vast amalgam of interests, and furthermore, like our elections, they are organized according to geographic lines, which means they must consider sectional interests when they make public policy. Interest groups, however, give functional representation to a certain portion of the public (albeit the more prosperous rather than the poorest) which wants to be heard on social, economic, and political issues that may cut across geographic lines. Interest groups provide *specific* representation, whereas parties represent aggregate interests.

TYPES OF INTEREST GROUPS

Most important interest groups have risen out of economic interests—James Madison's "most common and durable source of factions." Among the more powerful, for example, are the American Federation of Labor–Congress of Industrial Organizations (AFL-CIO), the United Auto Workers, the Teamsters, and the United Farm Workers Union, representing organized labor; the American Farm Bureau Federation, the National Grange, and the National Farmers Union, representing agriculture; and the National Association of Manufacturers and the Chamber of Commerce of the United States, representing business. These groups do not, however, represent their entire industries. For neither labor, agriculture, nor business speak with a single voice. The AFL-CIO and Teamsters, for instance, are often in conflict with each other, and within the AFL-CIO, interunion strife is common. The same is true among agricultural groups. Furthermore, only about one-third of American workers belong to unions and about one-third of the farmers belong to farm organizations. Businessmen are better organized, but they compete with each other and are frequently on opposite sides in political battles; certainly they do not form a homogeneous capitalist class.

Almost all businesses have their interest groups: for example, the American Bankers Association, the American Petroleum Institute, the Automobile Dealers Association, the Institute of Life

Insurance, the National Association of Home Builders of the United States. Likewise so do most professions: the American Bar Association, the American Medical Association, the National Education Association. Furthermore, many businesses are so large and have such elaborate interests that they maintain their own representatives in Washington to try to influence government; examples are American Telephone and Telegraph, General Motors, and several large oil and steel companies.

There are also veterans', racial, religious, women's, and student groups whose interests are largely other than economic. The strongest veterans groups are the American Legion, the Veterans of Foreign Wars, the American Veterans of World War II (Amvets), the Catholic War Veterans, and the Jewish War Veterans. Important racial-ethnic interest groups are the National Association for the Advancement of Colored People (NAACP), the Urban League, the Southern Christian Leadership Conference (SCLC), B'nai B'rith (Jewish), Sons of Italy, Ancient Order of Hibernians (Irish-American), the Mexican-American Political Association (MAPA), Asian Involvement, and the Congress of Racial Equality (CORE). As with other interest groups, members of these racial-ethnic groups are not of one mind on all matters; like all of us, they disagree on methods and goals. Among the stronger religious lobbies are the National Council of Churches and the Roman Catholic Church. Examples of women's groups are the Association of University Women and the National Federation of Business and Professional Women's Clubs. The largest student group is the National Student Association.

The list of other groups runs the gamut from the John Birch Society to the Students for a Democratic Society; from the Sierra Club (conservation) to the National Rifle Association; from the American Civil Liberties Union to the Minutemen; and from the National Organization for Women (NOW—women's lib) to Men Are Our Masters (MOM—antifeminist). A complete list of groups and their interests would run into the thousands, but Table 9-1 shows the twenty-five top spenders for 1969.

There are even "anti-pressure" groups. Examples are the League of Women Voters, the National Committee for an Effective Congress, Common Cause, and Nader's Raiders. Many join these groups out of concern that, because of group pressures,

194

Table 9–1

THE TWENTY-FIVE TOP SPENDERS FOR LOBBYING IN 1969
AND THE AMOUNTS THEY REPORTED SPENDING*

National Association of Letter Carriers (AFL-CIO)	$295,970
United Federation of Postal Clerks (AFL-CIO)	250,827
Reality Committee on Taxation	229,223
AFL-CIO (headquarters)	184,938
American Farm Bureau Federation	146,337
National Committee for the Recording Arts	139,726
National Association of Home Builders of the United States	138,472
United States Savings and Loan League	126,421
Record Industry Association of America Inc.	115,334
American Legion	114,609
Council for a Livable World	112,603
National Education Association, Office of Government Relations and Citizenship	97,537
National Housing Conference Inc.	95,562
American Medical Association	91,355
Railway Labor Executives Association	86,286
National Association of Theatre Owners	84,049
Citizens Committee for Postal Reform	83,951
Brotherhood of Railway, Airline & Steamship Clerks, Freight Handlers, Express and Station Employees (AFL-CIO)	80,985
American Trucking Associations Inc.	80,896
Liberty Lobby Inc.	79,927
National Federation of Independent Business Inc.	75,528
National Farmers Union	73,264
National Association of Postal Supervisors	68,365
National Council of Farmer Cooperatives	62,496
National Federation of Federal Employees	61,269

* These are the twenty-five top spenders of the 269 organizations that filed lobby spending reports for 1969 with the Clerk of the U.S. House of Representatives and the Secretary of the U.S. Senate.

Source: *Congressional Quarterly Guide to Current American Government*, Fall 1970, p. 110.

government may serve special interests to the disadvantage of the general public. Although lacking the financial capabilities of many pressure groups, anti-pressure groups have appreciably aided the cause of better government.

TARGETS AND TACTICS

Typically, interest groups have a number of targets and tactics. Among their favorites are exerting pressure on the electoral process and on legislators, executives, and courts. Interest groups do not, of course, confine their activities to the national government; they influence all branches of state governments as well. In fact, they may be even more active there, if they are unsuccessful at the national level; they may even try to defy the federal government by influencing the states. And if they are ineffective at the state level, they may lobby with local governments. A group may also, of course, go the opposite direction, or it may lobby two or three levels and various branches simultaneously. Furthermore, it is not only private groups that lobby. Government agencies also engage in lobbying activities on behalf of their own special interests, and cities increasingly lobby with their state governments and in Washington for legislation and funds.

Exerting Pressure on the Electoral Process

Interest groups do not nominate candidates for public office or draft political party platforms. However, many send representatives to appear before the platform resolutions committees of the major parties to urge endorsement of their programs, and many actively work for the nomination and election of candidates to political offices. Many also *assist* interest representation by informing their members about candidates and issues.

An interest group will usually support a candidate of *either* major party if his general outlook is similar to the group's. However, since the group usually chooses to reward friends and punish enemies, some labor, farm, business, and professional groups find most of their friends in one party and most of their enemies in the other. Furthermore, some groups tend to associate with one or the other major parties.

The usual way interest groups participate in an election campaign is by contributing money. Although unions and corporations are prohibited by law from making "a contribution or expenditure in connection with any election" involving the President, Vice-President, or member of Congress, both get around this by buying television, radio, and newspaper advertising for a party or candidate, publishing political material in their organs, and paying salaries to employees who work full time for a candidate or party.[1]

Influencing Legislators

Business interests, labor unions, racial and ethnic groups, professional associations, citizens' groups, and government executive agencies all try to influence state and national legislators. Usually, of course, they seek some special financial interest for themselves; however, sometimes they pressure to further their particular conception of the national interest.

The methods of lobbyists (that is, interest group agents) and pressure groups are depicted in the illustration below (Figure 9-1). Essentially these methods are the same as they were in the past. Interest groups carry on "grass roots" propaganda and educational campaigns to try to create a general climate of opinion in which their favored legislation will have a better chance of enactment and unfavorable legislation will fail. They urge their members to write Congressmen for or against a particular bill or policy. They also may directly contact Congressmen by sending letters and public statements of their positions on legislation. The major organized groups maintain permanent staffs of professional lobbyists, press agents, and researchers in Washington, and similar staffs in most state capitols, particularly during legislative sessions. (Groups having only an incidental interest in proposed legislation generally do not employ a full-time lobby staff, but may hire a lobbyist to represent them when legislation arises of interest to them.) These people keep watch on bills introduced, deciding which to support, which to oppose, and which to try to have amended. Customarily, they help expedite the passage of bills they favor (e.g., by providing legislators data upon

---

[1] Testimony before a Senate subcommittee investigating the 1956 election revealed that corporations permit the padding of expense accounts and give pay bonuses to employees with the understanding that they will make contributions to particular political campaigns.

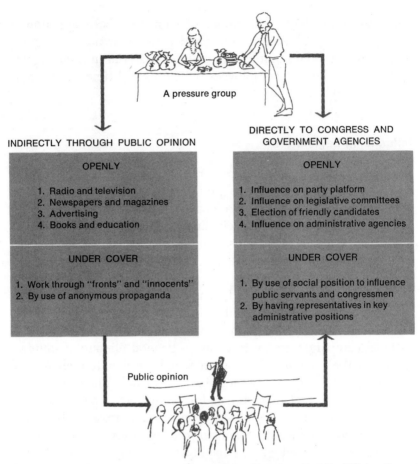

Figure 9-1. How pressure groups work. (Source: Public Affairs Committee, *Government Under Pressure,* Public Affairs Pamphlet No. 67 [out of print]. Reprinted with permission.)

which the bills are based, or by continuously encouraging favorable action). They may even originate the bills themselves.

Interest groups may seek to impress legislators with their ability to reward or punish them by giving or withholding voting support, campaign contributions, or other things they value. In pressing vigorously for favorable consideration by lawmakers (or bureaucrats, the President, or political parties) of the needs or concerns of their members, they are engaging in *interest representation.* The representation may, of course, be imperfect, but if it is too much at variance with the points of view of the members of the groups, the leaders may experience a revolt or mass exodus of members.

Influencing the Executive

A favorite target of interest groups is the chief executive, whether the President or a governor, since he has more influence over government than any other official. Aware that his recommendations on budgets and legislative policies normally carry considerable weight, interest groups may urge the executive to include or omit specific measures from his proposed legislative programs, to increase or decrease a particular agency's budget requests, or to sign or veto particular bills passed by the legislative branch.

How do interest groups gain the chief executive's support? Probably the most effective way is to help him get nominated, elected, or reelected. Another way is to support his programs or policies, particularly when he badly needs it, or at least refrain from criticizing him and his policies in hopes of gaining his future cooperation. There are also indirect routes—for instance, if a group can gain popular support, this might influence the White House or state house.[2] Often they inundate the chief executive with telegrams, letters, statements, and personal appeals.

In recent years, organized interests have begun to pay close attention to whom the executive selects for administrators. Naturally, these groups hope to see persons friendly to their organization appointed to administrative positions that affect their interests. This increased attention has come about because of the vast expansion of government regulation of economic life and because legislatures have tended to grant broad discretionary

[2] A classic example was the full-scale drive by the oil industry in 1956 and again in 1958 to secure passage of legislation to strip the Federal Power Commission of authority to regulate prices of natural gas sold in interstate commerce. A public relations firm got $100,000 to plan the drive. All the mass media were used and 3000 oil and gas company employees took part in the campaign. The industry's lobbyist made campaign contributions to several Senators who favored the bill. Unfortunately (for the oil industry), one Senator repudiated an oil lobby campaign contribution of $2500 and charged that it was an attempted bribe. Citing the "arrogant lobbying" for the bill, President Eisenhower, who had favored the bill, vetoed it.

powers to government administrators. Thus, groups with friends in high administrative posts may be able to secure special favors and privileges in such matters as licenses, subsidies, and contracts.

Interest groups also try to influence administrative agencies by appearing before them at hearings to testify for or against proposed rules or permits. In fact, they lobby these agencies in much the same way as they lobby Congress or the state legislatures. Interest groups may try to influence an agency by urging the legislature to cut or up its budget or to amend the laws by which it operates. Sometimes they even try to get legislators to investigate an agency to punish administrators for unfriendly actions toward the group. Generally, however, the relationship between private groups and administrative agencies is not antagonistic. In fact, oftentimes we find interest groups, administrative agencies, and legislators working together in harmony for their mutual benefit.

Influencing the Courts

Most interest groups spend much less energy trying to influence the judiciary than they do the executive or legislature. But they do often participate in the selection of judges, whether appointed or elected, by carefully scrutinizing the records of candidates and opposing the confirmation or election of those considered biased against the groups' interests. Furthermore, they sometimes turn to the courts for support. Here they may advance the cause of their members by initiating litigation to test the constitutionality of a law or of the actions of public officials—the NAACP, for instance, for a number of years relied on litigation as the principal means of securing Negro rights. Some groups often file briefs to support those involved in litigation—the American Civil Liberties Union, the American Jewish Congress, and the National Lawyers Guild, for example, have actively used this *amicus curiae* ("friend of the court") device. Most often the courts are used for vetoing rather than for positive innovation; however, it was litigation in the U.S. Supreme Court which in 1954 started the country toward racial integration, and which in 1962 shifted legislative power from rural and small-town America to the cities and suburbs.

200

Using the Initiative and Referendum

In many states, interest groups use the initiative and referendum to try to pass laws and constitutional amendments or to block unwanted legislation. The *initiative* is a device whereby the voters may propose statutes or constitutional amendments; the *referendum* is a means whereby they may approve or reject measures passed by their state legislature.[3]

In fact, these two devices are used almost *exclusively* by interest groups: political parties ordinarily do not need to use them, and no single individual could do so because of the organization required to draft propositions, circulate petitions, raise funds, distribute literature, and engage speakers to campaign.

SHOULD INTEREST GROUPS BE REGULATED?

There is also, of course, the *social lobby* (e.g., the furnishing of sumptuous free meals and great quantities of liquor) and the use of illegal or unethical methods.[4] Unscrupulous lobbyists have used this from the beginning of the republic, and some do today. Yet, the total impact of social lobbying, minor favors, and corrupt lobbying pactices is probably not so great as in earlier times.

Actually, there is little effective regulation of interest groups. Outright bribes are illegal, of course, and limitations have been placed on financial contributions to political campaigns. Furthermore, most states require lobbyists to register, many requiring that those who lobby before the legislature must also file statements of amounts spent in promoting legislation.

In 1946, Congress passed the federal Regulation of Lobbying Act, which requires that every person whose "principal purpose" is to try to influence Congress on the passage or defeat of any

[3] The initiative and referendum are discussed in more detail in Chapter 20.
[4] A recent case involved the Monarch Construction Company of Silver Springs, Maryland, and Democratic House Member John Doudy of Texas. On March 31, 1970 Doudy was indicted by a federal grand jury for allegedly accepting a $25,000 bribe from the company to intervene in a Justice Department investigation of it. Not since 1962 had an incumbent Congressman faced criminal charges.

bill must register with the Clerk of the House and the Secretary of the Senate, stating how much he is paid. Every three months he must file a statement indicating the bills he opposes or supports and a list of the publications that have printed his publicity. Failure to register may result in fine, imprisonment, or suspension of the privilege of lobbying. But registration requirements are not regulation; they merely publicize what a lobbyist is doing. And if their intent is to reduce lobbying activity, they have failed: hundreds of lobbies, including such large groups as the National Association of Manufacturers and the National Bankers Association, claiming that lobbying is not their principal purpose, have not registered and the extent of lobbying has not lessened.

Should lobbying activities be strictly regulated? Some think so. However, it is not likely that Congress will do this. In the first place, regulation might violate the First Amendment rights to freedom of speech and to petition the government. Furthermore, were lobbyists severely limited, they might simply go underground, and their influence might become insidious. Besides, although they represent special interests, interest groups provide our only specific functional representation.

NEW RADICAL GROUPS: THE RIGHT AND THE LEFT

There have been both radical right and radical left groups in the United States for many years. Some, such as the Ku Klux Klan and the Communist Party, have been thought radical because of their far-out programs or their commitment to revolution or violence. Others, such as the socialist parties, have been considered radical only because of their unorthodox programs. Radical groups have proliferated during all times of social change and crisis, but since World War II the continuous international crises and major social changes have produced them in unprecedented numbers.

The Radical Right

Today, most radical right groups are possessed with an extreme fear that the United States will be or is being subverted by communism and they view most problems from this perspective. Generally, they support states' rights and old-style laissez faire capitalist economics, and tend to equate the development of the welfare state with socialism, and socialism with communism. Among their targets have been the U.S. Supreme Court, the United Nations, the income tax, urban renewal, civil rights legislation, foreign aid, and fluoridation of public drinking water. Their leaders believe that history is changed by conspiracy and hold that government, labor unions, colleges, public schools, and some churches are controlled by communist or allied conspirators. This, they assert, justifies the frequently undemocratic counter tactics of the right. Among the great number of radical right organizations are the Minutemen, American Nazi Party, Christian Anti-Communist Crusade, Young Americans for Freedom (YAF), and John Birch Society.

The Radical Left

Historically, the American radical left has been represented primarily by small Marxist and socialist parties—among the most prominent the Communist, Socialist, Socialist-Labor, and Socialist-Workers parties. Never very significant politically, they declined markedly after World War II until the early 1960s, when several "New Left" groups became prominent, drawing much of their membership and support from college students. More committed to direct action and specific issues than the older communist and socialist organizations, they have organized mass demonstrations in opposition to the Vietnam war, the draft, poverty, pollution, "white racism," ROTC, campus military recruiting, and certain college administrations and curriculums. Several groups support the policies of the Soviet Union and the People's Republic of China and oppose American intervention in left-wing revolutions in underdeveloped countries. Like their counterparts on the radical right, some groups do not adhere to the democratic process nor the tolerance nor moderation of democracy and have resorted to various forms of intimidation and violence. Among the more prominent New Left groups are the Students for a Democratic Society, the Black Panthers, the Weatherman, the W.E.B.

Dubois Clubs, the Young Socialist Alliance, and the Progressive Labor Party.

NONVIOLENT AND VIOLENT POLITICAL PROTEST

Political protest is action that seeks to call public attention to a grievance of a group or individual. The protest may be about an existing policy or about failure to devise a policy. It may be non-violent or violent, organized or unorganized.

Nonviolent Political Protest

Organized nonviolent political protest, one of many pressure group tactics, embraces a wide assortment of actions: passive resistance, heckling of speakers, picketing, economic boycott, freedom rides, sit-ins, strikes, and mass demonstrations.

American workers have long employed nonviolent direct action in the form of strikes to gain concessions from employers. However, recently the most prominent use of nonviolent direct action has been in the civil rights movement, beginning in 1955 with the boycott organized by Martin Luther King, Jr. against racially segregated buses in Montgomery, Alabama. Many of these leaders took their text from India's Mohandas Gandhi (interestingly, Gandhi got many of *his* ideas from the American pacifist Henry Thoreau), who used nonviolent methods in obtaining India's 1947 independence from Great Britain. Sometimes, like Gandhi, the actions of these leaders have produced situations (either consciously or unconsciously) in which violence occurred—as in Chicago in 1965 when working-class whites attacked blacks marching in front of Mayor Richard Daley's home and protesting against what they considered segregation of the schools. Since 1955, a variety of protest tactics, often involving civil disobedience, has been used to try to arouse public support for civil rights legislation and black voting rights and opposition to racial discrimination in jobs and housing and to incidents of police brutality toward minorities. Although, on the one hand, some militants now argue that this nonviolent protest accomplished little and, on the other hand, some conservatives decry civil disobedience, these tactics certainly hastened integration of public facilities and advanced the cause of equal rights and opportunity.

Nonviolent direct confrontation with authority has also been widely used by militant student (and faculty) groups opposing the Indochina war and United States military policy or supporting the demands of militant blacks. They have used picketing, boycotts, sit-ins, strikes, and mass demonstrations—and with considerable success, particularly in such matters as getting colleges to provide more black studies curriculums, hire more minority teachers, and admit more black students.

Violent Political Protest

Organized violent political protest in America is older than the republic. The Boston Tea Party was a violent protest. So was Shays' Rebellion (1786–1787). And so was the 1794 Whiskey Rebellion in Western Pennsylvania against the federal excise tax on whiskey.[5] The 1860s produced the greatest violent political protest of them all, of course—the Civil War—and in our century there has been the bloody organized violence of gangsters and labor disputes. But if organized violence is not new, making it a moral credo is.

While most of today's minority groups and students reject violence, some endorse it. Some members of racial minorities, for instance, believe nonviolence is not enough to achieve racial justice or fundamental social reform, that only violence will command enough attention to make the "insensible white middle class" confront problems and support remedial action. Some white students also endorse violent action, notably those obsessively opposed to the Indochina war or what they believe are American imperialistic ventures and racist government policies. Remarkably, as Table 9-2 shows, the United States ranks *first* in civil strife among eighteen democratic nations.

[5] This was a revolt of farmers, who distilled their grain and sold the liquor, against a federal excise tax on the liquor. They argued that the tax was a burdensome tax on the farmers for the benefit of the capitalists. Washington and Hamilton put the revolt down with 15,000 troops from four states, thus making a strong show of force against elements which wished to destroy the new government.

Table 9–2
SOME GENERAL CHARACTERISTICS OF CIVIL STRIFE IN THE UNITED STATES, 1963–1968, COMPARED WITH STRIFE IN OTHER NATIONS, 1961–1965

	UNITED STATES	AVERAGE FOR 17 DEMOCRATIC EUROPEAN NATIONS	AVERAGE FOR 113 COUNTRIES
Pervasiveness: No. participants per 100,000 population	1,116	676	683
Rank of the U.S.		7th	27th
Intensity: Casualties from strife per 10 million population	477	121	20,100
Rank of the U.S.		3rd	53rd
Duration (sum of all events):			
Rank of the U.S.		1st	6th
Total magnitude of civil strife:			
Rank of the U.S.		1st	24th
Rank of the U.S., 1961–1965		5th	41st

Source: Ted Robert Gurr, "A Comparative Study of Civil Strife," in Hugh Davis Graham and Ted Robert Gurr *The History of Violence in America: A Report to the National Commission on the Causes and Prevention of Violence* (New York: Bantam Books, 1969), Table 17–2, p. 578, and Table 17–3, p. 579.

In the last two decades, unorganized violent protest has had considerable attention; it has even been studied by four presidential commissions.[6] Such protest has taken two forms. First

[6] Three of the commissions—the Warren, Kerner, and Eisenhower—were appointed by President Lyndon Johnson. The fourth, the Scranton Commission, was appointed by President Richard Nixon. *The Warren Commission* (President's Commission on the Assassination of President John.F. Kennedy), appointed in 1963, fastened the guilt for the assassination of the President upon Lee Harvey Oswald alone. However, it has been suggested that the "truth" the Warren Commission revealed was only a byproduct of a political goal of calming the public in the wake of national disaster, and that the Commission seemed to overlook the deeper truth. (See in particular E. J. Epstein, *Inquest: The Warren Commission and the Establishment of Truth*, 1966.)

The *Kerner Commission* (National Advisory Commission on Civil Disorders), created in the summer of 1967 following urban riots of 1966 and 1967, and chaired by then Illinois Governor Otto Kerner, concluded that "our nation is moving toward two societies, one black, one white—separate and unequal," and that "white racism" was the chief cause of increasing racial polarization.

The *Eisenhower Commission* (National Commission on the Causes and Prevention of Violence), created in 1968 and headed by Milton S. Eisenhower, concluded that it is time we faced up to the fact that, contrary to the

is *assassination,* as tragically happened with John F. Kennedy, Robert F. Kennedy, and Martin Luther King, Jr. Although these certainly are not new phenomena—four Presidents have been killed by assassins[7]—political murder nevertheless has risen sharply in recent years. We must note, however, that these assassinations have not been *group* tactics, but the tactics of one or so persons acting on their own. Second is *collective violence,* as in the black ghetto riots of 1964 through 1968 in Harlem, Watts, and Newark. Such uprisings were apparently unorganized, though militant agitators *may* have helped create a general atmosphere that contributed to the violence.

Can Violent Protest Be Avoided?

Those who would influence government are always urged to organize. Effective expression of different, *organized* viewpoints, in fact, strengthens democracy, and group advocacy helps make up for inadequacies in our system of representation.

But what is to be done when this advocacy takes a violent form? Although the Constitution protects the rights to organize freely, speak, protest, and demonstrate, it also protects the public order and the rights of others. Somehow these conflicting rights must be reconciled.

A strict repression of violent protest would not be democratic; nor, probably, would it be effective. Most studies, in fact, have recommended programs directed at reducing social tensions plus concurrent development of strategies to contain disruption. However, while this dual approach seems reasonable, it assumes that

---

American ideal, collective violence is so much a part of our culture that it has become reinforced in our society. In a sense, the commission was reflecting the turbulent politics of 1968 when Robert F. Kennedy and Rev. Martin Luther King, Jr., the leaders most closely identified with the black and the poor, were assassinated.

The Scranton Commission (President's Commission on Campus Unrest), headed by former Pennsylvania Governor William W. Scranton in 1970 following the Kent State and Jackson State shootings, urged the President to act on pressing social problems and to stop the harsh rhetoric of certain members of his administration. It also condemned equally the violence committed by students and the "brutality and excessive force by officers and troops called to maintain order."

[7] Abraham Lincoln, 1865; James Garfield, 1881; William McKinley, 1901; and John Kennedy, 1963.

legislatures and executives will give the same support to massive, costly reform measures that they will to measures of control. In the long run a democratic society cannot allow force to be an answer to solving legitimate and longstanding grievances. Yet it is a simple fact of life that not every demand of every protester can be met—not everyone can always be satisfied, and the frustrated may always be tempted to resort to violence. Still, on balance, considerable and widespread social and political reform *must* be undertaken if we are not to resort to maintaining order at the expense of justice and law.

Suggested Additional Reading

Ali, T. (ed.). *New Revolutionaries: Left Opposition*. 1969.

Bell, D. (ed.). *The Radical Right*. 1964.

Blaisdell, D. C. *American Democracy Under Pressure*. 1957.

Clark, R. *Crime in America: Observations on Its Nature, Causes, Prevention and Control*. 1970.

Dexter, L. A. *How Organizations Are Represented in Washington*. 1969.

Key, V. O. *Politics, Parties, and Pressure Groups*. 1964.

Lipset, S. M. *The Politics of Unreason: Right Wing Extremism in the United States, 1790–1970*. 1970.

Mahood, H. R. (ed.). *Pressure Groups in American Politics*. 1967.

McConnell, G. *Private Power and American Democracy*. 1966.

Millett, K. *Sexual Politics*. 1970.

Nieburg, H. L. *Political Violence: The Behavioral Process in American Society*. 1969.

Silverman, S. (ed.). *The Black Revolt and Democratic Politics*. 1970.

Skolnick, J. H. *The Politics of Protest*. 1969.

Zisk, B. H. *American Political Interest Groups: Readings in Theory and Research*. 1969.

Part 3

Principal Decision-Making Organizations

10 Congress: Members and Organization

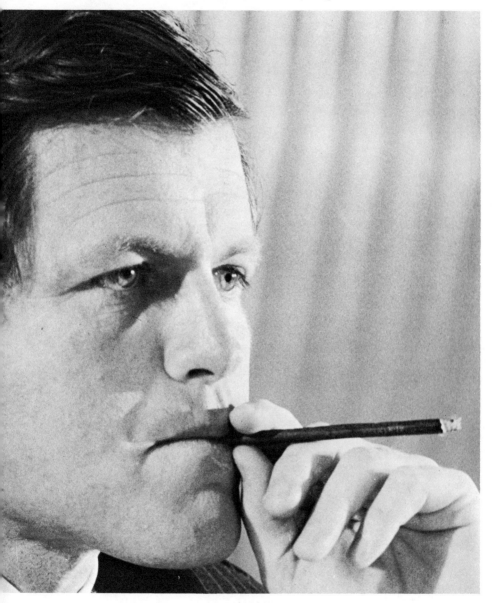

Steve Northup, Camera 5

The validity of both the national and the local viewpoints found in the executive and legislative constituencies is affirmed by the federal principle. . . . Despite their imposing differences, no one branch, ex- ecutive or legislative, can claim inherent superiority in articulating the national or public interest.

—*Louis W. Koenig*

According to Article I of the Constitution, "All legislative Powers herein granted shall be vested in a Congress of the United States, which shall consist of a Senate and a House of Representatives." This straightforward statement holds a certain attraction, for Americans like to believe their government is simple and tidy. They assume, incorrectly, that it is the undertaking of three *co-equal* branches: the legislature passes laws, the executive enforces them, and the courts interpret and apply them.

CONGRESS: ITS DISTORTED IMAGE

Americans think the President and Supreme Court Justices are generally above "politics," that dirty word. Only Congress, whose complex organization and functions the public does not comprehend, is believed to be wallowing in "politics." Not surprisingly, therefore, Congress is the least revered and least understood of the three branches.

More realistically, however, we must be aware that government is a disorderly, confusing struggle between fluctuating and nebulous elements of power, and that Congress is primarily an institution for working out compromises and formulating policy. Also involved in the *application* of rules (e.g., in overseeing the bureaucracy) as well as in making rules, it performs a particularly significant role in *interest representation*. The primary pressure center of American democracy, Congress is an amphitheatre where pressures converge from political parties, interest groups, and, yes, even the President and the courts.

CONGRESSMEN: VILLAINOUS POLITICIANS OR SOLONS?

Congressmen are often favorite whipping boys of journalists and other commentators and some members of the public. They are variously derided as ignorant, lazy, and power hungry. They are cited for taking "junkets" to various pleasure spots of the world at taxpayers' expense, loading the public payroll with incompetent friends and relatives, taking kickbacks from their appointees, accepting "gifts" or maintaining business connections which could lead to conflicts of interest, failing to enforce an effective code of ethics on themselves, and lacking interest in modernizing or otherwise improving congressional organization.

Some of these criticisms are, in fact, valid. Some ignorant, greedy, incompetent, and dishonest individuals *do* get elected to Congress. However, many of these complaints are unfair in describing Congressmen as a group. Congressmen have the usual quota of human faults; however, they do not seem a particularly perverted group. One study concluded that Congressmen are "substantial, conscientious, hard-working, well-educated men and women."[1] It does not mean, of course, that they are quite the wise and skillful lawgivers as the Solon of Athenian democracy. Although, like most people and institutions, Congressmen and Congress are vulnerable to criticism, it is worth noting that much of the complaining comes from those who primarily disagree with the legislative product Congress puts out.

CHARACTERISTICS OF CONGRESSMEN

Most Congressmen are men of late middle age (average age in 1971 was fifty-two) white, Protestant (see Table 10-1), war veterans, native born, and of upper-middle-class origin. Almost all have had previous political experience. More than half are lawyers, and most of the rest are businessmen, bankers, and educators (see Table 10-2).

Senators are, on the average, about five years older than Representatives[2] and have had more successful experience in politics. Because of their six-year terms, smaller membership, greater freedom of debate, and role in approving treaties and appointments, Senators have greater public prestige than do House members.

[1] Committee on Congress of the American Political Science Association, *The Reorganization of Congress* (Washington, D.C.: Public Affairs Press, 1945), p. 86.
[2] In 1971, the average age of Senators was 56.4 and Representatives 51.9.

Table 10–1
RELIGIOUS AFFILIATIONS OF MEMBERS OF THE
NINETY-SECOND CONGRESS

| RELIGION | HOUSE | | | SENATE | | | CONGRESS |
	D	R	TOT.	D	R	TOT.	TOTAL
Apostolic Christian	0	1	1	0	0	0	1
Baptist	32	10	42	5	3	8	50
Central Schwenkfelder	0	0	0	0	1	1	1
Christian and Missionary Alliance	0	1	1	0	0	0	1
Christian Churches	8	2	10	1	0	1	11
Churches of Christ	5	3	8	1	0	1	9
Christian Science	1	3	4	0	1	1	5
Eastern Orthodox	5	0	5	0	0	0	5
Episcopal	27	22	49	4	13	17	66
Evangelical Covenant	0	1	1	0	0	0	1
Evangelical Free	0	2	2	0	0	0	2
Jewish	10	2	12	1	1	2	14
Latter-Day Saints	3	3	6	2	2	4	10
Lutheran	2	9	11	3	0	3	14
Methodist	33	32	65	13	7	20	85
Presbyterian	26	41	67	10	6	16	83
Roman Catholic	77	24	101	9	3	12	113
Seventh Day Adventist	0	1	1	0	0	0	1
Society of Friends	0	4	4	0	0	0	4
Unitarian	3	0	3	3	2	5	8
United Brethren	1	0	1	0	0	0	1
United Church of Christ and Congregationalist	6	13	19	2	5	7	26
Unspecified Protestant	12	5	17	1	1	2	19
None	3	1	4	0	0	0	4
Total	254	180	434	55	45	100	534

Source: *Congressional Quarterly Weekly Report*, January 15, 1971, p. 126.

Blacks and women are badly underrepresented. Although blacks account for about 12 percent of the population, they constitute less than 3 percent of the Congressmen, and women also less than 3 percent.[3] The poor, the young, and the trade unionists

[3] Thirteen blacks were seated in the Ninety-second Congress, three more than in the Ninety-first Congress; and the largest number since Reconstruction. From 1961 to 1971, the number of women seated in Congress has declined from seventeen to thirteen.

Table 10–2
OCCUPATIONS OF MEMBERS OF THE
NINETY-SECOND CONGRESS

OCCUPATION	HOUSE D	R	TOT.	SENATE D	R	TOT.	CONGRESS TOTAL
Agriculture	19	17	36	5	8	13	49
Business or banking	70	75	145	15	12	27	172
Educator	39	22	61	6	5	11	72
Engineering	2	1	3	2	0	2	5
Journalism	17	13	30	5	2	7	37
Labor leader	3	0	3	0	0	0	3
Law	150	86	236	41	24	65	301
Law enforcement	1	0	1	0	0	0	1
Medicine	4	2	6	1	0	1	7
Public service/politics	222	141	363	55	44	99	462
Minister	1	1	2	0	0	0	2
Scientist	1	0	1	0	0	0	1
Veteran	185	131	316	41	32	73	389

Source: *Congressional Quarterly Weekly Report*, January 15, 1971, p. 129.

are also underrepresented. Congress is not and never has been a true cross section of the American people; however, Congressmen do reflect their constituencies in one respect: if they are not what their constituents are, Congressmen at least are what their constituents appear to want or what they will settle for.

The social characteristics of Congressmen do not precisely determine their behavior, but they do influence it. No doubt Congressmen understand and respond more readily to the needs and ideas of people similar to themselves. They may also tend to feel little compulsion to change a system through which they successfully ascended. In any event, very few Congressmen are radical firebrands.

LEGAL QUALIFICATIONS AND TERMS
OF CONGRESSMEN

There are 535 members of Congress: 100 Senators and 435 Representatives. A Senator must be at least thirty years old and a citizen of the United States for nine years. When elected, he must be an inhabitant of the state from which he is chosen.[4]

The term of office of Senators is six years. Terms are so arranged that one-third of the total Senate membership is elected every second year, and the terms of both Senators from the same state do not terminate at the same time. If a Senator resigns or dies during his term, the governor of his state may appoint a successor, if the state law allows (nearly all states have so provided). The appointee may serve until the next general election, when the voters select a candidate to serve the remainder of the unexpired term. Often a governor resigns and the succeeding governor appoints him to the Senate vacancy.

A House Representative must be at least twenty-five years old, a U.S. citizen for seven years, and an inhabitant of the state from which he is elected. According to custom, he must also be a resident of the district he represents. This custom is so strong, in fact, that Representatives who do not actually live in their districts usually maintain an address of some sort there. If a Representative resigns or dies in office, the governor of his state calls a special election to choose a successor to serve out his term. The term of office is two years.

Each house may judge the qualifications of those elected, and occasionally they refuse to seat members. In 1967, for example, the House voted to exclude Adam Clayton Powell, Representative-elect from a black Harlem district in New York, even though he satisfied the constitutional requirements of age, inhabitancy, and citizenship.[5]

PRIVILEGES, SALARIES, AND PERQUISITES OF CONGRESSMEN

For good reasons, the Constitution (Article I, Section 6) gives Congressmen two special privileges not accorded ordinary citizens or other officials: they enjoy, first, virtually unlimited freedom of

[4] The candidate must be an inhabitant of the state but not necessarily a "resident." As shown in the 1964 election of the late Robert F. Kennedy, a native of Massachusetts and frequent resident of Virginia, as Senator from New York, the term "inhabitant" may be broadly construed.

[5] On January 31, 1969 the House voted to fine Powell $25,000 and to remove his twenty-two year seniority. It then allowed him to take the oath of office. On June 16, 1969, the Supreme Court ruled that the House had improperly

speech and, second, some freedom from arrest when discharging their official duties.

Freedom of Expression

A Congressman may not be held legally responsible in any place except in Congress for anything he says—so long as he says it in Congress. This immunity protects any speech or debate, whether on the floor or in congressional committees, in the *Congressional Record*, and any written report he may make. A member may take advantage of his immunity and defame private citizens and public officials without risking a slander or libel suit. He is, however, accountable to the congressional house of which he is a member. For a particularly slanderous remark he may be called to order (i.e., required to desist) by the House's presiding officer. In an extreme case, his colleagues may censure or even, by a two-thirds vote, expel him.

Censure or expulsion for improper remarks is rare. Not since 1862 has a member of Congress been expelled for this (or any other reason). Not since 1954, when the Senate voted to censure Wisconsin's Senator Joseph R. McCarthy, has either house censured a member for improper language,[6] although in 1967 Connecticut Senator Thomas Dodd was censured for inappropriate use of campaign contributions. Although some Congressmen abuse their privilege of free expression, most observers believe that the cause of democratic government is better served when the people's representatives are able to speak freely.

Some Freedom From Arrest

A member of Congress is free from arrest while going to, attending, or returning from sessions, except for treason, felony, or

---

excluded him. Chief Justice Earl Warren, speaking for a Court majority of 7–1, held that the House was without power to exclude Powell because he possessed all constitutional requirements for membership.

[6] Senator McCarthy was cited specifically for contempt of a Senate elections subcommittee, for abuse of its members, and for insults to the Senate. However, it was McCarthy's accusation that the Department of the Army was "soft" on communism, and the Department's counter charges about the Senator's efforts to use his influence improperly within the Army, which was the last straw which led to his censure. A legislator who is censured suffers the ostracism of colleagues and loses much of his effectiveness as a legislator.

breach of the peace. This exempts him from civil summons so that he is not, for example, required to serve on a jury while Congress is in session or to appear in court as a defendant in a civil suit. Though he may be arrested for most criminal offenses, he may not be for nonindictable offenses such as minor traffic violations. Obviously, the major reason for this immunity is so Congressmen cannot be kept from their legislative duties while Congress is in session.

Salaries

Congressmen fix their own compensation and perquisites. The present salary of Senators and Representatives is $42,500 a year.[7] On the whole, they have been cautious about increasing their salaries, since the voters would oppose it if they gave themselves too large a raise. In fact, as a result, Congressmen have been paid less than persons of similar attainments in law, finance, and business.

Since it is not the monetary reward that has caused people to seek election to Congress, what has? The primary attractions seem to be prestige, power, and the opportunity to serve. There is also opportunity for advancement, since Congressmen often move to higher posts in government. In addition, many ex-Congressmen have profited on their return to private life from the connections they made while in Congress.

Perquisites

Congressmen also enjoy certain perquisites or "fringe benefits" of their office. They receive a travel allowance and $750 for trips to their home districts (including trips of a Virginia Congressman who lives seven miles from his office in the Capitol). They also get free use of the mails; allowances for staff pay, stationery, and telegrams; free office space in Washington and in their home states; free use of a complete gym; low-cost insurance and health plans; a tax-free living allowance of $3000 a year; very generous

[7] The President is currently paid $200,000 a year, the Vice-President $62,500, Cabinet members $60,000, Supreme Court Justices $60,000, and the Chief Justice $62,500.

retirement plans;[8] and a telephone allowance of 300 hours of free long-distance calls annually.

THE DIFFERENT CONSTITUENCIES OF SENATORS AND REPRESENTATIVES

At the 1787 Constitutional Convention, the delegates early decided to create two legislative chambers with different kinds of representation. A Senator was to be elected by the legislature of his state, a Representative by popular vote in his state. The Convention delegates thought that, in this way, Senators would be spokesmen for the states and would check the more democratically elected House. However, since the adoption of the Seventeenth Amendment in 1913, Senators, like Representatives, have been elected by popular vote. There remains, though, the check of the two chambers on each other.

BICAMERALISM

The bicameral system—that is, having two legislative houses—has often been criticized. Opponents lament the delays and deadlocks that happen because legislation must be approved by both houses. They also criticize the diffusion of responsibility in two houses, which facilitates buck passing. In addition, they fault the bicameral arrangement for being undemocratic: the Senate formula of giving each state two votes, they say, gives overrepresentation to less populous states and rural interests, so that Alaska, for instance, has the same vote as California, which has sixty-seven times more people. However, if this formula seems to work to the disadvantage of urban interests, it may be more apparent than real. By now, most states are at least industrialized to the point that their Senators cannot ignore the city voter.

Despite the criticisms of bicameralism as an obstruction to the majority will, it will not be abandoned for unicameralism (a one-

---

[8] Upon retirement a member may receive up to 80 percent of his salary each year. As his contribution to the fund, an 8 percent deduction is made in his salary each month he serves.

house legislature) in the foreseeable future. Congressmen are unlikely to propose a constitutional amendment to eliminate the house they belong to. Nor will any small state want to relinquish the equal representation in the Senate specifically guaranteed it in the Constitution. Moreover, though Americans are quick to criticize Congressmen and the rules by which they operate, they would probably regard such tampering with their basic institutions as akin to subversion.

AUTOMATIC APPORTIONMENT OF HOUSE SEATS
AMONG THE STATES

House seats are apportioned among the states according to their populations. The Constitution does not set the number of seats, although it limits them to one seat for every 30,000 persons and guarantees each state at least one Representative.[9] The total number of seats, however, is set by Congress. If the maximum representation permissible were allowed, there would be more than 6000 Representatives—and a body this size obviously would be unworkable. Some feel that even the present membership of 435, set "permanently" by Congress in 1929, is too large.

Congress has reapportioned the House seats every ten years following the census except that of 1920.[10] On some occasions reapportionment was achieved only after furious congressional battles. However, the Automatic Reapportionment Act of 1929 (amended in 1941) seems to have avoided this difficulty. Under this law, the President sends Congress, at the beginning of the January session following every decennial census, the new reapportionment figures. The Clerk of the House then informs each state governor how many Representatives his state may have in the next Congress.[11] Nine states gained seats in the House and sixteen lost seats after the 1960 census. California gained the most—eight—bringing its total to thirty-eight. The 1970 census figures indicated that

[9] The states having only one Representative are Alaska, Delaware, Nevada, North Dakota, Vermont, and Wyoming.
[10] Because of the shifts in population between 1910 and 1920, either the size of the House had to be increased or seats had to be taken from some states. Reluctant to do either, Congress did nothing.
[11] There is a new Congress every even-numbered year.

220

California's delegation increased to forty-three, four more than New York's (see Table 10-3).

DISTRICTING HOUSE SEATS AND GERRYMANDER

The district system for electing House members was established by Congress in 1842; however, the actual arrangement of districts within a state is made by the state legislature. Unfortunately, legislatures have often *gerrymandered* congressional districts— that is, the party or interests in power within the legislature have arranged the size and shapes of districts to give themselves an unfair advantage by guaranteeing the election or reelection of Representatives favorable to their cause. The resulting inequities have led some observers to refer to the House—and not too unfairly—as the House of Unrepresentatives.

Table 10-3
CHANGES IN HOUSE OF REPRESENTATIVES
REFLECTING 1970 CENSUS FIGURES

STATE	NO. OF REPRESENTATIVES BASED ON 1960 CENSUS	CHANGE FROM 1960 APPORTIONMENT
Alabama	8	−1
Arizona	3	+1
California	38	+5
Colorado	4	+1
Florida	12	+3
Iowa	7	−1
New York	41	−2
North Dakota	2	−1
Ohio	24	−1
Pennsylvania	27	−2
Tennessee	9	−1
Texas	23	+1
West Virginia	5	−1
Wisconsin	10	−1

Source: U.S. Bureau of the Census.

Rural interests have usually benefited most from gerrymandering, gaining representation far more than fairly due to them. This has happened because state legislatures, generally dominated by rural interests, have drawn congressional districts so that Congressmen from urban areas have had to be responsive to many more people than have Congressmen from rural districts. This benefited farmers over city people. This unfair arrangement has been relieved, however, by the 1964 Supreme Court decision (*Wesberry* v. *Sanders*) that all congressional districts must be substantially equal in population.

ORGANIZATION OF CONGRESS

Sessions

According to the Twentieth Amendment, the two houses of Congress must assemble each year at noon on the third day in January (unless by law they establish a different day). Neither house may, however, call itself into special session no matter how pressing the emergency. Only the President may order this—and when he does, it is to alert Congress and the public to his proposals on issues *he* considers pressing.[12] Should Congress adjourn the special session, the President may call it again.

Congress does, however, have full authority to adjourn a *regular session*—in odd-numbered years, usually by middle or late summer; in even-numbered years, usually by early summer so members may campaign. The President may adjourn Congress only if the two houses fail to agree on a date. Not wishing to appear weak, Congress has carefully avoided this.

The Committees: Little Legislatures of Congress

First-time visitors to Congress expecting to see American Democracy at Work are frequently shocked by what they view from the

[12] President Truman used his power to embarrass the Republican majority in Congress by calling Congress into special session in 1948 on the eve of the presidential election to redeem pledges made in the Republican Party platform. This was the last special session. Apparently, the fact that the President *may* call special sessions (as in 1948) has largely eliminated the necessity to do so.

galleries. Although, if lucky, they may witness a great debate attended by nearly the full membership, more likely the proceedings will be uninspiring and only a few Congressmen will be present. Congressmen may be seen reading the daily newspaper, paying no attention to the legislator who has the floor. Sometimes only the stenographer listens, since he must record the floor remarks for the *Congressional Record*. The reason for this disappointing scene is that the main work of Congress is done in smaller units, its committees.

Congress adopted the committee system early in its history because of its large membership and the heavy volume of work—now nearly 20,000 bills to consider each two-year session. But congressional committees are far more than means of apportioning the work load; despite the increase of presidential and party influence, these committees are real power centers of American government. The awarding of approximately 300 committee and subcommittee chairmanships is an important system of prizes for many individual Congressmen.

Standing Committees

The Senate has sixteen standing committees. As Table 10-4 shows, they are uneven in prestige, but among the most important are Appropriations, Foreign Relations, and Finance. The House has twenty-one standing committees, of which the Rules, Appropriations, and Ways and Means committees are the three most powerful.

Some subcommittees are also very powerful—a subcommittee of an appropriations committee, for instance, may have more influence on a given matter than its parent committee because of the subcomittee's involvement in appropriations for that area. The House Appropriations Committee subcommittee, for instance, has greatly affected State Department projects by its parochial and extremely conservative attitude on State Department appropriations.

Standing committees as a whole enjoy great powers: all bills are referred to them, and they can kill them, fail to report them out, amend them, or write their own. Only a few bills (about 10 percent) are eventually reported out for final consideration on the floor of the House or Senate.

Table 10-4
STANDING COMMITTEES
(RANKED IN GROUPS, BY ORDER OF IMPORTANCE)

SENATE COMMITTEES	HOUSE COMMITTEES
I. Appropriations Foreign Relations Finance	Rules Appropriations Ways and Means
II. Armed Services Judiciary Agriculture and Forestry Interstate and Foreign Commerce	Armed Services Judiciary Agriculture Interstate and Foreign Commerce Foreign Affairs Government Operations
III. Banking and Currency Labor and Public Welfare Public Works Interior and Insular Affairs Aeronautic and Space Sciences	Banking and Currency Education and Labor Interior and Insular Affairs Space and Astronautics Public Works
IV. Post Office and Civil Service Government Operations	Post Office and Civil Service Merchant Marine and Fisheries Veterans Affairs Internal Security [was Un-American Activities]
V. District of Columbia Rules and Administration	District of Columbia House Administration

Source: Ranking by H. Douglas Price, in Stephen K. Bailey, *The New Congress* (New York: St. Martin's Press, 1966), pp. 54–55. The House Standards of Official Conduct Committee was created subsequent to this ranking.

Committees are, of course, made up of members from both parties. The chairman and a majority of the members belong to the majority party (presently the Democrats), but the minority party is represented on most committees in about the same proportion as its membership bears to the total membership in that house. House committees average about thirty members, Senate committees are about half as large.

Many standing committees have subcommittees, either permanent or temporary—usually between 250 and 300 in both houses of Congress. Necessary because of the complexity of legislative business, subcommittees allow able, industrious Congressmen to gain early recognition and experience in congressional work.

In a formal way, each house determines the composition of its standing committees. In practice, however, Democratic members are selected by the Democratic Steering Committee in the Senate and Democratic members of the Ways and Means Committee in the House, and Republican members are selected by a Republican Committee on Committees in each house.

When considering important bills, standing committees often hold open hearings at which spokesmen for executive agencies, lobbyists for interest groups, and private citizens may present information and opinions. However, much of the actual decision making is done in closed sessions where Congressmen can feel freer to exchange ideas and reach agreement without the public watching, although these secret sessions probably reduce the possibility of popular control.

The Powerful Chairmen

Chairmanships of the standing committees are much coveted. The reason is that these chairmen enjoy tremendous power: they may defy other congressional leaders and even stifle the President's legislation. Other Congressmen, constituents, lobbyists, and the President cultivate their friendship.

The chairman controls the agenda of the committee meetings, and can frequently even prevent the committee from meeting. He appoints subcommittees and their chairmen, controls their jurisdictions, and appoints and controls most of the staff. If he chooses, he may represent the committee on the floor and in conference committees with committee members of the other house. Much of his power comes from the tradition that Congressmen must support committee chairmen and because newer members do not wish to antagonize these key old-timers.

The Seniority System: Longevity and Localism

Chairmen get their posts because of their long seniority. The majority party member with the longest continuous period of service on the committee normally becomes its chairman. As Table 10-5 shows, of the thirty-seven standing committees of both houses, twenty-three are headed by men who are at least sixty-five years old, the customary retirement age in private industry. Since they are not really chosen by their own committees, or by their party, or by the House or Senate, but by the voters of their state or dis-

225

Table 10–5
STANDING COMMITTEE CHAIRMEN SIXTY-FIVE AND OVER
(AS OF JANUARY 1971)

SENATE COMMITTEES	CHAIRMEN	AGE	YEARS OF SERVICE*
Aeronautical and Space Sciences	Clinton Anderson, N.M.	75	26
Agriculture and Forestry	Allen Ellender, La.	79	34
Appropriations	Richard Russell, Ga.†	73	38
Armed Services	John Stennis, Miss.	69	23
Banking and Currency	John Sparkman, Ala.	71	34
Commerce	Warren Magnuson, Wash.	65	34
Foreign Relations	J. William Fulbright, Ark.	65	28
Government Operations	John McClellan, Ark.	74	32
Judiciary	James Eastland, Miss.	66	28
Public Works	Jennings Randolph, W.Va.	68	26
Rules and Administration	B. Everett Jordan, N.C.	74	13

HOUSE COMMITTEES

Agriculture	W. R. Poage, Texas	71	34
Appropriations	George Mahon, Texas	70	36
Armed Services	F. Edward Hébert, La.	69	30
Banking and Currency	Wright Patman, Texas	77	42
District of Columbia	John McMillan, S.C.	72	32
Government Operations	Chet Holifield, Calif.	67	28
Interior and Insular Affairs	Wayne Aspinall, Colo.	74	22
Judiciary	Emanuel Celler, N.Y.	82	48
Merchant Marine and Fisheries	Edward Garmatz, Md.	67	24
Rules	William Colmer, Miss.	80	38
Science and Astronautics	George Miller, Calif.	80	26
Standards of Official Conduct	Melvin Price, Ill.	66	26

* Includes House service where applicable
† Died January 21, 1971.
Source: Copyright *Newsweek,* January 25, 1971, p. 19.

trict who send them back to Congress term after term, committee chairmen are responsible to local interests even though making national policy.

Not surprisingly, the seniority system is much criticized; mainly because, while no correlation has been demonstrated between seniority and ability, there is a direct relationship between seniority and a "safe" district. Such districts or states—dominated by a particular interest group, political machine, or one party—return the same member to Congress again and again. Thus, for example, in the Ninety-first Congress, Senators from Southern one-party states achieved chairmanships of ten of the sixteen standing committees; Midwest Senators held none and Eastern Senators only two.[13] Most chairmen of House committees were also from Southern and Western states. They tend to be conservative, rural-oriented, and least likely to support the national policies promoted by the President. The seniority system is also criticized for not allowing young and able Congressmen to use their talents by heading committees.

Despite recent stirrings, major reform is not likely to be quick in coming. Chairmen are not inclined to give up power willingly. Morever, no one has suggested an alternative acceptable to most Congressmen. Thus, the seniority system will probably continue, at least through this decade, to provide independent power centers which can determine the fate of policies and congressional careers.

However, conservative regional powers are on the decline. A number of committees chaired by conservative Southerners have a non-Southerner as ranking majority member—that is, next in line of succession. Also, in both houses those who wield party power—the majority leaders—are selected on grounds other than seniority. Moreover, seniority is not even now the sole basis for selecting committee members and subcommittee chairmen; all freshman Senators, for example, now get a major committee assignment and in both houses a member's background, abilities, and how hard he works frequently determine which committee he is assigned to or whether he is made a subcommittee chairman.

Special Committees

Both houses of Congress have special committees (e.g., the Senate Special Committee on Aging), with members selected by the

[13] Perhaps the most significant concentration of Southern seniority has been in the subcommittees of the House Appropriations Committee, which holds the purse strings on many of the basic operations of government.

presiding officers, whose task is to make investigations or to deal with some special area. The House Un-American Activities Committee was a special committee from its creation in 1938 until it was made a permanent committee in 1946. However, the use of such committees has declined in recent years, and the Legislative Reorganization Act of 1946 sought to make them unnecessary.

Joint Committees

Occasionally Congress creates joint committees composed of members from both houses, for closer coordination between Senate and House, and between Congress and the President, on national issues. Sometimes they make investigations and sometimes they supervise some congressional business (e.g., overseeing the administration). Examples of joint committees are those on Atomic Energy (the most powerful), on Internal Revenue Taxation, and on the Economic Report (of the President).

Conference Committees: The Third Houses

Conference committees, which are both special and joint, are so powerful that they are often called the "third houses of Congress." Composed of members of both parties of both houses, they meet in secret, and no records are kept of their proceedings. Their purpose is to reconcile the different versions of bills on the same matter passed in each house.[14]

Conference committee members are usually leading members of the standing committees responsible for the bills upon which agreement is sought. They are appointed by the presiding officers, and most represent the views of the majority of the house to which they belong. Usually the conferees achieve agreement among themselves, and the two houses generally approve the bill

[14] However, the conference committee does not simply split the difference between the houses. A case in point is the conference committee action on the supplementary appropriation bill for the Elementary and Secondary Education Bill of 1965, the most significant victory for federal aid to education in a struggle which spanned more than a century. The committee approved an appropriation of $1.223 billion, the amount stipulated in the original House version of the bill. The Senate had subsequently authorized $184 million over the House version and requested a conference with the House.

THE LEGISLATIVE REORGANIZATION ACT OF 1970

What It Did

1. *Reduced secrecy* by providing that all roll call votes in committee are to be made public, that teller votes in the House's Committee of the Whole are to be recorded if at least twenty members request, and that House committee hearings may be broadcast or televised (as the Senate already permits) if a majority of the committee approves.
2. *Expedited proceedings* by providing that House committees be allowed to sit during House sessions (except when a bill is being read for amendments), eliminating the right of a single member to require the reading of the previous day's *Journal*, and shortening the procedure for quorum calls.
3. *Reduced the arbitrary power of committee chairmen* with a long list of rule changes (e.g., by requiring that committee meetings and hearings be open—unless *the committee* votes to close them).

What It Failed to Do

1. *Failed* to modify the *seniority system.*
2. *Failed* to require that the *Congressional Record* report the proceedings of the two houses as they take place, without insertions or later modifications.
3. *Failed* to limit the power of the Rules Committee to report bills and propose special orders (e.g., one not permitting amendments) to govern the course of floor debate.

Prospects for Its Implementation

It appears that the degree to which Congress' senior members, who rule congressional committees, are faithful to or disregard the revised rules—and the vigor of the newer members' demands that the rules be adhered to—will decide if this congressional reform act, the first in twenty-four years, has substantial and lasting effect on Congress's operations. History shows that changing the rules of Congress has been easier than redistributing power among members.

they report back. Some observers argue that a major advantage of a unicameral system (only one legislative house) is that it would eliminate these committees, which many believe are excessively powerful.

PARTY ORGANIZATION AND LEADERSHIP IN CONGRESS

Needless to say, practically all Congressmen are elected as Democrats or Republicans, but this is an important fact because party membership is indeed a prerequisite for achieving positions of leadership and influence. Moreover, the parties are more than simply avenues to power, for they ensure the direction, coordination, and continuity of the formal institutions of congressional leadership.

Party Caucuses

The *party caucuses*—or conferences, as the Republicans call them —are the source of authority for party government in Congress. Each party in each house holds a caucus of its members before the beginning of each new Congress. In theory the caucus produces a party position on legislation, but in practice this only happens as a last resort. Both party leaders and members prefer this, one reason being that deciding party policy this way might well produce a dispute within the party, and the caucus decision would be almost impossible to enforce. Another reason is that party members would not readily submit to party discipline. Still, party members in caucus do approve committee assignments, discuss important legislation, and designate the party's choice for presiding officer, floor leaders, Clerk, and other party officers of Congress. These decisions are considered binding on party members.

Each caucus in each house has what is called a *steering* or *policy committee*.[15] Although theoretically responsible for formulating party legislative programs, they have never done so.

[15] In the House the Democrats call it *steering committee* and the Republicans call it *policy committee*; in the Senate both parties use the term *policy committee*. These Senate bodies handle committee appointments only.

Individual members of steering committees may be powerful, but the committees themselves exercise little control. In fact, they seldom meet.

House Party Leaders

The *Speaker*, the presiding officer of the House, is the most powerful political leader in the House and the single most important leader in Congress. He is not only the leader of the majority party in the House, he also is a parliamentary umpire.

His official powers are impressive. He may, for instance, refer all bills to standing committees, and thus can influence how a bill will get treated in the committee stage by referring it to a favorable or unfavorable committee. He may also recognize or refuse to recognize anyone who wishes to speak to an issue on the floor or to call up a measure for debate, and he may call members out of order and rule on points of parliamentary procedure—although his ruling may be appealed to the House. In addition, he appoints members of conference, special, and joint committees.[16]

Although formally chosen by the House, the Speaker is actually picked by a caucus (or conference) of the members of the majority party. Along with his staff, the Majority Floor Leader, and the party whips, he provides the members of the majority party with a party line on important matters. Thus, he is an important broker between the President and the majority party members in the House. Sometimes he has truly tremendous power. For instance, the late Sam Rayburn, who (except for four years) was Speaker from 1940 to 1961, had enormous influence because of his good relations with fellow Democrats. His successors, John McCormack and Carl Albert, while also powerful, have not had the same kind of personal influence.

The *Majority Floor Leader* is the second most important party leader in the House, and, like the Speaker, is chosen by the majority party caucus. His task is to keep close touch with House rank-and-file party members to learn their opinions and gain their

---

[16] Powerful as today's Speakership is, it is a weak reflection of what the post was in the late nineteenth and early twentieth centuries. In 1910, the members removed the Speaker from the Rules Committee and took away his power to appoint the members and chairmen of standing committees.

support for measures promoted by party leaders. He is influential in determining who shall speak on bills and other measures, makes lists of speakers the Speaker will recognize, and helps divide the time set aside for debates.

The principal leader of the minority party is the *Minority Floor Leader,* who is the legislative manager of his party and who usually becomes Speaker when his party gains a majority in the House. Each floor leader is assisted by a *whip* and several (sixteen to eighteen) assistant whips, all House members, who help the leaders maintain contact with party members and inform members of the strategy and tactics of party leaders. They also do the leg work needed to get out the vote on important issues, and help the floor leaders prepare lists of speakers. Whips are much more the gatherers of information than party discipliners.

Senate Party Leaders

The Senate has no counterpart to the Speaker of the House. The presiding officer is the *Vice-President of the United States,* but he does not have, in the Senate at least, the power or influence that the Speaker has in the House. Ordinarily he is not the leader of his party in the Senate, and he cannot even vote, except in the event of a tie.

When the Vice-President is absent, the *President Pro Tempore* presides. A Senator chosen by the majority party and then elected by the Senate, his position more closely approximates the influence of the Speaker, for he too is partisan and promotes the program of the majority party. However, he is only one of several leaders of the majority party in the Senate, and exercises nothing like the House Speaker's influence.

Senate rules are not nearly so strict as House rules, the reason being that the House is over four times larger. The House floor would be chaos without tight control by the presiding officer. In the Senate, on the other hand, most business is conducted by unanimous consent after consultation between majority and minority leaders.

Insofar as there is a paramount power in the Senate, it is the *Majority Floor Leader,* who has a leading role in controlling the flow of business to the floor, much as does the Rules Committee in the House. His power derives primarily from his party leadership, but his success or failure (as with most party leaders) is based largely on his ability to persuade, for he has no power to discipline and no patronage to distribute. The resourceful Lyndon Johnson, while in the Senate, built his power base around this position, and Hubert Humphrey, before he became Vice-President, gained wide respect as majority whip. As *Minority Floor Leader*, the late Everett Dirksen virtually established himself as an American institution.

The Problem of Congressional Staff

Congress employs about 25,000 people, ranging from congressional pages to responsible professionals with impressive experience and technical expertise. Congress could not function without this help. Moreover, the quality of the legislative product greatly depends on these people, particularly those at or near the professional level. One of the most invaluable aids is the *Congressional Research Service* of the Library of Congress (formerly the Legislative Reference Service). It employs lawyers, political scientists, economists, and other professionals to do research and supply information to committees and individual members of Congress. It also analyzes and evaluates bills and prepares summaries and digests of public committee hearings. In 1971 it had a staff of about 300. Its work is monitored by the Joint Committee on the Library and Congressional Research, which was created by the Legislative Reorganization Act of 1970. Another important source of assistance is the *Office of Legislative Counsel*, which helps Congressmen draft bills. Professional and clerical staff members are also assigned each standing and special committee by the Appropriations Committees. Currently this staff numbers over 1300. Congressmen also have professional and clerical assistants—now numbering about 5000—on their personal staffs.

Probably the main problem of congressional staff, and it is an important one, is the matter of *how much*. Without capable staff, neither the leadership, the committees, nor individual members could function effectively. Nor could Congress expect to balance the power of the executive branch, with its myriad information-gathering systems and professional civil servants. But if Congress has too much staff, and particularly too many experts, its decisions may be made by staff people instead of by elected representatives.

Suggested Additional Reading

Bailey, S. K. *The New Congress*. 1966.

Clapp, C. L. *The Congressman: His Work as He Sees It*. 1963.

Davidson, R. H. *The Role of the Congressman*. 1969.

Froman, L. A., Jr. *The Congressional Process: Strategies, Rules, and Procedures*. 1967.

Hinckley, B. *The Seniority System in Congress*. 1971.

Keefe, W. J., and M. S. Ogul. *The American Legislative Process: Congress and the States*. 1968.

Matthews, D. R. *U.S. Senators and Their World*. 1960.

Saloma, J. S., III. *Congress and the New Politics*. 1969.

11 Congress: Policy Making

I think it can be said that the Congress of the United States is the last really important legislative body.

—*Denis Brogan*

Understanding Congress takes some systematic analysis, for it is composed of intricate forms and structures which often conceal how it really works. Congress operates in two ways or according to two kinds of expectations: on the one hand, to promote the personal goals—that is, the status and careers—of Congressmen, particularly those with effective influence (*internal expectations*), and, on the other hand, to deal with the often-conflicting goals of the President, of interest groups, and of constituents (*external expectations*).

THE REPRESENTATION FUNCTION: SERVING LOCAL CONSTITUENTS

The typical Congressman's chief hope is to keep the support of voters in his district and thus remain in office. How does he try to do this? Principally he tries to please those in his district who helped him get elected—mainly organized groups that supported him, who are interested in how he votes on measures that benefit their members, and local party leaders, who are most interested in favors and patronage. Since both expect him to do his best for them, often this means a Congressman behaves more like an ambassador from his constituency than like a representative of the entire nation. This is especially apparent in the general scramble by Congressmen to get "pork barrel" legislation, such as rivers and harbors appropriations for their districts, and in the "logrolling" over things like farm relief and tariff restrictions to protect local industry.

A Congressman is not likely to be as attentive to the President's wishes (even if he is of the same party) as he is to his constituents', and his regard for the national party is even less. Although in succeeding elections he may be judged somewhat on how much support he gave the President, and although the national party does give him some patronage to dispense and perhaps some help in his campaign, basically a Congressman knows that how he voted on matters closely affecting his district is what really determines whether he will be reelected. A Congressman does not, of course, react like a computer, for he has his own personal beliefs and may often vote his convictions or his view of what is the common good. Nevertheless, for a Congressman to ignore the local basis of congressional elections is to court personal disaster.

Congressmen also act as errand boys to service their constituents' myriad requests for helpful intercession with executive agencies such as the Veterans Administration, the Selective Service System, or the Immigration and Naturalization Service—a role that has grown more demanding as government has become larger and more complicated. A Congressman may also find this role distasteful. Alben Barkley, a Senator and later Vice-President, told a story that illustrates the range of services rendered—and the occasional quixotic response of the recipient:

> I called on a certain rural constituent and was shocked to hear him say he was thinking of voting for my opponent. I reminded him of the many things I had done for him as prosecuting attorney, and county judge, as congressman, and senator.

I recalled how I had helped get an access road built to his farm, how I had visited him in a military hospital in France when he was wounded in World War I, how I had assisted him in securing veteran's benefits, how I had arranged his loan from the Farm Credit Administration, how I had got him a disaster loan when the flood destroyed his home, etc. etc.

"How can you think of voting for my opponent?" I exhorted at the end of this long recital. "Surely you remember all these things I have done for you?"

"Yeah," he said, "I remember. But what in hell have you done for me lately?"[1]

There are, however, more positive sides to this errand-boy activity. It may, for instance, help the constituents involved to understand administrative rules and practices and the need for them. Moreover, though such intervention on behalf of constituents may be sporadic and irresponsible—and even harmful to good administration—it may also improve the performance of insensible, autocratic, or capricious lower administrative officials, as well as revealing to them popular dissatisfaction.

THE PRESIDENT AS CHIEF LEGISLATOR

The President and the executive departments and agencies are a major force in congressional life. The reason is that the initiative, setting of priorities, and continuing legislative leadership are predominately in their hands. Basically, the executive branch sets the legislative agenda and rides herd on bills the President considers important. The executive also dominates national security policy and can make decisions daily that affect the economy and the personal lives of constituents in every congressional district— facts that every Congressman recognizes. This reliance on the executive has so increased, in fact, that some observers fear Congress may become merely a rubber stamp for the executive's programs. No doubt this concern is exaggerated, for Congress has very significant powers of its own. It must be noted also that, in struggling with the President, Congress often finds allies among

[1] Alben W. Barkley, *That Reminds Me* (Garden City, N.Y.: Doubleday, 1954), p. 165. Reprinted by permission.

the interest groups and even within the executive branch itself. Nevertheless, Congress must definitely operate within the context of presidential influence.

THE LAW-MAKING FUNCTION: CONGRESS IN ACTION

Obviously, the most important function of Congress is to make laws. The law-making process is complex, but the pattern of procedures is rather uniform: as Figure 11-1 shows, a bill is written, introduced, studied, perhaps amended, and passed in one house; is similarly handled in the other house; differences in the two versions are resolved; the identical version is finally passed in the two houses; and the result is submitted to the President for his signature. This outline of the process is developed further below.

Writing a Bill

The volume of legislative traffic is immense—as noted earlier, about 20,000 bills and resolutions are introduced in a two-year session. Only a fraction emerge from committee, however, and even fewer ever become law. The rest perish along the way, a fate most doubtless deserve.

Bills come from several sources. Some, of course, are conceived by individual members of Congress, based on promises they made during their campaigns, or on their experience after being in office, or in response to proposals from constituents, either individuals or groups (professional organizations, farm groups, chambers of commerce, labor unions, etc.). Interest groups also write bills.[2] So too do committees of Congress—most tax bills, for instance, are prepared by the House Ways and Means Committee. In recent years, however, most major legislation has originated in the executive branch, usually in the form of letters from a Cabinet member or agency head, or even from the President himself, directed to the Speaker of the House and the

[2] The veteran's lobby, led by the American Legion, has written, had introduced, and claims credit for the enactment into law of many pension, bonus, and veterans' benefit bills since World War I. For an account of the process used by the Legion to get laws on the statute books see Karl Schriftgiesser, *The Lobbyists* (Boston: Little, Brown, 1960), pp. 50–51.

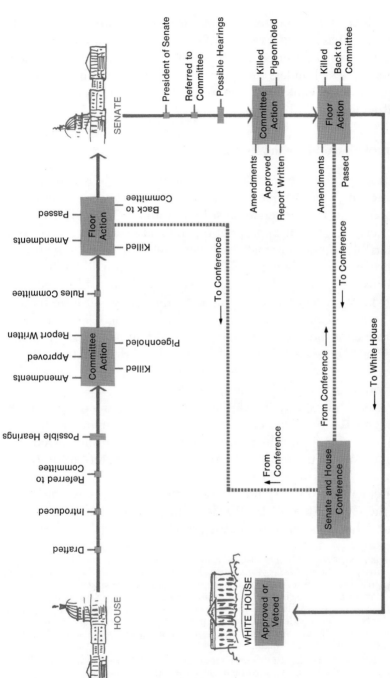

Figure 11-1. How a House-originated bill becomes law. (Source: California State Chamber of Commerce.)

President of the Senate. Many such proposals are sent after the President has given his annual State of the Union message.

Whatever the source, a bill is not likely to survive, especially if controversial, unless the sponsor is influential and has the strong support of relevant interest groups, affected government agencies, and legislators in both houses.

Introducing a Bill in the House

Bills may originate in either house, and similar bills may be considered in both chambers at the same time.[3] However, those bills proposed to raise revenue must be introduced in the House, and, by custom, general appropriations bills also originate there—not a terribly significant fact, however, since the Senate must also approve revenue bills and may amend them just like other bills.

Only a member of Congress may introduce a bill[4] and only into his own legislative chamber. In the House he introduces it by simply placing it in the "hopper" beside the Clerk's desk. To introduce it, however, does not mean he will necessarily promote it. The Congressman may ask that it bear the notation "by request" to signal he is introducing it by request of some other person or group and has no particular interest in it.

After a bill is introduced, the Clerk assigns it a legislative number and the Speaker refers it to a standing committee. It is no longer customary in the House to read aloud a freshly introduced bill, even by title; instead the title is simply entered in the *House Journal* and printed in the *Congressional Record*. Only when a bill emerges from a standing committee and is being considered in the Committee of the Whole or in the House itself is it ever read. This constitutes *second reading*. *Third reading* takes place

---

[3] Legislative proposals may also take the form of resolutions which may originate in either house. *Joint resolutions* differ very little from bills (the two are often used indiscriminately) and except for those proposing amendments to the Constitution, are subject to the same procedures. *Concurrent resolutions*, which are not normally legislative in character, are used merely for expressing facts, opinions, principles, and purposes of the two houses. *Simple resolutions* concern the operation of either house alone and are considered only by the body to which they relate.

[4] An exception is the Resident Commissioner from the Commonwealth of Puerto Rico, who may introduce bills into the House and who has the privileges of a member except he cannot vote.

after debate on specific items of a bill and is by title only. In the Senate, introduction procedures are similar, though somewhat more formal.

Committee Action on a Bill

The most crucial phase in the history of a bill is its treatment in committee; it is here that its destiny is usually decided. Much depends on the committee chairman's preferences: he may have his committee consider the bill; he may "pigeonhole" it (file it away and not consider it at all); or he may send it to a subcommittee for consideration. As a matter of course he sends copies of the bill to the executive departments or agencies concerned with its subject matter, and he and his committee usually weigh their reports when deciding the ultimate fate of the measure.

Pigeonholing is a bill's usual fate; it is simply not reported out of committee. And since pigeonholing generally prevents action on a bill, committees rarely have to report out a measure unfavorably. Still, if a committee refuses to report out a bill at all, it may be forced out—in the House, if a majority of members sign a petition, and in the Senate, if a majority of members so vote. Such *discharge action* is rarely taken, however, because members are reluctant to oppose the powerful chairman.

If a bill is important, and particularly if it is controversial, the committee usually holds public hearings about it, where spokesmen for interest groups, government departments and agencies, private individuals, and even members of Congress may appear and testify. They may attend voluntarily or at the request or summons of the committee. Hearings may be impressive sessions at which committee members sincerely seek advice and assistance and the information presented is valuable to the Congress; or they may be carefully staged proceedings by which the committee confirms and publicizes its own prejudices. In any event, since Congress accepts so many committee recommendations, interest groups find hearings favorable places for promoting their causes, and they are as active here as anywhere else in the governmental process.

Following public hearings, the committee members meet in closed executive session to determine what to do about the bill.

If they favor it, they usually rework it, making whatever revisions they want, and prepare a formal report on it. These committee decisions are crucial, and actually determine the final legislative product more than do the deliberations of the two houses, since floor action consists essentially in approving or modifying the committee's decisions.

The committees are thus great strongholds of congressional power, some of them powerful enough to challenge their whole chamber and the President. Despite recent clamors that they represent special privileges, they are beneficial in that they help Congress remain independent from executive domination: if committees and Congressmen have no power, Congress has no power.

Rules Committee Action on a Bill

When bills are reported out of House committees, they are scheduled for debate by being assigned a calendar number and placed on one of three legislative calendars: the Union, the House, or the Private.[5] According to House rules, bills are supposed to be considered in the order they appear on the calendars, and bills from certain calendars must be considered on particular days of the week. These rules are repeatedly set aside, however, and bills are taken from calendars regardless of their chronological order. One reason is that privileged business—such as appropriations and revenue measures or reports of conference committees—is given priority. Bills considered important by the Rules Committee also need not wait their turn. Moreover, there is the overall problem of time: the House simply has not time enough to consider all bills, whether in calendar order or otherwise.

Thus it is that the Rules Committee is perhaps the most power-

[5] The *Union Calendar* is for bills raising revenue, general appropriations bills, and public bills directly or indirectly appropriating money or property. The *House Calendar* receives all other public bills. The *Private Calendar* is, as the name indicates, for private bills—usually for relief of claims against the United States or for private immigration bills. Noncontroversial bills may be transferred from the Union or House Calendars to the *Consent Calendar*. This is done by the Clerk on the request of a member of the House. On specified days the Clerk calls bills from the Consent Calendar in numerical order. Unless there is objection from as many as three House members, a bill so called is immediately considered. The occasional bill on which the discharge rule has been successfully invoked is placed on the *Discharge Calendar*.

ful committee in the House, with nearly life-and-death power over bills, for it is this committee that is responsible for altering calendar order. Working with the majority party, the Rules Committee controls: (1) when a bill can be considered, (2) how long it can be debated, (3) how time for debate can be divided between opponents and proponents of the bill, and (4) what, if any, amendments can be offered from the floor. The highly strategic position of this committee is therefore obvious.

While the Rules Committee often cooperates with the House leadership, if it opposes a measure it may use its power to keep it bottled up—at least for twenty-one days, after which the Speaker may force it to bring the bill to the floor. A majority of House members may also petition to discharge the bill—although this is extremely rare, since an individual member is reluctant to antagonize the committee that will later decide whether to permit consideration on one of *his* bills.

Committee of the Whole Action on a Bill

Most debate takes place in what is called the *Committee of the Whole,* which is simply the House itself sitting in a different capacity that makes it easier to consider bills and resolutions.

When the House resolves itself into the Committee of the Whole, it may act with a much smaller quorum—100 members instead of the required 218. A quorum usually consists of a majority of those chosen and sworn. Procedures allow maximum participation and critical debate, no roll call (i.e., publicly recorded) votes are taken, and generally no member may speak more than once or longer than five minutes. The committee chairman later reports back to the House what action was taken, and these decisions are then voted upon by the House sitting officially.

House Floor Debate on a Bill

Unlike in the Committee of the Whole, debate in the House is carefully restricted. A member may not be able to gain the floor at all to speak on an issue; even if he does, he may not speak for more than an hour, except by unanimous consent. Moreover, at any time a member recognized by the Speaker may "move the previous question." If this motion carries, debate ends and a formal vote is taken on the issue.

Actually, whatever one may think, debate on bills is *not* the most important phase of the legislative process. Although there are some floor deliberations in the nature of great national debates and although many debates afford the public communication so necessary to a representative systsem, the words spoken in debate usually do not influence many votes. Members generally make up their minds behind the scenes or outside the House, and their decisions are more apt to be influenced by representatives of interest groups and government agencies and by congressional leaders than by anything said in debate. Furthermore, extended debates, whether in the House or in the Committee of the Whole, take place on only the more important bills. Others are debated only in a limited way or not at all.

Voting on a Bill

A bill is voted on after debate, but how individual representatives voted is seldom recorded. Usually passage or not of a bill is decided by "aye" and "nay" voice vote, because other methods of voting take more time.

A *roll call vote* may be forced (as the Constitution allows) if one-fifth (currently twenty in the Committee of the Whole, at least forty-four in the total House) of a quorum calls for each member's vote to be recorded in the *House Journal.*

Another method, the *rising vote,* in which the supporters on each side stand and are counted, can be secured by any member who feels that the Speaker's announcement of the result of the "aye" and "nay" voice vote is incorrect.

A fourth method of voting is also available: when at least one-fifth of a quorum demand, *tellers* will count those voting for and those voting against. Members file past the tellers to be counted. Since 1971, one-fifth of a quorum in the Committee of the Whole may request that the names and positions of members on a teller vote be recorded. This partial lifting of secrecy was a result of the Legislative Reorganization Act of 1970. Normally, Representatives will not support the call for such a vote, unless they see it as some personal advantage (e.g., if the recording of their vote would reveal their close adherence to majority opinion in their constituency), want to use the roll call as a delaying tactic, or demonstrate their popular position on an issue.

Members often try to avoid having their votes recorded in the *Journal,* since they are reluctant to take sides on an issue that might divide their constituents politically or that is in conflict between the demands of their constituents and the demands of the national party. Members also resent being put in the position of having to duck a vote, because the public can learn almost as much from studying a Congressman's nonvoting record as from looking at his voting record. Most voters are not aware how their representatives voted (even on roll calls), but interest groups, party leaders, and election opponents are.

Electronic voting systems would solve the time problem (a roll call takes about half an hour), and are now used effectively by about half the state legislatures. However, since neither house of Congress has availed itself of these handy devices, it would appear Congressmen do not want constituents too well informed about their votes.

Senate Action on a Bill

A bill that passes the House is sent to the Senate (and vice versa, of course), where it is (usually by the parliamentarian, but subject to the intervention of the presiding officer) then referred to the appropriate standing committee. Procedures in Senate committees are quite similar to those in House committees. Floor procedure, however, is very different and much simpler. There are only two calendars—the *Calendar of General Orders,* which contains measures to be acted on, and the *Executive Calendar,* which contains all nominations for office and all treaties awaiting Senate action. Calendar order is also followed much more closely, and Senate leaders and the Committee on Rules have less power than their House counterparts over the calendars. Still another difference is that the Committee of the Whole is not used, except when the Senate considers treaties. Finally, a bill in the Senate gets two readings (as opposed to one in the House) before going to committee, with Senate debate on the third instead of second reading. As in the House, the bill is not normally read to the members in its entirety; reading of the title only is considered a reading

The principal difference between the two houses' floor procedure is in debate rules. Senate closure rules on debate (discussed below) are not strict, there is no time limit on speeches, no procedure for "moving the previous question," and the speaker on the floor need not even make his remarks pertinent to the matter before the chamber. This greater freedom of debate is possible because of the smaller membership of the upper house.

Free Speech and Filibuster

Freedom of speech is a cherished Senate tradition, as a result of which Senators have a notable feeling of independence. The price of this freedom of debate, however, is that Senators holding a minority viewpoint may talk a bill to death, simply by gaining the floor and refusing to yield until the bill's proponents agree to remove it from debate. This tactic of *filibustering* has killed dozens of bills and caused the delay or amending of many more. A filibuster may be used by any Senator or Senators, conservative or liberal, Northern or Southern. And the variety of motives for which it may be used partly explains why the Senate has failed to establish a strong closure rule.

The individual filibuster record was set by Southern conservative Strom Thurmond, who talked for over twenty-four hours against the Civil Rights Act of 1957. Earlier, in 1953, Northern liberal Wayne Morse talked twenty-two hours against the Tideland Oil Bill, seeking to tack an anti-poll-tax rider onto the bill. More commonly, filibusters are by a *group* of Senators, and Southern Senators, in particular, have used it to try to prevent passage of civil rights bills. Their filibuster of the Civil Rights Bill of 1964 was the longest in history—eighty-three days.

Halting a filibuster is difficult. The present closure rule (adopted in 1917) is that one-sixth of the Senators present must first sign a motion for closure and then, after two calendar days, two-thirds of the Senators present must approve the motion.[6] Since 1917 only eight of thirty-nine attempts at closure have suc-

[6] In speaking of majority (or other) votes, it is assumed, unless otherwise stated, that a quorum is present for the vote.

ceeded; in fact, until 1964, the Senate failed every attempt to vote closure against Southern Senators filibustering civil rights bills.[7] Many more times, the majority, seeing the futility of a closure attempt, has simply not tried it at all. The usual effect of the closure rule has been that civil rights bills have required not just a majority vote, but a two-thirds vote in order to overcome Southern filibusters.

Conference Committee Action: Resolving Differences

Before a bill can be sent to the President for signing, it must pass each house in *identical* form. Often, however, it comes out of each house with similar but not identical provisions. If the differences cannot be readily reconciled, the bill must go to a *conference committee* composed of members of each house appointed by the presiding officers to iron out the differences.

The action of conference committees is extremely critical, for nearly all important public bills are referred to them. A committee may alter provisions, add new ones, or even write a wholly new bill on the subject. If the committee cannot reach agreement, either the bill fails or a new committee must be formed to try again at agreement. Usually, however, since at this stage there is considerable pressure to pass the bill, agreement is reached and both houses accept the conference committee's decisions.

The President's Action on a Bill

After a bill is passed in identical form by the two houses, the Speaker of the House and the President of the Senate sign the bill and send it to the President of the United States. He may sign it, thus making it law, or he may *veto* it and return it to Congress, stating his reasons. When the President vetoes, his legislative power is (at least in the negative sense) equal to two-thirds that of Congress, since this is the majority needed to over-

[7] In recent years closure has been successful on debate of the 1964 Civil Rights Bill, 1965 Voting Rights Bill, and the 1968 Open Housing Bill.

249

ride his action—a fact Congressmen keep in mind when legislating.

The President may also *pocket-veto* a bill, neither signing nor vetoing it. In this event, the bill still becomes law ten days after he receives it. However, if he pocket-vetoes a bill delivered to him less than ten days before Congress adjourns, the bill dies.

Speculation about the President's possible action is frequently intense, with interest groups, executive officials, state party leaders, Congressmen, and voters trying to influence his decisions, for his choice may vitally affect vested special interests, his administration, the country in general, and the outcome of future elections.

SEMI-LEGISLATIVE AND NONLEGISLATIVE FUNCTIONS

Besides law making, Congress has several important semi-legislative or nonlegislative activities. Among them are the electoral, constituent, and representative, and the roles of the Senate in treaty making and appointments, which are explained elsewhere in this book. Here we will describe three other functions: investigation, overseeing the executive branch, and impeachment.

Investigating: A Powerful Congressional Strategy

Over a hundred congressional investigations are conducted every session, mostly by standing committees. Usually they are concerned with legislative proposals, inspection of government agencies, inquiries into the problems and conduct of government, and review of treaty negotiations and proposed appointments.

Investigations by the regular standing committees, or their subcommittees, are useful in gathering information and opinions. When used to inquire on administrative action they are also important applications of the checks and balances system. The power to investigate, however, is frequently misused: many inquiries are largely political, and sometimes a committee already has the information it is supposedly seeking and is hoping the investigative drama and fanfare will mobilize public opinion in its favor. They may even threaten the constitutional balance of power. For instance, Senator Joseph McCarthy's confrontation with Secretary of the Army Robert Stevens in 1954 over what McCarthy, as chairman of the Senate Internal Security Subcommittee, charged to be the indifference of General Zwicker (Commanding Officer of Camp Kilmer) to communist infiltration and subversion threatened the President's effective control of the executive branch. However, McCarthy overreached himself and was censured by the Senate.

Inquiries are also conducted by *special investigating committees*,[8] which, though they normally may not introduce bills, have the same powers as standing committees. Both may subpoena witnesses and require them to testify. Both may prosecute witnesses for contempt of Congress if they refuse to answer questions—provided the matter being investigated is reasonably related to the function of Congress and the committee's questions are pertinent.[9]

Legally, committee witnesses are not in jeopardy of life or limb, and so all the safeguards of the judicial process need not be accorded them. The theory is that if such safeguards were available to a witness, he could use them to deny essential information to Congress and the public. However, witnesses do have some protections. Those willing to brave possible public censure may invoke the Fifth Amendment protection against self-incrimination to legalize their refusal to answer questions. Also, the Supreme Court once ruled, in 1957, that the First Amendment limits Congress's power to investigate, and that congressional committees may not expose for the sake of exposure nor attempt to punish individuals (*Watkins* v. *United States*).[10] However, the Court later retreated from this position because of strong op-

[8] The most important special investigating committees are the House Committee on Internal Security (formerly the House Committee on Un-American Activities) and the Senate Internal Security Subcommittee. The Committee on Internal Security is a standing committee, and the Internal Security Subcommittee is a subcommittee of the Senate Judiciary Committee.

[9] Each house may itself determine a witness's guilt and have that witness kept in custody for as long as it is in session. Also, each chamber may certify contempt cases to the appropriate United States attorney for presecution before the courts.

[10] While recognizing that the "power of the Congress to conduct investigations is inherent in the legislative process," the Court warned that the power is not unlimited and that "abuses of the investigative process may imperceptibly lead to abridgement of protected freedoms."

position by a coalition of conservative Congressmen, and it now appears, regardless of its 1957 decision, it will not intervene in congressional investigations even when the goal is simply to expose.

Some congressional investigators, eager for sensational revelations, have so abused the investigative function that they have brought it and even Congress itself into disrepute. Witnesses have been defamed, bullied, and otherwise mistreated, and the behavior of committees has bordered on the totalitarian.

The House has partly corrected such abuses by limiting defamatory testimony to closed sessions, by forbidding one-member subcommittees, by granting witnesses the right to have counsel present, and in other ways restricting committee action in the interest of fairness. Some reformers want further limitations, even suggesting that special investigating committees be abolished altogether and that all investigations be by subcommittees of the regular standing committees. The most common proposal, however, is for stricter procedures: prohibiting one-man hearings, disclosure of both the sources and nature of the charges against witnesses, the right of the accused to confront his accusers, and stricter control of television and radio publicity. Thus far, neither house has enforced such procedures, and until they do, such investigations are likely to remain one of the most controversial aspects of American government.

Overseeing the Administration

Overseeing the executive branch is now a principal function of Congress, largely because of the greater emphasis on government as the provider and protector of individual and social good through its economic and social programs and the increase in the administration's powers to make policy decisions within the framework of the laws.

There are many ways Congress may control the administration. Few of the President's powers, for example, can be exercised without funds—and for this money the President must depend on Congress, which annually reviews his appropriation requests. Congress also determines the basic administrative machinery: it may create agencies, abolish them, strip them of previously granted authority, tie strings to their appropriations, and cut off or reduce their funds. In addition, congressional control extends over executive branch personnel. It takes four major forms: (1) Senate confirmation of appointments, (2) laws governing the civil and military services, (3) informal pressures, and (4) the ultimate weapon—impeachment.

All of this keeps administrators sensitive to congressional thinking and helps to halt the diminution of congressional power. It also helps maintain a balance between the executive and Congress.

Impeachment

Though used infrequently, the authority of Congress to impeach and remove is a potentially significant power. The President, Vice-President, and all civil officers of the United States are subject to this control (Congressmen and military men are not civil officers).

Authority to impeach is vested in the House by the Constitution and the power to try impeachment cases, in the Senate. The grounds for impeachment and removal are "treason, bribery, and other high crimes and misdemeanors." Any member or group in the House may prefer charges. These are referred to a House committee which then reports its findings. If a majority in the House votes to impeach, articles of impeachment are drafted, indicating the grounds for removal. Members of the House then serve as managers to present a case for conviction in the Senate, which becomes a court for this purpose. If the President is tried, the Chief Justice of the U.S. Supreme Court presides. The Senate votes in secret, a two-thirds vote of the members present being required for conviction.

If convicted, the guilty person is removed from office and cannot again hold any position of trust with the government. This is as far as it goes, however, for he cannot be otherwise punished unless he is tried and convicted in a court of law. Since 1787 only twelve officers—nine of them judges—have been impeached by the House, though only four were convicted in the Senate and removed.

By far the most notable impeachment was of President Andrew

Johnson. Although the charges against him were political and he had committed no legal offense, the House voted to impeach him, and only one member less than the two-thirds of the Senators present voted to convict him. It is no doubt fortunate that President Johnson was not convicted: had he been removed from office for political reasons, the Presidency would have been greatly weakened and a precedent would have been set destructive to the principle of separation of powers.

Suggested Additional Reading

Bailey, S. K. *Congress Makes a Law.* 1950.

Bolling, R. *House Out of Order.* 1965.

Clark, J. S. *Congress, the Sapless Branch.* 1964.

Hinckley, B. *Stability and Change in Congress.* 1971.

Huitt, R. K., and R. L. Peabody. *Congress: Two Decades of Analysis.* 1969.

Matthews, D. R. *U.S. Senators and Their World.* 1960.

Polsby, N. W. *Congress and the Presidency.* 1964.

Rieselbach, L. N. (ed.). *The Congressional System.* 1970.

Robinson, J. A. *Congress and Foreign Policy-Making.* 1967.

Schneier, E. V. *Policy Making in American Democracy.* 1968.

Taylor, T. *The Grand Inquest: The Story of Congressional Investigations.* 1955.

White, W. S. *The Citadel: The Story of the U.S. Senate.* 1957.

12 The President: Policy Making

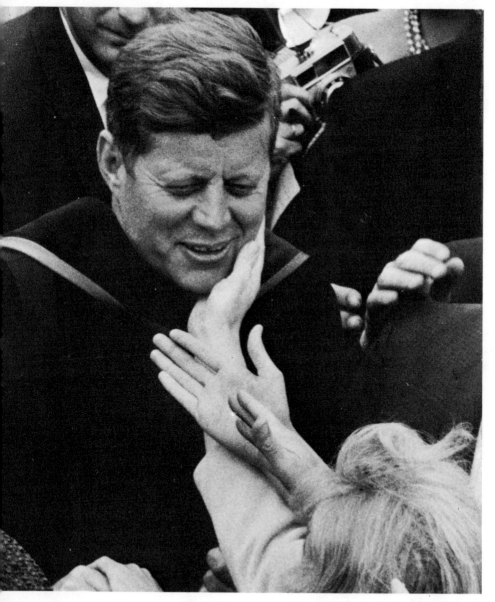

Jon Lewis, Photofind, S.F.

The President is the greatest majority
weapon our democracy has thus far
shaped.

—*Max Lerner*

The presidency—the most distinctive creation of the American
governmental system—is partly the product of the delegates to
the Constitutional Convention of 1787, but much more the product of evolution.

The 1787 delegates established the presidency as a single
executive, elected separately from Congress, and assigned important powers—most (but not all) executive power[1] and some
important legislative and judicial powers. The Convention made
him commander in chief of the army and navy and gave him
authority to make treaties, appoint federal executive and judicial
officers, grant pardons and reprieves, enforce federal laws, recommend legislation to Congress, and veto any bill passed in Congress.

[1] Many of his powers are enumerated in Article II, Sections 2 and 3 of the
Constitution.

PRESIDENTIAL AND PARLIAMENTARY SYSTEMS COMPARED

The American Presidential System

The chief executive is elected for a fixed term. He is also elected independently of, is not politically responsible to, and has separate powers from the legislative branch. He cannot be a member of the legislative branch. He tends to be the central figure in the system.

Chief advantages of the system are that separation of powers between the legislative and executive branches is a protection against tyranny, the voters get to select the nation's chief executive, and it encourages strong executive leadership and stability (because of the four-year term).

Chief disadvantages, critics say, are that it disperses responsibility and encourages deadlock between the executive and legislature, leading to paralysis and political futility.

Although the presidential system is widely copied in Latin America, the parliamentary system is more popular elsewhere.

The British Parliamentary System

Authority is vested in the legislative body and in the cabinet, which is headed by the Prime Minister. In Britain, when voters elect a new House of Commons, the leader of the majority party is automatically the new Prime Minister. Cabinet ministers, selected by him, are largely drawn from Parliament. There is little separation of power between the legislative and executive branches, and the Prime Minister can be toppled at any time if he loses the support of his majority in Commons.

Chief advantages are the ease with which the system produces policy, its clearer accountability to the electorate, and its putting national administration in the hands of tried and tested leaders.

Chief disadvantage is that the checks and balances of the presidential system are lost.

Clearly, most Convention delegates believed the national government needed a strong executive to achieve stability and efficiency. Yet, aware that executive power can be dangerous, they were careful to place checks on him so he would not be too strong. For instance, he was made to share treaty making and the appointing of high officers with the Senate. His vetoes could be overridden by a two-thirds vote in Congress. He was forced to rely on Congress for legislation that would create, organize, and finance the agencies of the executive.

The presidency today, though anchored in provisions of the Constitution, is far different from what it was envisioned in 1787. It is the most powerful office of any democratic government—in fact, the President could well be the key to American survival. His powers and responsibilities are immense. He is the architect of our foreign policy, commander in chief of the most powerful military in history, director of an administrative establishment of 2.9 million civilian employees which yearly expends over $225 billion, chief law enforcement officer, chief legislator, and leader of one of the nation's major political parties. He is also expected to be the chief engineer of economic stability and prosperity. In short, he is the center of national power and attention, the symbol of national unity, aspirations, and security, and often a representative for our society's chief concerns.

HOW THE PRESIDENCY HAS GROWN

The tremendous growth of the presidency since 1787 is largely due to three factors: (1) the personalities and talents of the Presidents, (2) recurrent domestic and foreign crises, and (3) rapidly changing, increasingly complex economic and social conditions.

Although nineteenth-century Presidents—especially Jefferson, Jackson, and Lincoln—advanced the power of the office, its most rapid and sustained growth has been in this century. Not all twentieth-century Presidents have been strong leaders, of course —certainly Taft and Harding were not. Still, in more recent years even President Eisenhower, who preferred sharing power with Congress, realized that the times required vigorous presidential leadership and was compelled to act accordingly. Today, no

President could sit idly by during a world crisis, or with a recession looming, or with our major cities wracked by crises and turmoil. In such troubled times, people tend to turn to the President rather than to relatively unknown legislators as the single commanding leader. They want an authoritative figure to lead—perhaps even to produce miracles—and certainly to give powerful and responsible direction.

Thus, the expansion of presidential power is partly circumstantial. In a crisis he can respond more quickly and effectively than can the two houses and 535 members of Congress. Even more, he *must* act—especially in foreign affairs, where only he has the information and ability to move with coordination, secrecy, and dispatch to protect American interests.

THE PRESIDENT'S LEADERSHIP ROLES

The President's principal job is to lead. It is he, not Congress, who sets the fundamental goals of the political system and who goads and coaxes to get them accomplished. It is on his proposals that Congress spends most of its time, and it is his office that most often impels Congress to take action. It is also often through his urging that the bureaucracy can be changed or can be made to take needed action. And in times of national crisis, it is the President to whom the nation looks for leadership and direction. Leadership, the basic differentiating function of the presidency, is also critical for the health of the political system: it furnishes much of the thrust and vigor needed to accomplish major changes.

To get an idea of the scope and complexity of the President's job, let us consider his many different roles. A word of caution, however: the roles discussed below are segments of a whole, performed concurrently and in practice inseparable. We must view them this way to appreciate the full power of the President.

Chief Administrator

The men who wrote the Constitution intended that the President primarily be the country's chief administrator; in Article II, they provided that "The executive power shall be vested in a President of the United States of America." They further enjoined him to "take Care that the Laws be faithfully executed" and to "nominate, and by and with the Advice and Consent of the Senate, . . . appoint Ambassadors, other public Ministers and Consuls, Judges of the supreme Court, and all other Officers of the United States, whose Appointments are not herein otherwise provided for, and which shall be established by Law." The Philadelphia delegates also gave him the power to "require the Opinion, in writing, of the principal Officer in each of the executive Departments, upon any subject relating to the Duties of their respective Offices."

Powers and Restraints

Even the sweeping grants of executive authority are incomplete, limited, or circumscribed. Although *the* executive power is conferred on the President, the term "executive power" itself is not clearly defined—and Congress, of course, also has executive power. (For instance, it can create administrative machinery, review the executive branch's requests for appropriations, and approve executive appointments.) Moreover, the President obviously cannot execute all laws himself; he must depend on subordinates, to whom he must give considerable latitude because of the complexity of matters with which the laws are concerned and the varied circumstances under which they must be applied. Also, one person could never direct and coordinate all the work of the approximately 1800 executive agencies, even if he gave all his time and energy, and with all the other work he has to do, the President has little enough time to supervise. In addition, many independent agencies—for instance, the Federal Reserve Board, the Interstate Commerce Commission, and the Federal Trade Commission—are largely free of presidential control; and others, because they have a close relationship with powerful Congressmen or pressure groups, may safely ignore his wishes. Finally, the President must share control of the other federal agencies with Congress, which creates and finances them, defines their functions, and frequently details their structure and procedures.

Formal Methods of Control

The President's primary means of formal administrative control is his power to appoint and remove his subordinates. Yet even

261

this power is limited. Ninety percent of the civilian employees in the executive branch are not political appointees but civil servants appointed under the merit system, and most of the others are hired by agency heads. In addition, with some exceptions, the President's key appointments are subject to Senate confirmation. However, it is the quality and tone of his administration, not anything the Senate might do, that establishes the caliber of his appointees: only once since 1925, when Charles Warren was not approved for the post of Attorney General, has the Senate rejected a President's Cabinet appointment, and appointees to ambassadorships are nearly always approved. Most other appointments requiring Senate approval (e.g., judgeships in the lower federal courts, collectors of customs, and United States attorneyships) are handled by the custom of *senatorial courtesy;* that is, before sending the appointee's name to the Senate, the President consults with the senior Senator in his party who represents the state in which the appointee will be assigned. If the President forgets this "courtesy," the Senator may declare the appointment "personally obnoxious" to him, and ask the Senate to withhold confirmation—and it usually will oblige. The net result, therefore, is that Senators in the President's party actually have the power to fill most vacancies in federal posts in their states.

The President does have considerable freedom to promote, demote, or transfer, especially at the top levels of administration. He may also remove executive officers (e.g., heads of departments) at will, but not officials whose functions are partly legislative and partly judicial (e.g., members of independent regulatory agencies),[2] nor civil service employees except in accordance with civil service regulations. A President is reluctant in any event to use his removal power, especially if he appointed the official, since removing him may appear to indicate an error in judgment. The official may also have powerful supporters or a national following, so that his removal might occasion major controversy and political repercussions. Finally, the President may wish to avoid public airing of scandal in his administration.

[2] In 1958, the Supreme Court (*Wiener* v. *United States*) went so far as to rule that the President may not remove these officers unless Congress has especially empowered him to do so.

Other Methods of Control

A more effective way the President may control his administration is superintendence over spending, a very sensitive matter with agency heads. He does this when drafting his budget, which determines how much money agency heads will have for their different programs. After Congress approves the budget, the Office of Management and Budget maintains continual watch over the agencies' expenditures, generally ensuring their cooperation with the President's wishes. The President may also exert influence by reorganizing an agency. He simply submits his proposed reorganization to Congress, and it goes into effect sixty days later unless one of the two houses rejects it.

The President's considerable administrative powers do not match his responsibilities. Accordingly, he must supplement his authority with his powers of persuasion, which consist largely of suggestions, rational arguments, and the atmosphere he sets for his administration. Still, a former aide of President Franklin Roosevelt once wrote:

> Half of a President's suggestions, which theoretically carry the weight of orders, can be safely forgotten by a Cabinet member. And if the President asks about a suggestion a second time, he can be told that it is being investigated. If he asks a third time, a wise Cabinet officer will give him at least part of what he suggests. But only occasionally, except about the most important matters, do Presidents ever get around to asking three times.[3]

Chief of State

As chief of state, the President symbolizes the unity and dignity of the country. In this capacity, he performs many of the ceremonial roles and functions that are performed by the monarchs of Britain, Sweden, and Holland. They rank above their prime ministers, who are the heads of government but not heads of state.

The President is the official host for visiting heads of state, foreign ambassadors, and other dignitaries from abroad. He re-

---

[3] Jonathan Daniels, *Frontier on the Potomac* (New York: Macmillan, 1946), pp. 31–32.

ceives delegations from many groups, decorates war heroes and astronauts, proclaims national holidays, lights the nation's Christmas tree at the White House, and throws the first ball into the field to begin the major league baseball season. Some of these activities may seem trivial, but their significance should not be underestimated. In performing them, the President can enhance his standing as a representative of all of the American people, not simply as the leader of a partisan coalition. Most Presidents are aware that a good performance as chief of state adds to their overall effectiveness and act accordingly.

Chief Legislator

Although the delegates to the Constitutional Convention did not deliberately try to make the President the chief legislator,[4] they assigned him significant legislative powers. The Constitution grants him veto power over bills passed in Congress and requires him "from time to time [to] give to the Congress Information of the State of the Union, and recommend to their Consideration such Measures as he shall judge necessary and expedient." He may also call Congress into special session "on extraordinary Occassions [sic]." Actually, these important powers were intended primarily to check Congress, not to make the President the chief legislator. But over 180 years of national growth, development of a party system, intermittent crises, and the increased complexity and rapid change of our society have made him so.

The so-called message power of the President is very important. This includes the annual *State of the Union message* and the large number of *special presidential messages* sent to Congress during a session. In his State of the Union message, the President can bring his entire program to the attention of the nation. Generally he delivers it to Congress in person, taking full advantage of radio and television exposure. Equally if not more important are his numerous written messages to Congress, which cover many topics and are usually accompanied by drafts of laws he wants passed. Today they comprise the most significant parts of Congress's legislative agenda.

[4] The President's legislative functions were also described in the previous chapter.

The President also has a potent tool in his *veto power,* which he can use to protect himself and the executive branch from congressional invasions and to defeat legislation he considers undesirable. The two houses are seldom able to get up the two-thirds vote necessary to override his veto, and the President can threaten to use the veto at any time during the legislative career of a bill in order to secure alterations he favors. However, one weakness in the veto power is that the President must veto *all,* not just parts, of a bill he opposes. Thus, Congressmen can often avoid vetoes of their pet projects by attaching them as amendments (sometimes called *riders*) to bills the President vitally needs.

The President has some legislative powers delegated to him by Congress, which is incapable of enacting detailed legislation to cover all the complicated, fluctuating situations of modern life. Of necessity Congress must be satisfied with establishing general standards and delegating to the President and his administrators the power to fill in details of the laws—and even, in some cases, to decide when a law should be applied at all. So long as Congress prescribes the general standards, however, this delegation is legal under the Constitution.

Chief of Party

By tradition, the President is head of his national party from the time he is nominated until he leaves office. He thus can select the party's national chairman and control the national committee. His program becomes the party program, and his pronouncements become party policy. He may also influence his party's candidates for office by deciding whether to campaign on their behalf. He is further able to influence some campaign contributions. He cannot, however, control nominations for Congress or for state and local offices, and he cannot exercise party discipline over incumbents. American parties are too decentralized for that.

The relationship between the President and his party is more cooperative than authoritarian, based largely on mutual need. The President needs the party to be elected and to secure the enactment of his program; the party and its candidates need the patronage and other rewards the President may dispense. Moreover, much of the party's success at the polls depends on the success of his programs as well as his popularity.

Still, there is normally a basic conflict between the President and his party, for neither national nor state party interests are identical to those of the White House. As a result, the President generally establishes and depends on his own personal organization within the party. Frequently, it is necessary for him to negotiate with other elements in his own party. Although when dealing with Congress or with the nation at large he may often find it effective to appeal to bipartisanship and play down his own party association, he must perform as expected of a party leader or face serious disaffection within the party.

Commander in Chief

If he wants, the President can always don a uniform and lead the troops in the field during wartime as head of the armed forces, but until the Civil War it was assumed that his powers as commander in chief[5] extended *only* to military matters. President Abraham Lincoln, however, assumed that as commander in chief he was responsible for warring not only against a military enemy but also against *domestic* insurrection and for maintaining public order, and that therefore his power extended to control of *civilian* matters. In the two world wars in this century, Presidents have assumed that the Lincoln Doctrine of warring on the domestic front applies during wars with a foreign enemy. In 1942, President Franklin D. Roosevelt, for instance, asserted that the President has authority under the Constitution and acts of Congress to "take measures necessary to avert a disaster which would interfere with the winning of the war." He specifically warned Congress that he would act to stabilize prices and wages if it did not do so. He also, by executive order, created numerous emergency agencies. He further used this power of executive order, in his capacity as commander in chief, to seize and to operate scores of industries and plants that were struck or threatened by strikes and to determine much of the military strategy of the Allies. He also ordered the detention of 110,000 Japanese-Americans liv-

[5] This role of the President is also discussed in Chapter 18.

266

ing in Western states (but, interestingly, not in Hawaii) into "relocation camps." Justice Murphy called this detention "an unconstitutional resort to racism" (*Ex parte Endo*, 1944). However, the Supreme Court, in a much criticized decision, voted 6–3 to uphold the detention on grounds of military necessity (*Korematsu v. United States*, 1944). The Lincoln Doctrine probably could also be asserted in Cold War conflicts (as in Vietnam), where there is no official congressional declaration of war.

Obviously, the President's role as commander in chief has become more crucial with the advent of tremendously destructive nuclear weapons and the complex new circumstances of international relations. Today, even military decisions—particularly those with extensive political implications—become the responsibility of the President, not of the professional military. For instance, President Truman in Korea and Presidents Johnson and Nixon in Vietnam asserted their responsibility by imposing restrictions on the use of nuclear weapons and by defining the extent of American involvement in the conflicts; and President Kennedy took full command during the United States–Soviet confrontation of the 1962 Cuban nuclear missile crisis. The President's power as commander in chief is mainly undefined, but it is considerable.

Under the Constitution, the President's military powers are shared with Congress to the extent that only it can "raise and support armies" and "provide and maintain a Navy." Not only does Congress provide all funds for the armed services, only it can officially *declare* war—though it has never declared war unilaterally nor refused a President's request for a war declaration. Nor has it refused the requests of recent Presidents for "authorization" to proceed militarily—such as Eisenhower's request in 1955 for action in Formosa and the Pescadores Islands and in 1957 for the Middle East, Kennedy's in 1962 for the Cuban missile crisis, and Johnson's in 1964 for reprisals against North Vietnam—while not legally (under the Constitution) going into war. In fact, however, the President may act *without* a congressional resolution at all—as did President Nixon in 1970 in ordering the U.S. "incursion" into Cambodia—though he usually will seek it for psychological or political reasons. Indeed, despite the constitutional restraints that only Congress can declare war, in actuality the President may deploy American troops anywhere in the world and conduct American foreign relations and undertake military actions in such a manner that war would be inevitable and a congressional declaration unnecessary.

Chief Diplomat

The President's control over foreign policy is given by the Constitution, which assigns him responsibility to negotiate with foreign powers and authority to make commitments on behalf of the United States.[6] The Constitution also empowers him to send and receive ambassadors and to extend diplomatic recognition to (or withhold it from) foreign governments. The 1787 constitutional delegates lavished this power on the President because they realized that secrecy, quick action, and a single voice are often needed in dealing with other countries. There are, however, limits on the President's powers in foreign affairs. For instance, he must depend on Congress for funds to support his policies, many of which are based on the amount of money available for foreign military and economic aid.

Judicial Officer

The Constitution, of course, assigns "the judicial power of the United States" to the federal courts. Nevertheless, the President also has some judicial powers. He appoints all federal judges (including Supreme Court Justices) and the United States attorneys, subject to confirmation by the Senate, which may reject his choices. He can also set aside some decisions of federal courts, as follows: he may *pardon* a person convicted of crime, lighten a sentence by granting a *commutation,* or postpone punishment by granting a *reprieve* so that further investigation may take place. In addition, he (as well as Congress) may grant group pardons or *amnesties,* as President Andrew Johnson gave amnesty to Confederate soldiers, relieving them of the offense of treason against the Union during the Civil War. The President's pardoning

---

[6] The President's role in foreign affairs is also discussed in Chapters 18 and 19.

268

power, however, extends only to federal crimes; he may not pardon anyone convicted for an offense against a state or local government. Nor may the President pardon anyone who has been impeached.

Interdependence of Presidential Roles

All roles of the President are interdependent, and how effectively he performs each role determines his effectiveness with the other roles. Doing well as commander in chief, for example, may complement his performance as chief diplomat, since American military posture and diplomacy are interdependent. But his performance as chief diplomat or chief legislator may conflict with his role as party leader, and his role as chief of state may be at the expense of his role as political leader.

The President's power flows from the immense prestige that resides in his office and from the rewards and sanctions he may use; yet his actual power fluctuates according to how broadly he interprets and effectively exercises his formal powers. Events and popular attitudes also affect the extent of the President's power—in time of war he exercises more power as commander in chief and chief diplomat; at other times, public opinion may impel him to take a less activist posture.

THE VICE-PRESIDENT'S ROLES

Described by John Adams, the first Vice-President of the United States, as "the most insignificant office that ever the invention of man contrived or his imagination conceived," and dormant through most of the nineteenth century, the vice-presidency has acquired special usefulness in the last three decades.

Administrative and Political Roles

Recent Presidents have invited their Vice-Presidents to attend Cabinet meetings and have given them significant executive responsibilities. As Vice-President, Richard Nixon presided over President Eisenhower's Cabinet and the National Security Council during the President's absence. Lyndon Johnson, as Vice-President in the Kennedy administration, was made chairman of interdepartmental committees concerned with the application of civil rights policies in government space and defense contracts; he was also a member of the National Security Council's executive committee.

When Johnson became President, he made Vice-President Hubert Humphrey responsible for promoting Johnson's "Great Society" legislation on Capitol Hill, keeping in touch with farm and urban affairs programs, and maintaining liaison with mayors, governors, and major interest groups. Like other Vice-Presidents, Humphrey assisted the chief executive by taking over some of his ceremonial duties and making good-will tours abroad. Later he gained greater prominence by using his long-standing popularity with liberals to counter the criticism of Senators Robert Kennedy and Eugene McCarthy, who reflected liberal disenchantment with the President's Vietnam war policy and cutbacks in poverty programs; he finally won the Democratic nomination for President.

Vice-President Spiro Agnew was relieved of many ceremonial duties to enable him to concentrate, in President Nixon's words, on "major line responsibilities," such as helping in federal relations with state and local governments and performing specific assignments for the President in international relations. He has had a particularly conspicuous role in Republican Party efforts to reassure its conservative backers and to win more partisans, especially in the South.

Constitutional Role

The Vice-President has only two constitutional functions: to preside over the Senate, and to succeed to the presidency if the President resigns, is removed (that is, impeached and convicted), is disabled, or dies. The first three events have never happened. However, as Table 12-1 shows, on eight occasions Vice-Presidents have assumed the presidency because of the death of the incumbent. Also, at three other times—when Presidents Garfield, Wilson, and Eisenhower were incapacitated—Congress earnestly considered whether presidential duties should be transferred.

Table 12–1
INCOMPLETED TERMS OF PRESIDENTS AND VICE-PRESIDENTS

The following are the Presidents and Vice-Presidents who died in office and their terms of service:

PRESIDENT	TERM	SUCCEEDED BY
William Harrison	Mar. 4, 1841—Apr. 4, 1841	John Tyler
Zachary Taylor	Mar. 5, 1849—July 9, 1850	Millard Fillmore
Abraham Lincoln	Mar. 4, 1865—Apr. 15, 1865	Andrew Johnson
James Garfield	Mar. 4, 1881—Sept. 19, 1881	Chester Arthur
William McKinley	Mar. 4, 1901—Sept. 14, 1901	Theodore Roosevelt
Warren Harding	Mar. 4, 1921—Aug. 2, 1923	Calvin Coolidge
Franklin Roosevelt	Jan. 20, 1945—Apr. 12, 1945	Harry Truman
John Kennedy	Jan. 20, 1961—Nov. 22, 1963	Lyndon Johnson

VICE-PRESIDENT		PRESIDENT
George Clinton	Mar. 4, 1809—Apr. 20, 1812	James Madison
Elbridge Gerry	Mar. 4, 1813—Nov. 23, 1814	James Madison
William King	Mar. 4, 1853—Apr. 18, 1853	Franklin Pierce
Henry Wilson	Mar. 4, 1873—Nov. 22, 1875	Ulysses Grant
Thomas Hendricks	Mar. 4, 1885—Nov. 25, 1885	Grover Cleveland
Garret Hobart	Mar. 4, 1897—Nov. 21, 1899	William McKinley
James Sherman	Mar. 4, 1909—Oct. 30, 1912	William Taft

The Vice-President who resigned his office was John C. Calhoun, who served from March 4, 1829 to December 28, 1832, and resigned to become a United States Senator. The President at the time was Andrew Jackson.

Source: Adapted from *Congressional Quarterly Guide to Current American Government,* Spring 1969.

The person who is, as the phrase goes, "a heartbeat from the presidency" should, one would think, be a man of undoubted presidential stature. But many have not measured up, principally because vice-presidential candidates are generally chosen to "balance" the party's national ticket. Another reason is that the office has been considered a political dead-end, to be avoided by those with promising political futures.

New circumstances, however, have made the office more attractive. The Twenty-second Amendment limiting a President to two full terms has made the vice-presidency a better position from which to run for President. And the Twenty-fifth Amendment, adopted in 1967, might also make the office more desirable. This amendment provides that the Vice-President shall become acting President if the President is incapacitated and unable to discharge the powers and duties of his office, and Congress is so notified in writing either (1) by the President himself or (2) by the Vice-President and a majority of the Cabinet secretaries. Later, if the President notifies Congress in writing that no disability exists, he can resume his office—unless the Vice-President and a majority of the Cabinet still disagree, in which case Congress must decide the matter within twenty-one days. If both houses determine by two-thirds vote that the President is incapacitated, the Vice-President continues as acting President; otherwise the President resumes office. This amendment also recognizes the importance of the vice-presidency by directing the President to appoint a replacement if that office becomes vacant, subject to confirmation by a majority vote of both houses of Congress.

If both the President and Vice-President were to die, the Speaker of the House would act as President. Next in line are the Senate President *Pro Tempore* and Cabinet secretaries in the chronological order in which their departments were created. A Cabinet member would serve only until a Speaker or a President *Pro Tempore* is available to act as President, but the Speaker or President *Pro Tempore* would be acting President until the next regular presidential election.

THE PRESIDENT'S TOP ASSISTANTS

Directly under the President are the heads of the eleven executive departments. These department heads—plus the U. S. Ambassador to the United Nations and whatever other top officials the President may designate—are the *President's Cabinet*. Generally, the President uses the Cabinet to help promote his program and give coherence to his administration, not to formulate policies. Usually the President deals not with the entire Cabinet but with one, two, or three of its members at a time. Because department secretaries are often selected to accommodate political interests—factions of the party; sections of the country; farm, business, or labor groups —and because they are often rivals, the President usually depends much more on members of his personal staff in the *White House Office*, who are selected for their ability and experience and for their loyalty to the President. These staff members bear such titles as: press secretary, foreign policy aide, military aide, legal counsel, political assistant, science advisor, political consultant, legislative assistant, administrative assistant, correspondence secretary, and appointments secretary. They are, as one writer points out,

> ... the President's "lengthened shadow." They help prepare his messages, speeches, and correspondence; arrange his appointments; oversee the inflow and outflow of his communications; analyze and refine the problems confronting him; advance his purposes with legislators, departments, private groups, and party officialdom. Although White House aides cherish their anonymity, they cannot escape importance. Only a few cabinet Secretaries can rival leading White House Staff members in influence and authority. Collectively, the staff tends to be more powerful than all other groups in the executive branch, including the Cabinet and the National Security Council.[7]

THE EXECUTIVE OFFICE OF THE PRESIDENT

Just outside the President's inner circle in the White House Office are a number of agencies which report directly to the President and which together constitute the *Executive Office of the President* (see Figure 12-1). Besides the White House Office it includes the following:[8]

The Office of Management and Budget. This agency assists the President with his budget. It studies each federal agency's budget estimates, holds consultations and hearings with the agency, and finally formulates the budget. The budget must, of course, be in keeping with the President's preferences and then be approved by Congress. The Office of Management and Budget also performs an important service for the President by seeing that legislative proposals from executive agencies conform with his policies. In addition, it recommends improvements in organization and management and coordinates statistical services. In short, by working at

[7] Louis W. Koenig, *The Chief Executive* (New York: Harcourt Brace Jovanovich, 1968), p. 159.
[8] The *United States Government Organization Manual*, revised annually, contains a description of the organization and functions of these and other bodies in the federal government.

273

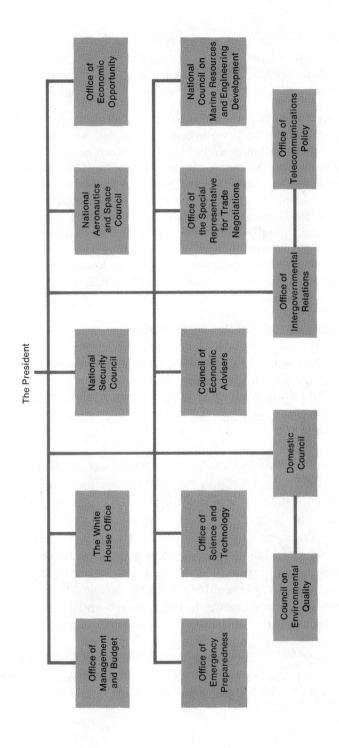

Figure 12-1. Executive Office of the President. (Source: *U.S. Government Organization Manual, 1970–1971.*)

the very heart of the governmental process, it helps the President control administrators who could frustrate his programs.

The Council of Economic Advisers. This agency consists of three economists who help prepare the President's annual economic report to Congress, study trends, and advise the President on economic policies.

The Domestic Council. Established in 1970, this is a Cabinet-level forum which is chaired by the President and includes the Vice-President, most Cabinet members, and other agency heads the President designates. The council advises the President on pressing domestic issues, recommends policy choices to him, and maintains a continuous review of the policies involved in ongoing programs.

The National Security Council. Composed of the President, the Vice-President, the secretaries of State and Defense, and the Director of Emergency Preparedness, the NSC has the momentous task of bringing together all important military and political factors in planning for national security, and advising the President "with respect to the integration of domestic, foreign, and military policies relating to national security."[9]

The Office of Emergency Preparedness. This office is primarily responsible for civilian mobilization and defense.

The Office of Economic Opportunity. OEO coordinates and supplements a number of antipoverty programs, among them *VISTA*, the Volunteers In Service To America, the domestic equivalent of the Peace Corps.

Council on Environmental Quality. Created in 1969, the council recommends to the President national policies to promote environmental quality, and helps him prepare the annual Environmental Quality Report to Congress.

The Office of Intergovernmental Relations. The purpose of this

[9] The NSC and its intelligence agency, the Central Intelligence Agency, are discussed in Chapter 18.

agency is to strengthen federal, state, and local relations. The OIR is headed by the Vice-President, who thus became the chief liaison between the federal government and state and local governments on such matters as federal aid and federal integration programs.

The National Aeronautics and Space Council. This agency helps the President develop programs in aeronautics and space, for example, by developing, testing, and operating aeronautical and space vehicles.

The Office of Science and Technology. This office advises the President on how science and technology can be used to further national security and the general welfare. As a link between the President and the scientific community, it symbolizes the new importance of science in the formulation of national policies.

The Office of Special Representative for Trade Negotiations. This agency assists the President by participating in trade negotiations with other countries and administers the U.S. trade agreements program (e.g., the General Agreement on Tariffs and Trade under which numerous tariffs between fifty-three nations were reduced or eliminated).

The National Council on Marine Resources and Engineering Development. Created in 1966, this office advises the President on how marine science and technology can be used to help the national interest and general welfare.

Office of Telecommunications Policy. Established in 1970, this office coordinates the telecommunications activities of the federal government.

Suggested Additional Reading

Bailey, T. A. *Presidential Greatness: The Image and the Man From George Washington to the Present.* 1968.

Feerick, J. D. *From Failing Hands: The Story of Presidential Succession.* 1965.

Hargrove, E. D. *Presidential Leadership.* 1966.

Hughes, E. J. *The Ordeal of Power: A Political Memoir of the Eisenhower Years.* 1963.

Kallenbach, J. E. *The American Chief Executive: The Presidency and the Governorship.* 1966.

Koenig, L. W. *The Chief Executive.* 1968.

Neustadt, R. E. *Presidential Power: The Politics of Leadership.* 1960.

Rossiter, C. *The American Presidency.* 1960.

Schlesinger, A. M., Jr. (ed.). *A History of American Presidential Elections.* 4 vols. 1970.

Sorenson, T. C. *Kennedy.* 1965.

13 The Federal Bureaucracy

Stan Wayman, *Life* Magazine, ©Time Inc.

Power [in American government] is nowhere concentrated; it is rather deliberately and of set policy scattered amongst
many small chiefs. These petty barons,
some of them not a little powerful, but
none of them within reach of the full powers of rule, may at will exercise an almost
despotic sway within their own shires. . . .

—*Woodrow Wilson*

Like the ideal bureaucracies of corporations, labor unions, and
educational institutions, a model government bureaucracy would
be a big organization having: (1) a hierarchical structure; (2)
well-defined division of labor; (3) uniform, formal regulations
governing operations; (4) rational, impersonal officials; and (5)
merit employment and promotion to ensure efficiency.

Naturally, government bureaucracy falls somewhat short of this.
As in all bureaucracies, informal relationships and rules develop,
which can impede (though they may assist) the organization's
effectiveness. Some displacement also occurs; the organization's
original goal is replaced by the goal of following regulations and
rules. Still, government bureaucracies are not quite as incompetent, uncreative, and useless as we are sometimes led to believe.

Nearly all upper-level people in the bureaucracy are college
graduates, about half with advanced degrees. If many come from

perhaps rather humble backgrounds, a disproportionate number are from high-income and professional families. Moreover, contrary to popular ideas, these career bureaucrats not only climb to the top more quickly than their counterparts in business, but usually serve in more organizations on the way up. The idea that the bureaucrat is a stolid, narrow, ossified person simply is not true. In any case, such bureaucracies are inevitable, for administering according to established bureaucratic precepts is more efficient than any other way.

The primary purpose of bureaucracy is to *apply rules*—that is, the general rules made by Congress and the President—to particular circumstances and individuals. Inevitably this process demands discretion and making decisions which allot advantages and disadvantages; hence, the bureaucracy clearly participates in making policy.

The bureaucracy also has three other functions: it *represents interests* when its agencies and officials act as spokesmen for special interests. It *initiates rules* when it recommends policies to Congress and the President and when it makes general rules as authorized by Congress. Finally, it *interprets rules* when its agencies try cases to decide if regulations or laws have been infringed.

MAIN AGENCIES OF ADMINISTRATION

As Figure 13-1 shows, the federal bureaucracy (unlike Congress, the presidency, and the courts) is not a united or integrated system. Each sector has a separate sphere of responsibility, and generally the sectors operate independently of each other. Thus, we must for the most part discuss them separately as the executive departments, government corporations, independent regulatory agencies, and independent agencies.

Executive Departments

The executive departments comprise most of the federal bureaucracy. By nearly any criterion, they are the most significant administrative organs: they have more personnel, spend

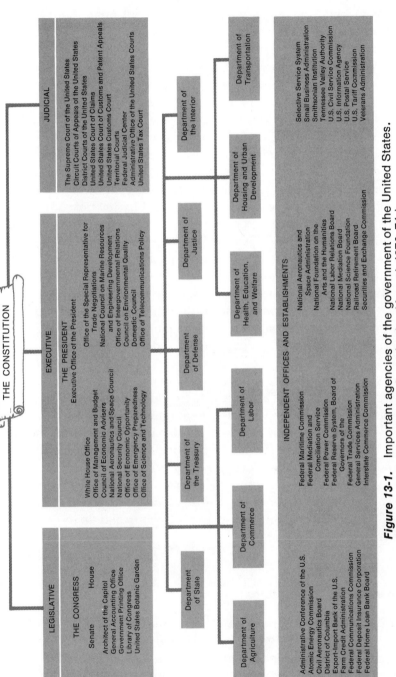

Figure 13-1. Important agencies of the government of the United States. (Source: *U.S. Government Organization Manual, 1970–71.*)

more money, and apply more laws than all other bureaucratic sectors combined. They also provide most of the services and enforce most of the rules of the political system.

The executive departments differ in size and in certain other respects, but they have much in common. Department heads (called *secretaries*, except for the Attorney General, who heads the Justice Department) are members of the President's Cabinet and report directly to him. All are paid the same: $60,000 a year. Most departments also have at least one undersecretary or deputy secretary to take part of the secretary's administrative load, and several assistant secretaries responsible for certain areas (e.g., a geographic region) or functions (e.g., public relations). Department heads also have a personal staff to assist them, much as the President does.

Currently there are eleven departments (in the order of their creation): State; Defense (renamed from the War Department in 1949); Treasury; Justice; Interior (originally Home); Agriculture; Commerce; Labor; Health, Education, and Welfare; Housing and Urban Development; and Transportation. (In 1970 the Post Office Department became an independent agency called the U.S. Postal Service.) Departments are divided into subdivisions bearing names such as bureaus, divisions, branches, sections, and units. Theoretically, similar functions and clientele services should be grouped for greater efficiency into a relatively few departments. However, several departments (but principally the Department of Health, Education, and Welfare) perform functions not related to their primary purposes, and many activities are scattered among two or more departments (e.g., the Bureau of Reclamation, the Corps of Army Engineers, and the Department of Agriculture construct dams and in other ways develop water resources).

Government Corporations

Government corporations have been used since 1791, when Congress established a Bank of the United States, but this kind of organization has become particularly prominent in the twentieth century; there are now more than eighty of them. Such corpora-

THE NIXON REORGANIZATION AND REVENUE-SHARING PLAN OF 1971

George Washington administered nine federal programs. No one knows exactly how many President Nixon administers, but there are over 1400 grant-in-aid programs alone. Since the early 1930s, government has become such a welter of narrow and overlapping programs that they cannot efficiently serve the public. To remedy this, President Nixon made two proposals—reorganization of federal agencies, and revenue sharing.

Reorganization of the Federal Bureaucracy

This proposal would reduce the present eleven Cabinet departments to eight. The departments of State, Treasury, Defense, and Justice would remain intact. The other seven would be consolidated into four:

Department of Natural Resources—land, energy, mineral, water, and marine resources, and recreation.

Department of Human Resources—health services, education, manpower, income maintenance and security, and social and rehabilitation services.

Department of Economic Development—food and commodities, labor relations and standards, domestic and international commerce, science and technology, and economic statistics.

Department of Community Development—metropolitan and community development, metropolitan renewal, and transportation.

Revenue Sharing

This plan would provide $16 billion of general-purpose grants to states and cities by adding $6 billion of new funds to $10 billion which would be diverted from existing federal programs. President Nixon proposed revenue sharing to give Americans "a new chance to . . . participate in government," and to give states and localities "more money and less interference." To increase popular participation, the plan would shift power from Washington bureaucrats to politically accountable local officials and transfer federal authority from senior bureaucrats to field officials.

tions are designed to provide a businesslike environment in which to perform their functions, and they are also given somewhat greater latitude in their fiscal arrangements. Although they submit annual budgets to the Office of Management and Budget, the corporate budget should be (in the words of the Government Corporations Act of 1945) a "business-type budget, or plan of operations, with due allowance given to the need of flexibility." Usually they may borrow money and use revenues gained through sales or loan payments. They may be set up for such purposes as to manufacture and distribute electric power (Tennessee Valley Authority), buy farm surpluses (Commodity Credit Corporation), make direct and indirect loans to farmers (Federal Land Banks and Federal Intermediate Credit Banks), insure bank deposits (Federal Deposit Insurance Corporation), and construct and manage navigation facilities (St. Lawrence Seaway Development Corporation). Most government corporations are attached to a federal department or agency and have varying degrees of independence; though a few, such as the Tennessee Valley Authority, are independent in fact as well as in name. The TVA Board of Directors is appointed by the President and reports directly to him.

Independent Regulatory Agencies

A product of the past eight decades, independent regulatory agencies are truly independent and are modeled after the Interstate Commerce Commission, which Congress created in 1887. The ICC was made relatively free of presidential influence so that it could freely exercise its quasi-legislative, quasi-judicial functions of setting rates, making rules, and judging whether these had been violated.

A regulatory commission has from five to eleven members with overlapping terms. Although members are appointed by the President, the membership is bipartisan and the President's power to remove commissioners is limited. Supposedly these agencies were established so as to be outside direct political control so they could perform their generally technical functions without interference; even so, they must decide many political questions not related to technical matters. Some observers argue, therefore, that regulatory commissions are a questionable institution in a democratic political system. However, the commissions are located in the executive branch and thus do not entirely escape presidential influence. They are also somewhat influenced by Congress and the enterprises they are supposed to regulate. Whatever their merits, independent regulatory agencies have gained general acceptance and promise to be permanent fixtures within the bureaucracy.

Besides the ICC, other important regulatory agencies are: the Federal Trade Commission, the Securities and Exchange Commission, the National Labor Relations Board, the Civil Aeronautics Board, the Federal Communications Commission, the Federal Power Commission, the Federal Maritime Commission, and the Federal Reserve System. All these agencies were created because of public demand for more government services, the need for increased government regulation of private enterprises, the lack of time for and expertise in these matters by Congressmen, and a need for nonpolitical direction.

Independent Agencies

Independent agencies are not located within the eleven executive departments, although actually, in structure and function, they resemble the executive departments more than they do the independent regulatory agencies. Generally speaking, all agencies that are not regulatory commissions or government corporations and that are not within an executive department (such as Interior or State) are independent agencies. Many, however, are no more independent than are the executive departments. Among the more important independent agencies are: the Atomic Energy Commission, the Tariff Commission, the Civil Service Commission, the Veterans Administration, the National Aeronautics and Space Administration, the United States Information Agency, the General Services Administration, and the Selective Service System.

A major difference between the executive departments and the independent agencies is that the agencies are usually more specialized than the departments. Also, many of the independent agencies were created to avoid interference from the existing departments. For instance, various foreign aid and information agencies were given separate status to guarantee against control by the State Department (which is not entirely trusted by some Congressmen and interest groups as a defender of American interests). Also, independent agencies (e.g., the Office of Economic Opportunity and the Peace Corps) were created to pioneer new and imaginative programs with new personnel, hiring, and management procedures.

THE CIVIL SERVICE

The federal government, by far the largest employer in the United States, employs more than 6 million persons full time in civilian and military jobs covering practically all the same occupations found in nongovernment life (see examples in Table 13-1). About half are in the "civil service," a term which means all civilian government employees except elected officials, high-ranking policy-making officers appointed by elected officials, and judges. About 8 percent of these are stationed outside the United States, another 10 percent serve in Washington, D.C. The rest are scattered throughout the United States—as many are located in California, for instance, as in the nation's Capitol. As Figure 13-2 shows, 43 percent of the civil service personnel serve in the Defense Department and about 24 percent are in the U.S. Postal Service.

For the first century of our nation's existence, Presidents made their appointments virtually without legal limitation, but generally staffed on the basis of competence. However, with the development of the party system, and especially during and after the Jackson administration, Presidents increasingly made appointments with a view to strengthening their partisan positions.

The case for the so-called "spoils system" was strong in Jackson's time. Government work was simple and the rotation-in-office principle, the basis of the system, brought a representative quality to government service which before had been largely absent. But the broad practice of the spoils system in the mid-1800s created widespread bribery, embezzlement, and incompetence, and cost the President and other officials time and decorum as office seekers contested for jobs. Finally, following the assassination of

Table 13–1
BEGINNING SALARIES, U.S. GOVERNMENT AND
INDUSTRY COMPARED, JULY 1969

U.S. CIVIL SERVICE GRADE	POSITION	PAY	PAY FOR COMPARABLE JOB IN INDUSTRY
18	Top career official	$33,495	—
17	Engineer	28,976	$23,280
16	Lawyer	25,044	28,841
15	Chief chemist	21,589	25,416
14	Chief accountant	18,531	19,046
13	Personnel director	15,812	16,005
12	Accountant, experienced	13,389	13,531
11	Buyer	11,233	12,431
10	Engineering technician, experienced	10,252	9,788
9	Secretary, experienced	9,320	7,251
8	Accountant, beginning	8,449	7,451
7	Engineer, beginning	7,639	9,023
6	Secretary, beginning	6,882	5,563
5	Junior draftsman	6,176	6,110
4	General stenographer	5,522	4,861
3	Typist, experienced	4,917	4,890
2	Keypunch operator, beginning	4,360	4,566
1	File clerk, beginning	3,889	3,674

Source: Adapted from U.S. Department of Labor figures.

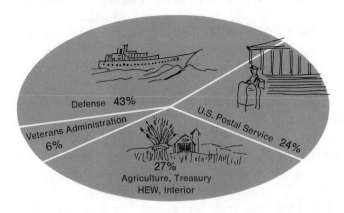

Figure 13-2. Percentage distribution of federal civilian employment by selected agencies. (Source: United States Civil Service Commission, 1969.)

287

President James Garfield in 1881 by a disappointed office seeker, Congress overturned the spoils system and passed a merit system law, the 1883 *Pendleton Act*. This act, and subsequent merit system legislation, was based on three principles: (1) competitive examination for entry into the civil service, (2) relative job security for civil servants, and (3) political neutrality of the public service.

Persons in the bureaucracy with career positions get their jobs initially by achieving a high grade on a competitive examination and are later promoted on the basis of merit evaluations by their supervisors. Such civil service people are secure from arbitrary dismissal, although they may be fired for cause (e.g., incompetence or taking a bribe). When the Pendleton Act was passed, only about 10 percent of the employees in the executive branch were under the merit system. Now about 90 percent are covered, either under the merit system administered by the Civil Service Commission or under the different merit systems of the various executive agencies.

The Civil Service Commission supervises the recruiting and examination of applicants and makes civil service rules. It is composed of three members (only two from the same political party) appointed by the President with Senate confirmation for six-year terms.

For lower-level positions, the commission uses written and oral examinations to screen applicants. For higher positions, it uses oral examinations and appraises the candidate's education, experience, and other personal characteristics. The names of applicants who pass (military veterans are given extra points and certain preferences) are entered on a civil service register which is circulated to government agency heads, who may select from the list. The agency head may fire an employee if doing so will "promote the efficiency" of his department, although the employee must have written notice and be given a public hearing. The agency head may also take disciplinary action (e.g., reprimands, loss of seniority, suspension, or demotion) short of removal.

Civil service people in top career positions are significant in formulating government policy. Being highly educated and experienced in their particular areas, they can give the appointed officials above them the information and insights they need to make policy decisions.

APPOINTED EXECUTIVES

If top career bureaucrats have considerable discretion and independence, their superiors, politically appointed bureaucrats (e.g., department secretaries and sub-Cabinet departmental officials, agency heads, and chiefs of bureaus) have even more, since they set general guidelines and can contravene their subordinates' decisions. In fact, the main job of these appointed bureaucrats is to make sure that the President is not only *formal* head but *actual* head of the federal bureaucracy. Because they are appointed by (and removable by) the President, they presumably share his goals and can thus help bring about coordination within the bureaucracy and bring public influence to bear on it. More than 500 of these top positions are filled by presidential appointees, who in turn appoint another 700; all are exempt from the civil service system.

Suggested Additional Reading

Cary, W. L. *Politics and the Regulatory Agencies.* 1967.

Daniels, J. *Frontiers on the Potomac.* 1946.

Downs, A. *Inside Bureaucracy.* 1967.

Mosher, F. C. *Democracy and the Public Service.* 1968.

Reagan, M. D. *The Administration of Public Policy.* 1969.

Redford, E. *Democracy in the Administrative State.* 1969.

Tullock, G. *The Politics of Bureaucracy.* 1965.

14 The Judiciary: Organization and Policy Making

Michelle Vignes, Photofind, S. F.

The power vested in the American courts of justice of pronouncing a statute to be unconstitutional forms one of the most powerful barriers that have ever been devised against the tyranny of political assemblies.

— *Alexis de Tocqueville*

The courts are major participants in policy making; like the President, Congress, and the executive agencies, they proclaim rules. It is easy to lose sight of this policy-making role, since court procedures and traditions *appear* to be nonpolitical.

JUDICIAL POLICY MAKING

In form, most court decisions simply determine the respective obligations and rights of parties to a dispute. However, these decisions often become precedents for deciding similar cases. Thus, a series of court decisions in a particular area may produce general policies to which everyone is expected to conform.

Although judges in other countries are also involved in policy making, American judges are much more so. The reason for this is that our judges not only interpret the law of torts, contracts, and crimes, but also interpret political law—the Constitution.

Interpreting the Constitution

Much of the prestige of American courts derives from their power of *judicial review*. This is particularly true of the final arbiter, the United States Supreme Court, which (like lower courts) may declare acts of Congress, the President, or the states unconstitutional.

Did the Constitution provide that the Supreme Court exercise this power? Certainly it did not specifically authorize the Court to judge the constitutionality of congressional and presidential acts. But it left no doubt that the Court had the power to review *state acts,* and the first Congress recognized this in the Judiciary Act of 1789. This power to review state acts is, in fact, imperative. As the eminent Supreme Court Justice Oliver Wendell Holmes noted, well over half a century ago, the Union would not come to an end if the Court were deprived of its power to nullify laws of Congress, but it *would* be imperiled if it lost its authority to invalidate state legislation.

In 1803, Chief Justice John Marshall successfully asserted, in the famous case of *Marbury* v. *Madison,* that the Court also had the power to declare acts of Congress unconstitutional. The case developed when outgoing President John Adams, a Federalist, appointed Marbury a justice of the peace for the District of Columbia. The appointment was signed and sealed shortly before Adams left office in 1801, but the commission was not delivered by the Federalist Secretary of State.[1] When President Thomas Jefferson, a Republican, took office, he instructed his Secretary of State, Madison, not to deliver Marbury's commission. Marbury then filed a petition for mandamus with the Supreme Court to require Madison to deliver it. In refusing delivery, the Republicans charged that the Federalists, defeated in the election of 1800, were attempting to retreat to the judiciary, from which to plague the new administration.

Marshall's thinking in this case was masterful. He realized that

[1] The Federalist Secretary of State, in fact, was none other than John Marshall himself, who earlier had been appointed and confirmed Chief Justice, and who held both offices at once for more than a month.

if the Court issued the writ, Madison and Jefferson would refuse to obey it, and the Court would have no way of compelling them. If, on the other hand, the Court refused relief to Marbury, it would be an admission of its weakness in controlling the executive. Either way the Court and the Federalists would have been humiliated.

Therefore, Marshall ruled that the Judiciary Act of 1789—which gave the Court authority to issue writs of mandamus—was void, because it added to the Court's original jurisdiction, an act not permitted by the Constitution.[2] With the Court declining to issue the writ, Madison and Jefferson had no opportunity to defy a court order. The writ was refused not because the Court lacked power to compel executive officers, but because the Court was exercising the much greater power of declaring an act of Congress unconstitutional.

Marshall's argument involved three basic assertions: (1) the Constitution is the supreme law of the land; (2) the powers of the branches of government are limited by it and are subordinate to it; and (3) the judges have sworn to enforce the Constitution, and must therefore refuse to enforce any legislative act that conflicts with it.

Although general acceptance of judicial review did not come easily, it has now become an established principle of American government. Why have the American people accepted this doctrine? One reason is that Supreme Court decisions have satisfied the preferences of enough people enough of the time: the Court has kept its constitutional doctrines safely within the limits of public tolerance. Furthermore, in our political culture, judges and courts have been able to sustain the image of being dispassionate arbiters of the law, while elected legislators and executives seem to be wallowing in politics. When the judges base their decision upon the Constitution—considered especially inviolate in the public mind—and couch it in legal terms, the public generally accepts it. The public view of judges and courts may not square with reality, but it is the myth that counts.

The Supreme Court uses its power of judicial review quite

---

[2] The Judiciary Act of 1789 had authorized the Supreme Court to issue a writ of mandamus in original jurisdiction. Marshall declared that Article III, Section 2 of the Constitution permitted the Court to issue the writ only when exercising appellate jurisdiction.

sparingly. Between 1937 and 1971 it declared only twenty-four federal laws unconstitutional; most were comparatively minor laws. However, several Court decisions on the constitutionality of state and local laws have been highly significant. Outstanding examples are the 1954 school desegregation case (*Brown* v. *Board of Education*), a number of cases in the 1960s requiring apportionment of the state legislative and House of Representatives districts on a strict population basis,[3] and the 1966 decision (*Miranda* v. *Arizona*) specifying rights of suspects in police interrogations.

Interpreting Statutes

Because the Supreme Court's decisions interpreting the Constitution are so publicized, its principal role in interpreting federal statutes is sometimes overlooked. An act of Congress is often ambiguously worded. Sponsors of legislative proposals often find that spelling out precisely what they intend will cost them votes needed for passage, but even when great care is taken to assure clarity, legislation may still be ambiguous and inexact. Thus, the Court must formulate policy by making clear in its decisions that which Congress could not or would not make clear.

OUR TWO COURT SYSTEMS

There are two distinct court systems (see Figure 14-1)—state and federal—the result of the creation, in 1789, of federal courts to operate along with the already existing state courts. Neither system is an appendage of or subordinate to the other, but judges in the state courts are limited in that they must observe the Constitution and federal laws and treaties, even if they conflict with their state constitution or laws. Their decisions denying claims based on the federal Constitution, laws, or treaties may also be overturned by the U.S. Supreme Court. Moreover, they are bound by federal court interpretations of state laws whose constitutionality is questioned. Nevertheless, state courts hear the great preponderance of criminal cases and civil disputes, and de-

---

[3] *Baker* v. *Carr* (1962), *Wesbury* v. *Sanders* (1964), and *Reynolds* v. *Sims* (1964).

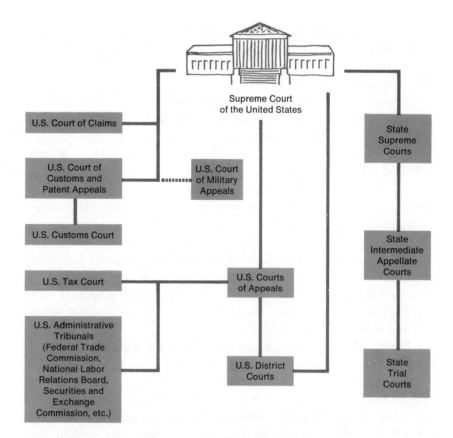

Figure 14-1. Organization of our two court systems.

cide nearly all of them with as much finality as if there were no federal courts.

OUR HIERARCHY OF LAWS

Article VI of the Constitution, the "supremacy clause," mandates a hierarchy of laws for the country. The United States Constitution is the highest law, next are treaties and laws of Congress, and next are federal administrative ordinances.[4] Below this are

[4] Authority for administrative ordinances (orders and directives) is derived from federal statutes, or the President, who may act in certain areas in the absence of federal legislation.

the state constitutions, then other state laws and executive orders, then administrative rulings and ordinances of local governments. State and local law is not inferior to federal law, but if they conflict, state and local law must give way.

In the states, common law and equity, as well as statute law, are applied in the courts. *Common law* is a system of judge-made law brought to this country from England and modified by decisions of American judges. It is based on the principle of *stare decisis*, which means that as far as possible a case is decided on the basis of earlier similar cases. Until about the turn of the century it was much more important than statute law. Even today, though largely superseded by state statutes, the spirit of this ancient law is pervasive in legislative halls and in courthouses.

Although there is no federal common law, federal judges do apply the rule of *stare decisis* where applicable and also state law —either statute or common law—where it pertains. A federal judge may apply common law, for instance, in a case where a citizen of one state is suing a citizen of another.

Equity developed with common law and supplements it. Its purpose is to provide substantial justice in cases where the strict application of common law would result in injustice or hardship. An example would be a court forbidding certain actions (e.g., for a union to go on strike) that would cause irreparable damage. Another example would be a court order requiring specific performance (e.g., that a person fulfill a contract). In statute law or common law, on the other hand, the typical remedy is money damages, but they are awarded only *after* the hurt has been done and the injured party can show what he suffered.

THE JURISDICTION OF FEDERAL COURTS

Federal courts have jurisdiction only over those types of cases specified in Article III of the Constitution and those conferred by Congress. All other cases are considered by state courts, which also share most of the jurisdiction Congress has conferred on the federal courts.

Unlike some state courts, federal courts do not render advisory opinions upon questions of law when requested by the executive or the legislature; they give opinions only in connection with legal

TOTAL JURISDICTION OF FEDERAL COURTS

Federal Questions

1. Cases arising under the Constitution
2. Cases involving federal laws
3. Cases involving treaties of the United States
4. Admiralty and maritime cases

Status of the Parties

1. Cases affecting ambassadors and other public ministers and consuls
2. Controversies to which the United States is a party
3. Controversies between two or more states
4. Controversies between citizens of different states (if the amount involved exceeds $10,000)
5. Controversies between citizens of the same state claiming lands under grants of different states
6. Controversies between a state (or its citizens) and foreign states or their citizens

EXCLUSIVE JURISDICTION OF FEDERAL COURTS

1. Cases in which the United States is a party
2. Cases to which a state is a party*
3. Cases against a representative of a foreign government
4. Crimes against the United States
5. Admiralty, maritime, bankruptcy, copyright, and patent cases

*Excepted is any suit against an American state by citizens of another state, or citizens or subjects or any foreign state. Also excepted are actions between a state and one of its citizens.

proceedings. Nor do federal or state courts initiate action; they wait until matters are brought to them.

THE STRUCTURE OF FEDERAL COURTS

Article III of the Constitution specifies that "The judicial power of the United States shall be vested in one Supreme Court, and in such inferior courts as the Congress may from time to time ordain and establish." Thus, although the Constitution provided specifically for a Supreme Court, it left it to Congress to decide the number, types, and jurisdictions of lower federal courts. Over the years, Congress has created many tribunals—district courts, courts of appeals, the Court of Claims, the Customs Court, the Court of Customs and Patent Appeals, and the United States Tax Court. All of these were created under Article III; thus, the independence of their judges is protected by the Constitution's provisions that they serve during good behavior and that their salary not be diminished while they are in office.[5]

Cases appealed from high state courts do not start at the bottom of the federal court ladder, but instead go directly to the United States Supreme Court; and all appeals from other federal courts or administrative tribunals go there or to the United States courts of appeals.

DISTRICT COURTS

The district courts constitute the lowest level of regular federal courts. Each state has at least one district. Some districts may have more than twenty judges, depending on the volume of litigation. In 1971 there were eighty-eight district courts in the fifty states, plus one in the District of Columbia and one in Puerto Rico.

Court is held at regular times in different cities within the district. Usually one judge sits on a case, but three may preside in some types of cases. Judges are appointed by the President with Senate confirmation.

Each district also has a federal district attorney who, under the direction of the Justice Department (see Figure 14-2), serves as court counsel and conducts criminal prosecutions. District courts also have federal marshals (also under the Justice Department), who execute court orders and serve papers; commissioners, who hold preliminary hearings in criminal cases; referees in bankruptcy; probation officers; and court reporters.

[5] However, Congress can show its displeasure by refusing to increase their salaries. It did this to the Supreme Court Justices in 1964 and 1965.

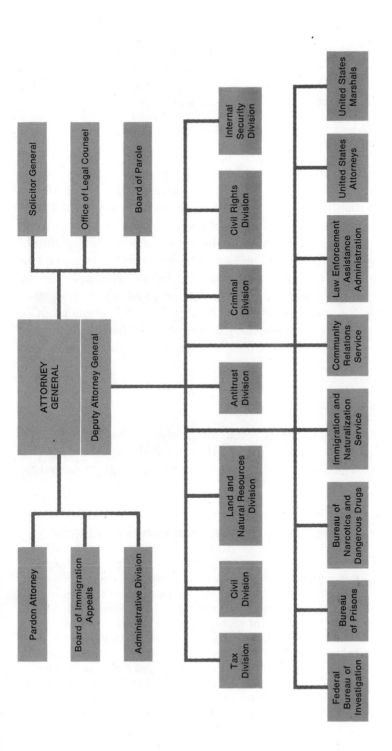

Figure 14-2. Department of Justice. (Source: *U.S. Government Organization Manual, 1970–1971.*)

District courts have *original jurisdiction* over both criminal and civil cases. They handle a great volume of business—more than 150,000 cases a year, about two-thirds of which are bankruptcy cases. They never hear cases on appeal.

Civil Procedure

Civil cases involve two or more private persons and proceedings to enforce a private right (e.g., a property right) or to obtain compensation for its violation. They are to be distinguished from criminal cases, which involve offenses against the law of the land. Legal action is started when one person (the plaintiff) sues another (the defendant) to get him to fulfill a contract or to get money from him for an alleged injury. The case may be heard by a judge alone or by a judge and jury. The parties must abide by the court's decision or risk being held in contempt of court and liable to a fine or jail sentence. Either an individual or the federal government may be a party—plaintiff or defendant —to a civil suit.

Criminal Procedure

In criminal cases, the government is always the injured party, and thus is the one which initiates proceedings. A person suspected of violating a federal criminal law is usually arrested by

---

THE CRISIS OF AMERICAN CRIMINAL JUSTICE

In 1971, according to the FBI, "serious crimes" (everything from car theft to murder) climbed past 5 million. However, less than half the crimes committed are ever reported. Recent Supreme Court decisions have also made the quality of criminal justice an inflamed issue; so have jail riots, the Chicago Seven and Black Panther trials (which turned courtrooms into arenas), and the arrests of civil rights and anti-war protestors, draft resisters, and pot users (now every second case on the Los Angeles criminal court docket), which made the middle class aware of a system of ramshackle justice the poor had long known.

The Most Difficult Areas

The Courts. The trial courts are in desperate disrepair, at every level mired in delay—chiefly because of the upsurge in crime (up 148 percent in the past decade), the increase in victimless offenses (drunkenness, homosexuality, marijuana possession) and the Supreme Court's broadening of defendants' rights (guaranteeing lawyers to the indigent and permitting more pretrial motions, postponements, and post-conviction appeals). Big-city courts generally have several times more cases than they could manage if they went to trial. As a result, most convictions in these courts are negotiated between judge, prosecutor, defense attorney, and defendant. In New York City only one arrest in thousands ends in trial. Sometimes, because of the long wait before a case comes to trial, an innocent man will plead guilty simply to get out of jail. Often, the guilty negotiate light sentences by pleading guilty to a lesser crime than the one they committed.

The Jails and Prisons. Of the 160,000 people in American jails, about half are not convicted offenders, but accused persons—mostly too poor to make bail—awaiting trial. Nevertheless, the accused and the convicted usually are not separated behind the jail walls. Jails usually lack educational and recreational facilities, and crime within them has become increasingly common. The prisons are often antiquated, overcrowded, and inadequately staffed. For every 4400 prisoners, there is only one full-time psychiatrist or psychologist. The average prison guard is paid only $6000 a year. Not surprisingly, there is very little rehabilitation: 85 percent of all crimes are committed by repeaters who have been "corrected." Yet prison sentences in this country are among the harshest in the Western world.

The Police. Poorly paid for taking increasingly high physical risks (their average wage is one-fourth *less* than what the government defines as the minimum standard of living for a family of four), resentful of being called "pigs," running athwart racial tensions with their use of such tactics as stop-and-frisk searches, and frustrated by a seemingly endless war against crime, the police, always clannish, have become increasingly alienated and now tend to look upon a large segment of society as their enemy.

What Can Be Done?

More of almost everything is needed—money, facilities, and especially people: legal aid lawyers, assistant prosecutors, judges, psychiatrists and psychologists, probation officers, and policemen. The money and manpower may not be forthcoming, but there are some other solutions to the more grievous problems:

Decriminalize Victimless Offenses. Relieving the system of crimes against morals and tastes, but which have no victims, would save enormous amounts of manpower, dollars, and time.

Keep Certain Offenders Out of the System. Taking alcoholics to treatment centers instead of jails, and having probation officers supervise offenders in the community instead of in prison can keep the jail population down and fight recidivism.

Upgrade the Competence of Judges, Attorneys, and Police. Nineteen states now follow the Missouri plan of having a nonpartisan board of lawyers and laymen help the governor appoint judges on the basis of merit, and seventeen states have watchdog commissions of lawyers and laymen to review the work of local judges; regular seminars can also help keep judges informed of latest innovations. More talented defense and prosecution attorneys might be attracted if bar associations and law schools helped upgrade the criminal law profession, now generally avoided by law students. The quality of police work might be improved if more money and attention were diverted to wages, recruitment, and basic research, and less to sophisticated weaponry like MACE, helicopters, and tanks.

Modernize Due Process. To reduce delay, the time between arrest and trial could be restricted. The "omnibus hearing," which requires defense and prosecution to state all their intentions early in the case, also has been successfully used to shorten trials and reduce post-conviction appeals. Many courts have begun giving the poor a break under the bail system by waiving bail for defendants whose reliability can be established. To reduce disparities in sentencing, some states have sentencing councils consisting of judges who review trial judges' recommended sentences.

federal law enforcement agents, often after extensive investigation by the federal district attorney working with the FBI. If the
suspect is indicted by a grand jury, the charges are read to him,
he enters a plea, and his trial date is set.

If the defendant wishes, he may, of course, have a jury trial.[6]
The district attorney presents the government's case; the counsel
for the accused pleads the defense case; witnesses testify and are
cross-examined; the defense counsel summarizes his case; and the
government's attorney follows with a final argument. The judge
then instructs the jury on the law applicable to the case, and the
jury—by unanimous vote—must render a verdict based on the
judge's instructions and the evidence. If the verdict is guilty, the
presiding judge passes sentence according to law—a fine, prison
term, or even death.[7]

Appeals From District Courts

Most federal cases not only begin but end in the district courts.
However, appeals may be taken as a matter of right to the courts
of appeals, and in some cases—for instance, where a federal law
has been held unconstitutional—directly to the Supreme Court.
The purpose of appeals, of course, is to reduce possible mis-
carriages of justice, but they also help keep interpretations of the
law uniform, since judges are influenced by rulings of other
courts, particularly those of the Supreme Court.

COURTS OF APPEALS

The eleven courts of appeals stand immediately above the district
courts and are presided over by ninety-seven judges, three of
which usually sit on a case.[8] They were first created in 1891 to

[6] The right to jury trial in federal courts includes all elements provided by
the common law at the time the Constitution was adopted. The most significant are a jury of twelve and unanimous verdict for conviction.
[7] He may also enter a verdict of acquittal (e.g., if he thinks the jury's verdict
is against the evidence) and free the accused, or declare a mistrial because
there was error in the proceedings.
[8] The United States is divided into eleven circuits, including the District of
Columbia as a circuit. Each state and territory is assigned to a circuit.

reduce the pressure on the Supreme Court of cases appealed from district courts.

A court of appeals is primarily an *appellate* court. It hears cases on appeal from district courts, from specialized courts, and from regulatory agencies such as the Federal Trade Commission and the National Labor Relations Board. Most cases come from the district courts.

THE SUPREME COURT

The Supreme Court, at the summit of the federal judiciary, is our most venerable tribunal. Initially, it showed little promise of playing a prominent part in the nation's development; however, under Chief Justice John Marshall (1801–1835) its prestige and influence expanded remarkably. Not only did it establish its power of judicial review in its own early rulings, over the years it also extended a pattern of centralization of national over state authority, and generally kept all branches and levels of government operating within the framework of the Constitution.

Organization and Sessions

The number of Supreme Court Justices is fixed by Congress. It has been as high as ten and as low as five, but since 1869 there have been nine—the Chief Justice and eight Associate Justices. They meet in the magnificent white marble Supreme Court building, 800 feet from the Capitol. Court sessions begin the first Monday in October and end the following May or June. Usually the Court hears cases for two weeks per month and then recesses for two weeks so that Justices may hold conferences on them and write their opinions. The Chief Justice presides at all sessions and conferences and announces the Court's decisions. He also usually decides which Justice will write the Court's majority opinion in a case, which sets forth the judges' reasoning in reaching their decision. Although more than 3000 cases are filled with the Court each year, it considers only a small proportion and writes opinions on only a few more than 100.

Decisions and Opinions

Six Justices constitute a quorum, and at least a majority of the quorum is needed to decide a case. If a decision is not unanimous, both *majority* and *dissenting opinions* will usually be written. *Concurring decisions* may be written if one or more Justices agree with the majority vote but for differing reasons. This often happens in complicated cases or those involving controversial issues.

Appellate Jurisdiction

The Supreme Court hears appeals from both federal and state courts. Most come from the United States court of appeals, a few directly from federal district courts, and a relatively small number from the highest state courts. This is because the Constitution confines federal judicial power to limited areas and because Congress, which defines the Supreme Court's appellate jurisdiction, has restricted the kinds of cases federal tribunals may hear. Another reason is that the Supreme Court often simply refuses to hear a case, even though it has jurisdiction. In general, cases reach the Court by one of three procedures: certification, appeal, or *certiorari*.

Certification, though rarely used, is a procedure whereby the court of appeals judges certify—that is, refer—to the Supreme Court a question of federal law they feel so difficult and momentous that it should be brought immediately to the high court's attention.

Appeal, more frequently used, may be made by the losing party in a case. He may, by right, appeal to the Supreme Court when a court of appeals strikes down a state law as being counter to the Constitution, a federal law, or a treaty. He may likewise, by right, appeal when a state high court declares a federal law or treaty unconstitutional, or upholds a state law against a substantial challenge that it conflicts with the Constitution or a federal law or treaty. However, the Supreme Court need take a case on appeal only if it feels a substantial federal question is involved.

Most cases are brought up to the Supreme Court because it has issued a writ of *certiorari*—an order of the Court to a lower court to send up the record of a case for review. The Court agrees to review the decision of a court of appeals or a state supreme court if a question of federal law is involved. The Court has the option of granting or denying review; the affirmative votes of four Justices are required before it can accept a case. The writ is granted only when there are important and special reasons, though the Court may avoid considering issues it prefers not to confront, whatever their importance. Of the nearly 3000 *certiorari* petitions received annually, it consents to hear only about 10 percent. However, these *certiorari* cases make up about 80 percent of the Court's business.

Original Jurisdiction

The Supreme Court's jurisdiction is almost entirely appellate. The *original jurisdiction* defined by the Constitution is meager, but it includes cases to which a state is a party and cases affecting representatives of foreign nations. Its only *exclusive* original jurisdiction (includes cases and controversies only it may hear and decide) involves controversies between states and actions brought *against* representatives of foreign nations. Actually, the few suits the Supreme Court has heard between states have been the only significant cases of its original jurisdiction.

SPECIAL CONSTITUTIONAL COURTS

Besides the three federal constitutional courts of general jurisdiction mentioned so far, there are four of special jurisdiction.

The *Customs Court* adjudicates disputed valuations placed by custom officers on goods entering the United States, upon which they collect tariffs and enforce quotas.

The *Court of Customs and Patent Appeals* hears appeals from decisions of the Customs Court and the Patent Office. It also reviews certain findings of the United States Tariff Commission as to unfair practices in import trade.

The *Court of Claims* has jurisdiction over suits against the United States for violation of contract or for property damage.

The *United States Tax Court,* made a court of record in 1969, tries and adjudicates controversies between taxpayers and the Commissioner of Internal Revenue.

Judges of all these courts are appointed by the President, with Senate approval, for terms of good behavior. As with other federal courts, their decisions all may be reviewed by the United States Supreme Court.

LEGISLATIVE COURTS

The three kinds of legislative courts are created by Congress and differ from constitutional courts in that their judges need not be appointed for life.

The *Court of Military Appeals,* established in 1950, has three civilian judges appointed to fifteen-year terms by the President with Senate confirmation. This court hears appeals of armed forces personnel from military courts-martial in serious cases, and although its power of review is not extensive, it may determine if a case fell under a military court's jurisdiction and if it gave justice fair consideration. In these trials defendants do not have most of the Fifth and Sixth Amendment rights of accused persons.

Territorial Courts have been created for U.S. territories—the Canal Zone, Guam, Puerto Rico, and the Virgin Islands. These courts have the same jurisdiction as federal courts and also (except in Puerto Rico, which has a separate system of local courts) handle all matters which in the states would be handled by state courts.

The minor *courts of the District of Columbia* are also legislative.

THE COURTS AND THE CONGRESS

Congress has ample power to curb the Supreme Court. It determines the Court's jurisdiction and may deprive it of power to hear cases—except for the Court's very minor, constitutionally defined original jurisdiction, which Congress may not enlarge or reduce (as Chief Justice Marshall determined in *Marbury* v. *Madison*). This did happen in 1866 when the post–Civil War Congress took away the Court's authority to rule on some important Reconstruction policies (later repealed).

Congress may also use its legislative power to "overrule" the Court. For example, after the Court decided that the federal government, not states, had authority to own underwater oil lands and to regulate insurance businesses, Congress ceded all or part of that authority back to the states. In addition, Congress may propose constitutional amendments which, if three-fourths of the states approve, can overturn Supreme Court rulings. This method has been used three times—with the Eleventh, Fourteenth, and Sixteenth Amendments. Neither legislative power nor constitutional amendment is commonly used.

By its power to set the number of Supreme Court Justices, Congress can influence the Court by decreasing or increasing its membership. It decreased the number in 1800, and again in 1866, when first the Federalists and later the radical Republicans wanted to keep opposition Presidents from filling Court vacancies. Congress increased the number at the request of President Lincoln, who hoped to pack the Court to secure favorable decisions in some Civil War cases. President Franklin Roosevelt made a similar attempt in 1937, but was rejected by the Congress.

Lower federal courts are actually creatures of Congress, which determines the number of courts and the number of judges assigned them. Congress can also determine the rules of procedure for all the courts, though it has delegated them some of this power.

Moreover, Congress sets the judges' salaries and retirement benefits and may impeach and remove them. Only four judges—all from lower courts—have actually been removed through impeachment, although Supreme Court Justice Abe Fortas and a number of lower court judges have resigned under threat of impeachment. Finally, the Senate may refuse to confirm the appointment of any federal judge, and through its custom of senatorial courtesy—not confirming prospective judges if they are objectionable to the Senator in whose state they would take office—it practically dictates the selection of lower court judges.

THE COURTS AND THE PRESIDENT

The President may influence the courts by his appointments of judges. Senate confirmation is required; but with the most important, the Supreme Court appointments, the choice is primarily his own. Furthermore, the courts—even the Supreme Court—must depend almost entirely on the President to enforce their decisions, and his discretion is quite large.

Presidents can also use their popular influence to battle the courts. President Jefferson, a frequent opponent of the Supreme Court, tried to encourage allies in Congress to impeach justices whose votes he disliked. President Theodore Roosevelt recommended that unpopular decisions be overruled by popular vote. In the 1930s, President Franklin Roosevelt attacked the anti–New Deal rulings of the "nine old men" on the Supreme Court and asked Congress to authorize him to appoint an additional Justice for each of the six who was past seventy. Although he failed, the Justices began thereafter to uphold the constitutionality of New Deal programs.

THE SELECTION OF FEDERAL JUDGES

Except for those on the Court of Military Appeals and the territorial district courts, all federal judges are appointed for life, assuming their good behavior. The formal selection procedure is relatively simple: the President proposes names and the Senate approves them. The entire selection process, however, is more complex.

District Court Judges

For a district court judge, the President normally appoints a person suggested by the Senator from the state in which the judge will serve. If both Senators are members of the President's party, he will confer with both. If neither Senator is of his party, he will generally defer to the state leaders of his party. The disadvantage of this method is that district courts are staffed with men more distinguished by party loyalty than by ability in law, although generally the judges have been reasonably competent. An advantage of this method is that both the judge and his decisions will tend to mirror the prevailing political forces of the area in which he presides.

Courts of Appeals Judges

Senators and other party leaders have less influence in selecting judges for the courts of appeals than for the district courts, since a court of appeals has jurisdiction over an area encompassing more than one state. Senators or state party leaders do not have so great a stake in the appointments, and thus the President has greater latitude in selecting these judges. Generally, more distinguished judges with more judicial experience are appointed to these courts than to the district courts.

Supreme Court Justices

Because of the Supreme Court's importance in policy making and in making the acts of the political system legitimate, the quality of the persons the President appoints is of immense and enduring significance. What criteria do Presidents follow in making selections? Not surprisingly, they choose men who tend to share their political philosophy. Of the 100 Court appointments made between 1789 and 1971, only twelve did not belong to the President's party. Although this kind of selection has been defended as keeping the Court in tune with the times, it assumes the President himself is attuned to the times and that the judges he appoints vote as he wants. But this assumption is not necessarily true: Chief Justice Earl Warren, appointed by politically moderate President Eisenhower, had a very liberal voting record. Also, Presidents have made some attempt to maintain a religious, geographic, and ethnic balance on the Court; such a balance helps legitimize Court decisions and gain support for them.

Traditionally, the Senate has exerted little influence on Supreme Court appointments and has gone along with the President's choices. In 1968 it turned down President Johnson's nomination of Abe Fortas as Chief Justice and Homer Thornberry as

310

Associate Justice, and in 1969 it rejected President Nixon's nominations of Clement Haynsworth and G. Harrold Carswell as Justices. But these rejections do not mean the Senate has ceased to rely on the President's judgment.

SUPREME COURT JUSTICES: PERSONAL QUALIFICATIONS

Although the Constitution does not state qualifications for Supreme Court appointments, in practice rather rigorous tests of fitness are applied. Justices are drawn from a narrow segment of the population, and of their various qualifications, three have been most common.

The first is *legal education*—all Supreme Court Justices have been practicing lawyers, law professors, or law school deans. No doubt, able persons from other occupations could serve well, since the Court considers broad policy questions; but having practitioners of the law has probably helped to give legitimacy to the Court's decisions: the public is impressed that such questions are decided by law experts, not laymen.

The second qualification is *high social status.* Most Justices come from high-status families, partly because such persons are more likely to have the education and contacts needed to be considered for the post.

This background also tends to implant a sense of public service which may lead to *public involvement,* the third qualification. Only *one* Justice in our history has not had previous political experience. Only one-third of the Justices, however, have had prior service as state or federal judges; most have served on state, not federal, courts. Clearly, appointment to the Supreme Court is not by advancing up through the federal courts.

Surely a Justice's educational, social, occupational, and intellectual backgrounds influence his decisions. Little wonder, then, that Supreme Court decisions tend to reflect upper middle-class values, feelings of individual social responsibility, and law training and professional legal connections—conditioned, of course, by political imperatives.

Suggested Additional Reading

Bickel, A. *The Least Dangerous Branch.* 1967.

Cardozo, B. N. *The Nature of the Judicial Process.* 1921.

Cox, A. *The Warren Court: Constitutional Decisions as an Instrument of Reform.* 1968.

Goldman, S., and T. Jahnige. *The Federal Courts as a Political System.* 1971.

Krislov, S. *The Supreme Court and Political Freedom.* 1968.

Lytle, C. M. *The Warren Court and Its Critics.* 1968.

McGowan, C. *The Organization of Judicial Power in the United States.* 1969.

North, A. A. *The Supreme Court: Judicial Process and Judicial Politics.* 1966.

Part 4

Policies of American Government

15 Civil Liberties: Evolution of First Amendment Freedoms

The more I advanced in the study of American society, the more I perceived that this equality of condition is the fundamental fact from which all others seem to be derived and the central point at which all my observations constantly terminated.

—*Alexis de Tocqueville*

That the drafters of the Constitution sought a balance between absolute authority and absolute freedom is shown by the political institutions they created. Although they gave these institutions real authority and power, they also dictated that official decisions follow specified procedures and that some decisions not be made by government at all. Yet, for determining the proper balance between authority and freedom, the Constitution has been only a guide which must be interpreted and applied to specific issues.

Constitutional interpretations may occasion major political disputes. In 1968, for example, Richard Nixon charged during his presidential election campaign that the United States Supreme Court had erred too much on the side of liberty in its recent interpretations of the Constitution's guarantees to persons suspected of crimes. Actually, there is universal agreement only about the *extreme* expressions of liberty and authority: nearly everyone agrees we cannot have the absolute freedom of the "law of the jungle" nor the absolute authority of a Nazi government. Between the two extremes, however, it is difficult to decide the proper balance between conflicting civil rights[1] and between liberty and authority—concepts that are often in opposition.

THE BILL OF RIGHTS: LIMITATIONS ON POPULAR ORGANS

When the architects of the Constitution finished their work in 1787, they had created a political system based firmly on the consent of the governed. However, they had failed to include specific guarantees of freedom of speech, press, and religion, and other basic liberties. These omissions aroused the suspicions of many Americans, who felt that representative government alone would not sufficiently guarantee their natural rights. They demanded the addition of a Bill of Rights.

Federalists tried to argue that such a list of limitations on the government (which had only enumerated powers, and no more) would be senseless—that individual liberties would be protected by the checks and balances system, by the general spirit of the people, and by their governments.[2] This logic failed to move the people, however, and faced with the prospect of the defeat of the Constitution in the states' ratifying conventions, the federalists acceded. Thus, in 1791 the American Bill of Rights was created, a document unique in that it stated limitations on popular rulers—the popularly elected Congress and the presidency— rather than on hereditary rulers.[3]

[1] "Civil rights" generally refer to *positive* acts of government intended to defend persons against discrimination or arbitrary treatment. Civil rights guarantees are sometimes found in constitutions, but more often they are written into statutes. The terms "civil rights" and "civil liberties" are often used interchangeably. However, the latter generally pertains to *restrictions* upon government interference with persons, opinions, and property which are written into bills of rights and other parts of constitutions. Civil rights also differ from "political rights," which usually refer to the rights to control government through such acts as voting.
[2] Six very important provisions, discussed in Chapter 16, were included in the original Constitution to protect individual liberties.
[3] The protection of life, liberty, and property against infringement by *individuals* was left essentially to the states.

Extending the Bill of Rights to the States

The Bill of Rights, which comprises the first ten of the Constitution's twenty-five amendments, applied solely to the national government and *not* to the states (a fact officially recognized by the Supreme Court in 1833 in *Barron* v. *Baltimore*). Clearly, in those days people feared the distant federal government, not their own state governments, which they felt confident of controlling. Moreover, they felt secure in that most state constitutions already contained a bill of rights.

These fears were largely misplaced, for the national government has been less inclined than state and local governments to curtail individual rights. As time went on, it became obvious that not applying the Bill of Rights to the states had been a mistake. Finally, after decades of court appeals, a major break came. In 1925 the Supreme Court ruled (*Gitlow* v. *New York*) that if a state deprived a person of his First Amendment rights of free speech or freedom of the press, it would be depriving him of liberty without due process of law—an action prohibited to the states by the Fourteenth Amendment. Within a few years, the remaining sections of the First Amendment were extended to cover the states, and in the next four decades, the Court—giving more weight to individual rights than to the federal-state relationship—made most of the Bill of Rights applicable in state courts.[4]

Popular Rights: An Impossible List

It is impossible to make a complete list of popular rights and their dimensions. They are forever in flux, being continuously redefined by constitutional amendments, legislation, executive orders, and court interpretations at all levels of government. Moreover, they are not absolute but *relative*: they may be exercised only in such a way and to such a degree that they do not impair the rights of others. Popular rights are also subject to limitations

[4] Today the Second, Third, and Tenth Amendments do not apply to the states, but the Fourteenth Amendment imposes on the states all the limitations the Bill of Rights imposes on the national government (except for jury trial in all civil cases involving more than $20, and grand jury indictment for serious crimes).

designed to protect the safety and well-being of the majority, particularly during emergencies.

The issues of individual rights are ultimately decided by the Supreme Court, which is more shielded from political pressures —and even from public opinion—than the popularly elected branches. Its decisions stand, unless overruled by the Court itself or by constitutional amendment. However, it cannot indefinitely maintain an interpretation that the public is resolved to reject; there are limits to what it can do in the face of determined, overwhelming popular opposition. As history shows, the effective protection of individual rights depends finally upon the support of public opinion.

THE FIRST AMENDMENT FREEDOMS

The First Amendment states: "Congress shall make no law respecting an establishment of religion, or prohibiting the free exercise thereof; or abridging the freedom of speech, or of the press; or the right of the people peaceably to assemble, and to petition the Government for a redress of grievances."

Freedom of Religion

Only in the First Amendment and in the prohibition against religious tests for public office (Article VI) does the word "religion" appear in the Constitution, and God is not mentioned at all. This does not mean the men who wrote the Constitution were not religious. They simply opposed a nationally established church and thought the national government should not have jurisdiction over religious matters.

How the Government Encourages Religion

The Constitution does not make the government the opponent of religion. In fact, probably following the dominant public opinion, the government actually encourages religion, especially the Christian faith. The words IN GOD WE TRUST are stamped on our coins, and the phrase "one nation, under God" appears in the national pledge of allegiance. The armed forces have chaplains, but at the same time have exempted from service ministers, theological students, and members of religious sects which believe it immoral to engage in warfare. Congress also has chaplains, and the Supreme Court opens its sessions with the supplication, "God save the United States and this Honorable Court." All states give Sunday legal holiday status and officially recognize the principal Christian religious holidays. Churches are, in fact, protected by the government: their property is generally tax exempt; their leaders are free to influence government and public opinion for or against government policies; and religious contributions by individuals are tax deductible.

The Supreme Court has exempted from prosecution persons who, for religious reasons, refuse to perform some general obligations or obey certain laws.[5] Conscientious objectors to military service may be excused for pacifist views unrelated to religion (*Welsh* v. *U.S.*, 1970) and on grounds of (broadly defined) religious belief (*U.S.* v. *Seeger*, 1965); persons who refuse for reasons of conscience to salute the flag in public schools are likewise excused (*West Virginia Board of Education* v. *Barnette*, 1943); and religious canvassers may generally proselytize without having to secure a license or pay fees.

The Doctrine of Separation Between Church and State

The words "separation of church and state" do not actually appear in the Constitution, but the Supreme Court has held that the Constitution creates such a wall. It explained this doctrine of separation between church and state in the landmark case of *Everson* v. *Board of Education* (1947):

> The "establishment of religion" clause of the First Amendment means at least this: Neither state nor the Federal Government can set up a church. Neither can pass laws which aid one religion, aid all religions, or prefer one religion over another. Neither can force nor influence a person to go to or to remain away from church against his will or force him to pro-

---

[5] However, religious reasons do not exempt one from the criminal laws (for example, those against polygamy) nor from paying taxes.

fess a belief or disbelief in any religion. No person can be punished for entertaining or professing religious beliefs or disbeliefs, for church attendance or non-attendance. No tax in any amount, large or small, can be levied to support any religious activities or institutions, whatever they may be called, or whatever form they may adopt to teach or practice religion. Neither a state nor the Federal Government can, openly or secretly, participate in the affairs of any religious organization or groups and vice versa. In the words of Jefferson, the clause against the establishment of religion by law was intended to erect "a wall of separation between church and state."

The Everson Doctrine was reaffirmed in 1948, when the Court (*McCullum* v. *Board of Education*) invalidated the so-called "released time" program of religious instruction in the public schools of Champaign, Illinois. Under the Champaign program, public school children whose parents approved were released from their classes to be given religious instruction—during school hours in public school rooms—by Protestant, Catholic, and Jewish teachers furnished by a private religious council. In ruling the program unconstitutional, the Court said it used "the tax-established and tax-supported public school system to aid religious groups to spread their faith."

The Court's ruling in the Champaign case was widely attacked, particularly by church groups. Whether or not consciously influenced by the criticism, the Court appeared to retreat somewhat when in 1952 (*Zorach* v. *Clauson*) it upheld New York City's released-time program. The circumstances were essentially the same as in Champaign, except that the religious-instruction classes were not held in public school buildings. Although the Court insisted it was not overruling its earlier decisions, the opinion appears not in keeping with the doctrine of separation. Nevertheless, writing for the Court, Justice William O. Douglas explained:

> The First Amendment . . . does not say that in every and all respects there shall be a separation of church and state. . . . We are a religious people. . . . When the state encourages religious instruction or cooperates with religious authorities by

adjusting the schedule of public events to sectarian needs, it follows the best of our traditions.

The Establishment Clause and School Prayers

The doctrine of separation may be interpreted in two ways: (1) that the "establishment clause" of the Constitution flatly prohibits the government from making laws "respecting the establishment of religion" or (2) that it means the government simply may show "no preference"—that is, it cannot grant aid to one religious sect over another. Which interpretation has the Court favored since 1952?

In 1961, the Court specifically disavowed (*Torasco* v. *Watkins*) the "no-preference" doctrine. In 1962, it reinforced this stand (*Engle* v. *Vitale*) when it ruled unconstitutional a "nondenominational" prayer prepared by the New York Board of Regents and recommended for use in the state's public schools. According to the Court, the Regents' prayer exercise violated the establishment clause of the Constitution by bridging the separation between church and state. Justice Hugo Black spoke for the majority on the Court:

> The First Amendment must at least mean that in this country it is no part of the business of government to compose official prayers for any group of the American people to recite as a part of a religious program carried on by government. . . . Neither the fact that the prayer may be denominationally neutral, nor the fact that its observance on the part of the students is voluntary can serve to free it from the limitations of the Establishment Clause as it might from the Free Exercise Clause.

In the following year the Court ruled (*Abbington School District* v. *Schempp*) that reading the Bible as part of the program of the public schools also violates the establishment clause. Said Justice Tom Clark for the Court:

> Violation of the Free Exercise [of religion] Clause is predicated on coercion while the Establishment Clause violation need not be so attended. . . . To withstand the strictures of the

Establishment Clause there must be a secular legislative purpose and a primary effect that neither advances nor inhibits religion.

However, the Abbington decision is not followed in many parts of the United States.

Subsidizing Parochial Schools

Government "aid" to religion is unconstitutional, but what *is* such aid? Direct subsidies to Catholic parochial schools? What is a subsidy? Is it using public funds to supply textbooks and bus transportation for parochial school children? The Supreme Court has ruled that such use of public funds for textbooks (*Cochran* v. *Louisiana,* 1930) or bus transportation (*Everson* case) are subsidies not to religious schools, but to the children themselves, and that nothing in the Constitution forbids aid to the education and welfare of children.[6] However, state payment of part of the salaries of teachers in religious schools would violate the establishment clause (*Lemon* v. *Kurtzman,* 1971).

Freedom of Expression

The Constitution dictates that "Congress shall make no law . . . abridging the freedom of speech, or of the press." Perhaps no constitutional guarantee is more indispensable. Without interchange of ideas and without the right to organize into groups, to question government decisions, and to campaign openly against them, democracy could not be preserved.

Rights Are Not Absolute

Although Justice Hugo Black and others hold that the prohibitions of the First Amendment are absolute limitations, even these

---

[6] Congress took advantage of this reasoning in 1965 to enact the so-called "School Aid Bill," a landmark development in church-state relations as well as in education. It provided public funds for almost everything—including acquisition of library books and textbooks and creation of "supplementary education centers"—except constructing classrooms and increasing teachers' salaries. All were made available to children attending public or private schools, including parochial schools.

rights are not absolute—and have never been interpreted to be. Picketing, for example, is protected by the guarantee of freedom of expression (*Thornhill* v. *Alabama,* 1940), but mass picketing, or picketing that applies physical force, is not. Yelling "fire!" in a crowded theater when there is no fire, publicly calling someone a "damned fascist," or calling the presiding judge in a courtroom dishonest—none of these expressions is protected. Nor is "obscene" speech, "fighting words" (words that provoke others to attack), or actual, overt, and direct language inciting persons to overthrow the government by force and violence. Using words intended to defame a person's (or group's) character or expose him to public hate, ridicule, or contempt is not allowed as free speech. If you speak these words, it is *slander*—if you write them, *libel*—and the injured party (or group—*Beauharnais* v. *Illinois,* 1952) is empowered by law to sue you for damages or even to bring criminal charges.

Sedition and Subversion

Before World War I, national limitations on free speech were uncommon. One exception was the Sedition Act of 1798, outlawing "false, scandalous, or malicious writing" against the national government, the President, or Congress—that is, writing with the intent to defame or bring them into contempt or disrepute. Thomas Jefferson and many others opposed the law, and it was allowed to expire during his presidency. Another exception was President Lincoln's effort to suppress pro-Southern expressions during the Civil War. During World War I, however, sweeping restrictions were placed on criticism of the government or its war policies. In general, the Supreme Court upheld these statutes, and before the war ended, nearly 2000 persons were confined in federal prisons for violating them.

The Clear-and-Present-Danger Test

Following World War I, state legislatures fearing subversion sought to repress communist, syndicalist, and socialist movements. In reviewing cases involving these restrictions, the Supreme Court developed the *clear-and-present-danger test.* Enunciated in 1919 by Justice Oliver Wendell Holmes in *Schenck* v. *United States* and in a number of subsequent dissenting opinions, the doctrine was as follows: Freedom of expression could be restricted in the interests of public safety only when the expressions—and the circumstances under which they were articulated—presented a clear and present danger of evils (e.g., overthrow of the government of the United States) which Congress or the state had a right to prevent. In later minority opinions, Justice Louis Brandeis held that the emergency had to be *grave*, and the evil *imminent*, if a finding of clear and present danger were to be supported.

The test of clear and present danger was not accepted as a majority opinion by the Court until 1940 (*Thornhill* case).[7] From then until the end of World War II, a majority of the Justices applied the standard consistently. They also joined it with a *preferred-status doctrine*, holding that First Amendment freedoms should have a preferred position in our constitutional values and that, accordingly, the Court should temper its usual inclination to interpret in favor of the constitutionality of legislation.

The Dangerous-Tendency Test

Another test which has at times been the official guideline of the Court is the *dangerous-tendency test*. This test is at variance with the clear-and-present-danger test and the preferred-status doctrine. It holds that government may outlaw speech that has merely a *tendency* to lead to an evil, and assumes rather than questions the constitutionality of laws regulating speech.

In 1951, the Supreme Court veered back toward the dangerous-tendency test of the 1920s when it supported the constitutionality of the Smith Act. The Smith Act—the first peacetime sedition act since 1798—outlawed specific aspects of political expression by making it unlawful to teach or advocate the overthrow of the government by force and violence, or helping organize or joining an organization that engaged in such advocacy, knowing its purposes. In upholding the conviction of eleven leaders of the

[7] The *Thornhill* case involved an Alabama law which forbade all peaceful picketing for any purpose it was ruled unconstitutional as a needless invasion of free speech.

324

Communist Party (*Dennis* v. *United States*) under the act, the Court pointed out that since the nation's security was threatened, the primary consideration was not simply how clear and present the danger, but the *gravity* of the evil.

The Smith Act was followed by the 1950 Internal Security Act (requiring communist-action and communist front organizations to register as such with the Attorney General), and the Communist Control Act of 1954 (which deprived the Communist Party, or any of its affiliates, of the privileges and immunities of legal bodies).

The Clear-Danger Test

In 1957, the Court reinstated the "clear" aspect of the clear-and-present-danger test in another interpretation of the Smith Act by distinguishing between mere *advocacy* of abstract doctrine and *conspiracy* to advocate concrete action to overthrow the government violently (*Yates* v. *United States*). Four years later, it ruled that a person may not be convicted under the Smith Act of membership in the Communist Party unless he is an "active" member and has demonstrated his specific intention to overthrow the government (*Scales* v. *United States*). Previously (1956), it had voided state laws forbidding advocacy of violent overthrow of the national government, holding that the Smith Act preempted the field (*Pennsylvania* v. *Nelson*)—a decision that occasioned widespread outcry against the Court.

Subsequently, in 1965, the Court held that the United States Attorney General's list of "subversive" organizations, which was compiled as part of the loyalty program established by President Truman in 1947, could not be used as a basis to bring charges against members of these organizations because the list did not constitute judicial proof of subversion (*Dombrowski* v. *Pfister*). That same year, the Court also ruled unconstitutional the law requiring individual Communist Party members to register with the Attorney General (as required by the 1950 Subversive Activities Control Act), holding that this violated the member's protection against self-incrimination (*Albertson* v. *Subversive Activities Control Board*), since a member would have been liable for punishment under the Smith Act.

War and Cold War Restrictions

The passage of the Smith Act in 1940 began a wave of legislative and executive restrictions on free speech and assembly. Besides being curtailed by the 1950 Internal Security Act and the 1954 Communist Control Act, communists and others advocating forceful revolution have also been denied government employment and positions in the armed forces. Starting with Senator Joseph McCarthy in the 1950s, congressional and state legislative committees have questioned hundreds of people about their associations, and demanded executive action against suspected subversives in public life.

Presidents also acted to control suspected subversion. President Truman, besides authorizing his Attorney General to prepare a list of subversive organizations, instituted a security program to remove from public service persons suspected of doubtful loyalty; President Eisenhower extended it to cover "security risks," including homosexuals and alcoholics. The program also covered "sensitive" positions in defense industries.

Among other actions aimed at controlling subversion were Post Office screening of publications mailed from other countries and the institution of federal and state loyalty oaths for public employees, school teachers, and military personnel.

In the 1960s, the anti-communist hysteria of the preceding two decades somewhat abated and the Supreme Court began narrowly construing the federal laws and executive orders dealing with security. It has, for instance, ruled unconstitutional laws denying communists passports and preventing them from being officers or employees of a labor union. The Court has also been less inclined to uphold the constitutionality of laws requiring private citizens to take loyalty oaths. Loyalty oaths for new federal employees were dropped in 1970.

Freedom of the Press

A free press has always been considered indispensable to democratic government, for reporting information and revealing conflict helps citizens ascertain the truth and serves the democratic ideal of popular consultation. As Thomas Jefferson observed, "Man may be governed by reason and truth. Our first object should therefore be to leave open to him all the avenues to truth. The most effectual hitherto found is the freedom of the press."[8]

The term "press" includes mimeographed materials, books, newspapers, magazines, radio, television, motion pictures, and even picket signs. All are entitled to the protection of the First Amendment, but the protection is not unlimited; as the English jurist Blackstone stated 200 years ago: "The liberty of the press ... consists in laying *no previous restraints* upon publications, and not in freedom from censure for criminal matters when published" [emphasis added].

A historic test of this principle of no previous restraint occurred in the 1971 case of the *U.S.* v. *The New York Times and Washington Post,* in which the government tried to stop, on grounds of national security, these newspapers from publishing the so-called Pentagon Papers—secret studies of how successive administrations from Truman to Johnson had involved the U.S. in an unsuccessful war against communism in Indochina, all the while withholding from the American people the grave implications of their decisions. The Court ruled 6–3 against the government, with three justices holding that the government's claim to censorship had no standing whatsoever and three others ruling that the press could not be muzzled except to prevent direct, immediate, and irreparable damage to the nation.

There are, however, some exceptions even to the rule of no previous restraint. Supreme Court decisions have implied, for instance, that considerable government censorship in time of war is permissible. Still, though federal agencies suppress information in peacetime as well as during war, neither the states nor federal government may prevent publication, require publishers to be licensed, or levy special taxes that discriminate against publishing. Nor may they permanently enjoin a libelous newspaper or magazine from publication. As Chief Justice Charles Evans Hughes wrote in 1931 (*Near* v. *Minnesota*), "the fact that liberty

---

[8] Saul K. Padover, *Thomas Jefferson on Democracy* (New York: Mentor Books, 1946), p. 163.

of the press may be abused by miscreant purveyors of scandal does not make any less necessary the immunity of the press from previous restraint."

Some censorship of publications has been exercised through the Post Office. For instance, during World War II, some radical and anti-war publications were denied the cheaper second-class mailing privileges. Also, Congress has barred foreign political propaganda, obscene literature, and lottery tickets from the mails. However, in 1965, the Supreme Court unanimously ruled unconstitutional legislation authorizing the Postmaster General to deliver "communist political propaganda" to an addressee only if he requested it (*Lamont* v. *Postmaster General*).

The courts themselves exercise some minor censorship. Although judges are generally permissive in allowing criticism of judicial proceedings, they have in recent years regulated news coverage of trials, primarily to help guarantee an unprejudiced jury. Probably a factor leading to tightened controls was the Supreme Court's reversal of the second-degree murder conviction of Dr. Samuel H. Sheppard (*Sheppard* v. *Maxwell*, 1966) on the basis that "virulent" newspaper publicity had denied him a fair trial.

Though protected by the First Amendment, movies, radio, and television are subject to more censorship than other mass media. Beginning in 1915, movies were precensored by state and local governments; this was permitted by the Supreme Court on the ground that they were spectacles or entertainment rather than information media. However, in 1952 (*Burstyn* v. *Wilson*), the Court changed its mind and brought movies under the protection of the First and Fourteenth Amendments. Yet it has not been willing to go all the way and apply the no-previous-restraint rule, which would make all movie censorship unconstitutional. In 1961 (*Times Film Corp.* v. *Chicago*), it ruled that state and local governments might require that films be licensed before their public showings. This does not mean that *any* previous restraint on movies is allowable; censorship may not be arbitrary and ideas in a movie may not be censored at all. In 1965, the Court (*Freedman* v. *Maryland*) established guidelines under which censors (1) must either issue a license promptly or seek a court order forbidding a showing; (2) must bear the burden of proof when they declare a movie obscene or objectionable; and (3) must allow for prompt court review of any restraint imposed.

Radio and television censorship is exercised by the Federal Communications Commission in the sense that it grants licenses to use the limited frequencies available to those who, in its opinion, serve the public interest, convenience, or necessity. These licenses are subject to renewal or cancellation every three years. The FCC may not directly censor political ideas in these media; but although denying it, the commission exercises some limited supervisory censorship over what it considers indecent, fraudulent, or seditious, and the Supreme Court has upheld this supervision (*NBC* v. *United States*, 1943). On the other hand, federal regulation of radio and television protects them from state regulation (*Dumont Laboratories* v. *Carroll*, 1950).

Obscenity is not protected by the First Amendment and is subject to censorship. In 1957, in the landmark case of *Roth* v. *United States*, the Supreme Court ruled that obscenity is not protected because it is "utterly without redeeming social importance."[9]

But what is obscenity? Certainly it is not entirely synonymous with sex. In the Roth case, the Supreme Court indicated that material relating to sex is not obscene unless "to the *average person*, applying *contemporary community standards*, the dominant theme of the material *taken as a whole* appeals to *prurient interest*" [emphasis added]. In the 1966 Fanny Hill case (*Memoirs of a Woman of Pleasure* v. *Massachusetts*) the Court went beyond the Roth test to declare that a book is not obscene unless it fails all the tests of the Roth case, is patently offensive, and without redeeming social importance. Under these standards, almost anything except "hard-core" pornography (also undefinable precisely) is protected. Nevertheless, in 1966 the Court upheld a conviction of a book publisher (*Ginzburg* v. *United States*) for sending obscene materials through the mails, emphasizing that he had used "titillating" advertising and was engaged in "commercial exploitation of erotica solely for the sake of prurient

---

[9] Mere *possession* of obscene matter, even if it is knowing possession, is not punishable (*Stanley* v. *Georgia*, 1969)—if it is in a person's home. If it is in the luggage of a returning traveler, however, it is not safeguarded (*U.S.* v. *Thirty-seven Photographs*, 1971).

appeal." In 1971 it upheld a statute prohibiting knowing use of the mail for delivering obscene matter (*U.S.* v. *Reidel*).

Freedom to Assemble, Associate, and Petition

The Constitution forbids Congress from abridging "the right of the people peaceably to assemble, and to petition the Government for a redress of grievances." The *right of assembly* covers not only peaceful assemblies in private homes, but also those in meeting halls, streets, parks, and other public places. It does not, however, give people the right to incite to riot or to disrupt traffic in a rush hour. The government may impose reasonable requirements to protect public order, although an ordinance giving public officials complete discretion would be unconstitutional (*Hague* v. *CIO*, 1939).

May police order an unpopular assembly to disperse or an unpopular speaker to be silent, if the response to them is so hostile that actual disorder is at hand? In 1951 the Supreme Court seemed to say that the police can control the targets of violence as well as those who threaten it. In this case (*Feiner* v. *New York*) it upheld the arrest of a sidewalk speaker who refused a police order to stop talking when it appeared his hostile audience would likely become violent. However, in 1963 (*Edwards* v. *South Carolina*), the Court ruled that "the Fourteenth Amendment does not permit a state to make criminal the peaceful expression of unpopular views," and it reaffirmed this position in 1969 (*Gregory et al.* v. *Chicago*). This hardly puts the issue to rest, for in local communities the police, reflecting local values, determine the extent to which people may assemble peaceably; when arrests are made, local courts decide guilt or innocence. In such matters, appeal to the Supreme Court is too slow and expensive to be of much practical use.

Freedom of association to promote political goals is not specifically mentioned in the Constitution. It has, however, been implied, and in 1958 the Court made it explicit (*NAACP* v. *Alabama*). Two years later (*Bates* v. *Little Rock*) it stated that "it is now beyond dispute that freedom of association for the purpose of advancing ideas and airing grievances is protected by the Due Process Clause of the Fourteenth Amendment from invasion by the States." The Arkansas city of Little Rock had required the NAACP to submit a list of its members to the city clerk. The Court held that this was not a reasonable regulation of a lawful group, because it would be likely that members would suffer reprisals.

The First Amendment *right to petition* government has involved few constitutional questions, except for issues growing out of lobbying activities. Most petitions to Congress are referred to committees, where they are pigeonholed. There is no guarantee in the amendment that Congress, its committees, or the President will *read* a petition, let alone act upon it.

Suggested Additional Reading

Chafee, Z. *Free Speech in the United States.* 1941.

Clor, H. M. *Obscenity and Public Morality.* 1969.

Emerson, T. I. *Toward a General Theory of the First Amendment.* 1966.

Emerson, T. I., D. Haber, and N. Dorsen. *Political and Civil Rights in the United States.* 2 vols. 1967.

Latham, E. *The Communist Controversy in Washington: From the New Deal to McCarthy.* 1966.

Meiklejohn, A. *Free Speech and Its Relation to Self-Government.* 1948.

Muir, W. K., Jr. *Prayer in the Public Schools.* 1968.

Report of the National Advisory Commission on Civil Disorders, 1968.

Stouffer, S. H. *Communism, Conformity, and Civil Liberties.* 1955.

Tresolini, R. J. *These Liberties: Case Studies in Civil Rights.* 1968.

U. S. Commission on Civil Rights, *Annual Report.*

Zinn, H. *Disobedience and Democracy: Nine Fallacies on Law and Order.* 1968.

16 Civil Liberties and Rights: Toward Greater Fairness and Equality

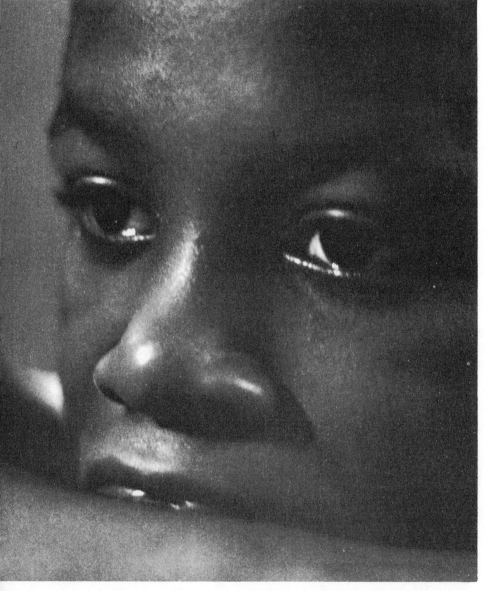

There are no necessary evils in government. Its evils exist only in its abuses. If it would confine itself to equal protection, and . . . shower its favors alike on the high and the low, the rich and the poor, it would be an unqualified blessing.

—*Andrew Jackson*

When the term "civil liberties" is used, the Bill of Rights (the first ten amendments) comes to mind. However, the original Constitution and its other amendments, especially the Fourteenth, also guarantee a number of civil liberties. In recent years, especially, the Fourteenth and Fifteenth Amendments have been the basis for much civil rights litigation and legislation.

CIVIL LIBERTIES OF THE ORIGINAL CONSTITUTION

To protect individual liberty, the original Constitution has several limitations on the federal government: enumerated powers, separate branches with each one checking the others, and division of powers between the nation and the states. The Constitution also defines many basic American freedoms: the writ of *habeas corpus,* prohibitions against bills of attainder and *ex post facto* laws, the right to jury trial, protection against loose definition of treason, and protection of contracts.

Writ of *Habeas Corpus* Guaranteed

"The Privilege of the Writ of Habeas Corpus shall not be suspended," the Constitution stipulates, "unless when in Cases of Rebellion or Invasion the public safety may require it." This is the so-called "great writ," derived from English common law, and it is perhaps the most important human right in the entire Constitution. Without it, a man could be imprisoned without explanation or having the opportunity for redress—and thus *all* his civil liberties would be impaired.

The writ of *habeas corpus* (literally, "you should have the body"—the opening words of the writ) is a court order, issued at the request of a person in jail, that he be brought before a civil judge to determine whether there are sufficient legal grounds for confining him. The writ applies to persons incarcerated by the national government only; however, federal courts have jurisdiction to determine if persons are being improperly held by state authorities.

Congress may suspend the writ, but the suspension is subject to review by the courts. Thus, when President Abraham Lincoln (not Congress) suspended it in parts of the North during the Civil War, the Supreme Court ruled (in *ex parte Milligan,* 1866) that he had exceeded his authority.[1]

Bills of Attainder Prohibited

A bill of attainder is a legislative act which inflicts punishment on specific individuals without permitting them a judicial trial. The Constitution expressly prohibits the government, national or state, from passing such a bill. Any person imprisoned on this basis can secure his release through a writ of *habeas corpus.*

Bills of attainder have not been common in our history. However, in 1946 (*United States* v. *Lovett*) the Supreme Court

[1] In 1946, the Court ruled that the United States Army had illegally suspended the writ in Hawaii during World War II (*Duncan v. Kohanamoku*).

voided a bill of attainder passed by Congress which consisted of a rider attached to an appropriations bill denying three Interior Department employees further compensation or salary. These employees had been denounced on the floor of Congress as "crackpot, radical bureaucrats" and affiliates of "communist front organizations." The same thing happened again in 1965 (in *United States* v. *Archie Brown*) when the Supreme Court voided a law of Congress making it a crime for a Communist Party member to be an officer or employee of a labor union. The Court pointed out that this act was a bill of attainder because it designated, by name, members of a political group and punished them. Chief Justice Warren, speaking for the majority, stated: "Congress possesses full legislative authority, but the task of adjudication must be left to other tribunals."

Ex Post Facto Laws Prohibited

The Constitution forbids the federal and state governments from passing *ex post facto*—that is, retroactive—laws. Interpreted literally, *all* retroactive legislation is prohibited. However, the Supreme Court has ruled (*Calder* v. *Bull*, 1798) that only retroactive *criminal* laws that would disadvantage *anyone* are prohibited. This means that Congress may not make laws which (1) make an act a crime that was not a crime when it was committed, (2) increase the punishment for a crime after it was committed, and (3) make it easier to convict a person of a crime after it was committed.

It is still constitutional, however, to pass retroactive civil legislation—for example, providing for retroactive income-tax increases. It is also legal to apply criminal laws retroactively benefiting the accused—for example, lightening a punishment.

Jury Trial Guaranteed

The Constitution states that all crimes except impeachment shall be tried by jury; all state constitutions also provide for jury trial. Based on common law, the jury usually consists of twelve persons who, in the presence of a judge empowered to instruct them on the law and to advise them on the facts of the case, arrive at a verdict by unanimous vote. As in the common law, however, the right to jury trial does not apply to contempt of court cases, cases in equity, or petty offenses. The jury is intended to give the accused more protection, but he may waive this right in federal courts and be tried only by a judge. Many states also allow this option.

Loose Definition of Treason Prohibited

The architects of the Constitution were technically traitors against the English government; thus, they were fully aware of the evils of a vague definition of treason. Accordingly, in the Constitution they carefully stated the crime of treason as consisting only of levying war against the United States or giving aid and comfort to its enemies. They also provided that the accused could be convicted only if he made a confession in open court or if two witnesses testified to seeing the same overt act. The consequences of guilt might not be extended beyond the person convicted—for instance, to his family.

However, this restricted definition of treason does not prevent the government from defending itself. Congress may provide punishment for a variety of disloyal acts, such as sabotage, espionage, attempted violent overthrow of the government, or conspiracy to do any of these.

Contracts Protected

The Constitution forbids any state from interfering in the obligation of contracts. This clause was included because the Constitution's framers were determined to place the sanctity of contracts beyond the reach of the debtor-dominated state legislatures. They had in mind the ordinary contracts between individuals, particularly contracts of debt. However, in early decisions, the Supreme Court gave a broad interpretation to the clause. In 1810 (*Fletcher* v. *Peck*) it ruled that the clause applied to public as well as private contracts, and in 1819 (*Dartmouth College* v. *Woodward*) that charters establishing corporations were also contracts. Thus, privileges that charters conferred on corporations could not be impaired by later laws.

336

For many years, the contract clause protected business against state regulation. Gradually, however, the Court changed its application, and in 1880 ruled (*Stone* v. *Mississippi*) that all contracts may be regulated by the state when necessary to protect the public health, welfare, safety, and morals. Then, in a 1934 ruling on a Minnesota law suspending mortgage foreclosures to avoid economic injustices and hardships caused by the Depression, the Court declared that even contracts between individuals could be modified by state law. Since then, the Court has tended to let the legislative branch decide whether circumstances warrant modifying or setting aside contractual rights. Furthermore, the contract clause has largely been supplanted by the due process clauses of the Fifth and Fourteenth Amendments in safeguarding property rights.

Other Safeguards

The Constitution provides that "no religious Test shall ever be required as a Qualification to any Office or public Trust under the United States." Nor may states require a declaration of belief in the existence of God as a test for public office (*Torasco* v. *Watkins,* 1961). The original Constitution also prohibits granting titles of nobility by either the United States or the states.

CIVIL LIBERTIES OF THE AMENDMENTS

Second Amendment: Limited Right to Bear Arms

This amendment guarantees that "A well regulated Militia, being necessary to the security of a free State, the right of the people to keep and bear Arms, shall not be infringed." This amendment was prompted by the fear that Congress might disarm the state militias, and must be interpreted in this light. Since it does not relate to individual rights, it does not prohibit Congress from taxing certain weapons (e.g., sawed-off shotguns). Nor does it confer a right to carry concealed weapons (pistols, daggers, sword-canes, etc.). The amendment also does not prohibit state and local governments from regulating the private ownership of firearms.

Third Amendment: Quartering of Soldiers Prohibited

This amendment states that "No Soldier shall, in time of peace be quartered in any house, without the consent of the Owner, nor in time of war, but in a manner to be prescribed by law." The amendment was thought important by the Constitution's framers because the forceful quartering of British troops in the homes of American colonials had been one of the grievances included in the Declaration of Independence. This prohibition seems so thoroughly in accord with our ideas that apparently there have been no cases of abuse.

Fourth Amendment: Unreasonable Search and Seizure Prohibited

That a man's home is his castle is a treasured inheritance from English common law. Indeed, the violation of this ancient right of privacy by colonial customs officials was one of the major causes of the American Revolution, and thus the practice of unreasonable seizures and "general" warrants was outlawed in the Fourth Amendment:

> The right of the people to be secure in their persons, houses, papers and effects, against unreasonable searches and seizures, shall not be violated, and no Warrants shall issue, but upon probable cause, supported by Oath or affirmation, and particularly describing the place to be searched, and the persons or things to be seized.

The amendment extends to letters and packages in the mails, to outbuildings around a person's home, and to any place one has a legitimate right to occupy—hotel rooms, rented homes, even a friend's apartment.[2] The papers and effects of corporations are also covered.

[2] In 1961, the Supreme Court declared that the Fourteenth Amendment also prohibits the states from engaging in unreasonable searches and seizures and from using evidence thus secured in a criminal trial (*Mapp* v. *Ohio*). In 1963 (*Kerr* v. *California*) the Court ruled that the Fourteenth Amendment imposed the same standards upon the states as the Fourth Amendment did upon the federal government.

Reasonable searches and seizures are not forbidden—that is, those based on a warrant issued by a judge having proper jurisdiction. Searches may also be made without a warrant, if the circumstances would not permit delay: an automobile, airplane, or boat could be so searched, if there is probable cause to believe a law has been broken, since otherwise a person could take advantage of delay and use these vehicles to escape (*Carroll* v. *United States,* 1925). In addition, a search may be made incident to a lawful arrest; however, the Court has been ambivalent about whether evidence of crimes not mentioned in a warrant may be introduced as evidence if obtained incidentally while making a lawful arrest or search.[3]

Does wiretapping of telephone lines or use of electronic eavesdropping devices violate the Fourth Amendment? In 1928, the Supreme Court ruled 5–4 that wiretapping is constitutional (*Olmstead* v. *United States*), but in 1934, Congress outlawed it in the Federal Communications Act, stating that "no person not being authorized by the sender shall intercept any communication and divulge or publish the existence, contents, substance, purport, effect, or meaning of such intercepted communication to any person."

The Supreme Court subsequently declared that the law made wiretapping a federal crime, and that evidence so secured was not admissible in federal court cases (*Nardone* v. *United States,* 1937; *Benanti* v. *United States,* 1957). Later in 1967 (*Berger* v. *New York*), it also ruled such evidence inadmissible in state courts. This so-called *exclusionary rule* was adopted because the justices felt it was the only effective way to prohibit illegal police tactics. As Justice Tom C. Clark wrote: "Few threats to liberty exist which are greater than that posed by the use of eavesdropping devices." In that same year, the Court also declared that the Fourth Amendment prohibited electronic eavesdropping as well as wiretapping (*Katz* v. *United States*).

In 1968, Congress enacted the Crime Control Act, requiring federal agents to obtain warrants to place taps, except in national security cases. In these cases, the President may authorize bug-

[3] However, the search may not extend beyond the person of one arrested except to the limited area into which he could reach to destroy evidence or to obtain a weapon (*Chimel* v. *California,* 1969).

ging. However, when Attorney General Mitchell entered office in 1969, he asserted that "national security" embraced domestic threats to public safety as well as foreign espionage. In effect he was assuming that federal law enforcement officials could use listening devices to exercise surveillance over such activist groups as the Black Panthers and the Students for a Democratic Society without prior court approval.

The act also allowed police—state and local, as well as federal— to secure permission from a court of competent jurisdiction to wiretap and eavesdrop in a wide variety of cases. For state and local officers the authority extended to the investigation of any crime punishable by more than one year in prison. This was the first time in the nation's history that police were permitted by federal law to make widespread use of these listening devices.

Although the provisions of the Crime Control Act of 1968 generally comport with the standards established in recent Supreme Court rulings, and forbid the use in any judicial process of evidence secured by illegal eavesdropping, the constitutionality of some of its terms appears questionable. First, the suspect need be notified of the surveillance only after it is accomplished, not when it is executed, as with a search warrant. Second, a search order can run for as many as thirty days, much longer than the usual warrant, which permits a search at one time only. Third, persons other than the one named in the order may have their privacy invaded, since the suspect may talk to and about many people.

Fifth Amendment: The Grand Jury
—The Most Ancient Safeguard

According to this amendment, the federal government may not hold any person to answer "for a capital or otherwise infamous crime, unless on presentment or indictment of a Grand Jury. . . ."[4]

---

[4] Excepted in the amendment are "cases arising in the land or naval forces, or in the Militia, when in actual service in time of War or public danger. . . ." The Supreme Court has interpreted this clause to read "except for persons serving in the land or naval forces." (See *Kinsella* v. *Singleton* and companion cases, 1960.) However, in 1969 the Court ruled (*O'Callahan* v. *Parker*) that, at least during peacetime and while serving in the United States, military personnel may not be subject to court-martial for "non-service-connected crimes."

The grand jury dates from the time of William the Conquerer (the trial jury, as we know it, is an offshoot). There are no more than twenty-three members on a grand jury, a vote of twelve being sufficient to return a "true bill" of indictment—that is, the decision that enough evidence exists to justify a trial. Proceedings are secret, and because the accused is not actually being tried, only the government is represented. The accused has no right to appear, but permission is sometimes given.

The advantage of the grand jury is that it spares both the accused and the government the expense and inconvenience of a trial based upon insubstantial charges. Yet more and more it is considered cumbersome, expensive, and unnecessary. England has almost completely abandoned it, and in the United States a defendant may waive it in a noncapital case. Many states have discarded it entirely and have substituted trial upon "information" —that is, upon a formal charge by a prosecuting officer.

Fifth Amendment: Double Jeopardy Prohibited

No person can "be subject for the same offense to be twice put in jeopardy of life or limb"—a Fifth Amendment protection against his being tried twice for the same offense by the same level of government. This protection is not so extensive as is popularly believed, however. A person may face civil as well as criminal proceedings, or he may be put in jeopardy for each of several offenses involved in a single act. He may also be tried in both state and federal courts for the same act, if the offense violated both state and federal law. Moreover, he may be tried again, if a jury cannot agree on a verdict or is dismissed because it includes persons incompetent to serve, or if the judge declares a mistrial.

Fifth Amendment: Freedom From Self-Incrimination

No person "shall be compelled in any criminal case to be a witness against himself." This famous clause of the Fifth Amendment is based on an ancient English law prohibiting the use of torture to force a person to testify against himself. In recent years the clause has generated heated controversy because witnesses have invoked it in congressional hearings on subversion, and because many people erroneously think the refusal to testify is tantamount to an admission of guilt. The Supreme Court has indicated that this clause protects the innocent as well as the guilty, though it has not denied the right of state and local governments and school boards to fire employees who invoke it. Today, the clause protects not only accused but also witnesses against almost any form of inquisition by any governmental agency.[5]

Under this amendment, no person may be forced to answer any inquiry if his answer would tend to incriminate him. A defendant in a criminal case may even refuse to take the stand to answer any questions, whether the answers would incriminate him or not; guilt is not to be inferred from this refusal. A person may not assert the right, however, merely because his answers would be embarrassing, impair his reputation, or incriminate others.

Many observers thought the right was undercut when Congress passed the 1954 *Compulsory Testimony Act.* Under this law, the prosecution may compel testimony from a witness at a congressional hearing or before a federal district court who "takes the Fifth Amendment'" when questioned on matters of national security, but he cannot then be prosecuted by the federal or the state governments for any matter included in his testimony. Congress passed the law because it was disturbed by the hundreds of witnesses who claimed self-incrimination when summoned to testify on national security matters. The Supreme Court upheld this procedure 7–2 in 1956 (*Ullman* v. *United States*).

Fifth Amendment: Life, Liberty, and Property Protected

The guarantee that no person may be deprived of "life, liberty, or property, without due process of law" is the broadest assurance of government fairness in the Constitution. It restricts both the federal government (Fifth Amendment) and the state governments (Fourteenth Amendment). Nevertheless, "due process of law" is not defined in the Constitution, nor has the Supreme

[5] In 1964 (*Malloy* v. *Hogan*) the Supreme Court ruled that the protection extends to state governments.

Court defined it, preferring instead to interpret its meaning as cases arise.

Due process has two major aspects: procedural and substantive. Until about 1890, the Court emphasized *procedural* due process—that is, the *manner* in which government acts. This interpretation means the government must provide persons with fair trials before properly constituted agencies and generally follow fair procedures. As a result, other constitutional guarantees are supplemented, especially those in the Fourth through the Eighth Amendments, for the judiciary has marked out the meaning of procedural due process so as to prohibit any procedure that shocks the conscience or makes a fair and enlightened system of justice impossible.

More recently the Court has also emphasized *substantive* due process—that is, it examines the laws in the cases it hears and decides if their *purpose* (not just the procedures by which they are enforced) is reasonable, fair, and just, and sets aside those that are not.

Before 1937, the Court often applied the doctrine of substantive due process to protect business liberty. It struck down federal and state laws regulating hours, minimum wages, workmen's compensation, price-fixing, and protecting workers from being fired for union membership. It held that these laws unreasonably interferred with the right of employees and employers to contract with one another. Since then, however, the Court has largely ceased applying this doctrine to laws regulating the economy, and has showed an increasing concern for protecting human rights.

Fifth Amendment: Power of Eminent Domain Limited

All governments have the power of eminent domain, the power to take private property for public use. The Fifth Amendment recognizes this prerogative, but limits it thus: ". . . nor shall private property be taken for public use without just compensation." The courts have even ruled that the government has in effect "taken" property when the title actually still remains with the owners. Land adjacent to an airport, for instance, could be considered unsuitable for residential use because planes take off or land over it; thus, it would have been "taken" and the government may be required to give just compensation, usually interpreted as reasonable market value (*Griggs* v. *Allegany County,* 1962).

Sixth Amendment: Guarantees to Accused Persons

The Sixth Amendment guarantees accused persons these important rights:

> In all criminal prosecutions the accused shall enjoy the right to a speedy and public trial, by an impartial jury of the State and district wherein the crime shall have been committed, which district shall have been previously ascertained by law, and to be informed of the nature and cause of the accusation; to be confronted with the witnesses against him; to have compulsory process for obtaining Witnesses in his favor, and to have the assistance of Counsel for his defense.

The Amendment thus repeats the right of jury trial guaranteed in Article III,[6] adding that it must be speedy, public, and impartial. The word "speedy" does not have a specific definition, but if the government fails to bring a person to trial within a "reasonable" time, it could bar him from being tried. The right to an impartial jury is, of course, relative, for no jury is completely impartial. Clearly partial, however, are juries from which members of the defendant's race, nationality, or religion—or, in capital cases, persons who do not believe in the death penalty—have been systematically excluded.

For protection, the defendant is accorded the right to a public trial. However, this is a right of the defendant, not of the news media. To protect the defendant further, trials are held in the state and district in which the crime was committed. However, if a defendant prefers and a judge agrees, he may be tried in

---

[6] In 1968, the Court held for the first time that the due process clause of the Fourteenth Amendment applied against the states the Sixth Amendment right to jury trial. This ruling applies in state cases which, if tried in the federal courts, the defendant would have the right to jury trial (*Duncan* v. *Louisiana*). The Seventh Amendment guarantees jury trial for common law suits in federal courts if they involve more than $20. The parties to the suit may dispense with a jury with the consent of the court.

344

another district if the community in which the crime took place is so prejudiced against him that it would be impossible there to select an impartial jury.

At his trial, the defendant must be furnished a copy of the indictment and a bill of particular charges. If it is a criminal case, he may cross-examine witnesses testifying against him. However, the Supreme Court has ruled that certain other government hearings (e.g., deportation or loyalty hearings) are not criminal prosecutions and that the testimony of unidentified informers is admissable. In such instances aliens may be deported and government employees fired without being able to confront their accusers directly.

The defendant also has the right of counsel for his defense. Since 1938, federal judges must not only inform the defendant in criminal cases of this right, but must secure an attorney for him if he cannot do so. In 1963 (*Gideon* v. *Wainwright*), the Court extended this federal rule to cases tried in state courts.

In 1966, the Court spelled out (in *Miranda* v. *Arizona*) by a 5–4 vote the rights of the accused to counsel during police questioning. Prior to any questioning, the person must be warned

> ... that he has a right to remain silent, that any statement he does make may be used as evidence against him, and that he has a right to the presence of an attorney, either retained or appointed.
>
> The defendant may waive effectuation of these rights provided the waiver is made voluntarily, knowingly and intelligently. If, however, he indicates in any manner and at any stage of the process that he wishes to consult with an attorney before speaking, there can be no questioning. Likewise, if the individual is alone and indicates in any manner that he does not wish to be interrogated, the police may not question him.

In 1971, however, the Court backtracked slightly when it ruled (in *Harris* v. *New York*) that voluntary statements made by an accused person before police had warned him of his rights could not be used as evidence, but could be used to impeach his credibility if he contradicted these statements while testifying in his own behalf. As Chief Justice Warren Burger put it, "the shield provided by *Miranda* cannot be perverted into a license to use perjury by way of a defense."

345

Eighth Amendment: Excessive Bail and Fines and Cruel and Unusual Punishments Prohibited

The Eighth Amendment mandates that "excessive bail shall not be required, nor excessive fines imposed, nor cruel or unusual punishments inflicted."

Requiring the accused to deposit bail money with the court is to help ensure that he will appear for trial. If he is jailed before being convicted, and excessive bail is set (or if he is too impoverished to pay bail), he may not only be imprisoned though innocent but also be seriously disadvantaged in preparing for his trial. Ironically, an accused person may be held in jail without being adjudged culpable, but if convicted he may be quickly released, as suspended sentences are often given by the courts for first offenders or in connection with a system of probation.

In an effort to reduce the discrimination against the poor which is involved in bail practice, Congress in 1966 passed the Bail Reform Act. This law *requires* federal judicial officers to discharge persons, on their own recognizance, who have been accused of noncapital offenses and who are not able to assemble bail, unless the officers have a substantial reason to feel that the accused will not appear at his trial. The act also guarantees the accused swift appellate court review of the decisions against his release and directs the Attorney General thenceforward to give the defendant time off any prison sentence for the time he spent in custody awaiting his trial.

The word "excessive" of the Eighth Amendment is not a specific guide. Much depends on the nature of the crime and the accused's reputation, and many believe it should also depend on his ability to pay. For some offenses—for example, capital crimes—bail may be denied. Those believed likely to commit another crime—homicidal maniacs, for instance—may also be held without bail. A fine may also be considered excessive when it is so large that it deprives a person of the possibility of making a living.

Barbaric punishments such as happened in the past—starvation, burning, quartering, crucifixion, and breaking on the wheel—would be cruel and unusual, though death by hanging, electrocution, lethal gas, and shooting are currently not considered so.

However, punishment that is all out of proportion to the offense—for instance, the death penalty for a misdemeanor—would be. So also would making drug addiction a crime (*Robinson* v. *California*, 1962).

Thirteenth Amendment: Slavery and Involuntary Servitude Prohibited

This amendment states that "Neither slavery nor involuntary servitude, except as a punishment for crime whereof the party shall have been duly convicted, shall exist within the United States or any place subject to their jurisdiction." This is the only amendment (besides the Twenty-first) which can be violated directly by an individual. Though directed against Negro slavery, it also applies to peonage—the requirement that a person work at a job against his will to pay off a debt. However, the amendment may not be invoked to avoid paying alimony, being drafted into the armed forces, or performing jury duty.

Fourteenth Amendment: State Abridgement of Privileges and Immunities of U.S. Citizens Prohibited

"No state shall make or enforce any law which shall abridge the privileges or immunities of citizens of the United States." This clause of the Fourteenth Amendment conferred no new rights on citizens but merely made explicit a federal guarantee that states could not abridge the privileges and immunities that American citizens have under the national government, the Constitution, federal laws, and treaties. Its purpose was to protect the Negro, but many hoped the Supreme Court would apply it so that the fundamental rights of the Bill of Rights could be enforced against the states. In fact, however, the Court has not done this; its narrow construction has made the clause insignificant.

Fourteenth Amendment: State Deprivation of Due Process of Law Prohibited

Because the Supreme Court rejected the contention that the privileges-and-immunities clause of the Fourteenth Amendment made the Bill of Rights enforceable against the states, some advocates argued that the amendment's due process clause served this purpose—as indicated by the word "liberty" in "No state shall . . . deprive any person of life, liberty, or property without due process of law."

Before 1925, the Court rejected this general view, though it ruled that the word "liberty" protected economic interests. But in a landmark decision (*Gitlow* v. *New York*), it finally decided that this Fourteenth Amendment "liberty" included freedom of worship, speech, press, assembly, and petition—the First Amendment freedoms—and made them limitations on the states.

Some jurists believe the amendment's due process clause incorporated *all* of the Bill of Rights—that its restrictions on the national government apply equally to the states. However, most of the Court has held otherwise, preferring to apply only those rights it considers "implicit in the concept of ordered liberty." Using this so-called "Palko test," developed in *Palko* v. *Connecticut* (1937), the Court has incorporated the entire Bill of Rights *except* the Second, Third, and Tenth Amendments (which do not apply to the states), indictment by grand jury, and jury trial in all civil cases involving more than $20. Beyond this, the Court has ruled, the rights the states extend to their citizens must simply be fundamentally fair and not arbitrary nor shockingly unjust.

Fourteenth Amendment: State Denial of Equal Protection of the Laws Prohibited

A state may not, according to the Fourteenth Amendment, "deny to any person within its jurisdiction the equal protection of the laws." This "equal protection," difficult to define, does not require that every law apply alike to all persons, but it does prohibit arbitrary and unreasonable classifications. Reasonable classifications, however, are allowed: for example, individuals may be classified according to income for tax purposes, or according to age for minimum standards for voting, or according to sex for military conscription.

But what about classifying people according to race, nationality, or religion? In 1896 (*Plessy* v. *Ferguson*) the Supreme Court upheld classifying by race, ruling that state-imposed racial segregation in public facilities was not discrimination if equal facilities were provided. The separate facilities for Negroes were definitely not equal, but not until the 1940s did the Court begin requiring them to be so, and not until 1954 (*Brown* v. *Board of Education*) did it hold that in public education, separate is not equal, and that segregation *is* discrimination.

The 1954 decision banned segregation in public education only, but it brought into question discrimination of all sorts. Civil rights advocates filed numerous suits testing other segregation laws in public transportation and accommodations, recreational facilities, and courthouses, and the Court also declared these laws unconstitutional.

Citing the equal protection clause, the Court has also ruled unconstitutional indictments or convictions of blacks by juries from which members of their race have been systematically excluded (*Hill* v. *Texas*, 1942; *Akins* v. *Texas*, 1945). Similar discrimination based on nationality or religion would be unconstitutional for the same reason. Equal treatment must also be accorded indigents accused of crimes.

Equal protection may not be denied city voters by giving rural voters greater representation than their numbers merit; except where the Constitution specifically states to the contrary, any system that makes one man's vote unequal to the vote of another denies him equal protection.

The clause does *not* prohibit discrimination by private individuals unless it is assisted or supported by state action. Private schools may therefore be discriminatory unless they receive public support. Restrictive covenants in deeds limiting the use of property to certain religions or races are not unconstitutional *per se,* but would become so if the state, through its officers or courts, helped enforce them (*Shelly* v. *Kraemer,* 1948). The same rule applies to owners of public accommodations, but if they refuse to serve blacks, they may be violating state or federal laws that cover certain accommodations involved in interstate commerce.

Interestingly, the federal government is not limited by an equal protection clause. However, the due process clause of the Fifth Amendment has been applied against its denials of equal protection. Under this process, which is similar to the one whereby the due process clause of the Fourteenth Amendment has extended most Bill of Rights restraints to the state governments, the Supreme Court has ruled unconstitutional the enforcement of racially restrictive covenants in the District of Columbia and segregation in its public schools (*McGhee* v. *Sipes,* 1948; *Bolling* v. *Sharpe,* 1953).

CIVIL RIGHTS: MOVES TOWARD POLITICAL AND SOCIAL EQUALITY

In recent years, civil rights advocates have become increasingly dissatisfied with the traditional ways of securing constitutional rights—that is, by going to court—and have demanded that the government be more vigorous in taking legislative and administrative action to prohibit discrimination.

Modern Presidential Initiatives

The federal government began to take stronger action on the problem of discrimination against blacks and other nonwhites at the start of World War II. Although President Franklin Roosevelt did not recommend any civil rights legislation as such, he did create—by executive order, since Congress would not have passed such legislation—a Civil Rights Unit in the Criminal Division of the Department of Justice, and established the first Fair Employment Practices Committee (FEPC). The FEPC, created at the behest of Negro leaders and other civil rights advocates (including Roosevelt's wife, Eleanor), eliminated some discriminatory employment practices in companies and labor unions working on defense contracts. However, Congress abolished it in 1946.

In 1948, President Harry Truman established a Fair Employment Board to see that all federal jobs were filled without regard to "race, color, religion, or national origin." In that same year he also banned "separate but equal" armed forces recruiting, training, and service. President Eisenhower continued Truman's civil rights policies, creating the 1953 President's Committee on Government Contracts to consider discrimination charges against government contractors; the committee had the authority to cancel contracts if necessary. In 1962, President Kennedy banned discrimination in housing built with federal assistance.

During the 1960s and after, however, most progress toward black equality has derived from the Supreme Court's historic 1954 school desegregation decision.

The 1957 and 1960 Civil Rights Acts

In the Reconstruction period after the Civil War, Congress proposed the Thirteenth, Fourteenth, and Fifteenth Amendments, and in the following decade enacted five major civil rights laws spelling out the rights of the new Negro freedmen. However, for many years afterward, it was unable or unwilling to legislate in this area, let alone initiate; nor did Presidents request such legislation.

Finally, in 1948, President Harry S Truman proposed the first comprehensive civil rights legislation of the twentieth century. A number of his proposals called for legislation to help realize the ideals of human dignity and equality—a real departure from the traditional view that government itself is the chief threat to human rights. But even with Truman's—and later Eisenhower's—repeated exhortations, it was not until 1957 that a civil rights statute actually reached the books. This was followed by a second act in 1960, and then by the comprehensive Civil Rights Act of 1964.

The civil rights acts of 1957 and 1960 were directed almost solely at returning the voting privileges illegally denied to Negroes in the South, and gave the Justice Department only moderate powers of intercession. Civil rights leaders came to regard the acts as too slow and cumbersome. Negro impatience intensified, until in August of the "long hot summer" of 1963, 200,000 people descended on the Capitol in the massive interracial March on Washington for Jobs and Freedom. Against this backdrop of mounting anger, threats, and sporadic violence, President Kennedy asked Congress for strong, expanded civil rights legislation; it was vigorously pushed by his successor, President Johnson, until it finally achieved success in 1964.

The 1964 Civil Rights Act

The Civil Rights (Public Accommodations) Act of 1964, passed after a seventy-five day filibuster by Southern Senators, consisted of eleven parts. The first part provided additional safeguards for Negro voting rights. The second part is generally considered the heart of the law. Called the *Public Accommodations Title*, it is based on Congress's power to regulate interstate commerce. It outlaws discrimination on account of race, color, national origin, or religion in hotels, restaurants, theaters, gas stations, and all other public accommodations related to interstate commerce and in all publicly owned facilities (such as parks and swimming pools). Other parts of the act empowered the Justice Department to file enforcement suits on behalf of persons whose rights had been violated in school segregation.

The Act also created a federal Fair Employment Practices Commission (FEPC) to enforce nondiscrimination by employers and labor unions, and authorized the federal government to withhold funds to state and local programs, public or private, that practiced discrimination. In addition, it established a Community Relations Service to help reconcile racial disputes at the local level.

The 1965 Voting Rights Act

Even after the 1964 Civil Rights Act, civil rights supporters demanded stronger federal legislation to protect Negroes registering as voters, especially in the South. Martin Luther King, Jr.'s voter registration drive in Selma, Alabama, and the violence attending civil rights demonstrations provoked a public clamor for action. President Johnson accordingly proposed the strongest voting rights legislation in nine decades. The Civil Rights Act of 1965, passed after yet another Senate filibuster, suspended literacy tests and other practices hindering Negro voting.[7] Although some key parts raised serious problems of constitutionality —largely because of the unclear division of responsibility for defining suffrage between the states and the federal government —the act's basic provisions were upheld by the Supreme Court (*South Carolina* v. *Katzenbach*, 1966).

The 1968 Open Housing Law

Housing, one of the areas of inequality identified by President Truman in 1948, was the last and probably the most politically sensitive. President Johnson requested open housing legislation

[7] Problems of black suffrage, and voting provisions of the various civil rights acts, are discussed in Chapter 6.

three times—in 1966, 1967, and 1968—before Congress finally passed it.

Fully effective in 1970, the Open Housing Law of 1968 prohibits discrimination in the sale or rental of 80 percent of all housing, including single-family residences. The only exceptions are owner-occupied dwellings of up to four units and privately owned single-family housing, if the sale or rental is made without a real estate agent or broker. In 1968, the Supreme Court (*Jones v. Mayer Co.*) ruled that an 1866 federal statute (never before interpreted by the Court) barring racial discrimination in the sale or rental of *all* property had the effect of removing the exemptions of the Open Housing Law of 1968. The law is enforced by individual civil suits, although the U.S. Attorney General may sue where there is a pattern of discrimination.

The law also provides criminal penalties for persons intimidating or injuring civil rights workers or others engaging in specified activities—voting; serving on a state or federal jury; participating in a state, federal, or federally assisted program; using the services of a labor union; working for a state, local, or private employer; or attending public school.

State Civil Rights Action

Many states and cities have also passed laws against discrimination in employment because of race, color, creed, national origin, or sex. Several states have statutes banning discrimination in public accommodations, including, in some instances, sales or leases of private homes and apartments.

Generally, these laws are enforced by special state agencies which emphasize education, prevention, and informal negotiated settlements, although sometimes they resort to criminal prosecution. States have ample legal authority to prohibit discrimination; the real problem is not legal or constitutional, but gaining political support for effective laws and for enforcing them.

Suggested Additional Reading

Bailey, H. A. (ed.). *Negro Politics in America.* 1967.

Barbour, F. B. (ed.). *The Black Power Revolt.* 1968.

Brophy, W. A. and C. C. Ferguson, Jr. *The Indian: America's Unfinished Business.* 1966.

Congressional Quarterly. *Revolution in Civil Rights.* 1965.

Cruse, H. *The Crisis of the Negro Intellectual.* 1968.

Grimes, A. P. *Equality in America.* 1964.

Grodzins, M. *Americans Betrayed: Politics and the Japanese Evacuation.* 1949.

Rosenberg, J. M. *The Death of Privacy.* 1969.

Westin, A. F. *Privacy and Freedom.* 1967.

X, Malcolm. *Autobiography.* 1964.

17 Domestic Policy

Ernest Lowe, Photofind, S. F.

When the poor have cried, Caesar hath
wept: Ambition should be made of sterner
stuff.

—Shakespeare, *Hamlet,* III, ii.

In domestic policy, the federal government uses three techniques
—manipulation, promotion, and regulation—to try to manage the
economy and control the society. *Manipulation* is exemplified
most vividly by the federal income tax law, which is graduated
to favor lower-income groups, and also by social welfare and
anti-discrimination laws (which manipulate social behavior), and
by government policies providing tight or easy money (which
manipulate the nation's financial structure). *Promotion* is illustrated by the federal outlay for farm income stabilization and
other policies that benefit specific groups: patents, statistical
services, research, protective tariffs, and aid to education. *Regulation,* widely used to police powerful interests such as business
and labor, is exemplified by anti-trust legislation, regulatory commission bans on unfair trade or labor practices, and court orders
prohibiting restraint of trade. All three techniques, of course, may

have more than one effect—regulating one interest, for instance, may in fact promote another.

Because of the variety of techniques and ways to apply them, it is difficult to study the politics of policy. Making individual case studies would help, but the number of studies needed would be nearly infinite. Instead, here we will simply try to describe government policy in several areas: the economy, agriculture, business, labor, health, education, welfare, and poverty.

THE ECONOMY

Decisions about the American economy—that is, about the production and distribution of goods and services—are largely made by private groups. In fact, no other highly industrialized country has so little government ownership and control of the economy, and what little government ownership (e.g., the Tennessee Valley Authority) there is occurred because of special circumstances, not because of any socialist theory that government ownership was necessary to assure social justice. Furthermore, industries developed by the government (e.g., atomic energy and space communications) have later been sold to private corporations for only a fraction of what it cost the government to develop them. Thus, the American approach to government management of the economy has been actively to promote the growth of private enterprise and, in recent years, to regulate it through legislation and government regulatory agencies.

Government Finance

Government taxing and spending have a major impact on the economy. About one-fourth of the spending is by national, state, and local governments—the federal government, with its more than $200 billion budget is by far the biggest spender, followed by California, New York, New York City, and then the large industrial states.[1]

[1] In 1967, state expenditures came to $39.7 billion and local expenditures to $67 billion.

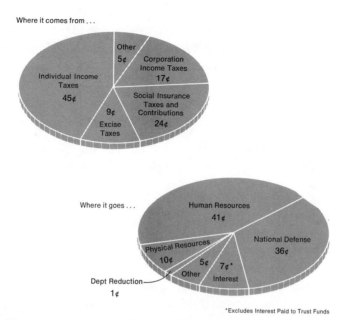

Where it comes from . . .

Other 5¢
Corporation Income Taxes 17¢
Individual Income Taxes 45¢
Social Insurance Taxes and Contributions 24¢
9¢ Excise Taxes

Where it goes . . .
Human Resources 41¢
Physical Resources 10¢
National Defense 36¢
5¢ Other
7¢* Interest
Dept Reduction 1¢

*Excludes Interest Paid to Trust Funds

Figure 17–1. The budget dollar—where it comes from, where it goes (fiscal year 1971 estimate). (Source: Bureau of the Budget.)

As Figure 17-1 shows, the principal federal revenue—about 62 percent—is the income tax, both individual and corporation. Social insurance taxes and contributions, and federal excise taxes—on such items as automobiles, alcohol, tobacco, jewelry, and telephones—are also important, and some income is derived from customs duties. The federal government also borrows money by issuing bonds and notes.

About 40 percent of total federal government revenue goes for military and security spending.[2] Most of the rest goes for income security, interest on the national debt, and health.

Federal government costs have increased incredibly in recent years, from $4 billion in 1932 to more than $200 billion in 1971—a fifty-fold increase. The main reason for this rise, other than defense spending, is the expansion in our population under eighteen and over sixty-five—the two groups with the greatest need for public services such as education and welfare. Contributing factors are also the increased urbanization, with its corresponding

[2] The 1970 defense budget amounted to about $80 billion.

demands for services, and popular demands for Social Security, reduced unemployment, and assistance to and regulation of business, agriculture, and labor.

The National Debt

When federal spending exceeds federal revenues the budget is said to be *unbalanced*. When this occurs, the government must borrow money to make up the deficit, usually by selling long-term bonds or short-term treasury notes.[3] Since 1930, the budget has often been out of balance, with the biggest deficits occurring during wartime or national crisis (see Figure 17-2). During World War II alone, the federal government borrowed over $200 billion. By 1971 the national debt stood at more than $400 billion.

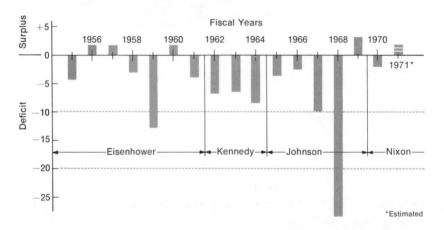

Figure 17–2. The story of the budget since the Korean War—surplus or deficit in billions of dollars. (Source: House Appropriations Committee.)

Little headway has been made on paying off the debt. Increasing taxes for this purpose is not popular, and economists disagree over whether it is even really necessary to pay off the national debt. More important than the size of the debt and the

[3] State constitutions limit the states' legal capacity to borrow, but there is no similar limitation on Congress.

interest payments (now about $14 billion a year) are the economic strength and resources of the nation.

Economists generally agree that during stable, prosperous times, balanced budgets are advisable, but that during times of international crisis or economic recession, unbalanced budgets help the economy: by borrowing money, the government may spend it on consumer or investment goods in such a way as to increase national income.

AGRICULTURE

American farmers have had a great deal of legislation enacted on their behalf, but through history they have been plagued with difficulties. At best, farming is a risky business, dependent upon weather and market conditions beyond the farmer's control. And although today American farmers are the most affluent farmers in the world, their incomes are low compared to those of other occupations.

Since the 1930s the federal government has tried to help farmers cope with their major problem—oversupply of their products, and resultant low prices—by supporting farm prices through regulating agricultural production. Several methods have been used. First tried, under the Agricultural Adjustment Act of 1933, were cash subsidies to farmers if they reduced production. The goal of the program was to provide *parity*—that is, the price for the farmers' products necessary to provide them a purchasing power equal to that which existed between 1909 and 1914. The program was supported by a special tax on the processors of agricultural products; however, three years after the program got under way, the Supreme Court (*U.S.* v. *Butler*) declared the process tax unconstitutional, stating it levied one group to give benefits to another.

A second program, the Agricultural Adjustment Act of 1938, which avoided the process tax, emphasized soil conservation: farmers were paid to reduce their acreage devoted to soil-depleting crops. By 1969 total payments to farmers amounted to $3.8 billion. However, a disproportionate amount of the money

went to the biggest farm operators (see box). In addition, if they
were approved by two-thirds of the farmers, voting in an election
conducted by the Department of Agriculture, the act allowed
marketing quotas and acreage allotments to be set up for cotton,
wheat, feed grains, and wool—all basic farm products which are
storable.[4]

The main agency for administering the price support program,
the *Commodity Credit Corporation,* works this way: It offers a
loan to a farmer against a particular crop he has planted but not
harvested. The amount the farmer receives is calculated according to the price support rate established by the Department of
Agriculture. If the market price stays up after he harvests the
crop, the farmer sells the crop and repays the loan. If, on the
other hand, the market price drops, he may store his crop permanently with the CCC, which then accepts the crop as payment
of the loan.

Since the 1950s the federal government has stored farm surpluses worth billions of dollars. Storage costs alone have run into
hundreds of millions of dollars. However, in the 1960s and 1970s,

[4] In 1956, Congress also established a "soil bank" plan under which farmers
were given cash payments for withdrawing farm acreage from production,
but keeping it ready for possible future tilling.

362

several domestic programs have helped decrease the government's surpluses. Among these have been the School Lunch Program (which provides matching cash grants to the states to subsidize school lunches, as well as lunches for needy children), the Special Milk Program (whereby government-purchased surplus milk is donated to schools), and the Food Stamp Program (under which poor people may buy—or receive free—food stamps and use them to purchase food that costs more than the amount paid for the stamps). In addition, the federal government distributes food to poor people living in cities not participating in the Food Stamp Program; it also buys perishable vegetables and fruits when surpluses impend and donates them to direct-distribution and school lunch programs. But if these programs have helped the government get rid of its surplus food, they have not erased malnutrition. In fact, a 1969 Senate committee found that "malnutrition has increased among Americans at all income levels."[5]

BUSINESS

Before the Civil War, regulation of business was mostly done by local government. Later, as business grew beyond the local market and thus beyond local jurisdictions, state governments took over. As transportation improved around the end of the nineteenth century, giant businesses burst across state boundaries, threatening small businesses, consumer interests, and even each other; since then only the federal government has been effectively able to regulate them.

But government has not only regulated business, it has also assisted it. In subsidizing mail service, for example, it made business advertising and transactions cheaper. It has also established protective tariffs, made internal improvements, given federal aid to railroads, issued patents to protect inventions and trademarks, made loans to businessmen, and established uniform weights and measures.

Today government promotes economic growth mostly by trying

[5] United States Congress, Senate Select Committee on Nutrition and Human Needs, *The Food Gap: Poverty and Malnutrition in the United States* (Washington, D.C.: Government Printing Office, 1969), p. 7.

to maintain a climate of confidence in the American economy and free enterprise. It also acts in more specific ways: facilitating domestic and foreign trade, regulating business and labor, curtailing inflation and deflation, granting tax incentives, expanding (or contracting) credit through the Federal Reserve System, restraining monopolies, aiding the marketing of farm products, conserving resources, supporting research, and compiling economic statistics.

LABOR

Although during the nineteenth century government aided business and agriculture, workers remained forgotten in the American economy. Not sharing the prosperity of their employers, they worked long hours under hazardous conditions for low wages. They had to battle against blacklists, employer-paid spies, company-created unions, and "yellow-dog" contracts that pledged them not to join a union of their own. Employers were backed by the courts, which issued injunctions against the unions' only weapons—picketing, boycotts, and strikes. The President and Congress failed to help working men, and even the Supreme Court was on the side of employers—as late as 1905 (*Lochner* v. *New York*) it overturned a New York law limiting bakers to ten working hours a day, declaring that the law violated the bakers' freedom to contract.

Not until the Depression years of the 1930s did government finally come to the aid of labor. In the last days of the Hoover administration, Congress enacted the *Norris-LaGuardia Act,* which stated that court injunctions against unions in labor disputes could be used only to prohibit direct union violence and intimidation; the act also declared yellow-dog contracts unenforceable in courts. The next year, 1933, Congress also passed President Roosevelt's *National Industrial Recovery Act,* which gave workers the right to organize unions and bargain collectively with employers over terms and conditions. However, the Supreme Court thought the act unconstitutional in 1935 (*Schechter* v. *United States*). Congress responded by passing the *National*

Labor Relations Act (popularly known as the Wagner Act), which contained all the earlier act's collective bargaining provisions and also outlawed several employer practices: discriminating against union members in hiring or firing, interfering with employee collective bargaining, refusing to bargain collectively, and attempting to dominate unions. The act also authorized unions and employers to enter into closed-shop agreements (one in which a worker must join a union before being employed) and established the National Labor Relations Board to enforce the law. Three years later, Congress followed with the *Fair Labor Standards Act*, which set minimum wages and maximum hours for most workers employed in manufacturing.[6]

Since the New Deal, most federal legislation has swung the other way, imposing new restrictions on labor—a result of the widespread opinion that labor has become too powerful and corrupt and that the employer has needed help. The 1947 *Labor-Management Relations Act* (Taft-Hartly Act) abolished the closed shop, required unions to bargain with employers, and required union officers to take a national loyalty oath. It outlawed featherbedding (requiring employers to hire more men for an operation than are necessary) and secondary boycotts (refusing to patronize or deal with anyone who does business with the employer with whom there is a dispute). It also changed the use of court injunctions so that the federal government, after an eighty-day cooling-off period, could seek injunctions against strikes and employer lockouts of employees which jeopardized the national health, general welfare, or safety. It has been chiefly used to avert nationwide rail and steel strikes. Further restrictions on labor were written into the 1959 *Labor-Management Reporting and Disclosure Act* (Landrum-Griffin Act), which established a "Bill of Rights of Members of Labor Organizations" and made union officials financially and organizationally accountable to their members. The "Bill of Rights" guaranteed the secret ballot in union elections, free speech in union meetings, the right of members to access to union records and to sue the union for unfair practices, and hearings in disciplinary cases.

[6] An amendment to this law, the Equal Pay Act of 1963, requires employers to pay equal wages to men and women who do equal work.

365

Until very recently, health care has been mainly the responsibility of individuals, private agencies, and state and local governments. However, since World War II, there has been a tremendous upsurge in federal health services.

Today, the *Public Health Service*, the major federal health agency, maintains specialized hospitals and helps state and local governments combat disease. It also supports research in the medical and related sciences, as illustrated by the Surgeon General's report describing cigarette smoking as a cause of lung disease, which spurred Congress to enact regulatory legislation (though less strict than the Public Health Service had recommended). Since 1946, and particularly since 1965, when Congress passed a comprehensive health research bill, research has shifted from communicable to chronic diseases and to disabilities such as heart disease, stroke, cancer, arthritis, and mental illness. Research has also increased on health problems related to the environment, principally water and air pollution and radiation. The increased activities of the Public Health Service have come mainly through expanded grants for research and training, not through the growth of its installations throughout the country.

Another important agency, *The Food and Drug Administration*, is designed to protect the public against adulterated, misbranded, and harmful drugs. Its responsibilities (e.g., to evaluate the effectiveness of all new drugs before they can be certified) have been much expanded since drug companies in 1962 experimented with distributing the tranquilizer thalidomide, later found to cause deformed babies when taken by pregnant women. In recent years the FDA has increasingly been accused of laxity in protecting consumers. In 1970, Ralph Nader, champion of consumer causes, and his Center for the Study of Responsive Law, after an extensive study of the agency, concluded that it was dominated by political pressures and that it was reluctant to or incapable of defending consumers.

Comprehensive medical care insurance was first provided by the federal government in 1965, when the so-called "Medicare" bill was enacted for persons over sixty-five. Medicare, financed by Social Security payroll taxes, covers hospitalization (ninety days), home nursing care (100 days), 100 home health care visits, and outpatient tests and diagnostic services. A supplementary, voluntary plan, available to the insured for a small monthly charge ($4.00) and matched by federal funds, covers physicians' fees and the costs of other health services and medical supplies. The plan takes care of 80 percent of the annual medical costs above the first $50, which the patient pays. In 1971, about 20 million persons were enrolled in Medicare.

The Medicare law also extended a program established earlier in the 1960 Kerr-Mills Act, which provided health care for needy aged, to cover all recipients of public welfare and other indigent people. This "Medicaid" program differs from Medicare in that it is not financed by Social Security taxes but by federal, state, and local matching funds, with the highest federal contribution going to the poorest states.

EDUCATION

Public education, traditionally a state and local activity, is mostly financed through and controlled by locally elected or appointed boards. Nevertheless, the federal government has not been a bystander. Sixty-eight colleges exist largely because of the 1862 Morrill Act, which gave states land grants to support the agricultural and mechanical arts. Since 1917, vocational education has also been subsidized by federal grants to states. Moreover, as a result of the federal G.I. Bill of 1944 and the Korean G.I. Bill, over 11 million veterans have received educational training. Among the many federal education programs operating today are those making loans and grants to colleges, universities, and medical schools for research, building construction, and student financial assistance; making grants to school districts located near defense facilities; educating Indians; educating handicapped children; and making perishable food available for school lunch programs.

The 1958 National Defense Education Act set aside funds to improve science teaching, later extended to social sciences and humanities. The *Elementary and Secondary Education Act of 1965* provided over $1 billion for elementary and secondary schools with economically deprived children—the first time federal funds had been used in a massive way for this purpose[7] —and for textbooks and library books for public and parochial schools and to finance supplementary education centers to furnish programs that individual schools cannot afford.

WELFARE

Since the landmark 1935 Social Security Act, the Social Security Administration has given states liberal financial aid for partly assisting dependent children (see Figure 17-3), the permanently

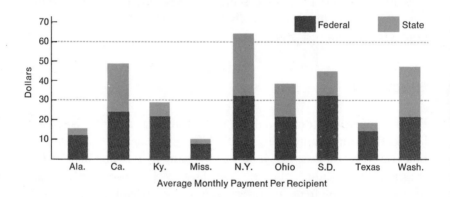

Average Monthly Payment Per Recipient

Figure 17–3. Aid to Families With Dependent Children. Average payments in selected states for recipients of Aid to Families with Dependent Children, showing federal and state shares. Graph is based on April 1969 figures. (Source: *Congressional Quarterly Weekly Report,* March 6, 1970, p. 704.)

disabled, the blind, and the aged, and for maternal and child health services. Although the federal government does not administer the program, it establishes minimum standards the states must observe to get federal funds. State and local governments must also continue to provide general relief and direct relief payments to other people needing help.

[7] In 1970 Congress passed a three-year, $24.6 billion extension of the ESEA.

TABLE 17-1
THE CITIES' WELFARE ROLLS:
PERCENTAGE OF CITY RESIDENTS RECEIVING PUBLIC
ASSISTANCE, FEBRUARY 1970, FOR CENTRAL CITY OR COUNTY
IN TWENTY LARGEST METROPOLITAN AREAS

Boston	15.3
New York	13.4
Baltimore	12.8
St. Louis	12.5
San Francisco	11.7
Philadelphia	11.5
Newark	11.5
Los Angeles	9.7
Atlanta	8.7
Chicago	6.8
Washington, D.C.	6.7
Cleveland	6.6
Detroit	6.4
Pittsburgh	5.8
Milwaukee	5.1
Seattle–Everett	4.1
Minneapolis–St. Paul	4.0
Dallas	3.6
Anaheim–Santa Ana–Garden Grove	3.2
Houston	2.9

Source: Department of Health, Education and Welfare, March 1971.

The Social Security program also provides *unemployment insurance,* which provides payment of funds for a limited time (currently a maximum of twenty-six weeks in nearly all states) to workers who are discharged or laid off for reasons beyond their control. Started in 1935, the program is funded by a federal payroll tax on industrial and commercial employers with four or more workers. Congress wrote the law in such a way that in states with approved state unemployment insurance laws, 90 percent of what employers paid into the state program could be credited toward their federal payroll tax assessment. Within two years, all states had such insurance programs, for had they not, employers would have had to pay the federal tax, but their employees wouldn't have been eligible for unemployment benefits.

Today, over 50 million workers are covered, including approximately 80 percent of those in nonagricultural jobs.

A third major part of the Social Security program is the *old-age, survivors, and disability insurance program,* administered directly by the federal government and now covering about 90 percent of those employed. Employees contribute, through payroll deductions, to an old-age insurance fund, which pays them monthly benefits when they retire at sixty-five (or at sixty-two with reduced benefits) or if they are permanently disabled and are over fifty.[8]

POVERTY

Although we live in the most affluent society in history, more than 10 percent of American families are poor.[9] In 1961, President John Kennedy began a vigorous campaign to alleviate this poverty. In that same year, Congress created the Area Redevelopment Administration to make grants and low-interest loans to poverty areas for developing industry and improving roads and other public facilities. The law also started a job-training program, later broadened by the Manpower Development and Training Act, to train the "hard-core" poor.

In the eleven-state area of Appalachia, the country's largest depressed area, the Area Redevelopment Administration operates together with the Appalachian Regional Commission (created by Congress in 1963), which represents the states affected and all the federal agencies involved. This area-development approach is a new idea in cooperative federalism. Most decision making and supervision is done by the states; although the federal government can veto decisions, it cannot dictate them: before an action is taken, it must be approved by most of the member states.

A serious weakness in the area-development approach is that

[8] The combined employer-employee rate of contribution, in 1971, was 10.3 percent on the first $9000 of the worker's earnings. The average monthly Social Security retirement check for a retired worker in 1970 was $116. In 1971 Congress raised monthly benefits by 10 percent.
[9] According to the Social Security Administration, the poverty threshold in 1970 for a nonfarm family of four was $3,700.

it bypasses some poverty-stricken *individuals.* These people may be helped by direct relief handouts, of course, but handouts have been criticized for making welfare recipients dependent on a dole and not allowing them to share the nation's general prosperity. One program designed to alleviate this was the 1964 *Economic Opportunity Act,* the cornerstone of President Lyndon Johnson's "war on poverty." This legislation opened a number of new fronts, as follows:

The *Job Corps,* intended to help disadvantaged sixteen- to twenty-one-year-old youths, provided urban and rural residence centers in which they could complete their education and gain vocational skills. The Job Corps operates in cooperation with states and communities, with the federal government providing up to 90 percent of the funds.

A program of part-time work, financed principally by the federal government, was instituted to help college students from low-income families.

The *Neighborhood Youth Corps,* was established to try to lower the high school dropout rate, to encourage those who had quit school to return (by providing part-time employment for students in low-income families), and to improve the employability of those who had finished school.

Head Start programs were launched to provide pre-school experience for children of low-income families so that they can enter school on a more equal basis.

Urban and rural *Community Action Programs,* federally financed but operated by private and public agencies with maximum participation of the poor (all told, they have about 29,000 nonprofessional employees, mostly from urban ghettos), were set up to develop a community's job opportunities and upgrade its physical and aesthetic environment. Long-term low-interest loans have been made available to low-income persons to finance small business enterprises and to acquire farm land. Federal assistance has been made available to state and local governments to improve living conditions for migratory farm workers.

The *Volunteers In Service To America* (VISTA), the so-called domestic peace corps, allows volunteers, eighteen years of age and older, to help states and communities to meet the health and education needs of impoverished groups such as migrant workers and Indians. Finally, the 1964 law provided legal aid for indigent criminal defendants in federal courts.

Most of the above programs are coordinated by the Office of Economic Opportunity (OEO), except the Job Corps, given in 1969 to the Department of Labor, and Head Start, assigned to the Department of Health, Education, and Welfare.

By 1971, the federal government was spending more than $30 billion dollars on various programs to assist the poor. Yet these efforts have made only a limited impression on hard-core poverty. Why is this?

First, notwithstanding the increasing expenditures for welfare and kindred programs considered in this chapter, most are under-financed. Second, the federal government has not developed a coordinated strategy to eliminate poverty. Third, while some of the programs are imaginative, many have been inherited from the Depression years of the 1930s and are inadequate to contend with the question of poverty in a relatively high-employment and affluent society.

In recent years, a new concept of public assistance, an *income supplement program* which guarantees cash payments to low-income families (in addition to existing programs providing training, education, and necessary goods and services), has received increasing attention. President Nixon's *family assistance plan*, based on this concept and presented to Congress in 1969, 1970, and 1971 represents a major effort to reorient federal welfare policy. Under this plan, a family of four would get some aid if its annual income were less than $3900. This plan would supply cash aid to the working poor for the first time, thus extending assistance to about 6 million families who previously were not included in public assistance programs.

Suggested Additional Reading

Cochrane, W. W. *City Man's Guide to the Farm Problem.* 1966.

Davies, J. C. *The Politics of Pollution,* 1970.

Dulles, F. R. *Labor in America: A History.* 1966.

Ewing, D. W. *The Practice of Planning.* 1968.

Harrington, M. *The Other America: Poverty in the United States.* 1962.

Kosa, J. A. *et al.* (eds.). *Poverty and Health.* 1970.

Kotz, N. *Let Them Eat Promises: The Politics of Hunger in America.* 1969.

Landis, J. M. *The Administrative Process.* 1966.

Mosher, F. C. *Democracy and the Public Service.* 1968.

National Urban Coalition. *Counterbudget: A Blueprint for Changing National Priorities, 1971–1976.* 1971.

Redford, E. S. *The Role of Government in the American Economy.* 1966.

Riessman, F. *Strategies Against Poverty.* 1969.

Tanzer, M. *The Sick Society: An Economic Examination.* 1971.

Theobald, R. (ed.). *Social Policies for America in the Seventies: Nine Divergent Views.* 1969.

U.S. Bureau of the Budget. *The Federal Budget in Brief* (annual).

Wilcox, C. *Public Policies Toward Business.* 1970.

18 Foreign Policy

Whom the gods would destroy, they first have go mad.

—Euripides

In the actual conduct of foreign relations the supremacy of the federal government is unchallenged. The President does not do it all, for Congress, state and local governments, and the Supreme Court also play significant parts. Even so, the President is its chief architect.

THE PRESIDENT AND FOREIGN RELATIONS

"I make foreign policy," said President Harry Truman, echoing Thomas Jefferson, who 150 years earlier had described the process as "executive altogether." Both were essentially correct.

But where does the President get this vast power? Much of it is derived not from the Constitution, but from custom, usage, laws of Congress, and especially the President's strategic advantages. Certainly, however, his constitutional powers here are considerable. With the advice and consent of the Senate he may make treaties, appoint high-ranking State Department officials, ambassadors, other public ministers and consuls, and receive foreign envoys. Some of these presidential powers have produced others—his power to appoint and receive ambassadors, for instance, has been broadened so that he may also extend diplomatic recognition to foreign governments or show disapproval by not recognizing them or by breaking off relations.

The President may also use his constitutionally given powers as commander in chief to achieve foreign policy goals, making important decisions of war and peace even without Congress's approval. Although, on one hand, Congress may pressure him to endorse a war policy, as it did President McKinley in 1898, it has never declared war without the President's consent. Nor may Congress negotiate peace. The President, on the other hand, may make wars or delay peace settlements if he wants. When in 1846 President Polk sent American troops into territory claimed by both the United States and Mexico, he left Congress no choice but to declare war. President Truman sent American forces to Korea, and President Johnson sent troops to Vietnam, committing the U.S. to war without official declarations of Congress. In Korea and Vietnam, the President did not ask Congress for a declaration of war partly because doing so would have imposed rigidities (e.g., the formal entry of American, North Korean, and North Vietnamese allies into the wars and the need for complicated negotiations to terminate the declared wars) that would make restoring peace difficult and partly because the United States did not diplomatically recognize its opponents, North Korea and North Vietnam.

Congress has declared war only five times: the War of 1812, the Mexican War, the Spanish-American War, and the two world wars. The six major undeclared wars are the naval war with France (1798–1800), the Barbary wars (1801–1805, and 1815), the Mexican-American conflicts (1914–1917), and the Korean and Vietnam wars.

The President need not even depend on the Senate for treaty approval, but may bypass it entirely and negotiate *executive agreements,* not treaties, with foreign powers. Presidents have often done this, although in the last two decades they have done so more cautiously, securing congressional or at least Senate approval for agreements involving important financial commitments or directly affecting foreign policy (e.g., the nuclear nonproliferation treaty approved in 1969).

The President also has much power because of his greater access to information and because of the need for secrecy and speed in conducting foreign relations. Moreover he has assets in his numerous opportunities (television, for instance) to appeal directly over the heads of his political opponents to his national constituency for support for his policies. In this way President Johnson, for example, was able to sustain his Vietnam war policies for many months despite opposition in Congress.

The State Department and Foreign Relations

The primary responsibility of the Department of State is to give the President information and counsel to help him formulate and carry out foreign policy. Among other things, the department also tries to protect American citizens abroad, receives reports from its foreign diplomatic staffs, represents the United States in international organizations, carries out public relations for the United States in other countries, promotes cultural relations, and issues passports and visas.

The head of the department, the Secretary of State (see Figure 18-1), is the President's chief adviser and first-ranking Cabinet member. He frequently acts as his spokesman and—officially, at least—helps him make decisions. Just how much influence he actually has depends on the President. Presidents Kennedy and Johnson, for instance, were virtually their own Secretaries of State as has been Nixon; none of these have found the State Department a useful source of policy ideas. Increasingly, the department has become more administrative, with the President depending more on his own foreign policy advisers for creative thoughts on policy.

There are, of course, other federal agencies involved in foreign affairs—the 1949 Hoover Commission listed forty-five, and others have been added since then. Most important is the Defense Department,[1] which has often overshadowed the State Department

[1] Discussed in more detail in Chapter 19.

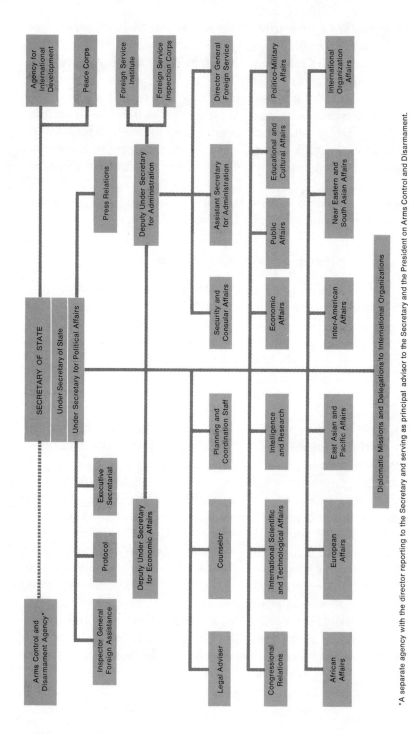

Figure 18-1. Department of State. (Source: *U.S. Government Organization Manual, 1970–1971.*)

in making foreign policy, particularly during the war in Southeast Asia. Many believe this is a lapse in civilian control and that it represents military solutions to political problems.

The National Security Council and Foreign Relations

The National Security Council advises the President on matters of national security—foreign, domestic, and military. Besides the President, its members are the Vice-President, Secretary of State, Secretary of Defense, Director of the Office of Emergency Preparedness, and the President's Special Assistant for National Security Affairs. Other persons attend at the invitation of the President.

Some Presidents—Eisenhower, for instance—have relied more on the NSC than have other Presidents. President Kennedy used it much less, although he did use a specially created executive committee of the NSC (and his brother Robert) to coordinate and direct his policies in the October 1962 Cuban missile crisis.

The Central Intelligence Agency and Foreign Relations

Like the Department of Defense, the Central Intelligence Agency has a special role in foreign affairs. Created in 1947, it serves directly under the National Security Council, relaying information it gathers from secret and open sources abroad and from other U.S. agencies.

The CIA has been frequently criticized for going beyond simple information gathering and actually making foreign policy—sometimes without even the Secretary of State knowing it. For example, it is supposed to have engineered the overthrow of unfriendly governments in Iran, Laos, and Guatemala. It also helped topple the Diem government in South Vietnam in 1963. The CIA planned and unsuccessfully attempted to overthrow Fidel Castro's government in Cuba in the abortive Bay of Pigs invasion in 1961. How many other governments it has tampered with or how many "failures" it has had is unknown because its operations are secret—even from Congress. Its budget is also secret, concealed from Congress by being distributed throughout the federal budget, but one guess is that the CIA spends from two to four times as much money as does the State Department.

After the 1961 Bay of Pigs disaster, President Kennedy tried to return the CIA to its original role of straight information gathering. An effort was made to set up a congressional watchdog to oversee the agency, but nothing came of it. In 1967, the CIA again came under fire when it was discovered to have found ways to give the money to political-action and research organizations— although the law forbade the agency from undertaking any functions within the U.S. Again Congress considered creating machinery to oversee the CIA but again failed to do so.

CONGRESS AND FOREIGN RELATIONS

The President is most responsible for foreign policy, but Congress also has many constitutional powers by which it can influence the conduct of foreign affairs. Its constitutional authority includes: providing for the common defense, declaring war, regulating commerce with foreign nations, establishing a uniform rule of naturalization, defining and punishing piracies on the high seas and offenses against the law of nations, raising and supporting armies and navies, making rules concerning captures on land and water, and making all laws necessary and proper for carrying these powers into execution. Most effective, perhaps, is its ability to withhold appropriations for the President's foreign military and economic aid programs.

The laws that Congress makes can directly affect the executive agencies that carry out foreign policy or even specific foreign policy matters themselves (e.g., tariffs). In addition, Congress can make declarations for or against the President's policies, and may even use its power of investigation to draw attention to the administration's foreign policy.

A case in point is the Senate's 1964 Tonkin Gulf Resolution, passed after North Vietnamese gunboats supposedly attacked an American destroyer. This resolution expressed support for President Johnson to order reprisals against North Vietnam, but its broad interpretation by the President to expand the Vietnam war later led to a great deal of soul-searching among members of the Congress. Subsequently, the Senate Foreign Relations Committee, headed by Senator J. William Fulbright, held hearings on Vietnam, signaling a breakdown of confidence between Congress and the White House and the end of twenty-five years of nonpartisanship in foreign affairs. The upshot was that the Senate in 1969 voted 80–9 to withhold funds for any U.S. "ground combat troops" introduced into Laos or Thailand; in 1970 it rescinded the Tonkin Gulf Resolution and passed the so-called Cooper-Church Resolution to deny funds for American ground forces in Cambodia or direct air support of Cambodian troops. In 1971 the Senate Foreign Relations Committee held hearings on the President's war-making powers. On the table were no fewer than three bills aimed at limiting the President's authority to commit U.S. troops abroad.

THE COURTS AND FOREIGN RELATIONS

The courts do not have much influence on foreign affairs. The Supreme Court holds that the judiciary is without the facilities or aptitude, and moreover, that foreign policy is a political, not a judicial, responsibility. The Court clearly recognized the President's primacy in foreign relations when in 1936 it asserted that he has "a degree of discretion and freedom from statutory restriction which would not be admissible were domestic affairs alone involved" (*U.S.* v. *Curtiss-Wright Export Corporation*).

Nevertheless, the Supreme Court has the *potential* to influence foreign policy. It could, for instance, decide the constitutionality of all international agreements as well as all other actions of the President and Congress (*Reid* v. *Covert,* 1957). However, should the Court void an important foreign policy decision of Congress or the President (e.g., by ruling presidential war-making unconstitutional) it could precipitate a constitutional crisis.

STATE AND LOCAL GOVERNMENTS
AND FOREIGN RELATIONS

State and local governments have far more influence on foreign affairs than most of us assume. Sometimes these are negative effects. In 1891, for instance, Italy severed relations with the

United States when a Louisiana mob lynched Italian citizens. For some time there was real danger of war, since the U.S. government was unable to make state or local authorities take action, even though they knew the mob leaders' identities. In 1906, Japanese and American relations were strained when the San Francisco Board of Education segregated Japanese in its public schools —despite several treaties with Japan in which the U.S. agreed to give Japanese citizens equal treatment—and the Secretary of State had to plead with San Francisco to modify its action. In 1935 the Secretary of State made an official apology to the Hitler government (at this time the U.S. still maintained diplomatic relations with Germany) when a New York magistrate disparaged it during a trial of six persons charged with disrespecting the Nazi flag. A more recent example occurred in 1965 when the mayor of New York, reflecting pressure from the large American Jewish community, snubbed Arab dignitaries visiting the city.

American foreign policy has often been frustrated by states' rights advocates fearing the authority of the national government. By blocking our ratification of the draft treaty of the United Nations Covenant on Human Rights, because they believe the covenant would allow the federal government to have greater control over civil rights here, they have limited America's world leadership ability in developing human rights.

Some states have also complicated our foreign relations somewhat by enacting laws denying aliens the rights to own land (e.g., the California law which forbade land title to aliens—mostly Japanese—ineligible for citizenship) or engage in certain businesses or occupations. However, such discrimination is not widespread—in fact, is definitely decreasing—and has not resulted in serious difficulties with other nations.

In recent years, there has been more cooperation between the federal and state (and even local) governments in foreign affairs. For instance, under the federally sponsored *Alliance for Progress* foreign aid program to Latin America, over two dozen states have joined with private groups to encourage economic development there: California has given assistance to Chile, Oregon to Costa Rica, and Texas to Peru. Some American cities have adopted foreign "sister cities"—Los Angeles, for example, has adopted

Eliat in Israel and other foreign cities—and exchange students, official visitors, and exhibits with them. Many state colleges and universities maintain overseas campuses, engage in student and teacher exchanges, and carry out international education programs at home.

Increasingly, state and local politicians are expressing themselves on foreign policy matters: governors and even mayors are asked by the President to support his foreign policies, and state legislatures and city councils send resolutions to the federal government. The principal reason for this interest is that foreign policy decisions often have a major impact on states and localities. Changes in trade agreements, for instance, directly affect local business, employment, and tax revenues.

PUBLIC OPINION, INTEREST GROUPS, AND FOREIGN RELATIONS

American elections often turn on major foreign policy issues—the Vietnam war, for instance, was a major issue in 1964 and 1968. Usually, we Americans are more concerned and better informed about domestic than foreign affairs. But Presidents and Congressmen who ignore public opinion on foreign policy may find themselves in trouble with the voters. Though leaders may manipulate public opinion for a while, they cannot sustain a long-term foreign policy program against the will of the voters, as witnessed by the rising clamor of public resentment against the Indochina war. It is also clear that the attitudes of ethnic and religious groups cannot be overlooked. Just as nineteenth-century presidential candidates had to avoid showing too much friendship with Britain, lest they lose the Irish vote, so today such candidates cannot ignore the feelings of American Jews about Israel.

Nor can they ignore economic interest groups—agriculture, labor, and business. All are vitally interested in foreign policy, especially trade policy, where their interests are most directly affected. Business is particularly active—for instance, in committing the U.S. government to private enterprise in its foreign aid grants, to being concerned about American investments abroad, and to intervening where necessary on their behalf.

TREATIES AND EXECUTIVE AGREEMENTS

Treaties and executive agreements with foreign countries, two instruments of foreign relations, are important in regulating the affairs of nations. Today these international agreements and the decisions involved in their execution not only comprise the basic source of international law (particularly important in this respect is the United Nations treaty), but also influence the daily lives of nearly all of us.

Treaties

A written document of the exact terms of an accord between contracting nations, a treaty may be *bilateral* (e.g., the proposed Okinawa treaty with Japan to return Okinawa to Japanese rule in 1972), binding two nations, or *multilateral* (e.g., the Southeast Asia Treaty), binding several nations.

Only the President or his agents may negotiate treaties. Usually the President negotiates them and seeks the advice and consent of the Senate afterward, although frequently he may consult important Senators and Representatives during the negotiation. For major treaties he may even put key Senators on negotiating teams, as with the 1963 nuclear test ban treaty, for instance.

The Senate may approve a treaty, if two-thirds of those present concur, reject it, or attach amendments to it. If the Senate amends a proposed treaty, the President, if he still wants it, must renew negotiations with the other treaty nations and get them to accept the amendments. There is an exception, however: if the treaty is multilateral, he may *ratify* it—that is, approve it with the other nations—but attach the Senate amendments as *reservations* to the terms of the agreement. These are not binding on other signatories unless they agree to them. In any event, the President may refuse to ratify a treaty, in which case the treaty has no effect.

384

Once a treaty is ratified by the contracting governments it is binding upon them in international law. When made public by the President, it becomes law in this country. If it conflicts with a federal law, the one that is later in date prevails. However, neither a law nor a court decision can dissolve a treaty as an international obligation.

Not all treaties are intended to be permanent; some provide a termination date. A treaty can also, of course, be ended by war, be replaced by another treaty, or be annulled by one of the governments involved in it.

Executive Agreements

Since 1900, American Presidents have negotiated more executive agreements than treaties. These differ from treaties in form and effect only in that they do not require Senate approval. Like treaties, however, these agreements are part of the supreme law of the land and need not be implemented by statutes.

Although many executive agreements deal with minor matters, several have made important international arrangements. Examples are the 1845 annexation of Texas, the 1889 Open Door policy for China, the 1940 agreement with Britain to exchange American destroyers for ninety-nine-year leases on naval bases; and the 1970 agreement with Mexico establishing the center line of the Rio Grande as a border between the United States and Mexico.

The President may handle an executive agreement in two ways: (1) he may submit it to both houses of Congress for approval by majority vote, or (2) he may disregard Congress entirely and make the agreement on his own authority—an authority derived from Congress's authorization, previous treaties, or by implication from his specific constitutional powers.

Executive agreements may be used instead of treaties—the choice is the President's. In fact, if the Senate refuses to approve a treaty, the President may make an executive agreement on the same matter. However, recent Presidents have been cautious about making executive agreements because of Congress's hostility to their overuse.

FOREIGN POLICY FROM WITHDRAWAL
TO COLD WAR LEADERSHIP

American diplomacy from 1789 to our assumption of Cold War leadership after World War II clearly demonstrates how foreign policy changes according to altered physical circumstances. Early American policies that limited the entanglement of a weak nation in the clashes of other nations gave way to those that reflected our later disposition to seize opportunities and take ventures for expansion and survival and finally to our recent arrogation of world leadership.

Washington's Foreign Policy and the Retreat
From European Politics

The foreign policies of our first President greatly influenced the subsequent conduct of our foreign relations. In fact, George Washington's *Farewell Address* to the American people signified the establishment of an American foreign policy. In it, he states the case for American isolationism from European affairs:

> Europe has a set of primary interests, which to us have none, or a very remote relation. Hence she must be engaged in frequent controversies, the causes of which are essentially foreign to our concerns. Hence, therefore, it must be unwise in us to implicate ourselves, by artificial ties, in the ordinary combinations and collisions of her friendships or enmities.

He further asserted: "It is our true policy to steer clear of permanent alliances with any portion of the world . . . [though] we may safely trust to temporary alliances for extraordinary emergencies."

Washington was giving specific counsel to a weak and divided nation, based on the United States' painful experiences with the entangling treaty of 1778 with France, which threatened our newly acquired freedom by drawing this country into the struggles between Old World powers in the Americas. In advising a retreat from European politics, Washington was, in effect, advocating a retreat from *all* power politics in foreign affairs.

American aloofness from Europe was an established political fact until the end of the nineteenth century. And it was a result of deliberate choice as well as of our favorable geographic location. Washington and other responsible observers emphasized this choice with "our detached and distant situation" in mind. "Why," he asked, "forego the advantages of so peculiar a situation?" Thus separated by the great oceans from the Great Powers, spectators from afar, Americans watched the international struggle in Europe, Africa, and Asia.

Monroe's Famous Doctrine

The 1823 *Monroe Doctrine*, or "the doctrine of the two hemispheres," extended Washington's foreign policy. The doctrine was an American reaction to a double threat by Spain—with the aid of the "Holy Alliance" of Austria, Russia, and Prussia—(1) to regain control of her former Latin American colonies, which had made themselves independent republics during the Napoleonic wars, and (2) to reestablish her monopoly over their trade. To the United States, the restoration of the monarchy meant a challenge to republican institutions in the Western Hemisphere, and a Spanish mercantile monopoly would have destroyed the profitable trade the U.S. had built up with the former Spanish colonies.

In August 1823, Great Britain proposed that the United States join with her to prevent action by the Holy Alliance, hoping thus to maintain her trade with the new republics and to guarantee her future influence in Latin America. President James Monroe, following the advice of his Secretary of State John Quincy Adams, refused the British offer. He not only feared the entanglements that might result with the British, but also calculated that England, with her mastery of the seas, would not permit the Holy Alliance to intervene in any event.

The noncolonization principle of the famous Monroe Doctrine, included in the President's annual message to Congress on December 2, 1823, was stated thus:

> . . . the American continents, by the free and independent conditions which they have assumed and maintain, are henceforth

not to be considered as subjects for future colonization by any European powers.

Later in his address President Monroe gave his views on possible intervention by the Holy Alliance. Their political system, he said,

> . . . is essentially different . . . from that of America. . . . We owe it, therefore, to candor and to the amicable relations existing between the United States and those powers to declare that we should consider any attempt on their part to extend their system to any portion of this hemisphere as dangerous to our peace and safety.

The President pointed out that the United States would consider unfriendly any attempt by a European power to control the destiny of any of the independent republics of the Western Hemisphere. For our part, he promised the United States would not interfere with existing European dependencies in the New World or the internal concerns of any European power.

Monroe's basic ideas were not original; they were shared by Washington, John Adams, and Jefferson. Monroe had simply formalized such existing ideas as those of the *two hemispheres, no transfer of territory, nonintervention, and nonentanglement.*

For more than a century, the United States generally followed the Monroe Doctrine of American *neutrality* in European wars and in keeping Western Hemisphere republics secure from interference by the Old World powers. In fact, even today, though the United States is deeply involved in the affairs of Europe and Asia, some people cite the doctrine as justifying American actions against the Communist government in Cuba.

Manifest Destiny and Imperialist Expansion

The term "manifest destiny" was coined in 1845 by a New York newspaper editor, John L. O'Sullivan, who claimed Americans had "the right of our manifest destiny to overspread and to possess the whole of the continent which Providence has given us for the development of the great experiment in liberty and federative self-government entrusted to us."

Embracing this idea, Americans believed that *all* North America was destined to become our territory—despite prior claims by France, Great Britain, Spain, Russia, Mexico, and American Indians based on rights derived from discovery, exploration, and settlement. This mystic conviction predated O'Sullivan's statement and, assisted by a combination of diplomacy, migration, and force, it figured in the 1803 Louisiana Purchase, more directly in the 1819 acquisition of Florida from Spain, in making Russia abandon claims to the Pacific Coast south of Alaska in 1824, and in forcing Britain's withdrawal of claims to Oregon territory in 1846. This concept also became a justification for the United States' war with Mexico in 1846–1848 over the territory between the Rio Grande and the Nueces River, which President Polk considered Texan.

Manifest destiny was slowed drastically by the Civil War and post-war reconstruction, the only major acquisition being the 1867 purchase of Alaska from Russia for $7 million. By the end of the nineteenth century, however, Americans again revealed an unmistakable desire for adventure and a wish to achieve new territory (and raw materials and markets for industrial growth) commensurate with the United States' bursting power. The immediate fruits of this rebirth of manifest destiny and a spur to further imperialistic ventures were the acquisitions of Hawaii in 1898 and of Samoa in 1899. Following these triumphs, propagandists of imperialism, including Theodore Roosevelt, urged further expansion, and preachers, professors, and newspaper publishers took up the cry. Their immediate goal was war with Spain. Anti-imperialists fought frantically to stem the tide but got no real hearing.

The Spanish-American War (1898) began ostensibly with the sinking of the U.S. battleship Maine in Havana harbor (Cuba was a Spanish colony), but the war was actually a result of manifest destiny combined at the start with the humanitarian motive of freeing the Cuban people. Spain was hardly a match. With a population of only 18 million (versus 75 million Americans), a navy of floating derelicts, and only the sympathy (not the support) of major European powers, Spain was soundly defeated. On December 10, 1898, the United States forced Spain to cede the Philippines, Puerto Rico, and Guam outright by treaty, and the U.S. asserted a form of protectorate over Cuba. The real meaning of the Spanish-American War, however, was something else. When the war began, Spain had the status but not the strength of a Great Power, whereas the United States was a Great Power in fact but not status. While the American victory assured the U.S. this coveted Great Power status, it also produced other unanticipated results. The forcible annexation of millions of people against their will not only did violence to the American Declaration of Independence, but also projected the U.S. into the Far East. This vastly increased the likelihood of European entanglements (or trouble with Japan) and lost us the strong moral position of our "doctrine of the two hemispheres."

Theodore Roosevelt's Imperialist Interpretation of the Monroe Doctrine

The original 1823 Monroe Doctrine expressed respect for the integrity of the sister republics of the Americas. It contained no hint that the United States was entitled to interfere in their affairs. But in 1904, President Theodore Roosevelt gave it precisely this interpretation. The chronic "wrong-doing" (e.g., not paying their debts to foreign lenders) of Latin American nations, Roosevelt said, ultimately required the United States, in keeping with the Monroe Doctrine, "to the exercise of an international police power." Since European powers were forbidden by the Monroe Doctrine to intervene, he said, it was the "sacred duty" of the United States to do so.

Thus, the Monroe Doctrine, designed to prevent European intervention in the Latin American republics, became the justification for American intervention in those countries. In ensuing years it was used to vindicate wholesale landings of marines in Central America and the Caribbean republics. Many of these assaults were undertaken to collect from these weak countries very high interest on loans made to them by wealthy Americans. They also served, as one historian puts it, as "assurances of protection to Wall Street"[2] for its investments in Latin America.

[2] Thomas A. Bailey, *A Diplomatic History of the American People* (New York: Appleton-Century-Crofts, 1946), p. 582.

Franklin Roosevelt's Good Neighbor Era

Reaction against American imperialism in Latin America reached such proportions in the early 1930s that newly elected President Franklin D. Roosevelt felt compelled to repudiate the imperialist interpretations of the Monroe Doctrine. To accomplish this, he devised the "Good Neighbor" policy, consisting of three specific commitments: *first,* that the United States would refrain from armed intervention in the Americas;[3] *second,* that maintaining the orderly processes of government in each Latin American nation was primarily the concern of that nation; but that, *third,* when these orderly processes broke down in a way that affected other nations in the hemisphere, it became the concern of the hemisphere. These principles were followed rather consistently and generally improved relations.

The wisdom of the Good Neighbor policy was borne out during World War II. Most of the Latin American nations cooperated with the United States in the war against the Axis and in the defense of the hemisphere. In recent years, however, the policy has been often strained by the United States' friendly relations with right-wing dictatorships in Latin America and by American interventions such as occurred in the Dominican Republic in 1965.

From Withdrawal to Involvement

When the United States was drawn into World Wars I and II, the principles of noninvolvement—enunciated by Washington, restated by Jefferson, and pledged by every President—were inevitably set aside. Actually, there was no choice. At stake was the domination of Europe, if not the world, by hostile powers. Both times, Britain, which for 400 years had prevented any power from totally dominating the European continent, was unable by herself to turn back the would-be conquerors.

After World War I, President Woodrow Wilson tried to depart from the peacetime noninvolvement policy by championing in-

[3] The foundations of Franklin Roosevelt's Good Neighbor policy were laid in the Coolidge and Hoover administrations, which abrogated the Theodore Roosevelt corollary to the Monroe Doctrine.

ternationalism and U.S. membership in the League of Nations. But he was frustrated by isolationists in the Senate, and in 1920 the voters showed they preferred "normalcy"—meaning isolation —when they elected Warren G. Harding as President.

For two decades after World War I, Americans turned their backs on the world, thinking that what happened outside the Americas was of little concern to them. By the 1930s, however, Americans began to watch with apprehension as dictatorships preyed upon weak countries in Europe, Asia, and Africa. By the fall of 1940, public opinion polls showed that most citizens favored giving American aid to Britain in her war against Germany, even though it might mean that the U.S. would become involved in the European war. A year later the United States was again at war.

During World War II the American people and their leaders, observing the new conditions of world affairs, became convinced that if world peace were to be maintained the U.S. would have to assume a position of world leadership. The different outlooks of the United States and the communist nations, the weakness of our European allies, and the defeat of the German-Italian-Japanese anti-communist alliance also impelled the United States to take the lead in trying to contain communism. The United States assumed an active role in the United Nations and took the initiative in forming the North Atlantic Treaty Organization. With these decisions the United States made a drastic and possibly an irreversible departure from the traditional American policy of nonintervention.

Suggested Additional Reading

Bailey, T. A. A Diplomatic History of the American People. 1946. The Art of Diplomacy. 1968.

Bemis, S. F. A Diplomatic History of the United States. 1965.

Chayes, A., and J. B. Wiesner (eds.). ABM: An Evaluation of the Decision to Deploy an Antiballistic Missile System. 1969.

Clark, K. C., and L. J. Legere (ed.). The President and the Management of National Security. 1969.

Cole, W. S. An Interpretative History of American Foreign Relations. 1968.

Hilsman, R. *The Politics of Policy Making in Defense and Foreign Affairs.* 1971.

Lerch, C. O. *Foreign Policy of the American People.* 3rd ed. 1967.

O'Leary, M. K. *The Politics of American Foreign Aid.* 1967.

Pusey, M. *The Way We Go to War.* 1969.

Radway, L. I. *The Liberal Democracy in World Affairs: Foreign Policy and National Defense.* 1969.

Rosenau, J. N. (ed.). *Domestic Sources of Foreign Policy.* 1967.

Sapin, B. M. *The Making of United States Foreign Policy.* 1965.

19 Foreign and Military Policy: The Search for Security

Justice without force is impotent. Force
without justice is tyrannical. We must
therefore combine justice with force.

—Pascal

The hopes that a postwar alliance could promote world order
and peace disappeared a few years after World War II. The
mutual fear and hostility of Russia and the United States, added
to their natural ambition and rivalry as two new Great Powers,
created the Cold War.

SECURITY THROUGH CONTAINMENT

In the early '50s, the Soviet Union began to wage a vigorous
foreign policy, along with militant promotion of the communist
ideology. Whether or not the Soviet plan was—or is—to "take
over the world," the U.S. reacted as if in fact it was. Following
a resurgence of an anti-communist mood much like that of the
'20s and '30s, the federal government under Harry Truman inaugurated a foreign policy whose dominant goal was the *con-*

tainment of the economic, ideological, and military expansion of communism. To do this, the United States established a system of collective defense arrangements, built up a massive inventory of weapons, began providing foreign-aid funds to other countries, started propagating anti-communist (and pro-American) propaganda—and finally used armed force.

Collective Defense Pacts

Since World War II, the United States has entered into eight regional mutual-defense agreements. As the accompanying map shows (Figure 19-1), these cover three general areas of the world: *Western Europe* is covered by the North Atlantic Treaty; the *Western Pacific* by the Southeast Asia Treaty, the ANZUS Treaty, and treaties with the Philippines, Japan, the Republic of (South) Korea and the Republic of (Nationalist) China; and *Latin America* by the Rio Treaty.

North Atlantic Treaty Organization (NATO)

When in 1949 the United States sponsored and then joined NATO, which is both a military and a political alliance, it was a major development in the new policy of containing Soviet expansion. It was also a major departure from the traditional American policy of noninvolvement; for, except for the 1947 Rio Treaty, this was the first time in over 150 years that the United States joined a peacetime alliance providing for mutual assistance in case of attack.

American participation in NATO assumed that U.S. security was tied to Western European security. In the treaty, we and the eleven other countries (now fourteen others, since Turkey and Greece joined in 1952 and West Germany in 1955) agreed that an attack against one was an attack against all and that all members would take action, including force, to protect the "Atlantic Community."

Besides the United States, the original members were Great Britain, France, Italy, Canada, Belgium, the Netherlands, Luxembourg, Norway, Portugal, Denmark, and Iceland. Under NATO command they have created an international army, continually consulting with each other to make their alliance effective.

Some feel NATO violates the spirit of the peaceful intentions of the United Nations Charter and its security arrangements. However, supporters insist that NATO is based upon the legal right of individual and collective self-defense. Whatever the merits of this debate, NATO is currently in trouble. Most of our European allies worry less than we do about the Soviet menace, and some, principally France and Britain, differ with us over the proper stance to take toward communist states and resent our preoccupation with Asia. Moreover, there is also considerable suspicion in Europe that the United States would not risk nuclear retaliation to defend West Germany against a Soviet invasion and that Europeans would have to make the greater sacrifices in terms of human lives. France in particular under President Charles de Gaulle—resentful that the United States has worked more closely with Canada and Britain and especially that this country has refused to share nuclear secrets with her—emphasized creating a "third force" ("force de frappe") in Europe, withdrew French forces from NATO commands, and had NATO headquarters (now in Brussels) removed from French soil.

Southeast Asia Treaty Organization (SEATO) and the Other Pacific Pacts

In the early '50s the United States concluded six collective defense treaties with nations of the western Pacific in order to improve the security of these noncommunist countries and to protect American interests there. While agreements vary, most of them provide for mutual defense against a threatened or actual attack on a member in the Pacific area.

The treaty with the largest membership (eight) is SEATO, modeled after NATO, and created in 1954 after the defeat of France in Indo-China. As the map (Figure 19-1) shows, besides the United States and France, members are the United Kingdom, Australia, New Zealand, the Philippines, Pakistan, and Thailand. Two large countries in the area, India and Indonesia—seeking to maintain neutral positions and anxious to keep Great Power confrontations out of the area—stayed out and fought the SEATO

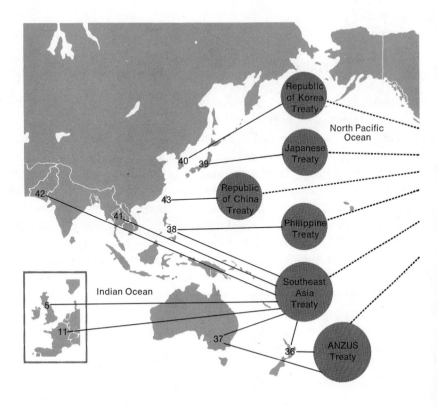

Figure 19-1. United States collective defense arrangements. (Source: U.S. Department of State.)

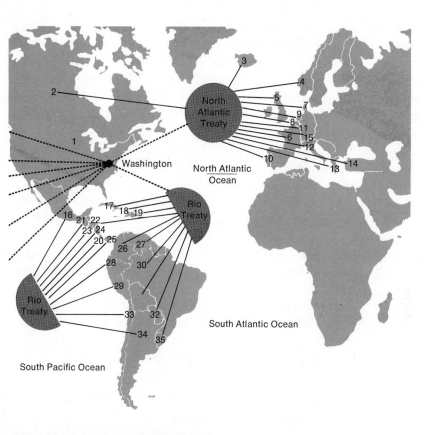

North Atlantic Treaty

Washington

North Atlantic Ocean

Rio Treaty

Rio Treaty

South Atlantic Ocean

South Pacific Ocean

33. Chile
34. Argentina
35. Uruguay

Southeast Asia Treaty (1954)
1. U.S.A.
5. Great Britain
11. France
36. New Zealand
37. Australia
38. Philippines
41. Thailand
42. Pakistan

ANZUS Treaty (1951)
1. U.S.A.
36. New Zealand
37. Australia

BILATERAL TREATIES

Philippine Treaty (1951)
1. U.S.A.
38. Philippines

Japanese Treaty (1951)
1. U.S.A.
39. Japan

Republic of Korea Treaty (1953)
1. U.S.A.
40. South Korea

Republic of China Treaty (1954)
1. U.S.A.
43. Nationalist China

idea. South Vietnam, Laos, and Cambodia, though not members, are also protected by the treaty.

SEATO differs from NATO in the obligations assumed by its members. Whereas NATO members regard an attack against one as an attack against all, SEATO requires each member merely to take action to meet an attack "in accordance with its constitutional procedures." SEATO also emphasizes giving assistance for economic and social development and for checking communist subversion. Unlike NATO, there is no standing army or real joint military command.

Contrary to popular belief, the United States was not committed under the Southeast Asia Treaty to intervene militarily in Vietnam. Because SEATO members have disagreed on the need for such action, the treaty has never been activated in this war, although another SEATO member—Australia—has sent combat troops to Vietnam.

Among its other Pacific treaties, the United States has entered into a trilateral security pact with Australia and New Zealand, called ANZUS (1951). It has also made bilateral security arrangements with the Philippines (1951), Japan (1951), South Korea (1953), and Nationalist China (1954).

The Rio Treaty of Reciprocal Assistance

This treaty was signed in 1947 by the U.S. and all of the Latin American republics. Like NATO members, these countries agree that "an armed attack against any American State is an attack against all," and all agree to assist, individually and collectively, the state under attack, until the United Nations intervenes.

The Rio Treaty also specifies that when the peace of the Americas is threatened, members are to consult with each other, and if necessary, employ sanctions, from severing diplomatic relations to using force. Before action may be taken, however, a two-thirds vote of the members is required.

Foreign Aid and Technical Assistance

To try to contain communism, the United States has also used its enormous economic power, giving other countries over $160 billion in grants and loans since the end of World War II.

The *foreign aid program* was begun in 1947, when President Truman asked Congress to give military and economic help to Greece and Turkey, both endangered by communist coups. The goal of this so-called *Truman Doctrine* was to prevent communism from taking over Western Europe. It reasoned that by bolstering the economies of European countries, we could lessen the appeal of the strong communist parties operating in many of them. The *Marshall Plan,* which grew out of the Truman Doctrine and which through economic and military assistance enabled many European countries to get back on their feet, was mostly successful and was discontinued in four years, although military aid has continued.

In recent years the aid program has been directed toward assisting underdeveloped and newly emerging nations, in order to help them try to reach the level of their rising expectations. The program has also emphasized new forms of aid such as development loans rather than outright grants.

Another kind of foreign aid for underdeveloped areas has been the *technical assistance program,* the so-called *Point Four Program* first put forth by President Truman as the fourth of several points in his January 1949 inaugural address. Again it was hoped that the influence of communism could be diminished by providing scientific and technical aid to underdeveloped countries. Since then, hundreds of experts have gone to help other countries raise their standards of living, and loans and subsidies have been provided for building factories, dams, and roads.

Two kinds of foreign aid programs are particularly worth mentioning, the Peace Corps and the Alliance for Progress.

The Peace Corps

Created in 1961 on the recommendation of President Kennedy as a semi-autonomous agency of the Department of State, the Peace Corps recruits and trains volunteers for underdeveloped nations (by 1971, there were about 9000 volunteers—average age under thirty—in sixty-one countries).

Peace Corpsmen are usually specialists in areas such as the sciences, teaching, or agriculture, and are trained by the Peace Corps in the language and culture of the host country. Currently about 40 percent are liberal arts graduates. In these countries, they work on projects for which there is a shortage of trained people—most often as teachers but also as agricultural, engineering, and public health experts—serving without much pay or special privileges. By helping people, they are also expected to help the image of the United States abroad. Even critics concede the Peace Corps has had some success, and some observers, such as historian Arnold Toynbee, believe that "in the Peace Corps the non-Western majority of mankind is going to meet a sample of Western Man at his best."

The Alliance for Progress

Launched by the Kennedy Administration in 1961, the Alliance for Progress was a ten-year $20 billion economic aid program for Latin America. This expensive program was greatly impelled by Fidel Castro's communist revolution in Cuba, which made the U.S. government fearful of another Cuba in Latin America.

The goal of the Alliance is nothing less than to solve the social and economic ills of Latin America. But the seriousness of the economic problems and the political instability make its chances uncertain. Moreover, as with most of our foreign aid programs, the abilities of our diplomats are limited because of Congress' insistence on involving private enterprise in the program. Congressional appropriations for the Alliance for Progress have been sharply reduced in recent years.

SECURITY THROUGH ARMS

The President dominates defense about as much as he does the rest of foreign policy.[2] It is he who exercises the war powers, even though the Constitution lodged them primarily with Congress. It is he who makes military decisions implementing Congressional policy, as when President Johnson ordered many heavy air strikes against North Vietnam following Senate passage of the Tonkin Gulf Resolution. Defense policy is so complex, however, that the President must depend a lot on others for decisions

[2] The President's role as commander in chief was described in Chapter 12.

on assignment of forces, weapons, strategy, and intelligence, and home-front matters such as recruitment, civil defense, and public relations. His recommendations are from several sources: the Defense Department, the National Security Council, the Atomic Energy Commission, the National Aeronautics and Space Administration, and the State Department.

If final defense policy reflects many sources, most of it comes from the *Department of Defense*, which, as Figure 19-2 shows, has many divisions. The department is headed by a civilian, the Secretary of Defense, who is advised by the Joint Chiefs of Staff and the Armed Forces Policy Council (composed of the civilian secretaries, the Joint Chiefs of Staff, the Director of Defense Research, and many civilian and military individuals, boards, and committees), and who in turn advises the President.

During World War II there were only two military departments—Navy and War—but because of wartime difficulties in coordination, Congress passed the 1947 Unification Act, which put the Army, Navy, and Air Force under the supervision of the Secretary of Defense. Unfortunately, this left each unit with so much autonomy that the Defense Department was unable to unfold an integrated military plan. Congress and a few presidential directives produced some improvement, but the greatest unification was accomplished by Robert McNamara, Secretary of Defense under Presidents Kennedy and Johnson. McNamara centralized authority in his office, shifting it from the military top brass and the civilian secretaries of the military departments. He also introduced new management procedures—systems analysis and program budgeting—to evaluate new weapons and to determine how to distribute money among the services. Most significant, he shifted funds so that our military defense no longer relied almost exclusively on nuclear weapons, but included conventional forces as well.

Despite McNamara's gains in unifying the services, civilian control of the military still is an urgent issue. Defense Department spending is now around $80 billion—about 8 percent of the Gross National Product and 41 percent of total federal spending. Employing about 1.3 million civilians, and including nearly 3.5 million military personnel, defense is the nation's largest industry. Since World War II its costs have amounted to more

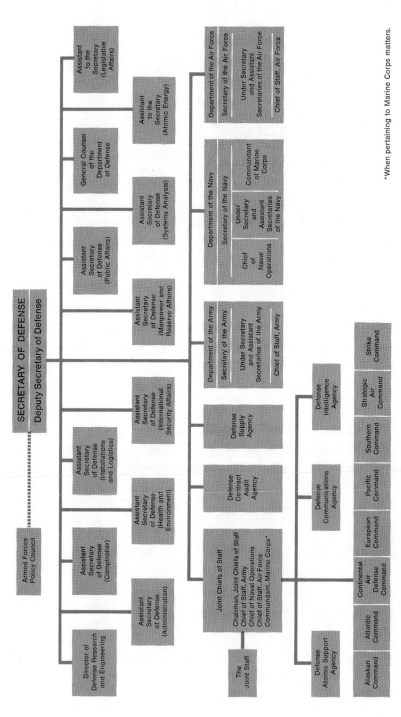

Figure 19-2. The Department of Defense. (Source: *U.S. Government Organization Manual, 1970–1971*.)

*When pertaining to Marine Corps matters.

than $1 trillion. This has produced a revolution in our economic life so that now one of nine wage-earners owes his livelihood to defense spending. Colleges and universities are only two recipients of this largesse. The result is that the military and its beneficiaries have become a very effective and self-interested pressure group in American society.

ARMS CONTROL AND DISARMAMENT

Since 1946, in pursuit of our stated goal of bringing national armaments under control, the United States has participated in numerous disarmament conferences and has even created an agency—the Arms Control and Disarmament Agency, established in 1961—to deal with the problem. The two major reasons for arms control are, first, to limit the tremendous cost of armaments, which burdens the economy and diverts money and manpower from other important tasks, and, second, to limit the risk of nuclear war, a risk that intensifies as more and more nations develop nuclear delivery and weapons systems. Presently, the nuclear powers are the U.S., U.S.S.R., Great Britain, France, and China, though West Germany, India, and Israel are capable of becoming so.

Many observers believe neither the United States nor Russia, the two great military powers, are sincere about disarmament, that there are powerful groups in both countries that distrust the motives of the other. Indeed it is true that only a small percentage of Americans believe that our unilaterally disarming (that is, without others disarming simultaneously) would lead to general world disarmament, and most feel a nuclear arsenal is necessary to deter a communist threat of war. The drawback of this "deterrence," however, is that the very existence of such weapons creates tensions (e.g., by raising the spectre in the U.S. of an attack from a Soviet "killer satellite," or in Russia of a preemptive American strike with multi-headed missiles). Moreover, should the weapons ever be used in a general war, it would be a war no one could win.

Some limitations have been established. The first major success was the 1963 *nuclear test ban treaty*, otherwise known as the Treaty of Moscow, which was signed by the United States, the

Soviet Union, and others, and which now has more than 100 members. Two notable holdouts, however, are the People's Republic of China and France, both nuclear powers. Treaty members agreed not to test nuclear weapons above ground (they may still test them underground) and to withdraw from the treaty only after giving three months' notice. An immediate result was to stop a lot of radioactive pollution of the atmosphere, pollution that could cause genetic damage to people throughout the world.

The test ban treaty encouraged other disarmament efforts. One success was the 1967 United Nations *Treaty Banning Weapons in Outer Space*—signed by sixty nations, including the U.S., the U.S.S.R., Britain, but not by France or China—which prohibited orbiting nuclear weapons in outer space and testing weapons on the moon.

Another success was the 1968 United Nations *Treaty on Nonproliferation of Nuclear Weapons,* which pledged nuclear nations not to disseminate nuclear arms to non-nuclear nations for at least twenty-five years, but required them to inform non-nuclear nations on nuclear developments not related to weapons. Non-nuclear nations in return agreed not to acquire or develop nuclear weapons. Although the United States, the Soviet Union, and Great Britain signed the treaty, France, Communist China, and India did not do so. The treaty is weak in its provisions for security and enforcement, but it does represent a diplomatic breakthrough in dialogue between the two major nuclear powers in that it led to their signing of agreements prohibiting nuclear weapons in Antarctica (1969) and on the ocean floor (1971), and to the preliminary secret Strategic Arms Limitation Talks (SALT) between them in 1969 and then to the open SALT negotiating sessions which began in the spring of 1970. Moreover, it could be a step toward decelerating the arms race, reducing the power of military establishments, and ultimately controlling the threat of nuclear war. A significant breakthrough came in 1971, after nineteen months of SALT negotiations. The United States and the Soviet Union agreed to concentrate first on limiting defensive antiballistic missile (ABM) systems and then, after reaching agreement on the ABM, to take up limitation of offensive strategic weapons. Before, the U.S. had insisted on negotiations to limit offensive as well as defensive weapons, while the Soviets insisted on the limitation or abolition of ABM systems first.

THE STATES AND DEFENSE

The men who wrote the Constitution clearly made the federal government responsible for national defense. But the states are also important here, both in peacetime and in war.

During peacetime, the states aid war veterans, giving them tax breaks, bonus payments, educational benefits, preference in public employment, and guaranteeing them home loans and maintaining places for the aged and disabled.

On the military side, each state has a *militia* for its internal defense. Though now called the National Guard and jointly financed by the federal and state governments, it is still a state organization, commanded by the governor unless during national emergency the President calls it into federal service. The governor is responsible for the Guard's organization, training and maintenance, with Congress making its regulations. In the '60s and '70s the Guard has been cast in a controversial role, being called on to maintain order in ghettos and on college campuses and to enforce school desegregation.

Civil defense, a task that has developed along with nuclear weapons, is planned by the federal government but carried out by the states, since actually CD is not only a civilian but a local matter. Civil defense is passive defense: saving lives and restoring communities. The state's responsibility rests with the governor and his civil defense director, though actual field operations are handled by local organizations. Developing an adequate program of protection has, however, been handicapped by the inability of the states and cities to bear the high costs and Congress's unwillingness to finance it because of public apathy and other demands on the defense dollar.

It is during wartime that states become most active in national defense. In World War II they administered the Selective Service System, merged their National Guard units with the federal military, recruited and trained defense workers, and helped carry out food and gasoline rationing.

THE UNITED STATES AND INTERNATIONAL ORGANIZATIONS

Since World War II we have partly tried to implement our foreign policy by participating in international organizations, often taking a leading, even dominant role here. Among the more than 200 international organizations we belong to, the most important to us are the United Nations and the Organization of American States.

The United Nations

The United Nations, chartered in San Francisco in 1945 by the victorious World War II allies, is not a world government but a world meeting to discuss the dangers of our day and to search for world peace. The overwhelming support (90–2) for it in the U.S. Senate at the time of formation was only one indicator of our new dedication to the principle of international cooperation.

When it first met at its New York headquarters in 1946, the UN had sixty-one nations; today it has 127 and lacks among the major powers only Communist China and West Germany. Until the mid-'50s the U.S. and the U.S.S.R. struggled to control it for their own purposes, with the United States gaining majority support for its policies, but with the Soviet Union using its Security Council veto to protect its interests. Since then, the Asian and African nations have played a dominant part, using the UN forum to air their grievances; India and other new nations have successfully used it to push nonalignment, peaceful coexistence, and disarmament.

The UN's purposes are to achieve: (1) world peace and security, (2) friendly international relations, (3) cooperation in solving international problems and in gaining human rights and freedoms, and (4) harmonious attainments of these ends.

As Figure 19-3 shows, the Charter provides for a General Assembly and a Security Council, and four other lesser organs: the Economic and Social Council, the International Court of Justice, the Trusteeship Council, and the Secretariat.

The General Assembly. The main deliberative body and forum

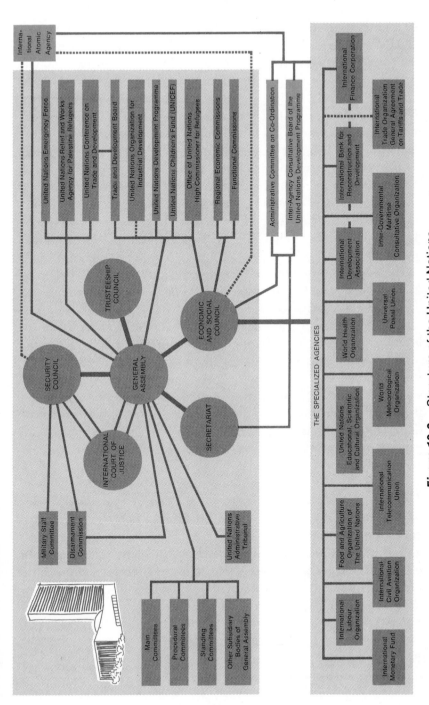

International Atomic Agency

United Nations Emergency Force
United Nations Relief and Works Agency for Palestine Refugees
United Nations Conference on Trade and Development
Trade and Development Board
United Nations Organization for Industrial Development
United Nations Development Programme
United Nations Children's Fund (UNICEF)
Office of United Nations High Commissioner for Refugees
Regional Economic Commissions
Functional Commissions

Administrative Committee on Co-Ordination
Inter-Agency Consultative Board of the United Nations Development Programme

TRUSTEESHIP COUNCIL

SECURITY COUNCIL

GENERAL ASSEMBLY

ECONOMIC AND SOCIAL COUNCIL

INTERNATIONAL COURT OF JUSTICE

SECRETARIAT

Military Staff Committee
Disarmament Commission

United Nations Administrative Tribunal

Main Committees
Procedural Committees
Standing Committees
Other Subsidiary Bodies of General Assembly

THE SPECIALIZED AGENCIES

International Finance Corporation
International Trade Organization General Agreement on Tariffs and Trade
International Bank for Reconstruction and Development
Inter-Governmental Maritime Consultative Organization
International Development Association
Universal Postal Union
World Health Organization
World Meteorological Organization
United Nations Educational, Scientific and Cultural Organization
International Telecommunication Union
Food and Agriculture Organization of The United Nations
International Civil Aviation Organization
International Labour Organization
International Monetary Fund

Figure 19-3. Structure of the United Nations.

for discussing world problems, the General Assembly includes all UN member states, each with one vote[3] (though each may have up to five delegates). It can signal the Security Council to any situation endangering international peace and make recommendations. It oversees all organs of the UN and considers their annual reports. It also considers the annual budget, apportions expenses among member states, and elects its own president, the UN Secretary General, nonpermanent members of the Security Council, members of the Economic and Social Council, and some members of the Trusteeship Council. So-called "important questions"—budgets, trusteeships, elections, suspensions, and expulsions—are decided by a two-thirds majority of those present and voting; all other matters are decided by a simple majority.

The Assembly's importance was particularly increased when in 1950 it approved the "Uniting for Peace" resolution, which bypassed the Security Council and recommended the UN take actions in the Korean war. Though of debatable legality, this resolution permitted the Assembly to recommend that UN nations take collective measures against aggressors if the Council failed to do so because of a Great Power veto. Despite this, the Assembly is limited in that it cannot make laws binding nations; it can only *recommend* (by two-thirds vote) on situations threatening international peace—and though a recommendation may express world public opinion, it takes the support of the Great Powers to enforce it.

The Security Council. Ready to meet at any time, the UN's enforcement agency is composed of fifteen members, each with one vote: the 1945 "Big Five" (the U.S., U.S.S.R., Britain, France, and Nationalist China), which hold permanent seats, and ten others elected by the Assembly for two-year terms. A procedural matter requires a "yes" vote of nine members to pass it; a substantive matter, such as admitting a new UN member, also requires nine votes, but it must include all of the Big Five mem-

---

[3] The U.S.S.R., however, in effect has three votes because two parts of it, the Ukraine and Byelorussia, are also UN members.

bers—a situation that gives each of the Great Powers a "veto" vote.

Responsible for maintaining international peace, it may negotiate, arbitrate, sever diplomatic relations, levy economic sanctions, and take military action (although it has not done so except in Korea). The Council is supposed to have a military force at its command, but it has been unable to agree on how to organize it. The Council also has control over regional security arrangements; if, for example, the Organization of American States wants to employ economic sanctions, it must first get the consent of the UN Security Council. (This does not always work, however; the 1965 U.S. intervention in the Dominican Republic was done outside the UN, but the Security Council took no official note of this.)

The Economic and Social Council. Composed of twenty-seven Assembly-elected members, ECOSOC tries to help eliminate some of the basic causes of war by improving health and living standards, promoting human rights, and encouraging international cooperation in science, education, and the arts. It has studied subjects ranging from the economic conditions of Latin America to the international opium trade. It has also made agreements with such specialized agencies as the Universal Postal Union and the World Health Organization.

The International Court of Justice. The UN's legal arm has fifteen judges elected for nine-year terms by the Assembly and handles disputes between nations and gives advisory opinions on international law and the UN Charter. It has no enforcement power, but if one party in a case fails to abide by its decision, the other may ask the Security Council to enforce it.

The Trusteeship Council. Members include all nations administering trusts (now only one, Australia, which administers New Guinea), the five permanent Security Council members, and three others elected by the Assembly. Under the trusteeship arrangement, a nation administering a trust territory must ensure

411

political, economic, social, and educational advancement in its trust territory and develop its capacity for self-government.[4]

The Secretariat. The Secretary-General, elected by the Assembly on the Security Council's recommendation, heads the Secretariat's 5500 international civil servants, most of whom staff the UN and manage its meetings at the UN New York headquarters. The Secretary-General is important in maintaining peace and security, since he may notify the Security Council of events that he believes may threaten the peace.

In policing Cyprus, the Congo, and the Gaza Strip, the UN has saved the United States money, possible misunderstanding, and abuse. UN procedures have also given the U.S. convenient face-saving devices, as demonstrated by President Kennedy's use of the UN to supervise the dismantling of Russian missile sites in Cuba following the 1962 Cuban missile crisis.

But the UN has been unable to bring peace to Southeast Asia and the Middle East, which has caused widespread disillusionment with the UN in this country. What this disenchantment fails to recognize, however, is that while the UN is useful for diplomatic consultation, for handling problems of world peace, and for rendering services to people and helping remove the causes of war, the organization has only moral force; it has no political or military power in its own right. It is not separate from and above the states which are its members, nor can it do more than its powerful members wish it to.

The Organization of American States

The OAS was established in 1948 by the United States and twenty Latin American republics (Canada is not a member; Cuba was expelled in 1962) at Bogotá, Colombia. The OAS charter, in the form of a treaty, set up machinery to protect

---

[4] The United States trusteeship over the former Japanese mandates of the Pacific—the Carolines, the Marianas, and the Marshalls—is classified as a "strategic area trusteeship," so called because of their military importance. It is not subject to control by the Trusteeship Council. UN functions relative to it (i.e., supervision of its administration by the U.S.) are lodged with the Security Council.

against intervention, settle political disputes, and provide for mutual security. The charter also calls for a general conference every five years. The OAS Organ of Consultation, composed of the member governments' foreign secretaries, reports on acts of aggression against OAS members. As discussed, the basis for the security system of the OAS is the 1947 Rio Treaty of Reciprocal Assistance.

FOREIGN POLICY OF THE '60s AND '70s

Under President Truman the containment policy simply meant opposing communism wherever it intruded into the noncommunist world. When Eisenhower became President in 1953, Secretary of State John Foster Dulles changed the doctrine to what became known as Massive Retaliation—blocking communist expansion by threatening to strike massively with nuclear weapons at the heart of the communist nations. For the technically advanced United States, with its superiority in nuclear weapons, the proposal seemed logical since it meant the U. S. would not have to use conventional forces to defend the vast expanse of the borders of the noncommunist world, could overcome the enormous manpower of China and the Soviet Union, and do it all with less drain on the American economy. But by 1957 the Russians had developed a large armory of nuclear weapons and were even ahead of the United States in developing an intercontinental ballistic missile. Suddenly, there was a balance of terror, for each nation could destroy the other, and it was obvious that nuclear weapons could be used only under the most wildly extreme circumstances. It was also apparent that they were particularly inappropriate in halting guerrilla wars of the sort based on Chinese Chairman Mao Tse-tung's experiences.

Thus, beginning in 1961 with President Kennedy—and continuing under Presidents Johnson and Nixon—the United States changed from a policy of Massive Retaliation to one of developing conventional military forces that could be used in limited wars, of trying to avoid falling behind the Russians in nuclear strength, of achieving a technical breakthrough (e.g., in ways of stopping incoming missiles or lessening radiation damage), and of aiding nations menaced by communist-assisted guerrillas—as in Vietnam.

These changes, however, are still in response to our basic policy of containing communism. Many critics assert that since communism is an ideology, not a thing, force and economic assistance cannot contain it; that by becoming so engrossed in anti-communism we have also become agents of reaction and repression; and that we have tried to assume more responsibilities than we can manage, overextending ourselves to the neglect of our domestic problems. Other critics, while not rejecting the policy of containment, counsel greater selectivity in applying it.

The containment policy succeeded in two early tests—in 1948 when the U.S. airlifted supplies to the people of West Berlin, breaking a year-long Russian blockade of that city, and in 1950 when President Truman sent American military forces to counter the Russian-backed North Korean invasion of South Korea. However, in the third great test, the Indochina war, the containment policy proved to be catastrophic.

Despite $120 billion in war costs and over 40,000 American dead by 1971 (there were 350,000 American casualties in all—more than in World War II and twice the number in the Korean war), the war produced at home high taxes and inflation; the neglect of our cities, public institutions, and environment; an increased distrust of government and growing use of violence as a political tool; and serious polarization between social classes—hawks against doves, blacks against whites, young against old. And in Indochina, despite the deaths of about 1 million Vietnamese soldiers and 325,000 Vietnamese civilians (30 percent under thirteen years old), and despite some tactical American military victories, South Vietnam had still not been secured for the government in Saigon.

As the war became increasingly unpopular with the American people, the U.S. bombing of North Vietnam was first reduced and then halted, there began the long process of negotiation in Paris, and the American presence in Vietnam was gradually scaled down. Then suddenly, in July 1971, President Nixon announced that he would visit mainland China before May 1972, and was enlisting China's assistance in settling the Indochina war. The new turn of events not only seemed to signify an improvement in U.S.-China relations after twenty-one years, but also, perhaps, the beginning of a new tripolar era, as opposed to the bipolar competition and maneuvering between the big powers.

Possibly in the 1970s the United States will move toward an "eclectic containment." That is, we would not involve ourselves in all cases where existing governments are being assaulted by indigenous communist elements (as in Vietnam), even those in which the Soviet Union or China are assisting the attack. The reasoning here is that even if indigenous communist movements gain control in some of these countries, their national interests would be different from those of Russia or China (as are Communist Yugoslavia's now) and they would be more a barrier than an aid to Russian and Chinese expansionism.

The cold war has now vastly altered. The danger of crude Soviet military action against the West appears to have subsided, replaced by Russian economic and ideological competition for influence with noncommunist states. U.S.-Soviet tensions have abated to the point, in fact, where both sides are now interested in arms control and disarmament. Moreover, because of the split between China and Russia and the increasing independence of some of the Soviet satellite countries in Eastern Europe (though chastened by Soviet repression of Czechoslovakia's attempt at independence in 1968), the Russian-dominated international communism of the '50s has given way to multi-centered communism.

Likewise, the relationship of the U.S. to its allies has changed. Britain, France, Germany, Italy, and Japan are still important powers, and Europe has become a resurgent and independent force. As a result of the reduced tensions between the U.S. and the U.S.S.R., these allies are charting a more self-directing role—particularly France, which has rebuffed American leadership and withdrawn most of its military forces from NATO.

There has also been a serious collapse of community and a rise in domestic crises in the United States, China, and the Soviet system. The racial revolution and the alienation of youth in this country, the alienation of intellectuals and the suppression of the Czechs in the Soviet system, and the great cultural revolution in China are all indicators.

Perhaps more significant, however, is what is happening to people in Asia, Africa, the Middle East, and Latin America. Influenced by Western concepts of progress, liberty, and equality, increasingly aware of what science may do for them, and no longer willing to accept as inevitable poverty, hunger, and ill health, these emerging nations are increasingly disturbed by nationalist movements, social ferment, and revolutions. Significantly, it is in this third world where the main confrontations between the United States and the communist giants occur: Korea, Southeast Asia, Cuba, the Congo, Nigeria, the Middle East, the Dominican Republic, and Guatemala. The most critical question facing the U.S. is how well our thinking keeps pace with the immense changes which are taking place in the world.

Suggested Additional Reading

Brogan, D. W. *Worlds in Conflict*. 1967.

Chase, S. *The Most Probable World*. 1968.

Cleveland, H. *The Obligation of Power: American Diplomacy in the Search for Peace*. 1966.

Feis, H. *Foreign Aid and Foreign Policy*. 1964.

Haas, E. B. *Tangle of Hopes: American Commitments and World Order*. 1969.

Halle, L. J. *The Cold War as History*. 1967.

Hardin, C. M. (ed.). *Overcoming World Hunger*. 1969.

Jordan, A. A., Jr. (ed.). *Issues of National Security in the 1970s*. 1967.

Kaplan, L. S. (ed.). *Recent American Foreign Policy: Conflicting Interpretations*. 1968.

Kennan, G. F. *Realities of American Foreign Policy*. 1966.

Morgenthau, H. J. *A New Foreign Policy for the United States*. 1968.

Pruitt, D. G., and R. C. Snyder. *Theory and Research of the Causes of War*. 1969.

Russell, R. B. *The United Nations and United States Security Policy*. 1968.

Scalapino, R. A. (ed.). *The Communist Revolution in Asia*. 1969.

Spanier, J. *American Foreign Policy Since World War II*. 1971.

U.S. President's Commission on an All-Volunteer Armed Force. *Report on an All-Volunteer Armed Force*. 1970.

Part 5

State and Local Government

20 State Government

Jeffrey Blankfort, BBM

Our states are designed to be our great centers for political experiment.

—Governor Nelson A. Rockefeller

Although the federal and the state governments influence each other, their decision-making processes are mostly separate and distinct, which is why we should discuss state government separately. The states are restricted, of course. The federal Constitution prohibits them from coining money, emitting bills of credit, passing *ex post facto* laws or laws impairing the obligation of contracts, denying their citizens equal protection of the laws, making laws abridging privileges and immunities of U.S. citizens,[1] or depriving any person of life, liberty, or property without

---

[1] These privileges and immunities, as E. S. Corwin and J. W. Peltason have pointed out in *Understanding the Constitution* (New York: Holt, Rinehart and Winston, 1967), p. 143, are only those "that owe their existence to the national government, the Constitution, and the laws and treaties of the United States, such as the rights of ingress and egress to and from the states, the right to visit the national capital, the right to engage in interstate and foreign commerce, the right to protection on the high seas and in foreign countries, and the right to vote in primaries and general elections in which congressmen and presidential electors are chosen and to have that vote properly counted."

due process of law. These federal restrictions continuously check the states; only by taking care in framing and administering programs affecting personal and property rights can the states stay within these provisions.

Although it is often claimed that one virtue of federalism is that it allows the states to experiment with their own forms of government, what is striking is not their variations but their uniformity. All states follow the American pattern of limited representative government. All have written constitutions, and they are all very much alike, featuring preambles asserting popular sovereignty, amendment clauses, and bills of rights similar to the federal Bill of Rights. Also, all states have separated powers, checks and balances, an independent judiciary, and a popularly elected governor. All but one have bicameral legislatures; only Nebraska's is unicameral.

STATE CONSTITUTIONS

Unlike the U.S. Constitution, which *grants* power to the national government, state constitutions generally *limit* power to their governments. There are, for instance, usually numerous restrictions on the legislature's ability to make law. It is restrained in the amount of debt it may incur and the kinds and rates of taxes it may levy. The state constitution's bill of rights directly limits the state's power to infringe on the basic privileges and freedoms of its citizens. The constitution also puts voter qualifications and terms and powers of officials beyond the legislature's jurisdiction, restricts its power to pass local and special laws, and specifies the procedures the legislature must follow when legislating. Finally, the state constitution (unlike the federal Constitution) delineates the structure and powers of local governments—the counties, cities, and special districts.

If the federal Constitution still serves well after 180 years, many state constitutions—most of which are over 100 years old—do not. Many constitutions contain too much detailed matter which should be handled by the legislatures. Often they shackle public officials so that they can deal with problems only by resorting to extraordinary procedures—political leaders, for example, sometimes simply ignore the constitution, if public opinion permits it, and judges deliberately interpret constitutional restrictions in such a way as to lower barriers.

Altering State Constitutions

State constitutions are elaborated and modified by interpretations of the governors and the legislatures, by judicial interpretations, and by custom, but they may also be altered in three formal ways: (1) by constitutional amendment, (2) by constitutional convention, and (3) by revisory commission.

Amendments to state constitutions are proposed either by the legislature, by popular initiative, or by constitutional conventions. Most commonly, it is the first way: an amendment is proposed by two-thirds of each house of the legislature and ratified by a majority of voters. Actually, however, amendments have contributed little to constitutional reform; as often as not, they have simply added yet more detail and burdened the voter with matters he knows little about.

To make a general revision of a state constitution or draft a new one, the most accepted way is to call a *constitutional convention*. This happens when the legislature places the matter as a referendum before the people, the people approve it, the legislature calls the convention, and delegates are then popularly elected. The constitutional changes proposed by the convention are then voted on by the people. Though such conventions are usually free to make their own rules and to propose an entirely new constitution, most have tended to suggest piecemeal reforms.

In recent years, several states have successfully used legislature-appointed *revisory commissions* to recommend constitutional revisions. Commission recommendations must then be approved by the voters. Though not employed on the federal level, the device has been used recently in California, Florida, Idaho, Kentucky, Pennsylvania, and Wisconsin.

Why Not All New Constitutions?

If state constitutions are so inadequate, why don't the states draft new ones or revise their old ones? Some have done so—conventions have been called or commissions formed in more than two-thirds of the states in recent years. But progress has been slow, since the people who want change are weaker politically than those with vested interests in present arrangements, and constitutional reformers have had difficulty rousing popular excitement for their campaigns.

Although there are disagreements as to what would make a good state constitution, there is at least one blueprint, the Model State Constitution, designed to encourage states to modernize and to otherwise improve their constitutions. First issued in 1921 by

---

THE MODEL STATE CONSTITUTION AND A TYPICAL STATE CONSTITUTION COMPARED

Model State Constitution*

1. Flexible constitution limited to fundamentals.
2. Unicameral legislature.
3. A single elected chief executive, integrated and centralized administration with a simple structure.
4. Unified court system with judges appointed by the governor.
5. Initiative and referendum.
6. Home rule for cities and counties.

Typical State Constitution

1. Relatively rigid and detailed constitution.
2. Bicameral legislature.
3. Multiple elected executives, relatively diffused administration with a cumbersome structure.
4. Decentralized and uncoordinated court system with judges popularly elected.
5. Neither initiative nor referendum.
6. Home rule for cities but not counties.

*National Municipal League, *Model State Constitution,* 1967. (Available in all large libraries and included as an appendix in some state government textbooks.)

---

the National Municipal League and revised periodically, it is short, concise, and modern, and concentrates executive power in the governor's hands. No state has adopted the model in its entirety, but its influence may be seen in recently altered constitutions, and particularly in the constitutions of Alaska, Hawaii, Michigan, and New Jersey. If nothing else, it at least encourages people to believe that government institutions and procedures can be improved.

THE GOVERNORS

Governors are far less powerful in their state governments than is the President in the federal government. A governor is not the only executive with constitutional powers; generally, he must share power with other executive officers and with boards and commissions. He cannot appoint all department heads nor dismiss them at will, but may remove them only if they fail their legal duties or violate the law. These department heads may be independently elected or appointed by boards, commissions, or the legislature, and may even belong to the opposition political party. Generally, they may act autonomously or, frequently, as handmaidens of interest groups operating in their areas. Even the indirect leverage the governor has over departments through his power to formulate their budgets and supervise expenditures depends on his legislative support.

The Governor's Roles

Today the typical governor serves a four-year term, is eligible to reelection indefinitely, and is paid over $25,000 a year (New York's governor receives the most, with $75,000). His various roles are described below.

Chief of State. Though the governor's role here is more modest than the President's nationally, there are many similarities. Most governors make the most of their *ceremonial* status, which allows them to appear as a representative of all the people of the state and provides favorable contacts with constituents. Though the role is necessarily time consuming, a governor's overall effectiveness may depend on how well he performs it.

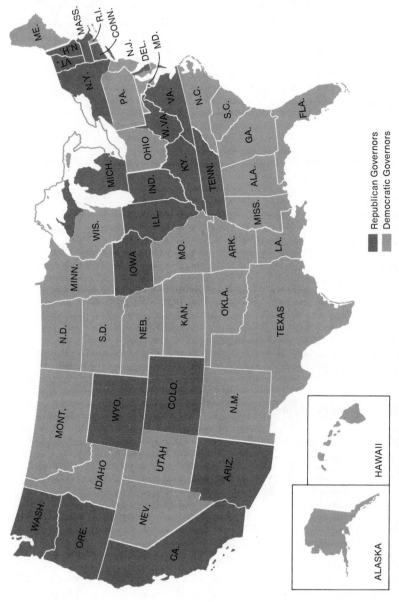

Republican Governors
Democratic Governors

ME.
N.H.
VT.
MASS.
R.I.
CONN.
N.Y.
N.J.
DEL.
MD.
PA.
W.VA.
VA.
N.C.
S.C.
GA.
FLA.
OHIO
KY.
TENN.
ALA.
MICH.
IND.
MISS.
WIS.
ILL.
MO.
ARK.
LA.
IOWA
MINN.
OKLA.
KAN.
NEB.
TEXAS
N.D.
S.D.
COLO.
N.M.
WYO.
MONT.
UTAH
ARIZ.
IDAHO
WASH.
ORE.
NEV.
CA.

HAWAII
ALASKA

Figure 20-1. Party affiliation of governors in 1971.

Chief of Party. Here the governor's position is much weaker than the President's, for often he must share party leadership with other elected state officials. Sometimes also, a United States Senator or even a mayor may have more party influence than he, or the party may be fragmented into local coteries more interested in local candidates. Still, the governor's personal influence and policy leadership within the party generally helps determine how effective he will be as governor. Likewise, his skill in exploiting radio, television, and press exposure is important.

Chief Legislator. A governor may substantially influence the legislative product by his formal authority to (1) call the legislature into special sessions, (2) address the legislature and send messages recommending legislation and policies, (3) submit the state budget, (4) veto bills, and (5) use his power of *item veto* to strike out any item of appropriations bills (though vetos can generally be overridden by a two-thirds vote of both houses). In addition, of course, his legislative influence depends on his personal popularity, his ability at informal negotiation and other means of persuading legislators, the quality of his staff, and the political circumstances under which he operates. A governor backed by strong party organizations has an obvious advantage, as does a governor of a large state whose potential as a presidential candidate can be translated into state political power.

Commander in Chief. The governor heads the state militia, the National Guard (except when the President calls it into national service); his state's civil defense apparatus; and, in about three-fourths of the states, the state police force. Generally, he will use the Guard when state and local police cannot cope with a situation, such as in quelling riots and strikes or in providing rescue and relief during tornadoes and floods. Hitherto, governors tended to delegate their responsibilities as commander in chief to an appointed adjutant-general and staff, but recently they have become more involved as the Guard has been increasingly used to enforce desegregation orders and to control disturbances, with the result that its effectiveness has become an important political issue.

Judicial Officer.   Like the President, the governor may grant executive clemency to convicted persons (during much of the last century, in fact, governors pardoned nearly half of all prisoners). In many states, he shares this power with pardon boards and is assisted by pardon attorneys, which investigate applications and make recommendations. Few governors like the responsibility of granting clemency, especially when they must decide on prisoners sentenced to the death penalty. A mistaken decision, such as releasing someone who later commits a major crime, may also be politically costly. As a result, executive clemency is being largely replaced by probation, the indeterminate sentence, and parole.

Chief Executive.   As noted, the typical governor shares his executive power with other officials—usually a lieutenant governor, attorney general, superintendent of public instruction, controller, treasurer, and secretary of state, all of whom are elected. However, despite this diffusion of executive power, it is to the governor that people look to enforce the laws and to supervise the state administration. It is from him that people demand more and better jobs, highways, schools, and recreation facilities; adequate welfare; cleaner air and water; and civil rights for everyone—all without raising taxes. No wonder, therefore, that the governorship is no longer a safe stepping-stone to candidate for President. To try to perform his difficult task, the governor must depend on his powers—often insubstantial even in the aggregate—such as his control over the state budget and his strengths as party leader and representative of all the people.

Other State Officers

The governor is supported or thwarted by (usually) about six other elected officers.

The *lieutenant governor,* who succeeds to the governor's chair if it becomes vacant, usually presides over the state senate and has some other minor administrative duties. Though the responsibilities of lieutenant governors have been expanded slightly in recent years, states lacking such an office do not seem to suffer much.

The *attorney general,* the state's chief legal officer, prosecutes for and defends the state, gives legal advice to state agencies, and oversees local law enforcement. The office is often a good base from which to make a bid for the governorship.

The *superintendent of public instruction* supervises elementary, secondary, and teacher-training schools. The *controller* authorizes payment of state funds; he also audits officers handling these funds. The *treasurer* is custodian of state funds and sometimes collects state taxes. The *secretary of state*, the caretaker of state records and the state seal, supervises election administration, issues corporation charters, and publishes laws.

Departments and Agencies

In most states, the governor is assisted by executive departments (generally headed by one person), but some states use boards and commissions for the same purpose. Boards are especially common in welfare and education, although they may be in addition to a departmental director.

Many states have a bewildering array of independent agencies, boards, and commissions—generally too many, in fact—whose activities could be more efficient if they were grouped into departments headed by a governor-appointed director.

Establishing an executive budget, if none already exists, is helpful, since with it (and the item veto) the governor can better govern the assignment of funds to the executive bodies and can thus direct their actions. It is also helpful to concentrate fiscal control in a finance department, and administration can be improved by reducing the number of elective officers or at least by transferring their most critical functions to governor-appointed officials.

The Governors and the President and Congress

Relations between governors and the President are not always smooth, of course. But as one writer observes:

> . . . the governors have often encouraged the national government to preserve or expand its programs, even on occasion, at the expense of State power. While the governors have been

prompt to argue with Presidents over programs which they felt belonged to the States, they have also urged Presidents to keep other responsibilities off the shoulders of the States.[2]

In regard to the governors seeking to influence Congress, the same writer points out:

> A glance at the resolutions passed by the Governors' Conference in recent years reveals how the governors have become absorbed in congressional policy issues. Between 1943 and 1959, 60 per cent of all resolutions passed by the Conference were addressed entirely or in part to the national government. Of these national policy resolutions, over two-thirds were aimed at Capitol Hill. In marked contrast, only 17 per cent of Conference resolutions were directed to State governments.
>
> The subjects of greatest concern to the governors during this period, judging from the contents of their resolutions, were national military and civil defense policy and general Federal-State relations.[3]

Another significant relationship between the governors and Congress derives from the fact that there are always a number of former governors (sometimes as many as thirty-five) in the Senate. This so-called "governors' bloc" often shows a high degree of unanimity on matters concerning the states, regardless of party affiliation.

THE LEGISLATURES

The state legislatures are like the U.S. Congress in structure and are likewise the main centers of decision. Unlike Congress, however, which has only the powers granted it, they have all powers except those denied them by state constitution or the U.S. Constitution. Moreover, they also have control over the structures and policies of local governments, which Congress does not.

Except for unicameral Nebraska, state legislatures are *bi-*

[2] Glenn E. Brooks, *When Governors Convene: The Governors' Conference and National Politics* (Baltimore, Md.: Johns Hopkins Press, 1961), p. 25.
[3] *Ibid.*, pp. 53–54.

428

cameral. Proponents of bicameralism believe that with two houses one can check the hasty, ill-considered acts of the other and that it helps balance diverse interests. However, those who advocate unicameralism (among them the Committee on Legislation of the American Political Science Association) counter that it is impossible to judge when legislation is really "ill considered," since bills are frequently rushed through anyway (particularly at the end of a session) and most bills, in fact, are not altered by the second house. They also argue that one house is cheaper and can pass bills faster, that two houses simply give special interests twice the opportunities to block legislation, and, anyway, what does the upper house represent that the lower house does not? No doubt, second houses have been less effective at checking bad legislation than have gubernatorial vetos, the courts, the press, and the electorate, but still the movement toward unicameral legislatures has made little headway. Americans are not quick to alter the basic structure of their government institutions.

Popular Representation: One Man, One Vote

All state constitutions require that legislative districts must be reapportioned periodically, usually by the state legislature. Since the U.S. Supreme Court has ruled that reapportionment must now be based on "one man, one vote," population rather than geography is now the major basis for determining the size of legislative districts.

Until the mid-'60s, urban and suburban voters were seriously underrepresented and rural voters overrepresented in most state legislatures.[4] In 1960 a city resident's vote was worth only half a farmer's vote in electing state legislators, and a suburban voter's was worth even less. The cause of this imbalance lay either in the state constitutions, which frequently favored rural interests, or in the state legislatures, which failed to reapportion legislative seats to reflect population shifts.

---

[4] It should be kept in mind, however, that both elected and appointed executives, and also judges, represent people, and that interest groups, political parties, the President and governors engage in interest representation, and that urban citizens have not been seriously underrepresented in the executive and judicial branches or in the parties or interest groups.

In its famous 1962 *Baker* v. *Carr* case, however, the U.S. Supreme Court moved to rescue urban and suburban voters when it ruled that "arbitrary and capricious" districts violated the Constitution's equal protection clauses and that federal courts had jurisdiction over cases challenging such districts. Although rural-dominated legislatures soon thereafter began reapportioning in hopes of forestalling more drastic action, the Supreme Court nevertheless ruled, in *Reynolds* v. *Sims* (1964), that "the fundamental principle of representative government in this country is one of equal representation for equal numbers of people." By the 1966 elections, forty-six state legislatures had taken steps to meet this one man, one vote test, clearly beginning to shift political power from rural to urban-suburban America.

State Legislators

Backgrounds. State legislators come from a variety of backgrounds and occupations; though lawyers are most common, some legislators are farmers and salesmen. There are few manual workers, few trade union leaders, few blacks, and few women.

Number of Legislators. State legislatures vary in size from Nebraska's 43 legislators (the smallest) to New Hampshire's 424 (the largest). Though most are much smaller than Congress (535), many are still too large. Generally, the lower house (usually called the *house of representatives*) has a little over a hundred members, the upper house (called the *senate* in all states) has about forty members.

Terms. In all but four states, representatives have two-year terms and most state senators have four-year terms. Both senators and representatives are popularly elected, and the turnover is high—over 50 percent per session.

Legal Qualifications. All states require that legislators be U.S. citizens and residents of the state. Law or custom also requires they reside in the districts they represent. In most states any qualified voter who is at least twenty-one is eligible to serve.

Pay. Compensation varies, with California legislators being highest paid ($19,200 a year), though still only half that paid U.S. Congressmen. Some states, in fact, pay as little in salary as $5 per day (plus expenses) each day the legislature is in session. In most states the pay is so inadequate that the only persons who can afford to serve are those who can combine their jobs with legislative duties.

Some people feel that the honor of being a legislator is payment enough; others would not pay them simply because they dislike legislators and their product. Most observers, however, favor paying salaries large enough to attract qualified people able to devote full time to the job.

Sessions. Whereas Congress meets for relatively long sessions (the 1969 Session lasted from January 3 to December 23), many state legislatures meet only about sixty days every *two* years. However, a growing number, now twenty-seven, meet annually, and there is a trend toward lengthening legislative sessions. Governors are also calling more special sessions. It is becoming more and more apparent that legislators simply cannot accomplish their work—especially in enacting realistic budgets—in short sessions held every two years.

Legislative Organization and Procedures

State legislatures operate much like Congress. Each legislative house has presiding officers, majority and minority party floor leaders, standing comittees, and conference and joint committees, rules committees, and party caucuses.

In the lower house, the speaker, chosen by members of the majority party, sometimes has more power than the Speaker of the U.S. House of Representatives—in California the speaker dominates the appointment of committees and chairmen and decides the order of legislative business. In most states, the upper house, the senate, is presided over by the lieutenant governor or, in his absence, by a senate-elected president *pro tempore*; in other states, the senate chooses its own president.

Legislative committees are similar to congressional committees, but not as well staffed, powerful, or effective. Nor do they follow the seniority rule as closely; because of high turnover in membership and short legislative sessions, legislative committee members do not acquire as much competence as do congressional committee members. Often, legislatures have so many committees that individual members have too many assignments and there is needless duplication, overlapping, and confusion.

How different legislatures operate varies much more than does their structure. In some states the governor is the central figure in the legislative process; in others he is relatively unimportant. In some states political parties and party caucuses are active in making policy; in others party responsibility is nearly absent.

How States Make Laws

Although Congress profoundly influences life within the states, it is the state legislatures that must enact comprehensive and detailed prescriptions for their government—and, as a result, they have truly immense responsibilities, broader even than those of Congress.

The functions of the state legislatures are similar to those of Congress and likewise they do far more than simply make statutes. They appropriate money, investigate government operations, and set up much of the state administrative machinery. They confirm or deny the governor's nominees for important offices and impeach and remove state officials. They establish their own forms of local government (e.g., various combinations of general-purpose municipalities—cities, boroughs, towns, and villages—as well as counties and special districts) and propose constitutional amendments to be approved by the voters. Finally, they may summon a convention to draft a new state constitution.

State legislatures have many powers by which they can deeply influence the economic and social affairs of their populations. They can administer elections, enact civil and criminal laws, assert eminent domain, and provide for education. They can regulate local commerce, professions, industry, agriculture, labor, and utilities. They can maintain roads and airports and establish and maintain institutions for the aged, the needy, the disabled, and the delinquent. In general, they can regulate persons and property in order to promote the public health, welfare, safety, and morals (called the "police power").

State legislatures act on bills much the way Congress does: a bill is introduced, considered by committees, by the two houses, then by conference committees, if needed, and finally signed by the governor. Leadership is provided by the party system, although in most states, party discipline is even weaker than in Congress. As with Congress, lobbyists for major economic and social groups abound.

There are, however, important differences in the ways state legislatures and Congress operate. Unlike Congress, few states keep records of debates, making it difficult for students of government to determine the history of laws. Debate is also not as strictly controlled as in the federal House nor as subject to filibustering. Most states require that amendments to bills be *germane*, that they deal with the same general subject as the bill itself; this helps prevent "riders." Some states require a record vote (a roll call vote of the entire chamber membership) on all legislation. The rush of legislation at the end of the session is much greater in most state legislatures than in Congress.

There also are differences in the ways governors and the President may handle legislation. Fewer than one-third of the states, for example, allow a pocket veto by the governor, but most states allow him an item veto over appropriations bills. Moreover, most governors veto more frequently than does the President.

Direct Democracy: The Initiative and the Referendum

Though voters cannot directly make federal laws or amend the U.S. Constitution, in twenty-two states (most in the West) they can make state law by using the initiative or referendum.[5]

The Initiative. In some states, the initiative may be used to enact either regular laws or constitutional amendments; in others, it may be used for only one or the other. The initiative is a petition (proposing either a bill or constitutional amendment) signed by

[5] The initiative and referendum are also used in cities and counties in several states.

433

5 to 10 percent of the voters. Once this many signatures are secured, the proposal is placed on the next election ballot for the voters' approval; generally, if a majority of those voting on the proposal approve, it is adopted. Some states have an *indirect initiative*, whereby the legislature votes on the initiated proposal. If it approves it, the proposal does not go on the ballot; if it rejects it, it does, so that the electorate has a chance to overrule the legislature.

The Referendum. The legislative referendum, of which there are three types, is a popular vote on a measure (either a regular bill or a proposed constitutional amendment) already passed by the legislature. *Referendum by petition* is used to prevent laws passed by the legislature from going into effect until they are approved by a majority of the voters.[6] The procedure is simple: if during a waiting period (usually sixty to ninety days) the required number of voters sign a petition requesting a referendum on a measure, it will not go into effect unless approved by the voters at the next election. The *optional referendum* enables the legislature, at its option, to provide that a measure it has passed cannot become law until it is approved by the voters at an election. The *compulsory referendum* is a device whereby constitutional amendments and bond issues passed by the legislature *require* the approval of the electorate.

Early twentieth-century reformers argued that the initiative and referendum would return government to the people and vanquish political machines and special interests; opponents protested they would destroy representative government and would open the door to a rash of radical and crackpot measures. Both have been only partly accurate. Popular initiative has allowed the citizenry to produce needed reform which the legislatures might never have brought about, but it has also made state constitutions more bulky and unwieldy, increased voter confusion, fostered some crackpot laws, and been manipulated by well-financed pressure groups who have found these devices easier to use than has the general public.

[6] Excepted from the referendum is "emergency legislation" and often tax measures and acts calling special elections.

The State Legislatures and Congress

What state legislatures do is of vital concern to Congress. They copy some federal laws, pass on constitutional amendments proposed by Congress, and enact cooperative legislation needed to qualify for federal grants-in-aid. Conversely, often Congress will in effect adopt the laws they pass—for example, those relating to elections, property, wills and estates, and marriage and dependency. In other words, Congress acts against the background of the body of state law much the way state legislatures do with the common law (which is assumed to apply unless altered by statute). Significantly, both houses of Congress have maintained a subcommittee on intergovernmental relations.

THE COURTS

With fifty-one sets of courts, systems of laws, and judicial precedents, we have the most complex legal system of any nation. Nevertheless, there are similar patterns: all the systems are hierarchical, most matters being considered by lower courts, after which there may be an appeal to a higher court, and finally to the highest court in the state. Most states have six types of courts, as described below.

Justice Courts

Justice courts are staffed by a *justice of the peace* (a carryover from the fourteenth-century English office) and now operate mainly in rural areas, though they once functioned in cities too. J.P.s decide minor civil cases (involving up to perhaps $500) and minor criminal offenses (misdemeanors). They spend much of their time dealing with traffic violations, but they also perform marriages, issue arrest warrants for persons charged with serious crimes, and hold preliminary hearings for suspects later bound over to a prosecutor or grand jury. Except in the most petty criminal and civil cases, their decisions may be appealed to the next higher court. J.P.s are usually popularly elected and lack law degrees.

Municipal Courts

Municipal courts (sometimes called "city courts," "police courts," or "magistrate courts") operate in incorporated areas and decide civil cases involving sums up to perhaps $5000 and minor criminal offenses. Most large cities have one centralized municipal court with divsions such as juvenile offenses, traffic, domestic relations, and small claims. Sometimes judges are elected, and sometimes they are appointed by the mayor or governor.

County Courts

County courts, often called "superior courts," are the major trial courts in state systems. It is here that trial by jury is generally encountered. Usually, two or three counties are grouped to form such courts. They handle all except petty criminal cases and all civil cases involving sums above perhaps $5000. Less than 5 percent of the cases they hear are appealed to higher courts. Most judges of these courts are elected and have law degrees.

Specialized Courts

Heavily populated counties use separate specialized courts. The *probate court* handles wills and estates; the *conciliation court* attempts to preserve family life and protect the rights of children; the *psychiatric court* hears petitions involving drug addicts, inebriates, and the mentally ill; and the *juvenile court* handles offenses by minors. Judges in these courts usually are trained or experienced in the areas involved, and procedures are more informal than in the regular county courts. In smaller counties their functions are performed by the regular judges of the county courts.

Intermediate Courts of Appeals

The more populous states have intermediate courts of appeals, distributed around the state in districts or regions, to relieve congestion in the state supreme court. Each court has three or more judges, and decisions are made by majority vote. Most of their cases are appealed from lower trial courts. Since only questions of law, and not of fact, are usually involved, juries are not employed. Judges in these courts are usually popularly elected.[7]

State Supreme Court

The state supreme court, the court of last resort in the state system, consists of five or seven judges, including a chief jutsice. They sit together when hearing cases, although some states permit them to sit in sections. Decision is by majority vote in the whole court or in a section. Judges are almost always popularly elected.

Except for issuing legal writs, the supreme court's work consists almost entirely of deciding appeals on questions of law from the lower state courts. Its decisions are final unless there is a possible conflict between state law (or its interpretation) and the U. S. Constitution or federal law. Then the U. S. Supreme Court, but no lower federal court, reviews its decisions.

Judicial Policy Making

In addition to being involved in adjudication, law enforcement, and specialized activities (probate, bankruptcy, or issuing business licenes), state courts are important in political decision making. For instance, though the legislature enacts laws, state judges interpret them and can thus dictate new meanings to constitutions and statutes. And though legislators shape legislative districts, state courts (under federal mandate) supervise this function. They also decide if laws are unreasonable or arbitrary, if local officials are complying with the law, or if the governor is exceeding his powers. In several states the highest courts render advisory opinions indicating if a proposed legislative or executive act is legal, and consequently antedate policy decisions. Obviously, the state judiciary can alter the rules of politics.

[7] In California, Missouri, and several other states, judges of the supreme court, the courts of appeals, and sometimes certain lower state courts are initially appointed by the governor (from a list supplied him by a commission composed of both members of the bar and laymen) but must, after a certain period in office, face a popular election to decide if they may continue in office.

Suggested Additional Reading

Beer, S. H., and R. E. Barringer. *The State and the Poor.* 1970.

Brooks, G. W. *When Governors Convene.* 1961.

Dye, T. R. *Politics in States and Communities.* 1969.

Heard, A. (ed.). *State Legislatures in American Politics.* 1966.

Jacob, H., and K. N. Vines. *Politics in the American States.* 1971.

Key, V. O. *American State Politics.* 1956.

Kilpatrick, J. J. *The Sovereign States.* 1957.

Ransome, C. B., Jr. *The Office of Governor in the United States.* 1956.

Sanford, T. *Storm Over the States.* 1967.

Zeller, B. (ed.). *American State Legislatures.* 1954.

21 Local Government

Howard Harrison, Photofind, S.F.

In our time, two giant and dangerous
forces are converging on our cities: the
forces of growth and decay.

—*Lyndon B. Johnson*

All local governments are legal creatures of their states, the
agents for exercising whatever powers the state entrusts them.
This legal relationship has been stated in what has become known
as *Dillon's Rule*:

> It is a general and undisputed proposition of law that a muni-
> cipal corporation possesses and can exercise the following
> powers and no others: First, those granted in express words;
> second, those necessarily or fairly implied in or incident to the
> powers expressly granted; third, those essential to the accom-
> plishment of the declared objects and purposes of the corpo-
> rations—not simply convenient, but indispensable. Any fair,
> reasonable, substantial doubt concerning the existence of
> power is resolved by the courts against the corporation, and
> the power is denied.[1]

[1] John F. Dillon, *Commentaries on the Law of Municipal Corporations*, 5th
ed. (Boston: Little, Brown, 1911), Vol. I, Sec. 237.

Although judge Dillon mentioned only municipal corporations (municipalities), his rule applies also to quasi-municipal corporations (e.g., counties and special districts). Furthermore, it is almost always interpreted strictly even in federal-local relations.

The subordinate position of local governments has only one major exception: about half the state constitutions have *home rule* provisions to give local governments greater autonomy. Supposedly, cities and counties thereby have full power over all activities, with the state intervening only in matters of statewide concern. In practice, however, state legislatures regard almost *every* significant function of local government (except charter adoption) to be of statewide concern—if only because state funds are nearly always involved. Counties—which are particularly dependent on state aid—and special districts are even more restricted than cities in their legal ability to act autonomously.

COUNTIES

All states have counties except Alaska (which has "boroughs") and Louisiana (which calls them "parishes"). The counties of Connecticut and Rhode Island no longer have government functions. There are more than 3000 counties in the United States and they vary widely in size and population. As administrative, judicial, and political subdivisions, counties generally have little legislative power; more than cities, in fact, they exist principally as administrative subordinates to enforce state legislation. They are the units of government for enforcing the law (through the sheriff, prosecuting attorney, and coroner), for education (through a superintendent of education), for recording births, marriages, divorces, deaths, deeds, mortgages, and licenses (through a county clerk); for welfare (through a department of social services); and for giving out agricultural information (through a county agricultural agent).

More counties are now moving toward the municipal pattern of government, with an elected—and stronger—county executive officer. But this mayor-like executive is still weakened by the practice of electing numerous other county officials, by his having to compete with an elected superintendent of schools, treasurer, clerk, sheriff, coroner, recorder, tax collector, auditor, and

442

highway superintendent. Modernization is also hampered by the widespread commission form of county government, which has three to five elected commissioners, often key political leaders, exercising both legislative and administrative power. County government is also weakened by counties and cities duplicating each other's functions.

SPECIAL DISTRICTS

Counties and municipalities are *multipurpose* governments, but special districts serve special purposes and have special revenue sources. Public schools are the most common and best known of such districts, but there are many others whose activities are not confined by city and county boundaries: fire protection, highways, libraries, cemeteries, and housing. In "water" matters alone there are special districts concerned with water supply, flood control, irrigation, drainage, port administration, sanitation, sewage disposal, soil conservation, even mosquito abatement.

MUNICIPALITIES

If counties are creatures of their state, municipalities (cities, boroughs, and villages) are creatures of their residents. Less state administrative units compared to counties, their functions are nonetheless sizeable—and are compounded by their frequently swelling populations. Among other things, they must protect their citizens from crime, fire, and disease; they are responsible for water supply, garbage disposal, public transportation, education and recreation; they must set tax rates, maintain streets, and decide on zoning.

There are several ways by which cities may organize themselves, as discussed below.

Types of City Charters

Weak Mayor–Council Plan. Under this system, the mayor, though popularly elected, is really only a figurehead. He usually presides at city council meetings, but often has no vote or veto. His power over the city budget and over appointments and removals is limited. The council, in fact, is the stronger part, not only enacting all legislation but often giving detailed directions to city agencies. Once, in the nineteenth century, this plan was the most prevalent municipal system, but now it is used chiefly in small municipalities—Los Angeles and Atlanta being the largest cities still organized according to this system.

Commission Plan.   Here the power, both executive and legislative, is concentrated in a policy-making commission. Often this body is composed of five elected members, each of whom heads one of the city's administrative departments and one of whom is mayor— although this title is ceremonial only, since he definitely is not a chief executive. Almost no cities have adopted the commission plan in the last three decades, but it is still used in large cities such as Memphis, Tenn., Portland, Ore., and St. Paul, Minn.

Council–City Manager Plan.   This system consists of a weak mayor and a strong, popularly elected city council which selects a professional administrator, a *city manager*, who serves for an indefinite period and who is responsible to the council. The council also selects the mayor from among its members to preside over the council and act as ceremonial head of the city.

The city manager supervises all departments, appoints and dismisses employees, prepares the budget for the council, spends city funds, and advises the council by presenting new ideas to cope with city problems.

Over half the cities with populations between 25,000 and 100,-000 are based on the council–city manager form of government. Many observers believe the plan is particularly suited to cities this size because it concentrates policy-making power in the hands of a few councilmen, making it easier to pinpoint responsibility and reducing rivalry between the city's legislative and executive branches. Other advantages are the expertise the manager brings to city administration and the separation between politics and administration.

Strong Mayor–Council Plan.   Common in large cities and patterned after the national and state governments, this plan separates the powers of the executive and legislative branches and includes a system of checks and balances. The mayor, who is elected independently of the city council, has important powers of his own: he may veto council ordinances, appoint and remove officials, and plan and execute the city budget. In addition, elected administrative officials and semi-autonomous boards are generally fewer than in cities with a weak mayor–council plan. In short, like the President, the mayor has a share in policy making and has an administration centralized under him.

Mayor-Administrator Plan.   A newer form of city government, this plan combines advantages of the strong mayor–council plan (e.g., its checks and balances and popular leadership by a mayor) and the council–city manager plan (professional administration). Under the system, the mayor keeps his potent powers but appoints a chief administrator, a professional manager, whe relieves him of much of his administrative load so the mayor can spend more time in his political role as a community leader. New York, New Orleans, San Francisco, and a number of other cities now use the plan.

The Big City Mayor

Today's mayor of a big city (over 500,000 population) faces the most urgent problems of domestic politics. If his formal powers resemble the President's, his actual power—though increasing in recent years—is much less. Though both chief executives must wrestle with such problems as civil rights, housing, transportation, health, and education, the President is able to maintain greater distance from them and balance them with nonurban concerns such as foreign affairs.

Big city mayors, as has been pointed out, reign but do not rule.[2] Most big cities now employ the strong mayor plan, which theoretically empowers the mayor to draw up a budget, propose legislation, veto city council measures, and appoint and remove officials. In practice, however, most big cities—New York, Chicago,

[2] Scott Greer, *Governing the Metropolis* (New York: Wiley, 1962).

and Detroit, for instance—require the mayor to share his administrative and budget powers with other government units that he
cannot control. Only in Cleveland and Boston, of the largest cities,
is he the sole elected executive officer.

Big and Bigger Cities

During the 1950s there was an astonishing shift of 26.4 percent
of our population to the central cities and suburbs of our 212
largest metropolitan centers. This population movement has
placed immense burdens on government. Roads and transit systems have become inadequate; air and water pollution and crime
have increased.

Because of the prevalence in the cities of black people (see
Figure 21-1), who suffer most from economic depression, both
industry and the more affluent whites have moved to the suburbs.
By 1995, according to the 1968 report of the President's National
Advisory Commission on Civil Disorders, the black population in
central cities is expected to increase by 71 percent. A great many
of these migrants to Northern cities are from the South and face
not only the same difficulties of adjustment suffered by earlier
European immigrants but also the disadvantages of segregation.
By using the ballot, however, they can make government aware

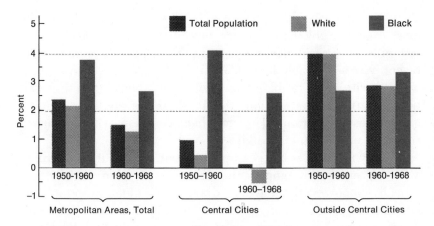

Figure 21-1. Average annual percent change in population in metropolitan areas, by race: 1950–1960 and 1960–1968. (Source: U.S. Bureau
of the Census.)

446

of their desires. Thus, it is no coincidence (or moral transformation) that Northern politicians have become interested in civil rights and the problems of the cities and their people.

An especially urgent problem facing urban government is an inadequate tax base (i.e., the unit of taxation, such as net income, or the value of an article or property) for services, aggravated by the loss of industry and affluent taxpayers to the suburbs. Another is interracial conflict, which reflects the problems of unemployment, crowded, segregated schools, poor police relations, environmental pollution, and general congestion.

Obviously, in the rapidly expanding megalopolises, traditional government is becoming more obsolete, for problems are not restricted to the jurisdictional boundary of the city, but involve neighboring cities, as well as all levels of government. The cooperation of local governments and major involvement by the state and national government are essential if the future of our big cities is not to be indeed grim.

Suggested Additional Reading

Clark, T. N. *Community Structure, Power, and Decision-Making.* 1968.

Dahl, R. A. *Who Governs? Democracy and Power in an American City.* 1961.

Danielson, M. N. *Metropolitan Politics: A Reader.* 1971.

Gans, H. J. *The Levittowners.* 1967.

Lindsay, J. V. *The City.* 1969.

Martin, R. C. *Grass Roots.* 1968.

Mumford, L. *The Urban Prospect.* 1968.

Ruchelman, L. I. (ed.). *Big City Mayors.* 1970.

Sherrard, T. D. (ed.). *Social Welfare and Urban Problems.* 1968.

Syed, A. H. *The Political Theory of American Local Government.* 1966.

Winter, W. O. *The Urban Polity.* 1968.

Constitution of the United States: The Original Constitution

Superseded portions of the Constitution are enclosed in brackets and are in italics.

We the People of the United States, in order to form a more perfect Union, establish justice, insure domestic tranquility, provide for the common defense, promote the general welfare, and secure the blessings of liberty to ourselves and our posterity, do ordain and establish this Constitution for the United States of America.

ARTICLE 1

Section 1. All legislative powers herein granted shall be vested in a Congress of the United States, which shall consist of a Senate and House of Representatives.

Section 2. The House of Representatives shall be composed of members chosen every second year by the people of the several States, and the Electors in each State shall have the qualifications requisite for electors of the most numerous branch of the State Legislature.

No person shall be a Representative who shall not have attained to the age of twenty-five years, and been seven years a citizen of the United States, and who shall not, when elected, be an inhabitant of that State in which he shall be chosen.

Representatives and direct taxes shall be apportioned among the several States which may be included within this Union, according to their respective numbers, [*which shall be determined by adding to the whole number of free persons, including those bound to service for a term of years, and excluding Indians not taxed, three fifths of all other persons*]. The actual enumeration shall be made within three years after the first meeting of the Congress of the United States, and within every subsequent term of ten years, in such manner as they shall by law direct. The number of Representatives shall not exceed one for every thirty thousand, but each State shall have at least one Representative; [*and until such enumeration shall be made, the State of New Hampshire shall be entitled to chuse three, Massachusetts eight, Rhode Island and Providence Plantations one, Connecticut five, New York six, New Jersey four, Pennsylvania eight, Delaware one, Maryland six, Virginia ten, North Carolina five, South Carolina five, and Georgia three*].

When vacancies happen in the representation from any State, the Executive Authority thereof shall issue Writs of Election to fill such vacancies.

The House of Representatives shall choose their Speaker and other officers; and shall have the sole power of impeachment.

Section 3.   The Senate of the United States shall be composed of two Senators from each State, chosen [*by the Legislature thereof*], for six Years; and each Senator shall have one vote.

Immediately after they shall be assembled in consequence of the first election, they shall be divided as equally as may be into three classes. [*The seats of the Senators of the first class shall be vacated at the expiration of the second year, of the second class at the expiration of the fourth year, and of the third class at the expiration of the sixth year*], so that one third may be chosen every second year; [*and if vacancies happen by resignation, or otherwise, during the recess of the Legislature of any State, the Executive thereof may make temporary appointments until the next meeting of the Legislature, which shall then fill such vacancies*].

No person shall be a Senator who shall not have attained to the age of thirty years, and been nine years a citizen of the United States, and who shall not, when elected, be an inhabitant of that State from which he shall be chosen.

The Vice President of the United States shall be President of the Senate, but shall have no vote, unless they be equally divided.

The Senate shall choose their other officers, and also a President pro tempore, in the absence of the Vice President, or when he shall exercise the office of President of the United States.

The Senate shall have the sole power to try all impeachments. When sitting for that purpose, they shall be on oath or affirmation. When the President of the United States is tried, the Chief Justice shall preside: And no person shall be convicted without the concurrence of two thirds of the members present.

Judgment in cases of impeachment shall not extend further than to removal from office, and disqualification to hold and enjoy any office of honor, trust or profit under the United States, but the party convicted shall nevertheless be liable and subject to indictment, trial, judgment and punishment, according to law.

Section 4. The times, places and manner of holding elections for Senators and Representatives, shall be prescribed in each State by the Legislature thereof; but the Congress may at any time by law make or alter such regulations, except as to the places of choosing Senators.

The Congress shall assemble at least once in every year, [*and such meeting shall be on the first Monday in December*], unless they shall by law appoint a different day.

Section 5. Each House shall be the judge of the elections, returns and qualifications of its own members, and a majority of each shall constitute a quorum to do business; but a smaller number may adjourn from day to day, and may be authorized to compel the attendance of absent members, in such manner, and under such penalties as each House may provide.

Each House may determine the rules of its proceedings, punish its members for disorderly behavior, and, with the concurrence of two thirds, expel a member.

Each House shall keep a journal of its proceedings, and from time to time publish the same, excepting such parts as may in their judgment require secrecy; and the yeas and nays of the members of either House on any question shall, at the desire of one fifth of those present, be entered on the journal.

Neither House, during the session of Congress, shall, without the consent of the other, adjourn for more than three days, nor to any other place than that in which the two Houses shall be sitting.

Section 6. The Senators and Representatives shall receive a compensation for their services, to be ascertained by law, and paid out of the Treasury of the United States. They shall in all cases, except treason, felony and breach of the peace, be privileged from arrest during their attendance at the session of their respective Houses, and in going to and returning from the same; and for any speech or debate in either House, they shall not be questioned in any other place.

No Senator or Representative shall, during the time for which he was elected, be appointed to any civil office under the authority of the United States, which shall have been created, or the emoluments whereof shall have been encreased during such time; and no person holding any office under the United States, shall be a member of either House during his continuance in office.

Section 7. All bills for raising revenue shall originate in the House of Representatives; but the Senate may propose or concur with Amendments as on other bills.

Every bill which shall have passed the House of Representatives and the Senate, shall, before it become a law, be presented to the President of the United States; if he approve he shall sign it, but if not he shall return it, with his objections to that House in which it shall have originated, who shall enter the objections at large on their journal, and proceed to reconsider it. If after such reconsideration two thirds of that House shall agree to pass the bill, it shall be sent, together with the objections, to the other House, by which it shall likewise be reconsidered, and if approved by two thirds of that House, it shall become a law. But in all such cases the votes of both Houses shall be determined by yeas and nays, and the names of the persons voting for and against the bill shall be entered on the journal of each House respectively. If any Bill shall not be returned by the President within ten days (Sundays excepted) after it shall have been presented to him, the same shall be a law, in like manner as if he had signed it, unless Congress by their adjournment prevent its return, in which case it shall not be a law.

Every order, resolution, or vote to which the concurrence of the Senate and House of Representatives may be necessary (except on a question of adjournment) shall be presented to the President of the United States; and before the same shall take effect, shall be approved by him, or being disapproved by him, shall be repassed by two thirds of the Senate and House of Representatives, according to the rules and limitations prescribed in the case of a bill.

Section 8. The Congress shall have power to lay and collect taxes, duties, imposts and excises, to pay the debts and provide for the common defense and general welfare of the United States; but all duties, imposts and excises shall be uniform throughout the United States.

To borrow money on the credit of the United States;

To regulate commerce with foreign nations, and among the several States and with the Indian tribes;

To establish an uniform rule of naturalization, and uniform laws on the subject of bankruptcies throughout the United States;

To coin money, regulate the value thereof, and of foreign coin, and fix the standard of weights and measures;

To provide for the punishment of counterfeiting the securities and current coin of the United States;

To establish post offices and post roads;

To promote the progress of science and useful arts, by securing for limited times to authors and inventors the exclusive right to their respective writings and discoveries;

To constitute tribunals inferior to the supreme Court;

To define and punish piracies and felonies committed on the high seas, and offenses against the law of nations;

To declare war, grant letters of marque and reprisal, and make rules concerning captures on land and water;

To raise and support armies; but no appropriation of money to that use shall be for a longer term than two years;

To provide and maintain a navy;

To make rules for the government and regulation of the land and naval forces;

To provide for calling forth the militia to execute the laws of the Union, suppress insurrections and repel invasions:

To provide for organizing, arming, and disciplining the militia, and for governing such part of them as may be employed in the service of the United States, reserving to the States respectively, the appointment of the officers, and the authority of training the militia according to the discipline prescribed by Congress;

To exercise exclusive legislation in all cases whatsoever, over such district (not exceeding ten miles square) as may, by cession of particular States, and the acceptance of Congress, become the seat of the government of the United States, and to exercise like authority over all places purchased by the consent of the Legislature of the State in which the same shall be, for the erection of forts, magazines, arsenals, dock-yards, and other needful buildings;—and

To make all laws which shall be necessary and proper for carrying into execution the foregoing powers, and all other powers vested by this Constitution in the government of the United States, or in any department or officer thereof.

Section 9. [*The migration or importation of such persons as any of the States now existing shall think proper to admit, shall not be prohibited by the Congress prior to the year one thousand eight hundred and eight, but a tax or duty may be imposed on such importation, not exceeding ten dollars for each person.*]

The Privilege of the writ of habeas corpus shall not be suspended, unless when in cases of rebellion or invasion the public safety may require it.

No bill of attainder or ex post facto law shall be passed.

No capitation, or other direct, tax shall be laid, unless in proportion to the census or enumeration herein before directed to be taken.

No tax or duty shall be laid on articles exported from any State.

No preference shall be given by any regulation of commerce or revenue to the ports of one State over those of another: nor shall vessels bound to, or from, one State, be obligated to enter, clear or pay duties in another.

No money shall be drawn from the Treasury, but in consequence of appropriations made by law; and a regular statement and account of the receipts and expenditures of all public money shall be published from time to time.

No title of nobility shall be granted by the United States: And no person holding any office of profit or trust under them, shall, without the consent of the Congress, accept of any present, emolument, office, or title, of any kind whatever, from any king, prince, or foreign state.

Section 10. No State shall enter into any treaty, alliance, or confederation; grant letters of marque and reprisal; coin money; emit bills of credit; make any thing but gold and silver coin a tender in payment of debts; pass any bill of attainder, ex post facto law, or law impairing the obligation of contracts, or grant any title of nobility.

No State shall, without the consent of the Congress, lay any imposts or duties on imports or exports, except what may be absolutely necessary for executing its inspection laws: and the net produce of all duties and imposts, laid by any State on imports or exports, shall be for the use of the Treasury of the United States; and all such laws shall be subject to the revision and control of the Congress.

No State shall, without the consent of Congress, lay any duty of tonnage, keep troops, or ships of war in time of peace, enter into any agreement or compact with another State, or with a foreign power, or engage in war, unless actually invaded, or in such imminent danger as will not admit of delay.

ARTICLE 2

Section 1. The executive power shall be vested in a President of the United States of America. He shall hold his office during the term of four years, and, together with the Vice President, chosen for the same term, be elected as follows:

Each State shall appoint, in such manner as the Legislature thereof may direct, a number of electors, equal to the whole number of Senators and Representatives to which the State may be entitled in the Congress: but no Senator or Representative, or person holding an office of trust or profit under the United States, shall be appointed an elector.

[The electors shall meet in their respective States, and vote by ballot for two persons, of whom one at least shall not be an inhabitant of the same State with themselves. And they shall make a list of all the persons voted for, and of the number of votes for each; which list they shall sign and certify, and transmit sealed to the seat of the government of the United States, directed to the President of the Senate. The President of the Senate shall, in the presence of the Senate and House of Representatives, open all the certificates, and the votes shall then be counted. The person having the greatest number of votes shall be the

453

President, if such number be a majority of the whole number of electors appointed; and if there be more than one who have such majority, and have an equal number of votes, then the House of Representatives shall immediately choose by ballot one of them for President; and if no person have a majority, then from the five highest on the list the said House shall in like manner choose the President. But in choosing the President, the votes shall be taken by States, the representation from each State having one vote; a quorum for this purpose shall consist of a member or members from two thirds of the States, and a majority of all the States shall be necessary to a choice. In every case, after the choice of the President, the person having the greatest number of votes of the electors shall be the Vice President. But if there should remain two or more who have equal votes, the Senate shall choose from them by ballot the Vice President.]

The Congress may determine the time of choosing the electors, and the day on which they shall give their votes; which day shall be the same throughout the United States.

No person except a natural born citizen, [*or a citizen of the United States, at the time of the adoption of this Constitution*], shall be eligible to the office of President; neither shall any person be eligible to that office who shall not have attained to the age of thirty five years, and been fourteen years a resident within the United States.

In case of the removal of the President from office, or of his death, resignation, or inability to discharge the powers and duties of the said office, the same shall devolve on the Vice President, and the Congress may by law provide for the case of removal, death, resignation or inability, both of the President and Vice President, declaring what officer shall then act as President, and such officer shall act accordingly, until the disability be removed, or a President shall be elected.

The President shall, at stated times, receive for his services, a compensation, which shall neither be increased nor diminished during the period for which he shall have been elected, and he shall not receive within that period any other emolument from the United States, or any of them.

Before he enter on the execution of his office, he shall take the following oath or affirmation:—"I do solemnly swear (or affirm) that I will faithfully execute the office of President of the United States, and will to the best of my ability, preserve, protect and defend the Constitution of the United States."

Section 2.   The President shall be commander in chief of the army and navy of the United States, and of the militia of the several States, when called into the actual service of the United States; he may require the opinion, in writing, of the principal officer in each of the executive departments, upon any subject relating to the duties of their respective offices, and he shall have power to grant reprieves and pardons for offenses against the United States, except in cases of impeachment.

He shall have power, by and with the advice and consent of the Senate, to make treaties, provided two thirds of the Senators present concur; and he shall nominate, and by and with advice and consent of the Senate, shall appoint ambassadors, other public ministers and consuls, judges of the Supreme Court, and all other officers of the United States, whose appointments are not herein otherwise provided for, and which shall be established by law: but the Congress may by law vest the appointment of such inferior officers, as they think proper, in the President alone, in the courts of law, or in the heads of departments.

The President shall have power to fill up all vacancies that may happen during the recess of the Senate, by granting commissions which shall expire at the end of their next session.

Section 3. He shall from time to time give to the Congress information of the State of the Union, and recommend to their consideration such measures as he shall judge necessary and expedient; he may, on extraordinary occasions, convene both Houses, or either of them, and in case of disagreement between them, with respect to the time of adjournment, he may adjourn them to such time as he shall think proper; he shall receive ambassadors and other public ministers; he shall take care that the laws be faithfully executed, and shall commission all the officers of the United States.

Section 4. The President, Vice President and all civil officers of the United States, shall be removed from office on impeachment for, and conviction of, treason, bribery, or other high crimes and misdemeanors.

ARTICLE 3

Section 1. The judicial power of the United States, shall be vested in one Supreme Court, and in such inferior courts as the Congress may from time to time ordain and establish. The judges, both of the Supreme and inferior Courts, shall hold their offices during good behavior, and shall, at stated times, receive for their services, a compensation, which shall not be diminished during their continuance in office.

Section 2. The judicial power shall extend to all cases, in law and equity, arising under this Constitution, the laws of the United States, and treaties made, or which shall be made, under their authority;—to all cases affecting ambassadors, other public ministers and consuls;—to all cases of admiralty and maritime jurisdiction;—to controversies to which the United States shall be a party;—to controversies between two or more states;—between a State and citizens of another State;—between citizens of different States;—between citizens of the same State claiming lands under grants of different States, and between a State, or the citizens thereof, and foreign states, citizens or subjects.

In all cases affecting ambassadors, other public ministers and consuls, and those in which a State shall be party, the Supreme Court shall have original jurisdiction. In all the other cases before mentioned, the Supreme Court shall have appellate jurisdiction, both as to law and fact, with such exceptions, and under such regulations as the Congress shall make.

The trial of all crimes, except in cases of impeachment, shall be by jury; and such trial shall be held in the State where the said crimes shall have been committed; but when not committed within any State, the trial shall be at such place or places as the Congress may by law have directed.

Section 3. Treason against the United States shall consist only in levying war against them, or in adhering to their enemies, giving them aid and comfort. No person shall be convicted of treason unless on the testimony of two witnesses to the same overt act, or on confession in open Court.

The Congress shall have power to declare the punishment of treason, but no attainder of treason shall work corruption of blood, or forfeiture except during the life of the person attainted.

ARTICLE 4

Section 1. Full faith and credit shall be given in each State to the public acts, records, and judicial proceedings of every other State. And the Congress may by general laws prescribe the manner in which such acts, records and proceedings shall be proved, and the effect thereof.

Section 2. The citizens of each State shall be entitled to all privileges and immunities of citizens in the several States.

A person charged in any State with treason, felony, or other crime, who shall flee from justice, and be found in another State, shall on demand of the executive authority of the State from which he fled, be delivered up, to be removed to the State having jurisdiction of the crime.

[*No person held to service or labor in one State, under the laws thereof, escaping into another, shall, in consequence of any law or regulation therein, be discharged from such service or labor, but shall be delivered up on claim of the party to whom such service or labor may be due.*]

Section 3. New States may be admitted by the Congress into this Union; but no new State shall be formed or erected within the jurisdiction of any other State; nor any State be formed by the junction of two

456

or more States, or parts of States, without the consent of the Legislatures of the States concerned as well as of the Congress.

The Congress shall have power to dispose of and make all needful rules and regulations respecting the territory or other property belonging to the United States; and nothing in this Constitution shall be so construed as to prejudice any claims of the United States, or of any particular State.

Section 4. The United States shall guarantee to every State in this Union a republican form of government, and shall protect each of them against invasion; and on application of the Legislature, or of the Executive (when the Legislature cannot be convened) against domestic violence.

ARTICLE 5

The Congress, whenever two thirds of both Houses shall deem it necessary, shall propose Amendments to this Constitution, or, on the application of the Legislatures of two thirds of the several States, shall call a Convention for proposing Amendments, which, in either case, shall be valid to all intents and purposes, as part of this Constitution, when ratified by the Legislatures of three fourths of the several States, or by Conventions in three fourths thereof, as the one or the other mode of ratification may be proposed by the Congress; Provided that [*no amendment which may be made prior to the year one thousand eight hundred and eight shall in any manner affect the first and fourth clauses in the ninth section of the first Article; and that*] no State, without its consent, shall be deprived of its equal suffrage in the Senate.

ARTICLE 6

All debts contracted and engagements entered into, before the adoption of this Constitution, shall be as valid against the United States under this Constitution, as under the Confederation.

This Constitution, and the laws of the United States which shall be made in pursuance thereof; and all treaties made, of which shall be made, under the authority of the United States, shall be the supreme law of the land; and the judges in every State shall be bound thereby, anything in the Constitution or laws of any State to the contrary notwithstanding.

The Senators and Representatives before mentioned, and the members of the several State Legislatures, and all executive and judicial officers, both of the United States and of the several States, shall be bound by oath or affirmation, to support this Constitution; but no religious test shall ever be required as a qualification to any office or public trust under the United States.

ARTICLE 7

The ratification of the Conventions of nine States shall be sufficient for the establishment of this Constitution between the States so ratifying the same.

AMENDMENTS TO THE CONSTITUTION

AMENDMENT I. (ADOPTED 1791)

Congress shall make no law respecting an establishment of religion, or prohibiting the free exercise thereof, or abridging the freedom of speech, or of the press; or the right of the people peaceably to assemble, and to petition the government for a redress of grievances.

AMENDMENT II. (ADOPTED 1791)

A well-regulated militia, being necessary to the security of a free State, the right of the people to keep and bear arms, shall not be infringed.

AMENDMENT III. (ADOPTED 1791)

No soldier shall, in time of peace be quartered in any house, without the consent of the owner, nor in time of war, but in a manner to be prescribed by law.

AMENDMENT IV. (ADOPTED 1791)

The right of the people to be secure in their persons, houses, papers, and effects, against unreasonable searches and seizures, shall not be violated, and no warrants shall issue, but upon probable cause, supported by oath or affirmation, and particularly describing the place to be searched, and the persons or things to be seized.

AMENDMENT V. (ADOPTED 1791)

No person shall be held to answer for a capital, or otherwise infamous crime, unless on a presentment or indictment of a grand jury, except in cases arising in the land or naval forces, or in the militia, when in actual service in time of war or public danger; nor shall any person be subject for the same offense to be twice put in jeopardy of life or limb; nor shall be compelled in any criminal case to be a witness against himself, nor be deprived of life, liberty, or property, without due process of law; nor shall private property be taken for public use, without just compensation.

AMENDMENT VI. (ADOPTED 1791)

In all criminal prosecutions, the accused shall enjoy the right to a speedy and public trial, by an impartial jury of the State and district wherein the crime shall have been committed, which district shall have been previously ascertained by law, and to be informed of the nature and cause of the accusation; to be confronted with the witnesses against him; to have compulsory process for obtaining witnesses in his favor, and to have the assistance of counsel for his defense.

AMENDMENT VII. (ADOPTED 1791)

In suits at common law, where the value in controversy shall exceed twenty dollars, the right of trial by jury shall be preserved, and no fact tried by a jury, shall be otherwise re-examined in any court of the United States, than according to the rules of the common law.

AMENDMENT VIII. (ADOPTED 1791)

Excessive bail shall not be required, nor excessive fines imposed, nor cruel and unusual punishments inflicted.

AMENDMENT IX. (ADOPTED 1791)

The enumeration in the Constitution, of certain rights, shall not be construed to deny or disparage others retained by the people.

AMENDMENT X. (ADOPTED 1791)

The powers not delegated to the United States by the Constitution, nor prohibited by it to the States, are reserved to the States respectively, or to the people.

AMENDMENT XI. (ADOPTED 1798)

The judicial power of the United States shall not be construed to extend to any suit in law or equity, commenced or prosecuted against one of the United States by citizens of another State, or by citizens or subjects of any foreign state.

AMENDMENT XII. (ADOPTED 1804)

The electors shall meet in their respective states and vote by ballot for President and Vice-President, one of whom, at least, shall not be an inhabitant of the same State with themselves; they shall name in their ballots the person voted for as President, and in distinct ballots the person voted for as Vice-President, and they shall make distinct lists of all persons voted for as President, and of all persons voted for as Vice-President, and of the number of votes for each, which lists they shall sign and certify, and transmit sealed to the seat of the government of the United States, directed to the President of the Senate;—The President of the Senate shall, in the presence of the Senate and House of Representatives, open all the certificates and the votes shall then be counted;—the person having the greatest number of votes for President, shall be the President, if such number be a majority of the whole number of electors appointed; and if no person have such majority, then from the persons having the highest numbers not exceeding three on the list of those voted for as President, the House of Representatives shall choose immediately, by ballot, the President. But in choosing the President, the votes shall be taken by States, the representation from each State having one vote; a quorum for this purpose shall consist of a member or members from two-thirds of the States, and a majority of all the States shall be necessary to a choice. And if the House of Representatives shall not choose a President whenever the right of choice shall devolve upon them, [*before the fourth day of March next following*], then the Vice-President, shall act as President, as in the case of the death or other constitutional disability of the President.—The person having the greatest number of votes as Vice-President, shall be the Vice-President, if such number be a majority of the whole number of electors appointed, and if no person have a majority, then from the two highest numbers on the list, the Senate shall choose the Vice President; a quorum for the purpose shall consist of two-thirds of the whole numbers of Senators, and a majority of the whole number shall be necessary to a choice. But no person constitutionally ineligible to the office of President shall be eligible to that of Vice President of the United States.

AMENDMENT XIII. (ADOPTED 1865)

Section 1. Neither slavery nor involuntary servitude, except as a punishment for crime whereof the party shall have been duly convicted, shall exist within the United States, or any place subject to their jurisdiction.

Section 2. Congress shall have power to enforce this article by appropriate legislation.

AMENDMENT XIV. (ADOPTED 1868)

Section 1. All persons born or naturalized in the United States, and subject to the jurisdiction thereof, are citizens of the United States and of the State wherein they reside. No State shall make or enforce any law which shall abridge the privileges or immunities of citizens of the United States; nor shall any State deprive any person of life, liberty, or property, without due process of law; nor deny to any person within its jurisdiction the equal protection of the laws.

Section 2. Representatives shall be apportioned among the several States according to their respective numbers, counting the whole number of persons in each State, excluding Indians not taxed. But when the right to vote at any election for the choice of electors for President and Vice President of the United States, Representatives in Congress, the executive and judicial officers of a State, or the members of the Legislature thereof, is denied to any of the male inhabitants of such State, being twenty-one years of age, and citizens of the United States, or in any way abridged except for participation in rebellion, or other crime, the basis of representation therein shall be reduced in the proportion which the number of such male citizens shall bear to the whole number of male citizens twenty-one years of age in such State.

Section 3. No person shall be a Senator or Representative in Congress, or elector of President and Vice President, or hold any office, civil or military, under the United States, or under any State, who, having previously taken an oath, as a member of Congress, or as an officer of the United States, or as a member of any State legislature, or as an executive or judicial officer of any State, to support the Constitution of the United States, shall have engaged in insurrection or rebellion against the same, or given aid or comfort to the enemies thereof. But Congress may by a vote of two-thirds of each House, remove such disability.

Section 4. The validity of the public debt of the United States, authorized by law, including debts incurred for payment of pensions and bounties for services in suppressing insurrection or rebellion, shall not be questioned. But neither the United States nor any State shall assume or pay any debt or obligation incurred in aid of insurrection or rebellion against the United States, or any claim for the loss or emancipation of any slave; but all such debts, obligations and claims shall be held illegal and void.

Section 5. The Congress shall have power to enforce, by appropriate legislation, the provisions of this article.

AMENDMENT XV. (ADOPTED 1870)

Section 1. The right of citizens of the United States to vote shall not be denied or abridged by the United States or by any State on account of race, color, or previous condition of servitude.

Section 2. The Congress shall have power to enforce this article by appropriate legislation.

AMENDMENT XVI. (ADOPTED 1913)

The Congress shall have power to lay and collect taxes on incomes, from whatever source derived, without apportionment among the several States, and without regard to any census or enumeration.

AMENDMENT XVII. (ADOPTED 1913)

The Senate of the United States shall be composed of two Senators from each State, elected by the people thereof, for six years; and each Senator shall have one vote. The electors in each State shall have the qualifications requisite for electors of the most numerous branch of the State legislatures.

When vacancies happen in the representation of any State in the Senate, the executive authority of such State shall issue writs of election to fill such vacancies: *Provided,* that the legislature of any State may empower the executive thereof to make temporary appointments until the people fill the vacancies by election as the legislature may direct.

This amendment shall not be so construed as to affect the election or term of any Senator chosen before it becomes valid as part of the Constitution.

AMENDMENT XVIII. (ADOPTED 1919)

Repealed—See Amendment XXI.

AMENDMENT XIX. (ADOPTED 1920)

The right of citizens of the United States to vote shall not be denied or abridged by the United States or by any State on account of sex.

Congress shall have power to enforce this article by appropriate legislation.

AMENDMENT XX. (ADOPTED 1933)

Section 1. The terms of the President and Vice President shall end at noon on the 20th day of January, and the terms of Senators and Representatives at noon of the 3rd day of January, of the years in which such terms would have ended if this article had not been ratified; and the terms of their successors shall then begin.

Section 2. The Congress shall assemble at least once in every year, and such meeting shall begin at noon on the 3rd day of January, unless they shall by law appoint a different day.

Section 3. If, at the time fixed for the beginning of the term of the President, the President elect shall have died, the Vice President elect shall become President. If a President shall not have been chosen before the time fixed for the beginning of his term, or if the President elect shall have failed to qualify, then the Vice President elect shall act as President until a President shall have qualified; and the Congress may by law provide for the case wherein neither a President elect nor a Vice President elect shall have qualified, declaring who shall then act as Prsident, or the manner in which one who is to act shall be selected, and such person shall act accordingly until a President or Vice President shall have qualified.

Section 4. The Congress may by law provide for the case of the death of any of the persons from whom the House of Representatives may choose a President whenever the right of choice shall have devolved upon them, and for the case of the death of any of the persons from whom the Senate may choose a Vice President whenever the right of choice shall have devolved upon them.

Section 5. Sections 1 and 2 shall take effect on the 15th day of October following the ratification of this article.

Section 6. This article shall be inoperative unless it shall have been ratified as an amendment to the Constitution by the legislatures of three-fourths of the several States within seven years from the date of its submission.

AMENDMENT XXI. (ADOPTED 1933)

Section 1. The eighteenth Article of amendment to the Constitution of the United States is hereby repealed.

Section 2. The transportation or importation into any State, territory, or possession of the United States for delivery or use therein of intoxicating liquors, in violation of the laws thereof, is hereby prohibited.

Section 3. This Article shall be inoperative unless it shall have been ratified as an amendment to the Constitution by conventions in the several States, as provided in the Constitution, within seven years from the date of the submission hereof to the States by the Congress.

AMENDMENT XXII. (ADOPTED 1951)

Section 1. No person shall be elected to the office of the President more than twice, and no person who has held the office of President, or acted as President, for more than two years of a term to which some other person was elected President shall be elected to the office of the President more than once. But this Article shall not apply to any person holding the office of President when this Article was proposed by the Congress, and shall not prevent any person who may be holding the office of President, or acting as President, during the term within which this Article becomes operative from holding the office of President or acting as President during the remainder of such term.

Section 2. This Article shall be inoperative unless it shall have been ratified as an amendment to the Constitution by the legislatures of three-fourths of the several States within seven years from the date of its submission to the States by the Congress.

AMENDMENT XXIII. (ADOPTED 1961)

Section 1. The district constituting the seat of government of the United States shall appoint in such manner as the Congress may direct:

A number of electors of President and Vice President equal to the whole number of Senators and Representatives in Congress to which the district would be entitled if it were a State, but in no event more than the least populous State; they shall be in addition to those appointed by the States, but they shall be considered, for the purposes of the election of President and Vice President, to be electors appointed by a State; and they shall meet in the district and perform such duties as provided by the twelfth article of amendment.

Section 2. The Congress shall have power to enforce this article by appropriate legislation.

AMENDMENT XXIV. (ADOPTED 1964)

Section 1. The right of citizens of the United States to vote in any primary or other election for President or Vice President, for electors for President or Vice President, or for Senator or Representative in Congress, shall not be denied or abridged by the United States or any State by reason of failure to pay any poll tax or other tax.

Section 2. The Congress shall have power to enforce this article by appropriate legislation.

AMENDMENT XXV. (ADOPTED 1967)

Section 1. In case of the removal of the President from office or of his death or resignation, the Vice-President shall become President.

Section 2. Whenever there is a vacancy in the office of the Vice-President, the President shall nominate a Vice-President who shall take office upon confirmation by a majority vote of both Houses of Congress.

Section 3. Whenever the President transmits to the President pro tempore of the Senate and the Speaker of the House of Representatives his written declaration that he is unable to discharge the powers and duties of his office, and until he transmits to them a written declaration to the contrary, such powers and duties shall be discharged by the Vice-President as Acting President.

Section 4. Whenever the Vice-President and a majority of either the principal officers of the executive departments or of such other body as Congress may by law provide, transmit to the President pro tempore of the Senate and the Speaker of the House of Representatives their written declaration that the President is unable to discharge the powers and duties of his office, the Vice-President shall immediately assume the powers and duties of the office as Acting President.

Thereafter, when the President transmits to the President pro tempore of the Senate and the Speaker of the House of Representatives his written declaration that no inability exists, he shall resume the powers and duties of his office unless the Vice-President and a majority of either the principal officers of the executive departments or of such other body as Congress may by law provide, transmit within four days to the President pro tempore of the Senate and the Speaker of the House of Representatives their written declaration that the President is unable to discharge the powers and duties of his office. Thereupon Congress shall decide the issue, assembling within forty-eight hours for that purpose if not in session. If the Congress, within twenty-one days after receipt of the latter written declaration, or, if Congress is not in session, within twenty-one days after Congress is required to assemble, determines by two-thirds vote of both Houses that the President is unable to discharge the powers and duties of his office, the Vice President shall continue to discharge the same as Acting President; otherwise, the President shall resume the powers and duties of his office.

AMENDMENT XXVI. (ADOPTED 1971)

Section 1. The right of citizens of the United States, who are eighteen years of age or older, to vote shall not be denied or abridged by the United States or by any State on account of age.

Section 2. The Congress shall have power to enforce this article by appropriate legislation.

Index

470

Majority Floor Leader, 231–232
Manifest destiny, 388–390
Mansfield, Mike, 174
Mao Tse-tung, 413
Marbury v. *Madison*, 292–293
Marchetti v. *United States*, 99
Marshall, John:
 and Constitution, 69, 76, 103–104
 and doctrine of implied powers,
  102–105
 and judicial review, 76, 292–293
 and Supreme Court, 304
Marshall Plan, 401
Mason, George, 65
Massachusetts, 69
Massachusetts v. *Mellon*, 108
Massive retaliation, 413
Mayor, 445–446
McCarthy, Eugene, 270
McCarthy, Joseph R., 217, 251, 326
McCormack, John, 231
McCulloch v. *Maryland*, 102
McKinley, William, 376
McNamara, Robert, 403
Medicare, 366–367
Memphis, Tenn., 444
Men Are Our Masters (MOM), 194
Meredith, James, 114
Mexican-American Political
 Association (MAPA), 24, 194
Mexican-Americans, 3, 22–24, 130
Mexico, 15
Miami Beach, 167
Michigan, 140, 423
Middle East, 412
Military, 77–78
Military policy, 394–405
 arms control, 405–406
 containment, 395
 Department of Defense, 403–405
 North Atlantic Treaty Organization
  (NATO), 396–397
 and President, 402–403
 of sixties and seventies, 413–416
 Southeast Asia Treaty Organization
  (SEATO), 397–400
 states and, 407
Militia, 407
Minimum age for voting, 134–136
Minority Floor Leader, 232
Minutemen, 194, 203
Miranda v. *Arizona*, 345
Mississippi, 138, 180
Mitchell, John, 340
Model State Constitution, 422
Monroe, James, 387–388
Monroe Doctrine, 387–388, 390

Montesquieu, Baron d., 73
Morison, Samuel Eliot, 68
Morris, Gouveneur, 78
Morse, Wayne, 248
Mosca, Gaetano, 29, 30
Movie censorship, 328
Multi-party systems, 152
Municipal courts, 436
Municipalities:
 charters, 443–445
 mayor, 445–446
Murphy, Justice, 267

Nader, Ralph, 366
Nader's Raiders, 194
National Council of Churches, 194
National Aeronautics and Space
 Council, 276
National Association for the Advance-
 ment of Colored People (NAACP),
 194, 200
National Association of Home Builders
 of the United States, 194
National Association of Manufacturers,
 193, 202
National Association of State Attorneys
 General, 111
National Bankers Association, 202
National Commission on the Causes and
 Prevention of Violence, 206
National committee,
 of parties, 158–159
National Committee for an Effective
 Congress, 194
National Confederation of American
 Ethnic Groups, 25
National Conference of Commissioners
 on Uniform State Laws, 110
National Council on Marine Resources
 and Engineering Development, 276
National debt, 360–361
National Defense Education Act, 367
National Education Association, 194
National Farmers Union, 193
National Federation of Business and
 Professional Women's Clubs, 194
National government, 103
National Grange, 193
National Guard, 407
National Industrial Recovery Act, 364
National Labor Relations Act, 365
National Labor Relations Board v. *Jones
 and Laughlin Steel Corporation*, 97
National Lawyers Guild, 200
National Organization for Women
 (NOW), 194

474

National Rifle Association, 34, 194
National Security Council, 275, 379
National Student Association, 194
Nationalist China, 400, 410
Nationalists, 62, 68
Navy, 403
Nebraska, 420, 430
Negroes, see blacks
Neighborhood Youth Corps, 371
Netherlands, 396
New England, 129
New Hampshire, 430
New Haven, Connecticut, 32
New Jersey, 423
New Left, 30, 118, 203
New Mexico, 23
New states, 100–101
New York City, 358, 445
New Zealand, 397
Nineteenth Amendment, 86, 133
Nixon, Richard M., 118
    and birth control, 12
    and China visit, 414–415
    and civil rights, 315
    as commander in chief, 267
    and federal government, 107
    and grants-in-aid, 107
    military policy of, 413
    on minimum voting age, 136
    in nominations and elections, 166,
        169, 177, 178, 184
    and parties, 149, 150, 166, 169, 177,
        178, 184
    and public opinion, 125
    revenue-sharing plan of 1971, 283
    and sectionalism, 13
    and South, 150
    and State Department, 377
    as Vice-President, 269
    and voting, 124, 125, 136
No-party systems, 153
Nominations and elections, 163–188
    campaign, 176–178, 186–188
    conventions, 163–165, 167–175
    electoral college, 178–185
    popular election, 183–185
    presidential, 166, 176–178
    primary elections, 163–165, 169
    state presidential, 169
Nonpartisan primary, 164
Nonviolent protest, 204–205
Nonvoting, 129–132
Norris-LaGuardia Act, 364
North Atlantic Treaty Organization
    (NATO), 396–397
North Carolina, 69
Norway, 396

Nuclear test ban treaty, 405–406
Nuclear weapons, 405, 413

Office group ballot, 165
Office of Economic Opportunity, 275
Office of Emergency Preparedness, 275
Office of Intergovernmental Relations,
    275
Office of Legislative Counsel, 233
Office of Management and Budget,
    263, 273
Office of Science and Technology, 276
Office of Special Representative for
    Trade Negotiations, 276
Office of Telecommunications Policy,
    276
Okinawa, 384
One-party systems, 153
Open Housing Law of 1968, 352–353
Open primary, 164, 175
Oregon, 382, 389
Organization of American States, 412
Original jurisdiction, 306
O'Sullivan, John L., 388

Paine, Thomas, 59
Pakistan, 397
Palko v. Connecticut, 348
Parity, 361
Parliamentary system, 258
Parochial schools, 322
Partido Revolucionario Institucional,
    153
Parties, political, 145–188
    and campaign, 176–178, 186–188
    in Congress, 182–183, 230
    and conventions, 158, 163–165,
        167–175
    in democracy, 33
    district and county committees of,
        159–160
    evolution of, 146–149
    functions of, 145–146
    grass-roots organization of, 160
    ideological, 155
    interest, 155
    national committee of, 158–159
    in nominations and elections, 163–188
    and popular vote, 178–185
    pragmatic, 155
    and President, 166, 175–178
    pressure groups compared to, 192
    and primary elections, 163–165, 169
    state organization of, 159
    structure of, 157–188
    and two-party system, 149–154
Party caucus, 230–231, 432

477

Two-party system, 149–154
  in South, 150
Tyler, John, 113

Unemployment insurance, 369
Unification Act of 1947, 403
Uniform Narcotic Drug Act, 110
Uniform state laws, 110
Unitary and confederate systems, 72
United Auto Workers, 193
United Farm Workers, 193
United Nations, 408–412
  Economic and Social Council, 411
  General Assembly, 408–410
  Secretariat, 412
  Security Council, 410–411
University of Mississippi, 114
Urban League, 194
U.S. v. *New York Times and Wash-*
  ington Post, 327
U.S. v. *Reidel*, 330
U.S.S.R., *see* Soviet Union
Utah, 100

Vandenberg, Arthur, 136
Vermont, 129
Veterans of Foreign Wars, 194
Veto:
  by President, 249
  in Security Council, 410–411
Vice-President, 269–276
  administrative and political roles of,
    269–270
  constitutional role of, 270–272
  incompleted terms of, 271–272
  salary of, 218
  and Senate, 232
Vice-presidential candidate, in conven-
    tions, 172–173
Vietnam, 14, 205, 376, 380, 400, 402,
  414
Violent protest, 205–208
  U.S. compared to other countries, 206
Virginia, 138
Volunteers In Service To America
  (VISTA), 371
Voting, 122–142
  and blacks, 127, 130, 133, 136–138,
    141
  free elections, 132
  gerrymander, 138–139
  in House of Representatives, 246–247

Voting (*cont'd*):
  among Mexican-Americans, 23, 130
  minimum age for, 134–136
  nonvoting, 129–132
  party preference, 126–129
  qualifications for, 132–134
Voting machines, 165–166
Voting Rights Act of 1970, 133, 136

Wagner Act, 365
Wallace, George, 24, 149, 150, 180
War, 376
War Department, 403
War power,
  federal expansion through, 98
War restrictions, on freedom of
  expression, 326
Warren, Charles, 262
Warren, Earl, 217, 310, 335
Warren Commission, 206
Washington, George, 56, 58, 60, 69,
  102, 146, 386–387
"WASP," 3
Watkins v. *United States*, 251
Weatherman, 203
Welfare, 368–370
Welsh v. *United States*, 319
Wesberry v. *Sanders*, 222
West Berlin, 414
West Germany, 15, 405, 406, 408
Whigs, 147
Whip, 232
Whiskey Rebellion, 205
White backlash, 13
White ethnics, 24–26
White primary, 137
Williams v. *North Carolina*, 115
Wilson, Woodrow, 154, 174, 391
Wiretapping, 339–340
Women, 214
Wood, Robert C., 25
World War II, 392
Writ of *certiorari*, 305–306
Writ of *habeas corpus*, 334

Young Americans for Freedom (YAF),
  203
Young Socialist Alliance, 204
Youth, 19–22, 130, 214

Zwicker, General, 251

479